P9-CFO-620

Not Just Roommates

Not Just Roommates

Cohabitation after the Sexual Revolution

ELIZABETH H. PLECK

The University of Chicago Press
Chicago and London

Elizabeth H. Pleck is professor emerita of history and human development and family studies at the University of Illinois at Urbana-Champaign.

The University of Chicago Press, Chicago 60637
The University of Chicago Press, Ltd., London
© 2012 by The University of Chicago
All rights reserved. Published 2012.
Printed in the United States of America

21 20 19 18 17 16 15 14 13 12   1 2 3 4 5

ISBN-13: 978-0-226-67103-1 (cloth)
ISBN-13: 978-0-226-67104-8 (paper)
ISBN-10: 0-226-67103-8 (cloth)
ISBN-10: 0-226-67104-6 (paper)

Library of Congress Cataloging-in-Publication Data

Pleck, Elizabeth H. (Elizabeth Hafkin), 1945–
    Not just roommates : cohabitation after the sexual revolution / Elizabeth H. Pleck.
        pages ; cm
    Includes index.
    ISBN-13: 978-0-226-67103-1 (cloth: alkaline paper)
    ISBN-10: 0-226-67103-8 (cloth: alkaline paper)
    ISBN-13: 978-0-226-67104-8 (paperback: alkaline paper)
    ISBN-10: 0-226-67104-6 (paperback: alkaline paper)   1. Unmarried couples—United States—History—20th century. 2. Unmarried couples—Legal status, laws, etc.—United States—History—20th century.
3. Discrimination against unmarried couples—United States—History—20th century. 4. Common law marriage—United States—History—20th century.
I. Title.
    HQ803.5.P54 2012
    306.84'10973—dc23

                                                                 2011043369

♾ This paper meets the requirements of ANSI/NISO Z39.48-1992 (Permanence of Paper).

CONTENTS

ILLUSTRATIONS

ONE

Introduction

In 1972, Michelle Marvin, an actress and cabaret singer living with but not
legally married to the Hollywood actor Lee Marvin, brought a lawsuit when
their six-year relationship ended. She sought alimony and half of the income Lee Marvin had earned while the couple were together. In 1975, the
California Supreme Court in *Marvin v. Marvin* affirmed that a nonmarried
cohabitor such as Michelle Marvin had the right to enter into a legal contract with her partner; previously courts had held that because cohabitation
was somewhat akin to prostitution, there could be no right to contract for
what were essentially sexual services. It is often claimed that the California
Supreme Court decision in *Marvin v. Marvin* represents a milestone of the
sexual revolution and surely a key one in terms of the social acceptance of
cohabitation.

That's the myth of *Marvin*. The *Marvin* decision made palimony front-
page news and established the right of cohabitors to make contracts in
many states. However, most cohabitors did not enter into legal contracts,
verbal promises proved hard to enforce, and few cohabitors sued for palimony because these suits were lengthy, costly, and hard to win. Despite the
favorable ruling of the California Supreme Court, Michelle Marvin never
received a penny in proceeds from legal victory. In a few states considerably more conservative than California, the *Marvin* decision led to rulings
that contracts between cohabitors were invalid in that state. A legal victory
for cohabitors adopted in most states, but not all, a contractual approach
to living together fashioned by the courts turned out to be largely unworkable—that's the reality of *Marvin*.

On the whole, cohabitation has become a normative experience in
American society. In fact, the majority of American women have cohabited
at some point in their lives, and couples who do not live together before

their wedding day are now the deviants. Census figures on cohabitation suggest that there may have been about 230,000 couples cohabiting in 1960. In 2010, the US Census Bureau estimated that there were 8 million cohabiting households, of which about 516,000 were same-sex couples; in addition, more than 3 million children were being raised by parents who were partnered rather than legally married. These figures show a thirty-five-fold increase in the rate of cohabitation in the space of a half century, an astounding upward climb probably unparalleled in demographic history.[1] The spectacular growth in cohabitation and nonmarital childbearing are the least cyclical developments in family change in the last fifty years: divorce plateaued in the 1980s, the number of abortions has dropped in recent years—the growth of cohabitation and bearing children out of wedlock have proven unstoppable.

The very nature of courtship and marriage has been altered by this trend. By the 1990s, most engaged couples lived together before walking down the aisle. Between 1965 and 1975, only 9 percent of first unions began with cohabitation; between 1990 and 1995, the figure was 54 percent. By the 1990s, cohabitation had emerged as a family form for giving birth to and raising children. Indeed, many American children are now growing up with a cohabiting parent and the parent's partner. Two demographers estimated that as of 2008 almost half of all children in the United States at the time could be expected to spend some time in a cohabiting family. One can say that American attitudes followed behavior—and vice versa. The percentage of Americans who thought that living together outside of marriage was morally wrong declined from 86 percent in 1977 to 41 percent in 2001 and fell even more dramatically, to 27 percent, by 2007. The attitudes of high school seniors turned positive much earlier, reflecting the vanguard role of youth in the sexual revolution. The percentage of high school seniors who believed that living together prior to marriage is a good idea increased from 36 percent in 1975 to 70 percent in 2008. Girls were always more conservative in their attitudes than boys, but the gender gap between male and female high school seniors was closing, largely because young women were adopting a much more favorable view of cohabitation prior to marriage.[2]

Because of these changes in attitudes, one would expect that any sanctions against living together would long ago have been consigned to the dustbin of America's puritan past. However, cohabitation has not become completely approved of. Occasionally, a reporter stumbles across a law still on the books criminalizing cohabitation, fornication, or adultery, but quickly adds that the law is never enforced. But in fact, discrimination against cohabitors still exists, and couples continue to be punished for living together, despite the prevalence, even ubiquity, of these relationships. Here are seven examples for the years 2005 through 2010, when most people assume cohabitation had become completely accepted.

- A Catholic high school in Appleton, Wisconsin, dismissed a teacher because he had too much to drink and stayed overnight at his girlfriend's apartment in Green Bay.
- A trial court judge denied visitation to a divorced father in Michigan because he had a live-in girlfriend.
- The state parole board added three months to the sentence of a prisoner in West Virginia because he told them he planned to live with his girlfriend after he got out of prison.
- A mother on public aid in San Diego was convicted for welfare fraud for failing to report her abusive live-in boyfriend's income, even though he was not giving her any of his money.
- A North Carolina sheriff told a cohabiting dispatcher that she had to get married or lose her job.
- A California man was denied a job with a sheriff's department when they found out he was living with another man.
- A couple who had been together for thirteen years and who bought a house in suburban Missouri were denied an occupancy permit to live in town because they were cohabiting.[3]

Not a single example on this list comes from New York City, San Francisco, or Cambridge, Massachusetts, which is why living in college towns and gentrifying neighborhoods gives a false impression that tolerance for and acceptance of couples living together is universal. Although cohabitation has become commonplace and open in the United States, overt acts of discrimination against cohabitors—by employers, judges, parole boards, landlords, and localities—are still occurring, especially in more conservative regions of the country. Protection of the rights of cohabitors is largely related to geography: knowing the map of anticohabitation sentiment and politics pinpoints the hot spots in an ongoing culture war. Protection of the rights of cohabitors is also related to poverty: poor people on welfare do not have the same rights to privacy as self-supporting couples. And while poverty and geography affect the way cohabitors are treated, so does government policy; policies at all levels of government promote legal unions through a system of marital privilege in which cohabiting couples receive fewer employee and government entitlements as well as having fewer rights, such as the right to sue third parties when their partner is harmed or injured or the right not to testify against one's partner in a criminal proceeding.

The purpose of this book is to outline the features of American history, especially recent history, that explain why American law and policy have failed to accept the reality of cohabitation. This is the history of a cultural lag, a failure of beliefs, laws, and policy to keep up with changing reality and of a lack of interest or concern about that lag. This book argues that this lag is a product of the salience of marriage promotion as a traditional feature of American politics, which was revitalized with the emergence of the New Right in the late 1970s (what I refer to as the backlash against the sexual revolution or the culture wars). Cohabitation itself was unimportant enough in the culture wars that it was rarely a primary target of the clashing sides. Instead, it often became a target because it was related to other issues that were more emotionally charged. The existence of this culture war is important in understanding why, despite the growth of more open and accepting attitudes toward cohabitation, a kind of "coercive moralism" characterizes many aspects of American law and social policy toward cohabitation.

My undergraduate students are extremely interested in denial of the right of gay couples to legally marry; they have no interest whatsoever in denial of the right not to have to marry. A few lawyers, judges, and members of singles organizations believe family law must change to take into account the large number of cohabiting families because they have seen so many instances of vulnerable women and children harmed when they were denied their right to sue or were deemed ineligible for certain benefits. Some social scientists are concerned about cohabitation because so many children are being raised in what is deemed a fragile family form; cohabiting couples are more likely to break up than married couples, and cohabitation is often of shorter duration than marriage, bringing instability to the lives of children and increasing the risk of poor outcomes since some of the children of cohabiting couples will find it difficult to deal with so many changes while they are growing up.

I had no reform agenda in mind when I began my research. I was mainly interested in the ways the American family has changed since and because of the 1960s, and cohabitation seemed to be the least explored in a set of divisive new social trends, including divorce, the growth of single-parent families, and the rise of out-of-wedlock childbearing. It is only as a result of my research that I have concluded that cohabitors are indeed second-class citizens in the United States, even though most of them would shrug their shoulders at the idea. Marriage reflects and reinforces the notion of the state creating distinct classes of citizens, only some of whom receive special benefits. I include within the domain of sexual citizenship property and privacy rights and equal justice under the law; the right to political representation; the right to share in economic welfare and security; the right not to have to marry; and the right to recognition of a family form other than legal marriage. Thus, the history of cohabitation as "sexual citizenship" shows the way that policies in regard to and the punishment of sexuality have been used in creating the favored status of marriage in the United States. I agree that cohabitation can have negative consequences for some couples themselves but especially for children, because having many adults coming and going in children's lives during the early years of life increases the risk of psychological and behavioral problems in childhood and adolescence. A cohabitating partnership is usually not a stable home for a child, and all things being equal, stability is best for children. My response is not to deny that is so, but instead to make the following points. The first is that promoting marriage among cohabiting parents does not necessarily help the children. A recent review of the social science literature concludes, "encouraging marriage among at-risk populations may not translate into improved child outcomes."[4] With that caution in mind, I take the advice of the demographer Larry Bumpass when he advocates family "policy toward the amelioration of negative consequences, rather than toward attempts to reverse the tide."[5]

Cohabitation exists within the shadow of legal marriage; because legal marriage is the preferred state, families and the government seeks to promote it—even, I would say, coerce it. This book traces how the state, churches, and society did not simply pressure couples to get married but punished them for not doing so. Interracial or same-sex couples were not allowed to marry, but those in which the woman was pregnant were often pushed into exchanging vows. Often the man could leave town to escape going to the altar, or an uninformed family might not force the matter. But marriage promotion is a very long-standing American tradition, which begins with the belief that legal unions provide a kind of secure foundation for government and society and that sexual activity and childbearing should occur only within them. The further assumption is that there is a general moral consensus, which must be upheld by the law. These views are very old, defining features of the American character and American history, present even in the American colonies. After the Revolution, politicians, jurists, and ordinary Americans regarded stable marriage as the foundation for the new republic. They believed that the success of the nation depended on a particular form of marriage—monogamous, Christian, heterosexual, and intraracial. The historian Nancy Cott writes, "Observance of Christian-model monogamy was made to stand for customary boundaries in society, morality, and civilization; the nation's public backing of conventional marriage became a synecdoche for everything of value in the American way of life."[6] The rhetoric about marriage as the foundation of the nation appears as a leitmotif in the American symphony, with only slight changes in the notes. The Supreme Court enunciated this view in Victorian language in *Maynard v. Hill* (1887). The Court opined that "marriage is an institution, in the maintenance of which in its purity the public is deeply interested, for it is the foundation of the family and of society, without which there would be neither civilization nor progress."[7] In the Personal Responsibility and Welfare Opportunity Reconciliation Act of 1996, popularly known as welfare reform, *success* rather than *progress* was the watchword, but the means of achieving the goal was the same. The preamble to the act stated that "marriage is the foundation of a successful society" and that "marriage is the essential institution of a successful society which promotes the interests of children."[8]

Marriage promotion is more than a rhetorical flourish in court decisions and legislative preambles; it is ideology translated into policies that have real negative effects on cohabiting couples, their obligations, and, more important, their rights. Specifically, marriage promotion consists of four elements having to do with sanctions against cohabitation: (1) the punishment of cohabitation, including discrimination, such as in housing and jobs; (2) forcing couples living together to legally marry; (3) surveillance of cohabitors, including denial of the right to privacy; and (4) providing benefits to legally married couples that are denied to cohabitors. These elements of marriage promotion are not simply relics of an ancient past but persistent features of American law and policy up to the present day.

The punishment of cohabitation was not ancillary but central to the promotion of marriage. Punishment was first of all criminal; throughout colonial history, cohabitation was a crime; in most American states, cohabitation remained a crime, punished by a prison term and/or a fine. Cohabitation is still a criminal offense in five American states, although it appears that the last arrest for cohabitation was in 2003 (in North Carolina). Widely flouted, the criminal laws against cohabitation were also used to legitimate discrimination against cohabitors, including discrimination in housing and employment. In fact, many Americans did not want cohabitors as tenants, neighbors, schoolteachers for their children, probation and police officers, or Miss America contestants. The rationale for both the criminal punishment of cohabitation and for discrimination against cohabitors was that it was immoral (and the state had an interest in promoting morality) and that it constituted a threat to the sacred institution of marriage and therefore a threat to society. The sense of fear and threat is based on the belief that legal marriage is a relatively fragile institution, constantly under assault by people who are tempted to sin. Government, expected to embed the widely shared religious and moral principles in law and policy, was entirely justified in seeking to deter sin and uphold the institution of marriage.

Ferreting out couples who were engaged in a secret and hidden practice or who were pretending to be legally married is a second type of marriage promotion, which I call "surveillance." Cohabitors were not entitled to a right of privacy because it was believed that they were engaged in immorality that threatened marriage and public decency. They did not have to exhibit their nonconformity openly for their living situation to be brought to the attention of the authorities; many were quite discreet. Cohabiting women were ineligible for widows' pensions, from Revolutionary War pensions to Social Security survivor's benefits. Government agents fielded complaints from the public, talked to a woman's neighbors, and inspected her home to find out whether she had a man residing with her. If they found a live-in lover, she was declared ineligible for public aid. Because cohabitation was a crime, the police staked out the premises of those believed to be engaging in it. Both the police and inspectors for welfare agencies have pursued warrantless searches of the homes of cohabitors merely because a couple was living together. The evidence in this book will show that cohabitors have always had lesser rights to privacy than the general population. Overall, cohabiting women of color on welfare probably have had the most circumscribed right to privacy, but the examples in this book reveal stakeouts and intrusions in the homes of cohabiting police officers and school employees as well.[9]

My point is not simply that laws and policies influence couples to choose marriage over cohabitation; it is that government promotes marriage through "shotgun marriage," compelling cohabiting couples to legally marry, whether or not they want or are "ready" to do so. In a traditional shotgun marriage, a father, weapon in hand, compels a man to marry his daughter. The shotgun marriage is usually thought of as an action taken against a man who impregnated a young woman, but there were also shotgun marriages involving cohabitors. A father forced a boyfriend to get a divorce so that he could marry his daughter or decided not to prosecute a man for living with his runaway daughter so long as he married her. More important, judges, prosecutors, and other authorities insisted that couples marry. The legal scholar Ariela Dubler calls this coercion "the marriage cure"; it was based on the assumption that the state should promote marriage and that an unmarried couple living together should be prodded into doing what would be best for them and for society. City clerks enforced town zoning ordinances, telling couples living in town that they had to marry or sell their house. Landlords gave their tenants the option of getting married or being evicted. Family court judges insisted that divorced mothers marry their live-in boyfriends or ask them to move out if they wanted to retain custody of their children. Circuit court judges ordered short periods in jail for a convicted criminal who refused to stop cohabiting. Judges abrogated a prison sentence for illegal cohabitation if a couple married. Police chiefs warned cohabitors on the force to get married or else lose their jobs. Immigration officials urged cohabiting couples to marry, with the promise that if they did so they could avoid deportation. All of these authorities believed that it was acceptable to coerce couples into marrying, on the (unwarranted) assumption that once cohabitors wed, they would remain together for a lifetime.[10] As was true of surveillance, the shotgun marriage was not simply imposed on the poor or racial minorities; many of those forced to wed were middle class or even quite wealthy.[11] To be sure, some of these couples complained, asserting violation of their constitutional right to privacy, but their pleas were generally ignored and overruled.

Finally, the state as well as private employers promotes marriage through "marital privileging," granting benefits to married but not cohabiting couples, which makes clear not only that such unions are superior but also that marriage confers the right to make a claim on public funds. Thus, marriage was promoted by granting special economic benefits to married couples that nonmarried ones would be denied (because they were deemed immoral). An incredible number of benefits are available during the marriage, after it ends, and in the event of the death of one of the partners. Marriage privileging dates back to the early nineteenth century when the US government first began to award pensions to widows of veterans; before then marriage was not seen as the basis for entitlement to public funds. To be sure, although there is long-standing practice of providing special benefits to married couples and legally married widows, some state and federal policies have discouraged marriage by making it more beneficial to cohabit than to marry. Overall, however, when politicians become aware that the flow of benefits discourages marriage and encourages cohabitation, they try to correct the situation so as once again to right the moral balance in society.[12]

The old American tradition of marriage promotion was revitalized in reaction to the sexual revolution of the 1960s. The sexual revolution caused a huge backlash, in which changes in sexual attitudes and practices symbolized the decline in religion, morality, the family, and the nation. I define backlash as "the mobilization of sentiments initiated to some degree in opposition to an existing movement."[13] Whereas the Old Right saw itself defending the nation from the threat of Communism, the New Right was galvanized into action by what they perceived as the decadence and immorality of the 1960s; it emphasized religious principles embedded in law, crackdowns on criminals and welfare recipients, and opposition to the sexual revolution, feminism, and gay civil rights. The backlash meant not only that old laws and policies that promoted marriage and discouraged cohabitation were retained to reassure the public that the state stood behind morality; new laws and policies, post-1970, were enacted to undergird marriage and morality. The backlash had slightly different inflections over the course of several decades: an initial rallying cry about "law and order" at the end of the 1960s; a second, about "family values," with the emergence of the Christian Right at the end of the 1970s; and a third, "marriage promotion," which combined a desire to end the federal welfare program with opposition to same-sex marriage, beginning in the 1990s. The earthquake of the 1960s triggered aftershocks thereafter.[14] Politics, the sexual revolution, and the family were closely intertwined; thus, liberalism was central to the growth of cohabitation, and the right of privacy, so fundamental to cohabitation and to gay rights and feminism, also became increasingly important to liberalism. Similarly, mobilization against various features of the sexual revolution became a key element in conservativism by the 1970s.

The two social thinkers who first used the phrase *the sexual revolution* illustrate the opposite poles of thinking about its consequences. An Austrian psychoanalyst and colleague of Sigmund Freud, Wilhelm Reich, wrote *The Sexual Revolution* (1930). He argued that it had to precede a social revolution in order to challenge obedience to authority. Otherwise, he claimed, the family and sexual morality would stifle individual freedom. *The American Sexual Revolution* (1956) by the Harvard sociologist Pitrim Sorokin defended the social order. Sorokin argued that unless Americans reversed the dangerous trend toward "sexual promiscuity," the entire culture risked decline. If Wilhelm Reich originated the term, exactly when the sexual revolution came to denote a real change in behavior (as well as a change in values and norms and a decline in taboos and stigmas) is much in dispute among scholars. Some trace the origins of a large-scale sexual revolution to the freer atmosphere of World War II; others recognize the 1950s as a contradictory decade in which the revolution was channeled into more sexually satisfying marriages at precisely the same time that courts were voiding sexual censorship laws and the sexologist Alfred Kinsey and the *Playboy* publisher Hugh Hefner were championing sexual freedom outside of marriage. Still others (myself included) would pinpoint the early 1960s, when the Food and Drug Administration approved the birth control pill for prescription, Helen Gurley Brown heralded the emancipation of unmarried women in *Sex and the Single Girl* (1962), and popular magazines began to use the phrase *the sexual revolution*. Historians of the sexual revolution have cited almost every social and political change in the twentieth century as causes of it: the list includes the growth of a national consumer and media culture that used sexuality to sell products and gain viewers by putting sexuality on display; the expansion of the federal government; the importance of popularized Freudianism claiming that sexual repression was unhealthy; numerous legal challenges that expanded the domain of democracy to include sexual freedom. The long-range view of the sexual revolution is that decoupling sex from marriage did not occur in a single decade but over many centuries and was especially related to the decline in the need for large families, the emancipation of women, and the growth of individualism. Sexual liberalism was an earlier phase of the revolution, mainly concerned with enhancing heterosexual experience within marriage and legal access to birth control for married women. In the sexual revolution of the 1960s, marriage was only one context for sexual expression or childbearing, and adherents of the revolution favored increasing the options for sexual intimacy outside of marriage—some also favored discarding marriage entirely.[15]

Although there is little consensus about the causes of the sexual revolution, there is quite a bit about how the 1960s was related to the growth of cohabitation. The social movements of that decade from civil rights to welfare rights to feminism and gay liberation influenced one other and contributed both a language of "rights" and a language of "liberation" during the late 1960s. These 1960s social movements had religious and spiritual as well as secular dimensions, but the secular side was especially important because cohabitation up to that time had been considered living in sin. Many dimensions of feminism were important to the growth of cohabitation. For heterosexual women, the birth control pill and the legalization of abortion contributed to the decoupling of sex and marriage. Specifically, the availability of the birth control pill increased the certainty that a woman could have sex without becoming pregnant; it made a long-term sexual relationship less risky. Key components of feminism were the demand for reproductive freedom and the growth in women's education and employment, which were both causes of and results of women's quest for freedom. As women became more permanent wage earners, marriage became less of an economic necessity for women. They postponed marriage as they spent more years acquiring an education. The emancipation of women and the erosion of the economic necessity for women to be married contributed to the rise in divorce since the 1960s. Similarly, the growth of divorce made living together appear a sensible next step for those who had tried and failed at marriage and were reluctant to take another chance without first putting their new relationship to a test of residential compatibility.

Many people reading this book will think of cohabitors as the engaged couple next door, college educated and middle class. Cohabitation is linked to the 1960s, to its communes and crash pads and young women in tie-dye who referred to their partner as "my old man." Cohabitation among college students provoked the most shock in the older generation, the most stories in the press, and the largest volume of mail to Dear Abby. Because of the decline of parietal rules governing student residential life, college students were living together—often without telling their parents. But white, middle-class, opposite-sex cohabitation is only one form; cohabitation among the less well educated was and remains more common. By the 1980s, the sexual revolution and the feminist movement were slowing while the computer revolution and the globalization of manufacturing were taking off. Middle- and upper-class men and women were coming to grips with the sexual revolution by delaying marriage, accepting women's long-term participation in the workforce, and dividing up family responsibilities more equitably. At the lower socioeconomic levels of society, opposite-sex cohabitation has grown the most, where it is part of a general decline in marriage among less educated women, who are not only more likely to cohabit, but also more commonly do so several times. Such women are also more likely to bear children in a cohabitating relationship (which has a strong chance of not lasting). As a result of the decline in the stigma attached to nonmarital childbearing and the fear of divorce, the shotgun marriage became a relic of the 1950s. Moving in, or doing so when pregnant, has often replaced marrying young. Greater tolerance for nonmarital childbearing and diminished wage-earning prospects for men without college degrees has coincided with the hollowing out of opportunities for steady jobs for less educated men, encouraging cohabitation in what social scientists dub "a fragile family," one very likely to break up.[16]

A third form of cohabitation, distinct from the two described above, is living together among same-sex couples. When I tell people that the subject of my research is the history of cohabitation, the main question I am asked is whether I am including gay men and lesbians in my study, on the assumption that same-sex cohabitation would be a worthy subject of inquiry, but heterosexual cohabitation would not. In the social sciences, demographers are only beginning to survey lesbian and gay male cohabitors. In general, they find that patterns of cohabitation among gay men and lesbians are not the same as among straight people, since it is more common among white, older, well-educated couples. In general, then, the odds are that same-sex cohabitors are wealthier than opposite-sex cohabitors because they tend to be dual earner and have graduated from college. It seems likely that, given the widespread denial of legal marriage to gays, cohabitation is associated with stability—as the more committed relationship in a community that has until recently been barred from marrying. Nonetheless, this history of cohabitation primarily concerns broad patterns relating to the majority, most of whom are straight—according to the recent census figures cited earlier, 92 percent of cohabitors are opposite-sex couples.

To some extent, the assumption that the history of straight cohabitation is less interesting that the history of gay cohabitation reflects the reality that the forms of prejudice, punishment, and violence gays face is of a different magnitude than the kinds of discrimination and stigma straight cohabitors have been forced to confront.[17] Moreover, the option of getting legally married makes straight cohabitors appear unsympathetic: these are people who had the choice to legally marry but decided not to exercise it. Of course, the portrayal of straight cohabitors as free to marry overlooks the fact that many are separated but not divorced or would forfeit benefits if they married—they stand to lose Social Security or military health insurance, pension income, or access to financial scholarships for their children. It is true that straight cohabitors (who were not at the time still married) possessed a fundamental constitutional right, the right to marry legally. But it turns out that being in possession of such a right also made them vulnerable because they could be told to get married or else; gay couples were not coerced into marrying because gay marriage was illegal (and it was also assumed that for gays to marry was to encourage sin). Upon a few occasions recently, in states where gay marriage has been legalized, the same process of marriage coercion has also begun to occur.

Despite the fact that homosexuality is a more powerful stigma than straight cohabitation, straight cohabitors and gay and lesbian relationships suffer in many similar ways. Both groups have faced employment and housing discrimination, deportation, loss of child custody, and denial of the right to adopt children or serve as foster parents. Government, employers, and private individuals punish both groups for their status (being gay or not being legally married) as well as for their conduct. The concept of being in the closet is not exclusive to gays—cohabitors, straight or gay, were usually secretive about their living arrangements, sensing disapproval and possible discrimination if they were open, and were often encouraged to lie about their relationships. To be sure, Christian conservative groups take an entirely different attitude toward marriage promotion among the straight poor than among opposite-sex couples, poor or wealthy. They favor promoting marriage among cohabitors on welfare if they are straight, but totally oppose it if they are gay. Despite such different attitudes toward the promotion of marriage, conservative Christian groups do have a consistent view about immorality—cohabitation is sinful and so is homosexuality. Indeed, in targeting gays for persecution, religious right groups have passed legislation that restricted the legal rights of both gay and straight cohabitors. More important, gay liberation is an important motor of change for cohabitation. In fighting for the rights of their own group, gays have ended up benefiting others. If there is any group that straight cohabitors have to thank for the limited rights and benefits they now enjoy, it is the movement for the rights of lesbians and gay men.[18]

Indeed, this book shows the interplay between gay activism and the cause of cohabitors, revealing mutual influence. The gay liberation movement is an instance of identity politics among a sexual minority: collective action by a group with its own institutions, subculture, legal defense organizations, mobilization, insistence on public claims of pride rather than shame, demands for civil rights, and even the organization of parents of its members. There is clearly a relationship between the history of persecution and the formation of gay identity. In the case of cohabitors, however, government policing and punishment has not led to group identity. As the narrative of sexual history without sexual identity, the history of cohabitation reveals the legal advances and problems for a group that has no collective sense, no civil rights movement, no independent legal defense organization, no consciousness of being discriminated against, no separate institutions—no newspapers, bookstores, churches, or bars to call its own. Never marching on Washington for their rights, cohabitors only rarely picketed on their own behalf. If there is a cohabitor's separate world, it would have been that of prostitutes, interracial couples, bohemians, or the counterculture. Advocating respect for their living arrangement, some sought to decrease the stigma attached to cohabitation—in that sense, they were demanding social change, but not as part of a mass movement. Most cohabitors do not regard their situation as a civil rights issue or a matter of civil liberties; if anything, they often want to be left alone in a relationship they sought out because it seemed to be more egalitarian and to have "no strings attached." Since there is no legal defense organization for couples living together, they have often brought individual lawsuits with the aid of the American Civil Liberties Union (ACLU), usually on the grounds that they were denied their right to privacy or right to be free from unreasonable searches and seizures. The legal advances of cohabitors since the 1960s do not prove that a social group can achieve gains without an identity, but rather that a group without an identity can benefit as the result of a social movement's activism.

As part of the increasing openness and acceptance of cohabitation, the stigma against cohabitation has declined. Some couples still hide their living arrangement from their parents, especially if their parents believe that living together outside of marriage violates religious precepts. Even partners who have cohabited for decades willingly concede that "the stigma" against cohabitation is much less that it was decades ago. The dictionary definition of stigma is a mark of disgrace or infamy. The sociologist Erving Goffman defined stigma as "an attribute that is deeply discrediting" that reduces the bearer "from a whole and usual person to a tainted, discounted member."[19] Ancient Greeks originated the term to refer to a set of markings typically burned or cut into the bodies of criminals, traitors, and prostitutes. Prostitutes in ancient Rome were forced to wear special togas.

I reserve the term *stigma* to apply to the interpersonal communication of shaming, excluding, and shunning; it is used here to refer to informal sanctions against cohabitation. By contrast, formal sanctions are called punishment or the law against cohabitation. This definition is deliberately truncated, since in a larger sense laws and policies uphold, enforce, and perpetuate stigma. Any and all aspects of the punishment of cohabitation and the promotion of marriage no doubt compound the stigma of cohabitation, reinforcing the superiority of legal marriage and the inferiority of cohabitation. The law and public policy do appear to have a dualistic view, in which marriage confers dignity and respectability, and nonmarriage implies the absence of such desirable qualities. But I have deliberately stayed away from the position that the institution of marriage is inherently stigmatizing of all those who are not part of it, mainly because that seems a critique of marriage that is too global and ahistorical, not recognizing both the significant appeal of legal marriage to many as well as the changing nature of stigma. I have preferred instead to operationalize stigma as the social, psychological, and interpersonal processes that are intended to hurt, shame, demean, disrespect, and exclude.[20]

During the history I recount here, people other than those who lived together were also discredited by their association with cohabitation in what the sociologist Erving Goffman calls "courtesy stigma." Courtesy stigma extended to academic experts who spoke out in favor of cohabitation and state legislators who introduced bills to eliminate the criminal penalty against cohabitation. The most important courtesy stigma was that attached to a child born out of wedlock—and to the mother who gave birth to the child. Not until the 1960s did the Supreme Court grant children born out of wedlock the same legal status as children born to legally married parents. Before then, the offspring of parents who were not legally married were considered illegitimate—the term was *bastard* and the phrase was *nobody's child*—and were not allowed to inherit property from their fathers.[21] The decreasing frequency of the term *illegitimate* by the 1980s constitutes a further index of the decline of courtesy stigma.

Although "courtesy stigma" affected people who were not themselves cohabiting, punitive actions against cohabitation were mainly centered on coresident couples. Lengthy stories about cohabitors who were punished for living together appear in each chapter of this book to show the impact of stigma on their lives. When I had a choice about which stories to tell, I opted for couples I could locate and interview.[22] Since most cohabitors do not perceive themselves as targets of mistreatment, people whose stories are recounted here are those who had a genuine grievance. They were victims of discrimination who fought back, usually by taking their case to an administrative hearing or to the courts. In fighting for their rights, these couples were enlarging American ideas of sexual citizenship.

In these struggles there was a strong element of the double standard in the way women were treated. Women suffered more name calling (tramp, gold digger) than cohabiting men (who might be called pimps, parasites, and paramours). In family courts, cohabiting mothers were punished by losing custody of their children, whereas judges tended to hold divorced fathers with live-in girlfriends to a "lower" moral standard or even to view the presence of their girlfriends as assuring a man's children better care. But in the criminal courts, many more men than women were prosecuted for the crimes of fornication and cohabitation. In sum, there were quite a few heterosexual men who were stigmatized because they cohabited.

Stories of individuals are the only way to learn the personal price some cohabitors have had to pay. To be sure, adults with secure incomes, liberal employers, and liberal parents suffered little personal pain, proof that some people were insulated from the shame others experienced. I interviewed cohabitors who thought that the charges brought against them were a laughing matter, and others who were moved to tears. At the more severe end of the spectrum, a cohabitor experienced "internalized stigma," in that he or she absorbed "negative perceptions, beliefs, and experiences into his or her own self."[23] Internalized stigma manifested itself in loneliness, depression, and, in a few cases, suicide. The damage to reputation might not diminish even when a couple moved to another location but instead shadowed them in their new place of residence. I tell these stories to show not only that punishing cohabitation was personally damaging but that the experiences of these couples are connected to the history of the culture wars and the assertion of a right of personal privacy.

The long tradition of legal acknowledgment of common-law marriages (also called informal marriages) runs counter to the equally long tradition of promoting legal marriage and punishing cohabitation.[24] There were several reasons why the law might be tolerant of couples who did not legally marry, including that common-law marriage could shift the obligation to support a dependent woman from the public purse to a man. It should also be mentioned that common-law marriage was not about cohabitation, but rather about broadening the definition of legal marriage. American common-law unions were considered marriages, and the children from them were not regarded as bastards but were defined as legitimate; ending a common-law marriage required a divorce. The Swedish legal scholar Goran Lind defines common-law marriage "as a legal institution that gives the legal effects of formal marriage to qualified couples who without formally having entered into marriage, are in agreement and live together under marriage-like conditions."[25] For centuries, the Catholic Church tolerated informal marriage because it wanted to reduce out-of-wedlock childbearing and keep the faithful from leaving the church. The qualified couple exchanged words of consent, which the church considered the requirement for marriage. The Council of Trent (1545–63) sought to eliminate informal marriages and cohabitation at a time of Protestant defection from the Catholic Church. After Henry VIII broke with the Roman Catholic Church, Anglicans continued to recognize common-law marriage. In 1753, the British parliament passed legislation requiring that for a marriage to be valid it had to be performed by a minister of the church except in the case of Quakers or Jews. The legislation was designed to discourage elopement by young couples whose parents opposed the match and found an unscrupulous minister to marry them. Under the new legislation, a legal marriage required publication of banns, a license, a ceremony with witnesses and solemnized by clergy, and state registration.[26] In the United States before the Civil War, antebellum state appellate courts in some states not only accepted common-law marriage but also claimed that not to permit it would have the effect of declaring a large number of children illegitimate. The high-water mark for judicial acceptance of common-law marriage came in 1877, when the US Supreme Court in *Meister v. Moore* held that "common-law marriage is a marriage."[27]

At the local and state level, judges were usually confronted with a woman who had been deserted or brought a claim after her partner had died. They gave the woman the benefit of the doubt—except when it was a black woman claiming to be the common-law wife of a white man, in which case racial prejudice overrode notions of Victorian morality. Judges were especially sympathetic to the woman if the neighbors regarded the couple as married and were inclined to rule in favor of a dependent and virtuous woman who had had a long-term cohabitating relationship and was requesting a share of a dead man's estate. Difficulties arose when someone appeared in the court who knew that the couple was merely posing as married and disputed the woman's claim. The challenger might be the parents of a young girl who had run away from home to live with her boyfriend. Or the man could be shown to have a legally married wife from whom he had not been divorced. In such cases, cohabitors were punished, sometimes with a jail term. Whereas many nineteenth-century judges were sympathetic to a woman's claims of common-law marriage, many US government pension clerks were not. Judges and clerks shared the view that a woman was dependent on the family, not the public, for support. But US pension clerks, unlike judges, had to follow strict rules of eligibility about proof of marriage when dispensing public funds. [28] I trace in detail in chapter 7 the gradual demise of common-law marriage in the twentieth century, so that it can no longer serve as a rationale or safe haven for cohabiting couples who decide they want to seek the legal benefits of marriage. As of early 2011, common-law marriage is legal in eleven states and the District of Columbia. However, it is probably the legacy of the tradition of common-law marriage that explains the mistaken popular belief—common even among law students—that if a couple remains together seven years, they are legally married.

This book is organized according to a chronology of challenges to the second-class citizenship of cohabitation. Thus, I examine statutes against interracial cohabitation, welfare law, sanctions against college students living together, criminal prohibitions against cohabitation, denial of alimony, loss of child custody, and discrimination in housing and employee benefits. These topics constitute some but by no means all the ways that cohabitors have been discriminated against in law and policy, nor all the ways they fought discrimination. In all these areas, it is easy to show how regulation of cohabitation was intertwined with race, class, gender, generation, geography, and sexual orientation. Although some challenges to the denial of citizenship are coterminous, later struggles in domains such as child custody, housing, and employee benefits proceeded only after the greater visibility of student cohabitation and the assertion of legal rights of cohabitors in

Marvin v. Marvin. In turn, all of these challenges exist within the shadow of the language about rights and the victories of the civil rights movement. Because of the topical organization of the book, several chapters discuss events happening during the same period of time. Although the 1960s is the point of origin for the sexual revolution of cohabitation, the decade of the 1970s comes up in various chapters when the criminal punishment of cohabitation began to crumble and cohabitors insisted on their civil rights and liberties. It is therefore useful to keep in mind an overall periodization of changes in cohabitation as one considers specific forms of discrimination.

1. 1962–67: Cohabitation is seen as lower class and more common among minorities, interracial couples, and bohemians. It is against the law in most states and is highly stigmatized. The first attacks on laws against cohabitation and administrative procedures restricting cohabitation appear in the courts and in campus protests. Although occurring at the same time, the lawsuits and protests are unrelated, infrequent, and characterized by a language of rights that originated with the civil rights movement.

2. 1968: Meanwhile, college student cohabitation becomes visible in the press through the punishment of Linda LeClair at Barnard College for living off campus with her boyfriend. Campus activists, influenced both by hippie values and by a belief in confronting authority, were also protesting against college housing rules. Cohabitation is seen in a new light, as part of the counterculture, the generation gap, student unrest, and "the new morality" of the young. Cohabitation is still highly stigmatized and remains criminalized.

3. 1969–75: Revelation of cohabitation in cities and at colleges is no longer "a sex scandal," and as a result of its increasing visibility, cohabitation appears in popular songs, in Hollywood films, and on television, but still not in advertising. It remains scandalous in small towns and suburbs, where it provokes hostile reaction and punishment as part of a general backlash against 1960s protest and liberalism. Meanwhile, social scientists begin to study this new trend and help reinforce the view that it is mainly a phenomenon among college students. The social researchers engage in a scholarly debate on whether cohabitation is an alternative lifestyle for the young and a testing ground for marriage or whether it is harmful to women, a predictor of divorce, and a cauldron for domestic violence.

4. 1976–80: By the end of the 1970s, the generation gap had subsided and cohabitation was no longer a crime in most American states. With the end of the criminalization of cohabitation in many states, cohabitors insist on claiming new legal rights, defining cohabitation not simply as a form of dating or a testing ground for marriage but as a legitimate form of family

that involves rights as well as obligations between long-time partners. The judgment in the *Marvin* case adopts this view and leads to greater visibility of cohabitation, including on television and in more Hollywood films. Opposition to cohabitation becomes a minor part of the emergence of a national backlash against gay civil rights and feminism, and cohabitation is perceived as threatening marriage and contributing to the rise of divorce and the decline of the family. Still, despite the backlash, stigma against cohabitation lessens even more and tends to be concentrated in the Midwest and the South, where a few new legislative prohibitions are enacted.

5. 1980–95. When Ann Landers changes her mind about cohabitation and announces in a column in 1993 that it is a "sure way to avoid possible disaster," it is clear that dominant public opinion has shifted. The majority of American women in the early 1990s are living with a partner prior to getting married, delaying marriage until they finish their education and reach a desired level of financial stability. Cohabitation has become normative, rather than deviant, so much so that couples who did not live together before marrying are the new abnormals. Moreover, as cohabitation becomes a living arrangement common in the suburbs, and more children are being raised by cohabiting mothers, trial court judges are forced to determine custody, alimony, and visitation rules for the divorced who are cohabiting. The familiar pattern of acceptance and backlash, divided by region, is compounded by a national belief, regardless of region, that legal marriage is the key to overcoming poverty among the poor. The gay liberation movement begins to press for cohabitors' rights to employee benefits, also provoking opposition from the New Right. Stigma against cohabitation lessens even more and remains concentrated in select regions.[29]

6. 1995 to the present. Cohabitation is so common that it defies classification but instead serves a variety of different purposes: as a pathway into marriage; an alternative to marriage, especially among the poor; and a form of dating. Childbearing among cohabiting couples burgeons. The growing prevalence of cohabitation collides, however, with the strength of the "marriage movement," a more secular version of the conservative religious backlash against the sexual revolution, which emphasizes promoting legal marriage as the solution to poverty and/or opposes same-sex marriage. Both developments reinvigorate efforts to promote legal marriage in law, policy, and school abstinence-only curricula.[30]

The single point of origin here is the early 1960s, when individuals and couples first defied being punished for living together. Everything about the 1960s, but especially the sexual revolution was deeply unsettling and led to a defense of marriage and religious morality that affected American law, electoral politics, and family life. Cohabitation was seen as threatening not only the institution of marriage but also the nation. The sense of a threat to the nation has a long history: promotion of marriage serves as a rhetorical first line of defense against the disruptive impact of political, economic, and social change in the family and the nation. Republican politicians as well as religious conservatives led the rightward turn, which sought to defend marriage and family from the onslaught of the sexual revolution and rein in liberal decision making by the courts.[31] Fear about dramatic and unsettling change was often channeled into symbolic fights over sexuality, gender, marriage, and the family in which laws and judicial pronouncements often served as rhetorical assurance of stability and morality. Debates about cohabitation expressed broader social and political concerns about ideology, the right of privacy, the proper role of the state, and the health of the nation. Political ideology and the sexual revolution were mutually reinforcing: the sexual revolution strengthened the privacy side of liberalism, just as the threat to marriage, gender roles, and the family reinvigorated and reshaped American conservatism.

The history of cohabitation in recent decades is in a sense about the widespread denial of the reality that Americans will spend a growing proportion of their lives outside of legal marriage and that cohabitation has for many become a form of family. An enormous revolution in sex and marriage has swept throughout the developed world since the 1970s. The increase in the average age at first marriage, high rates of divorce, increased childbearing outside of wedlock, the rise of cohabitation, the increased economic independence of women who are changing the nature of marriage as well as singlehood are all features of the dethroning of marriage as the only option for adult life. In fact, cohabitation is far more common in Scandinavia, parts of Western Europe, and the Commonwealth countries than in the United States because the latter is more religious and more marriage-minded than these other countries. In a sense, where there is more reality, there is also more acceptance of it. In Scandinavian law and social policy, cohabitation is virtually indistinguishable from legal marriage; to a lesser extent, that is also the case in France, the Netherlands, and the Commonwealth nations. This book explains why the United States is such an outlier. Whereas most developed countries have focused on how they can best cope with this new reality of committed relationships and the way children are being raised, many Americans have focused on how they can make immorality disappear because it is such a threat to the nation.

Although the sexual revolution and the emergence of cohabitation were generational changes that spread across many countries, ideas about rights of the citizen, different understandings of the nation, and the political ideologies of liberalism and conservatism have profoundly shaped how each country responded. Cohabitation certainly had ties to free love, anarchism, and socialism, but as it became more common in the United States, its greatest defense was liberalism, including respect for the right of privacy, the recognition of plural forms of families, and the belief that the state should be neutral in matters of morality. Similarly, the greatest opponents of cohabitation were social conservatives who defended legal marriage and sexual expression only within the confines of marriage. One of the major areas of struggle in the United States has been about the legacy of the 1960s; it is a conflict of moral and family discourses and ideals, fundamentally connected not only to the social and regional divisions in American society but also to the political conflicts of emergent conservatism and liberalism, expressed in court decisions, law, public policy, and the growing polarization of the two major political parties. Liberalism proves the better defense for privacy rights and personal freedom, but it has nonetheless failed to provide workable solutions for the growth of cohabitation, suggesting that the rights framework is a necessary but not sufficient element for the genuine acceptance of cohabitation. Moreover, while greater tolerance for and acceptance of cohabitation is the strongest trend recounted here, the growing bifurcation of the nation along regional lines comes in a close second.

TWO

Night Falls in Miami Beach

Dismantling laws against interracial sex and interracial marriage was among the major victories of the civil rights movement in the mid-1960s. In 1964, an interracial cohabiting couple challenged an antimiscegenation law before the US Supreme Court and won. That decision was a victory both for civil rights and for the sexual revolution, although at the time the decision was understood entirely as a stepping-stone on the way to a declaration that legal marriage was a fundamental constitutional right that could not be abridged on grounds of race. The first couples to sue in court against laws punishing cohabitation included interracial couples who saw themselves not as taking on the cause of living together but instead as overturning statutes against interracial marriage. The civil rights movement was a necessary precondition for a sexual revolution that benefited cohabitors, but it did not attack the fundamental assumption that cohabitation was immoral and should be criminalized.

In 1962, Connie Hoffman and Dewey McLaughlin were arrested in Miami Beach, Florida, for the crime of "Negro Man and White Woman, not Being Married to Each Other, Habitually Living in and Occupying in the Nighttime, the Same Room." This crime (of an interracial couple living together in the nighttime) was a special offense compounded of race and sex found only in Florida, but interracial cohabitation was a separate crime in several other states. In 1964, the case of Hoffman and McLaughlin reached the US Supreme Court, which ruled that Florida's law against interracial cohabitation in the nighttime was a violation of the equal protection clause of the Fourteenth Amendment of the Constitution.

The US Supreme Court declared laws against interracial cohabitation unconstitutional three years before it declared laws against interracial marriage unconstitutional. The reason laws against interracial cohabitation were removed first was not that interracial marriage was the greater taboo—quite the opposite. The stigma against interracial cohabitation was much greater than the stigma against interracial marriage. Hoffman and McLaughlin did not want to claim that they were cohabiting but instead insisted that they had a common-law marriage; they wanted to appear before the courts as a respectable married couple. When tracked down by a reporter from *Jet* magazine as their case went to trial, they expressed the hope that the court would protect "the personal right to marry"; they never mentioned the right to cohabit. In fact, the NAACP (National Association for the Advancement of Colored People) lawyer for Hoffman and McLaughlin said before the Court, "The time has come to remove this stigma from the fabric of American law." He was referring not to the stigma of cohabitation, which, as far as one can tell, he believed should not be dismantled—but instead to the stigma against interracial marriage.[1]

The purpose of this chapter is to show that cohabitation is not simply about mostly white young people living together, but about race in American history. There were special and separate laws against interracial cohabitation in order to enforce white supremacy. But the very long history of the civil rights movement shows that the movement often tried to refute racial stereotypes about black people by insisting that contrary to racial and sexual stereotypes, many African Americans were sexually respectable, which proved that they were fit and ready to become first-class citizens. The civil rights movement, thus, was unwilling to attack the whole idea of sexual respectability and to insist that moral standards could not be used to make decisions about citizenship. Because of these attitudes, the Hoffman and McLaughlin case was not a good one to overturn the criminalizing of cohabitation. In fact, Florida still has a law against cohabitation on the books, a law that was last enforced in 1969. Although the majority of states removed laws punishing cohabitation as a crime in the 1970s, many others, including Florida, did not. Thus, the story in Florida begins with the civil rights movement, but continues with the growth of the New Right, which in a sense has replaced Jim Crow as the major force that supports the legal regulation of cohabitation in the Sunshine state.

The civil rights drama recounted here is not the familiar one of dogs, fire hoses, and bullhorns, since Miami Beach was not a bastion of the Old South; the policemen who arrested McLaughlin and Hoffman did not belong to the Klan—one was an Italian American, Nicholas Valeriani, and the other a Jew, Stanley Marcus. Although the Florida law against interracial cohabitation was a legacy of Jim Crow segregation in the South, the actual case that came before the US Supreme Court involved racial discrimination by an Orthodox Jewish landlady in a Jewish neighborhood in Miami Beach. As the lawsuit made its way to the Supreme Court, the constitutional issues posed kept changing. The Miami Beach police transformed a case of a landlady who wanted to evict an interracial couple because her neighbors objected into a criminal violation of an antimiscegenation law. In the Florida Supreme Court, the question was whether the state would be required to remove the last major barriers to interracial marriage left over from the Jim Crow era. In the US Supreme Court, the issue changed again to become a question of whether the law would permit the use of race as a system for classification and punishment.

In Florida, marital supremacy turns out to be a longer and more durable tradition than white supremacy—laws against interracial cohabitation lasted 132 years, whereas laws against cohabitation have endured for at least 178 years. Thus, *McLaughlin v. Florida* was both a great victory for civil rights and a highly conservative legacy for sexual freedom, since in a favorable decision the US Supreme Court also held that the state had a responsibility to preserve morality through the punishment of "illicit" sexuality. Ironically, the Warren Court, in one of its great liberal rulings, provided the rationale for the criminalization of cohabitation in Florida, that the state has an interest in punishing the immorality of promiscuity. Although the criminal law against cohabitation itself is no longer enforced, it has nonetheless been used multiple times to justify various forms of discrimination against cohabitors. None of these legal developments have, of course, had any impact on the thousands of couples throughout Florida who are openly living together, proving once again that punishing cohabitation does not deter people from doing as they please.

In 1962, interracial cohabitation was still a pattern generally found among poor white women who took as partners low-skilled, uneducated black men. According to liberal lawyers and judges, interracial couples were cohabiting *because* they were prohibited from legally marrying. Indeed, legally married interracial couples were sometimes charged with the crime of interracial cohabitation. But interracial couples living together were in fact often choosing a short-term relationship, and they often chose it several times, since they might be serial cohabitors, or one or both of them were legally married to someone else but were separated and had not divorced. Moreover, another distinctive pattern of interracial cohabitation was that it mainly consisted of white women and black men. White men who had black mistresses tended to visit rather than reside with these women, unless the woman could be camouflaged in the same household as a maid or a cook. If a white man had a child with a black woman, it was unlikely that he would acknowledge the child as his. White women who lived with black men were usually cut off from their families of origin, who doubtless would not have approved of the relationship. Similarly, the cohabiting black man was often isolated from his biological family and perhaps from friends as well. The relationship between Connie Hoffman and Dewey McLaughlin fit precisely in these common patterns.[2]

Connie Hoffman, a waitress originally from Birmingham, Alabama, where the NAACP was once banned, had a brother who belonged to the Ku Klux Klan. She left the Steel City when she was in the eighth grade, perhaps to live with another brother in Miami. Maybe she had always yearned for a freer life; perhaps she had to get away from her family. At any rate, even though she grew up in the segregated world of Birmingham, she met and fell in love with men from quite different backgrounds. By 1956 she was twenty-seven and pregnant with the child of Robert Gonzalez, probably a Cuban émigré. She took his name and called herself his common-law wife. This may have been accurate, or she may have wanted to make sure that her son, Ralph, was considered legitimate.[3]

When she was four months pregnant, Connie Hoffman left Robert Gonzalez and began to live with Fred Hoffman. He was white, in his fifties, and was willing to support her and Ralph; she may even have married him. They rented an efficiency apartment from Dora Goodnick in April 1961. Connie Hoffman broke up with Fred Hoffman seven months later; he moved to his own place nearby, but Connie, who remained Dora Goodnick's tenant, continued to go by the name of Hoffman. She could not control Ralph, and Fred Hoffman agreed to take him, though Ralph sometimes stayed overnight with her. Dora Goodnick was annoyed by Connie's inability to care for Ralph, but not enough to evict her.

Connie fell in love with Dewey McLaughlin, and by December of 1961 they were living together in her apartment. He was a merchant seaman born in La Cieba, Honduras. In Florida, McLaughlin was not classified as Honduran, however. The color of his skin made him an African American. Light-skinned Hondurans were considered Hispanics, who were not subject to Florida segregation laws, but dark-skinned Hondurans were considered blacks, who were. After twice being deported and then returning to the United States, he moved to Miami, where he found work as a porter at a Miami Beach hotel. He had married an African American woman, but they had separated, and apparently he was still legally married when he was living with Connie Hoffman.[4]

After spotting McLaughlin in the apartment, Dora Goodnick asked Hoffman, "Miss Connie, who is that gentleman?" Connie replied, "That is my husband." Dora Goodnick then asked Connie Hoffman to add the couple's name to the register; Connie signed as husband and wife. Dora asked no more questions even though Connie Hoffman had previously identified Fred Hoffman as her husband, presumably because she wanted to rent the apartment. In South Beach, many residents did not own cars; so a stranger waiting at the bus stop would be quickly noticed. Neighbors confronted Dora, asking her whether she knew that she had a "colored man" living in one of her apartments. Dora Goodnick entered apartment 8 and asked to speak to Connie. In Yiddish-inflected speech, she said to her, "I want you should move out; I don't want that business," but Connie Hoffman refused to leave.[5]

Later, Dora was hanging her laundry outdoors on a clothesline, and the screen door to apartment 8 was standing open. McLaughlin did not know that Dora was nearby. He had been taking a shower and stepped out of the shower naked; she saw him without clothes using the toilet. At the trial of Hoffman and McLaughlin, Goodnick testified, "That is why I moved her out."[6] Dora Goodnick viewed Dewey McLaughlin in terms of his naked body, which symbolized pollution and the contamination of the toilet in apartment 8. Nakedness conveyed sexuality, and a black man's use of the toilet stirred the fear that blacks spread venereal disease.[7] In glimpsing McLaughlin naked, Dora probably saw his genitals. The purported large size of a black man's penis had been a subject of the racist overheated imagination for centuries.[8]

Dora Goodnick could not accept a black man's use of the bathroom, his having sex with a white woman, or his being drunk on property she owned. In December of 1961, she complained about the couple at the police station across the street, but apparently the police did not respond. Finding Fred Hoffman in his apartment, she said to him, "Please move them out."[9] Complying with her request, he came to apartment 8 and put Connie Hoffman's clothes into his car. Filled with rage at Dora, Connie approached the open door of the Goodnick house and shouted, "I am going to kill you; I am going to kill you." Dora Goodnick closed her windows, did not answer, and padlocked the door to apartment 8.

Connie Hoffman and Dewey McLaughlin moved to an apartment in Miami for about three months, perhaps in a black neighborhood or a mainly Honduran area of Miami. In February of 1962, Connie returned to Dora Goodnick's; McLaughlin was with her again, but at first unnoticed. Dora was suffering from arthritis and bronchitis, and when she walked she needed to use a cane. The only explanation for why Connie Hoffman was allowed to rent the apartment again is that Dora's husband was desperate to find a tenant and acted without consulting his wife. Exactly why Hoffman and McLaughlin wanted to move back to an apartment where the landlady had forced them to leave is not at all clear. They may have preferred to live in Miami Beach, because it was closer to their jobs or to Ralph, who was probably living with Fred Hoffman. They seem to have miscalculated, thinking that Dora was too weak to threaten them again or that the police had already shown that they were willing to leave them alone.

When Dora Goodnick figured out that Dewey McLaughlin was living in apartment 8, she tried to evict him and Connie Hoffman. She and the neighbors complained to the Juvenile Aid Bureau of the Miami Beach Police Department that Ralph was wandering the streets at midnight. The police arrived at apartment 8 on the evening of February 23, 1962, to arrest Connie Hoffman for contributing to the delinquency of a minor. But it appears that the police had also decided that they might be able to accuse Hoffman and McLaughlin of the crime of interracial cohabitation. Connie Hoffman was not at the apartment because she was searching for Ralph. The Miami Beach detectives, accompanied by Dora, knocked on the front door of the apartment, but Dewey McLaughlin did not allow them entry.[10] Dora told the two detectives that the apartment had an exit in the back; they went there and cornered McLaughlin as he was trying to escape.

The detectives entered apartment 8 and questioned Dewey McLaughlin, asking him to produce his Miami Beach registration form. Employees of Miami Beach hotels and restaurants were required to carry identification cards, issued by the Miami Beach Police Department, with their photos and fingerprints. Blacks in greater Miami believed that the registration system was designed to monitor and police black workers on Miami Beach and that law officers singled them out for routine checks of their identity cards.[11] The registration system made it easy for the police to use the lack of a card as grounds for arrest, if other kinds of evidence were not immediately available. In examining McLaughlin, Detective Valeriani noted that McLaughlin's registration card had expired, and he and Marcus then arrested McLaughlin for violation of the civil registration law.

Marcus and Valeriani entered the apartment even though they did not have a search warrant. Why did McLaughlin let them in? Valeriani explained at the trial that he did so "at our request. He didn't offer any type of refusal of entrance."[12] Dewey McLaughlin knew the racial rules, that a black man did not tangle with white policemen. The officers had the power to inquire about sex and so they did. They quizzed McLaughlin as to whether he had

had sex with Connie Hoffman and told him that he had to answer honestly or he "had trouble."[13] McLaughlin, having been twice deported from the United States, understood the nation's unwritten racial rules. Detective Valeriani noticed that "you could see he was very hesitant, hesitated, and finally it was gotten across that he understood and that they were sleeping in the bed." McLaughlin told the detectives that he had had sex with Connie only one time, but the police could see the double bed, and McLaughlin's two shirts hanging nearby, and knew he was lying.

The detectives put McLaughlin in an unmarked police car and took him to the station house. They ran into Connie on the street and asked her to appear there as well. After the couple was fingerprinted and photographed, they were released. The next day, Detective Marcus appeared at a hearing in municipal court to testify against Connie Hoffman. As a result of that hearing, Ralph was temporarily removed from his mother's custody on the grounds of child neglect. The police asked Connie Hoffman if she was living with "a Negro male." Reflecting her misunderstanding of Florida law, she replied, "I don't know of any law prohibiting me from living with a Negro man. That is all I have to state."[14] She was then charged with contributing to the delinquency of a minor, and McLaughlin was charged with violating the civil registration law. (For some reason, they were still not charged with the crime of interracial cohabitation.)

Hoffman and McLaughlin were living at apartment 8 a week later, when Dora Goodnick and her neighbors complained again, this time to the Juvenile Aid Bureau. Lieutenant Farrell, a woman social worker with the Juvenile Aid Bureau, called the police, who went to the Cavalier Hotel where McLaughlin was employed as a porter. The manager of the hotel, Bernard Charkovsky, who liked McLaughlin, tried to stop the police from arresting McLaughlin; they told Charkovsky he was interfering with an arrest. Another policeman showed up at apartment 8 and arrested Connie Hoffman. She and Dewey McLaughlin were charged with violating Florida statute 798.05, the crime of a Negro man and white women living together in the nighttime. (The other half of the statute made it a crime for a Negro woman and white man to live together in the nighttime.) Thus it appears that the interracial cohabitation statute was not the first but the last resort, to be used if more common kinds of criminal charges did not carry sufficient penalties. Violation of this statute was also easier to prove than the crime of cohabitation, which, at least according to the law books, required catching the couple in an act of sexual intercourse. All told, the police undertook several punitive actions at the same time, since they brought Ralph to the police station where he was taken into custody by the Juvenile Aid Bureau and placed him in the care of the State Department of Public Welfare; it is not known what happened to Ralph. Miami Beach police also checked with the Immigration and Naturalization Service to find out whether McLaughlin was in the United States legally.[15] Therefore, use of the criminal law also involved loss of custody and threats of deportation.

Shtetl by the Sea

The irony of life in Miami Beach was that the victims of discrimination ended up practicing it. When he developed Miami Beach in the 1920s, Carl Fisher made sure that land sales were restricted by covenants that prohibited sale to Jews. Hotels on the beach liked to advertise "Always a View, Never a Jew." At the end of World War II, Jewish servicemen who had been stationed on the Beach during the war returned to settle there, shocked to find that signs restricting Jews had not been taken down. They, along with the Anti-Defamation League, sponsored an ordinance in Miami Beach that banned the "Gentiles Only" or "Restricted Clientele" signs. Even so, a survey by the Anti-Defamation League in the early 1950s found that about a fifth of Miami Beach hotels prohibited Jews.[16]

Real estate developers in South Miami Beach, however, were willing to sell property to any white person who could pay cash. Jews, some of whom were owners of hotels in the Catskills, had moved to Miami Beach in the 1930s and built small hotels and apartment buildings in South Beach. When Holocaust survivors from displaced persons camps emigrated to the United States in the late 1940s and early 1950s, they were attracted by the sunshine, beaches, cheap housing, and presence of a Yiddish-speaking community. Those who suffered from asthma or arthritis flocked to Miami Beach "like geese to rest and warm themselves in the sun."[17] Other Jews followed and established delis, kosher markets, Yiddish radio stations and theaters, and cheap cafeterias that were open day and night. In 1961, Miami Beach was 80 percent Jewish, and the average age was sixty.[18]

The Second Street neighborhood of Miami Beach housed hotel service workers and poor, largely Yiddish-speaking immigrant elderly Jews who were "almost solid Social Security," depending on their checks from the government and small additional pensions.[19] Dora Goodnick was a Holocaust survivor and an Orthodox Jewish woman who covered her hair with her scarf. In 1951, she and her husband had moved to Miami Beach where they bought a small bungalow facing Second Street and derived income from four efficiency apartments behind their house. Each efficiency consisted of a living room with a sofa and double bed, a small kitchen, and a bathroom. The Goodnicks's neighbors were also Orthodox Jews.

Interracial couples were not the only residents of Miami Beach who were living together outside of legal marriage, but cohabitation among the elderly was secretive: the man friend moved out if the children came to visit. But cohabitation among the elderly had become visible when the *Miami News* in 1964 disclosed "the tragic burden" of seniors not being able to remarry for fear of losing survivors' Social Security or veterans' death benefits.[20] The racial double standard was in that being forced to "live out of wedlock" was seen as a tragedy for older white couples but not for the younger interracial couples.

Miami Beach had one foot in Yiddishkeit and another in the segregation of the South. The black neighborhoods of Miami might contain interracial cohabiting couples, but the white neighborhoods of Miami Beach did not; such couples received stares and hostile remarks when they appeared together in public. The civil rights movement in Miami Beach dated back to the end of World War II when a black Bahamian immigrant trying to start a union among laundry workers organized the first "sit-and-swim-in" in Miami Beach in 1945. As a result of the protest, two of the city's beaches were desegregated.[21] Black doctors were permitted on the staff of Mount Sinai Hospital in Miami Beach by 1952.[22] When a black Methodist church group held its conference at a Miami Beach hotel, a local taxi company began to hire black drivers. Several of the small Jewish-owned hotels on the Beach were racially integrated by the mid-1950s, although black headliners at Miami Beach hotels were forced to find hotel accommodations across the causeway in Miami hotels.[23] The first small-scale efforts to desegregate the Miami Beach Public Schools began in 1959. Even so, according to Miami Beach informal racial etiquette, blacks were not supposed to be on the beach after sundown, swim in the ocean, or walk on the sand.[24]

The Legal Challenge

The McLaughlin case was part of and decided in an atmosphere of a national commitment to civil rights.[25] Congress passed landmark civil rights legislation barring discrimination in housing and employment in 1964. Student volunteers from the North arrived in Mississippi for Freedom Summer to register blacks to vote. Days after the Civil Rights Act was passed, three of the Freedom Summer workers were declared missing; President Johnson responded by initiating an FBI manhunt to locate them. After their bodies were discovered in an earthen dam in Neshoba County, many Americans believed that their murders could be avenged only by a rededication to the cause of ending racial discrimination through peaceful and legal means. The Supreme Court had already dismantled many of the laws and rationales supporting racial discrimination, but a few strands of legal apartheid remained.

The law making interracial cohabitation a special kind of crime was an expression of white supremacy; overthrowing the law was an important assault on the sexual underpinnings of Jim Crow. Statutes against interracial cohabitation were part of what were called antimiscegenation laws, which punished interracial sex, interracial cohabitation, and prohibited interracial marriage. In 1964, when the Supreme Court decided *McLaughlin v. Florida*, interracial marriage was against the law in nineteen states, including those in the Old Confederacy, the border states, Wyoming, Oklahoma, and Indiana. In two of the nineteen, Tennessee and Alabama, the antimiscegenation statute prohibited both interracial marriage and interracial cohabitation.[26] In 1964, five additional states had laws punishing interracial cohabitation (Arkansas, Louisiana, Florida, Nevada, and North Dakota). For the most part, these legal bans against cohabitation or marriage were state rather than city laws; however, in 1922, Houston passed a city ordinance banning interracial cohabitation in an effort to control the sexual behavior of newly arriving black migrants to the city.[27] The reason for the statute in Houston was that, throughout Texas, municipalities had wide latitude to enact their own segregation statutes.

McLaughlin v. Florida has usually been interpreted as a partial victory on the way to overturning laws prohibiting interracial marriage between heterosexuals.[28] Achieving the right to marry is seen as the central story, because the right to marry is regarded as a symbol of equality, a fundamental right of citizenship. The bar against cohabitation is not defined as the denial of a fundamental right to citizenship because of the assumption that cohabitation is sinful, that denial of rights to cohabitors is a necessary way to promote marriage, and that the right not to marry is not in fact a fundamental right of citizenship. Because the facts of the case were in dispute and the plaintiffs in *McLaughlin* were seen as somewhat disreputable cohabitors, the Supreme Court did not use this case to overthrow the extant laws barring interracial marriage.

Laws against interracial cohabitation were among the oldest legacies of American racial supremacy, passed in the colonies, north and south, and revived as a means of racial and social control after the restoration of white Democratic rule in the post–Civil War South. The regulation of cohabitation among people of the same race and class involved policing morality and promoting marriage; the regulation of interracial cohabitation used sexual regulation as a means of affirming white supremacy. In colonial Britain, there had been no laws prohibiting interracial sex or interracial marriage. The British colonists in North America were thus faced with a blank slate—blank as to law, but filled with assumptions about racial inferiority; race-specific laws were intended to draw stronger distinctions as to race. Laws against interracial fornication, interracial marriage, and interracial cohabitation were initially designed to reserve the rather small supply of white servant women as sexual and marriage partners for white men and punish those women who strayed. In fact, sexual relationships between white female indentured servants and African male servants, slaves, or free men were not uncommon. Masters of indentured servants wanted to claim the progeny of such unions as future servants and make up for the months lost while a white woman servant was pregnant. White servant women were discouraged from intimate association with African men; such laws helped to define the color line as the line most dangerous to cross.

The earliest miscegenation statutes did not single out interracial cohabitation for punishment because most white and black indentured servants were forced to live in the households of masters and could not reside together freely on their own. Only when many blacks and whites could dwell in their own households were anticohabitation laws passed.[29] Even for the South, Florida had an unusually well-developed arsenal of laws against interracial sex and marriage. The state forbade interracial marriage and interracial cohabitation in 1832 as a means of preventing white men from flaunting their black mistresses in public view.[30] There was seemingly little need to prevent black men from living with white women because the free black population was small and it was believed that slave men were prohibited from cohabiting with white women by the institution of slavery. During Reconstruction, white southerners wanted to clamp down on the freer sexual mores that had prevailed during the war. In 1868, the Florida legislature passed nonracial laws criminalizing fornication and lewd and lascivious behavior and added adultery as a crime six years later. In 1881, the ban on interracial marriage, temporarily shelved during Reconstruction, was put back in place. When the Redeemers, or mainly white Democrats, returned to power they passed another law that punished a black man and a white woman or a white man and a black woman who "habitually live in and occupy in the nighttime the same room," the law used against Hoffman and McLaughlin.[31]

As was the case in most southern states, the actual target of these crimes was not interracial liaisons but long-standing interracial relationships. The multiple laws of Florida sprang a perfect trap for such couples. By law, they were not permitted to marry legally, establish a common-law marriage, or cohabit. As in most southern states, the police and the courts selectively enforced such laws in Florida, focusing on punishing black men and white women in a committed monogamous relationship.[32] So long as a white man did not flaunt his relationship with a black woman, the law tended to look the other way. In the segregated South, those the police did catch could be treated very harshly. Thus, in 1958, an elderly black woman in Purvis, Mississippi, was sentenced to ten years in prison for interracial cohabitation with a white man recently discharged from the state mental hospital. A black handyman in Laurel, Mississippi, in 1959 served eighteen months in prison for "interracial cohabitation" with a wealthy, white, married woman. In Mississippi, cohabitation meant sexual relations, in this case, adultery, not actual living together.[33] Exactly how many arrests and convictions for the crime of interracial cohabitation there were in Florida in the 1950s and 1960s is unclear.[34]

The NAACP Legal Defense

While awaiting trial on the charge of interracial cohabitation, Connie Hoffman was called into the office of a social worker with the State Department of Welfare Board. Because she wanted to regain custody of Ralph, she willingly answered questions and insisted that she was the common-law wife of Dewey McLaughlin. While in jail, Hoffman had demanded an NAACP lawyer; G. E. (Grattan Ellesmere) Graves, Jr., forty-three, the attorney for the Miami NAACP, volunteered.[35] Graves, who had grown up in Washington, DC, knew Thurgood Marshall from his student days at Howard University Law School during the war. After finishing law school in 1946, Graves moved to Florida and became a prominent civil rights attorney in Miami, so visible that he was targeted for assassination by the White Citizens Council. He had opposed urban redevelopment that would have forcibly destroyed a downtown black neighborhood and helped write the legal briefs for several important civil rights cases in Miami. Graves sued to integrate Miami's beaches and public parks and fought to desegregate the railroad stations and the bus terminals. Black caddies, who wanted to play golf on Miami links, sought Graves's help in bringing a lawsuit to desegregate Miami golf courses.

Graves fully expected that McLaughlin and Hoffman would not succeed in a Miami criminal court or the Florida Supreme Court and that the case would have to be appealed to the US Supreme Court. He told that to Jack

Greenberg, the head of the civil rights litigation unit, the national office of the NAACP Legal Defense Fund; Greenberg assisted in mapping out the legal arguments for the trial. About four months after their arrest, McLaughlin and Hoffman went before a judge and jury in the criminal court of Dade County, Florida. Before the trial, the judge rejected Graves's motion to quash the indictment against his clients. Graves made two constitutional arguments, that Florida's interracial cohabitation law violated the due process and equal protection clauses of the Fourteenth Amendment and that the search of Hoffman and McLaughlin's apartment violated their constitutional right to privacy. Graves also offered the standard defense attorney argument at this time, that the state had failed to prove the racial identities of the defendants. Thus, Graves argued that the prosecution had not proven the "race" of either defendant because it relied on physical identification by detectives rather than documented verification of the ancestry of each defendant.

At the trial, Goodnick, the two Miami Beach police detectives, and a social worker with the State Department of Welfare testified against Hoffman and McLaughlin. Graves cross-examined the state's witnesses but put none of his own on the stand. At the end of the trial, Graves asked the judge to inform the jury that common-law marriage was legal in Florida. The judge complied and explained the state's definition of common-law marriage, which was a couple holding themselves out as married and recognized as such by their neighbors. But he also told them that Florida prohibited interracial marriage, so that an interracial couple could not claim common-law marriage. (At this point Graves made a fatal error in not objecting to the judge's instructions, which was necessary to make an effective appeal on constitutional grounds.) After a one-day trial, the jury took twenty-four minutes to return a unanimous verdict of guilty. Hoffman and McLaughlin were sentenced to thirty days in jail and a fine of $150 each; they served eighteen days of their sentence in county jail before the New York office of the NAACP Legal Defense Fund arranged for their bail pending appeal.

Graves immediately appealed the case to the Florida Supreme Court, which he knew would rule against him. In 1957, the court had tried to block desegregation of the University of Florida Law School, even after being required to desegregate it by the US Supreme Court.[36] The Florida Supreme Court justice Millard F. Caldwell, a former governor, known segregationist, and vocal opponent of the NAACP, wrote the court's unanimous decision reaffirming the conviction of McLaughlin and Hoffman, snidely dismissing the crime they engaged in as "integrated illicit cohabitation."[37] He referred to "the new found concept of 'social justice'" that might invalidate Florida law but was unwilling to establish any new law in the state. The Florida Supreme Court ruled that if "some new law is necessary, it must be enacted by legislative process or some other court must write it."[38]

Jack Greenberg of the NAACP Legal Defense Fund told lawyers in his office not to argue any case before the US Supreme Court unless it was winnable. The NAACP thought this case was not only winnable but could be used to dismantle the entire edifice of antimiscegenation law. In talking to the press, the NAACP spokesperson explained that *McLaughlin v. Florida* was about the "freedom to join in marriage with the person of one's own choice."[39] The NAACP's litigators believed that the judge's instructions to the Dade County jury had tipped the scales in their favor. By instructing the jury that interracial marriage was illegal in Florida, the judge had thrown down the gauntlet, inviting a challenge to the constitutionality of bans on interracial marriage. To present the arguments before the Court, Jack Greenberg contacted two lawyers who had long worked with the NAACP and had written legal briefs in the *Brown v. Board of Education* case. William Coleman was an African American with an eminent law firm in Philadelphia, and Louis Pollak was the dean of the Yale Law School. Both men were former clerks for Supreme Court justices, Coleman for Justice Felix Frankfurter and Pollak for Associate Justice John Rutledge. Coleman saw the goal of overthrowing laws against interracial marriage within reach and wanted to link Florida's prohibition against interracial cohabitation to the state's ban on interracial marriage by arguing that a common-law couple had to cohabit because they were not legally allowed to marry.

Although the NAACP had opposed extension of miscegenation laws as early as 1913, they had not taken the lead in litigation in the courts to challenge these laws. Instead, the Japanese American Citizens League (JACL), the Los Angeles Catholic Interracial Council, and the American Civil Liberties Union (ACLU) had advanced this cause and sought test cases that involved white servicemen married to Japanese or Korean war brides, where the man's citizenship rights had been proven by his service during the war. An attorney for the Japanese American Citizens League asked Jack Greenberg for more details about Hoffman and McLaughlin. After learning more about their situation, the attorney told Greenberg that he thought the couple were immoral, not the respectable young couple in love who made the most appealing plaintiffs. They were not the sympathetic public face of interracial cohabitation that would complement the Asian war bride married to the patriotic white GI who were presented as the public face of interracial marriage. The JACL wrote to Greenberg that the "facts of this case itself do not lend themselves readily to stirring social sympathy."[40]

The US Supreme Court had tried to avoid tackling America's deepest sexual fears. In 1954 and 1955, at the time it was issuing the two *Brown* decisions, the Court had deliberately skirted the issue of interracial marriage. Moreover, the NAACP had received many entreaties to bring lawsuits against miscegenation laws but always demurred because its litigators thought that the Supreme Court would rule against them. The NAACP always believed in an incremental strategy in approaching the Supreme Court, tackling the less provocative issues first. Thurgood Marshall thought that laws against interracial sex and marriage were morally wrong but did not want to raise the issue of sexual taboos that would threaten the school desegregation cases. In 1955, NAACP's executive director, Roy Wilkins, went even further, declaring in a public statement that marriage was a private matter and that the NAACP had no position on the subject of the constitutionality of antimiscegenation laws; they chose not to challenge sexual barriers directly. The whole tenor of the civil rights movement of the 1950s and early 1960s was to emphasize that blacks were deserving of full citizenship because they were sexually respectable and believed in the importance of legal marriage and fidelity within it.[41]

Thus, all the major parties delayed the moment of reckoning, but when it came, it was clear that the contest involved was about the legality of racial segregation. At the Supreme Court in 1964, the attorney general and the assistant attorney for the state of Florida conceived their Supreme Court brief in *McLaughlin* as a last stand for Jim Crow. By this time, criminal prohibitions on interracial relationships were almost exclusively confined to the South. Florida's attorney stated in his legal brief that "the races have better advanced in human progress when they cultivated their own distinctive characteristics and develop their own peculiarities."[42] He argued that the authors of the Fourteenth Amendment were explicitly opposed to interracial marriage. This claim fell on deaf ears since Earl Warren, about a decade earlier, had declared, "1866 is over." The Florida legal brief seemed rushed, since it contained many factual errors based on misreading the transcript from the original trial. But Florida's assistant attorney general found the weakness of the NAACP's case, pointing out that Hoffman and McLaughlin were not able to enter into a legal marriage since one or both of them were still legally married to someone else. He argued that since that they did not have a valid common-law marriage, it did not matter whether the state of Florida prohibited interracial marriage. But the Florida attorney also defended the state's interest in enforcing morality by insisting that Florida was trying to uphold "basic concepts of sexual decency." Lawyers for the state of Florida had inserted the remark that the "right to racially integrate at the altar or in the bed" was not a right conveyed by the Fourteenth Amendment.

The Florida attorney also voiced the common fear of segregationists, that interracial sexual relations lead to the birth of biracial children who are psychologically damaged by having to experience societal stigmas. This was the first time "harm to children" was introduced into arguments about punishing cohabitation, but it would not be the last. Lawyers for the state of Florida argued that barring interracial sex and interracial marriage served a public purpose in preventing the birth of such children. After the Civil War, it was commonly believed that blacks were an inferior race, destined for extinction, and that American race laws would be needed to protect the white race from inheriting the inferior qualities of blacks. The purity of the white race, scholars argued, was based on the purity of "white blood"; the birth of biracial children was seen as polluting good blood with bad. The fact that white Victorians feared that the physically frail mulatto would introduce weakness into the white race contradicted the other common assertion, that mulattoes were so frail as to be sterile. A Georgia court in 1869 held that offspring of interracial sexual relationships "are generally sickly and effeminate and that they are inferior in physical development and strength to the full blood of either race."[43] In 1964, it was no longer credible to claim publicly that a biracial child was doomed to physical weakness. Instead, the attorneys for the state of Florida relied on the more modern version of the argument, that cohabitation caused harm to children. In their view the state had a responsibility for the welfare of children and since biracial children were at a psychological disadvantage, it would be better for them not to be born.

The NAACP lawyer William Coleman was revolted by the eugenic arguments of the Florida attorneys. He told the Court, "I thought I was living in 1964—but during the last 10 minutes I trembled." He compared the arguments of the Florida attorneys to Hitler's speeches condemning offspring of Gentiles who intermarried with Jews.[44] Coleman and Pollak wanted a double assault on Florida's ban on interracial cohabitation as well its ban on interracial marriage. They argued that if Florida did not bar interracial marriage, Hoffman and McLaughlin could have been recognized as a couple married according to the common law, avoiding the questions of whether McLaughlin was already legally married to another woman and whether Connie Hoffman might also be married to someone else.

At the Supreme Court, the whole question of whether McLaughlin and Hoffman had a valid common-law marriage was muddled, and for this reason alone, the Court did not tackle overthrowing bans on interracial marriage. The state of Florida argued that it was up to McLaughlin and Hoffman to prove that they had a common-law marriage; the NAACP insisted that the burden of proof lay with the state of Florida to prove that they did not. Some of the justices, especially the ones who were ready to throw out interracial marriage bans at this time, were interested in this argument. Chief Justice Earl Warren, who belonged in this category, had not been paying close attention when the case was presented in court. He thought that McLaughlin and Hoffman had a common-law marriage. At conference, he asserted that he could not "see any justification for denying common law marriage to those of different race and granting it to other races." Justice Hugo Black, who had been listening more closely, told Warren, "The record indicates that both of these people are married."[45] The justices were left with an argument on behalf of two people who could not make clear that they deserved to be recognized as legally married.

After some deliberation, the Court crafted a decision that overturned Florida's law against interracial cohabitation without tackling the state's law against interracial marriage. The Court declared that Florida's provision against interracial cohabitation was an unconstitutional violation of the equal protection clause of the Fourteenth Amendment and further argued that invidious classifications based on race violated the Constitution, rejecting the view that race-specific laws were somehow acceptable, so long as they punished white and black equally.[46]

Dewey McLaughlin and Connie Hoffman were no longer criminals, but they still did not have the legal right to marry each other. They continued to live together as the case went to court, but soon after their victory, they split up. Connie Hoffman moved into Fred Hoffman's apartment behind the Miami Beach police station; Dewey McLaughlin found a room in a motel in the white section of Miami Beach; the fate of Ralph Hoffman is not known. Three years after the Supreme Court decision, Fred Hoffman called the police early one morning because Connie was breaking the furniture in their apartment. Two years later she was arrested by the Miami Beach police for stabbing a man on a street corner in an early morning fight.[47]

In 1969, Otha Favors and his girlfriend Sharon Clinkenbeard became the last couple arrested in the state of Florida for the crime of cohabitation. It was somehow fitting that five years after *McLaughlin v. Florida* an interracial couple was booked and convicted for cohabitation in south Florida. The Tampa police, along with the FBI, were reining in black militants by charging them with minor violations of the law. But it was not only the black power and antiwar activism of Otha Favors that led to the couple's arrest and conviction, but also the fact that he was cohabiting with a white girl. They were both sentenced to ninety days in jail for cohabitation and served a week of their sentences before their conviction was overturned, in part because they were married by the time they appeared before a judge.[48] In that sense, their situation was the result of racial progress, in that the Supreme Court in 1967 had ruled that laws denying interracial couples the right to marry were unconstitutional. Their arrest triggered a review of the enforcement of the law but generated no publicity. Thereafter, a few couples in Florida were threatened with arrest for cohabitation, but the authorities never followed through by booking anyone for the crime.[49]

Florida's Statute 798.02

McLaughlin v. Florida struck at the taboo against interracial sex, especially sex between a black man and a white woman. It demolished the long-standing but facile argument that special race laws were not discriminatory so long as they punished blacks and whites equally; the Court ruled that such laws remained racially discriminatory because they made race into a special category of classification and punishment and created a special crime depending on the race of those involved. As the legal scholar Reva Siegel notes, the case focused not on "how prohibitions on interracial relationships injured people or shaped their identities" but rather on the harm of race classification.[50] Nonetheless, the civil rights revolution was a limited victory for sexual freedom, since the Court attacked sexual taboos while adopting a highly conservative attitude toward sexuality and marriage.

The Supreme Court affirmed that the state had an interest in regulating sex—so long as it was even-handed in punishing blacks and whites equally and not making invidious racial distinctions in the criminal law. The Court was still upholding a single dominant moral code shaped by religion and respect for the traditional family and was still willing to use the police to enforce this code. The state of Florida, the Court agreed, could employ the criminal law to "prevent breaches of the basic concepts of sexual decency." A statute that punished a man and woman for living together in the nighttime, they believed, was punishing "illicit extramarital and premarital promiscuity." The Court referred in passing to a "general evil" to be corrected—a form of "promiscuous conduct" and "illicit behavior"—and characterized laws criminalizing cohabitation as "nondiscriminatory extramarital relations statutes."[51] Because the state had a responsibility to police morality, it also followed that cohabitors did not have a right to privacy. The Court had no quarrel with the state of Florida punishing such behavior as a crime; the problem was selecting only interracial couples for special punishment under a statute that classified a crime by the race of the people who committed it. It has long been assumed that the regulation of race and the regulation of sexuality are so intertwined that it is impossible to separate them. But the Supreme Court was seeking to dismantle the legal edifice that enshrined black inferiority and segregation while affirming what the Court must have regarded as a more legitimate undertaking of the state, its power to enforce morality.

Thus, while the Supreme Court ended the criminalization of interracial cohabitation, it did not declare—indeed, it has never declared—that criminal punishment of cohabitation is unconstitutional. As I write this, Florida still has a law criminalizing cohabitation: it is one of the five states in which cohabitation is still against the law. Even more recent victories for gay rights have not toppled such laws. The Supreme Court decision overturning sodomy laws used to punish gay couples, *Lawrence v. Texas* (2003), struck down sodomy laws as a violation of the constitutional right to privacy. The Court's opinion did not say anything about the constitutionality of the remaining laws prohibiting cohabitation, even though the lawyer for the defendants in *Lawrence* did insist that there should be a right to "private adult consensual intimacy" for straight as well as gay couples. The decision had none of the language about decency or morality found in *McLaughlin* but instead emphasized personal liberty and respect for individual choices; it was a major legal victory for gay civil rights, and a 180 degree turn from the Court's previous ruling on gay rights a little less than twenty years before. In 2005, a North Carolina Supreme Court, using *Lawrence v. Texas* as its model, ruled that laws criminalizing cohabitation violated a constitutional right to privacy. Still, a North Carolina Supreme Court decision is not the law of the land, and although sodomy, fornication, and cohabitation appear to be examples of consensual sex, protected by a constitutional right to privacy, the matter has not been put to a test.[52]

The Florida statute 798.02, which criminalizes cohabitation remains on the books. It consists of two sections, one criminalizing a man and woman living together as if they were married, and the other, criminalizing lewd and lascivious conduct. As of 2010, the second section, prohibiting lewd and lascivious conduct, was still being enforced—in fact, there were 392 arrests for lewd and lascivious cohabitation in Florida between 2005 and 2007 and 104 in 2010. This second section of the statute seems to be used to close down strip shows in private adult entertainment clubs, to raid gay bars, and to arrest child molesters. When defendants appeal their conviction on the crime of lewd and lascivious cohabitation, they invariably win. In contrast, the first section of the law, which punishes cohabitation with a maximum sentence of six months in prison, a $500 fine, or both and has not been enforced since Favors and Clinkenbeard were arrested in 1969.[53]

Still, the illegality of cohabitation in Florida was invoked dozens of times between 1974 and 1994 to justify employment and housing discrimination and denial of parole. Circuit court judges, police chiefs, and condo associations have insisted on punishing cohabitors because they believe the policy of the state of Florida is to promote marriage. None of these authorities are foolhardy enough to think they can stem the growth of cohabitation; instead, they want to exert moral authority within the sphere they control, backed up by the state criminal law. Some of the Florida cohabitors who faced discrimination were black or interracial couples, but most were white and ranged from a Canadian retired couple who bought an expensive condo on the beach in Fort Lauderdale to couples of moderate means who faced eviction from their mobile homes in trailer parks. Police chiefs and probation officers most strongly invoked the marriage cure, telling officers to get married or face suspension; some went so far as to stake out the apartments of cohabiting officers, defending their actions by pointing to Florida's criminal law against cohabitation.[54]

A couple recently harmed by Florida's criminal law against cohabitation is Michael Schiavo and his second wife, Jodi Centonze. Michael Schiavo's first wife was Terri Schiavo, a comatose woman being kept alive on a feeding tube and in a persistent vegetative state for the last thirteen years of her life. As the legal guardian of his wife, Schiavo had been pressing the courts for years to have his wife's feeding tube removed so that she could be allowed to die. Although he remained married to Schiavo, he had begun to live with Centonze, a woman he had met three years after his wife slipped into her permanent coma. Terri Schiavo's parents and other family members were devout Catholics who wanted to sustain their daughter's life by all means necessary. The pope, the president, and the governor of Florida all sided with Terri Schiavo's parents. As part of their court petition to have their son-in-law removed as his wife's legal guardian, Terri's parents pointed out that their son-in-law had a live-in "girlfriend," had fathered two children with her, and lived with her in a home Centonze owned. The petition of Terri Schiavo's parents claimed that by living with Centonze and their children Michael Schiavo was violating the Florida criminal statute against lewd and lascivious cohabitation, which they believed was "a disqualification for appointment as guardian." Most of the public furor over Terri Schiavo had nothing at all to do with cohabitation, yet Michael Schiavo's motives for wanting to allow his wife to die were suspect because of his living arrangement. Anonymous hate mail and bloggers called Centonze Schiavo's "personal whore" and described his children with her as bastards.[55] The name callers on the Web considered themselves pro-life or referred to themselves as homeschoolers, indicating that Centonze's attackers were mainly people who identified with the Christian Right. Thus, the retention of Florida's law against cohabitation strengthened the side of Schiavo's parents in a battle between two competing conceptions of morality.

The fact that criminalizing cohabitation has not been repealed by the Florida legislature is because of the success of Christian New Right activists, starting at the local level and targeting gay rights. A survey that appears to have been filled out mainly by the elderly in Miami in 1977 indicates that attitudes there were not very different from those nationwide: there was a large generation gap. The most remarkable thing about the survey is that no one in Miami was asked whether cohabitation should be against the law. But respondents to the survey clearly believed that cohabitation should be stigmatized. In response to the question, "If I were living with someone, my family would disapprove," eighty-nine people answered yes, and forty-one no. But plenty of people shared the view of one elderly couple who wrote the comment, "It's a sin, you turkeys."[56]

These views were not conducive to removal of the law against cohabitation. Anita Bryant's 1977 antigay "Save Our Children Crusade" was a local initiative, one of several points of origin for the New Right; it also reintroduced the stereotype of gays as child molesters who had to be restrained by general legislation. Bryant, a Florida Citrus Commission spokesperson and former Miss America, led a successful referendum campaign to repeal a gay rights ordinance in Miami's Dade County. Her victory spread, as citizens in Eugene, Oregon, St. Paul, Minnesota, and Wichita, Kansas voted to overturn their gay civil rights ordinances as well. Bryant's most important contribution to history was that these stunning antigay victories awakened gay activism in Miami and across the nation. As Tina Fetner notes, "It was only after the emergence of an anti-gay movement that the lesbian and gay movement grew into a large-scale, national social movement."[57] In Florida, gay activists devised a clever response to Bryant, a proposed state constitutional amendment about privacy, vaguely worded, that they hoped would decriminalize sodomy, cohabitation, and even smoking marijuana at home. Because of its general language, the amendment passed in 1980, but the Florida Supreme Court never used it to decriminalize sodomy or cohabitation.[58]

Beginning in the late 1970s, there were periodic failed attempts in the state legislature to remove the legal ban on cohabitation, which separated the issue entirely from homosexual rights but nonetheless always failed. The state organized a legal task force to consider overhaul of the state's marriage and family law, including the possible elimination of the law criminalizing cohabitation. A newly elected Barnard graduate and Jewish woman state legislator from Miami Beach sought to reform the state's marriage law on feminist and more egalitarian lines. But although the task force members seem to have favored repeal of the criminal law against cohabitation, they realized that they did not have the necessary votes in the state legislature. A Republican woman member of the task force quietly admitted, "We have more important things to do than look at this problem" and any attempt to eliminate the law would run up against "a law-and-order governor" and "a law and order legislature."[59] That was the same attitude a conservative state legislator confronted in his unsuccessful effort at repeal in 2010 and 2011.[60]

With the legislature uninterested in reform, and gay advocates in Florida marginalized as a result of Bryant's huge voter turnout against gay rights, cohabitors in Florida have turned to the courts for relief. In 1999, a few dissenting judges in the state supreme court, when overturning a conviction on lewd and lascivious cohabitation declared that the law was antiquated and suggested that the legislature needed to repeal it. But their argument fell on deaf ears. The courts required a test case, an individual who could show that he or she was personally harmed by the law. Enter Howard Fletcher, a sixty-five-year-old grandfather from Juneau, Alaska, and executive secretary of the National Sexual Rights Council. Backed by Hugh Hefner and the Playboy Foundation, he checked into a Boca Raton hotel with a woman family friend who was not his wife (he said that he had an open marriage) in 1999. He stayed three nights with her at the Doubletree Suites to make sure that he was challenging the part of the law that prohibited living in open adultery. Flanked by five hired models in bikini bottoms and T-shirts saying "Sex Instructor," he held a news conference to argue that the laws against cohabitation and other consensual sex crimes violated the right to privacy, due process, and individual liberty. A federal district court judge in Miami simply dismissed the lawsuit because Fletcher's lawyer missed a procedural deadline.[61]

Punishing immorality and promoting marriage proves to be a deeper and more longer-lasting societal concern than enforcing racial restrictions; belief in marital supremacy, not white supremacy, more enduring, and more deeply embedded in law and policy. Even at the moment of greatest liberalism in the Warren Court, the justices still upheld the fundamental beliefs in marriage promotion and state interest in enforcing morality. Thus, it turns out that the ideal of marriage as the best institution for sex and intimacy and legal marriage as the foundation for the nation is harder to tackle even than white supremacy. Promotion of marriage, rhetoric about "sexual decency," and appeals to "save our children" gained new life in the 1970s, succeeding in some states, such as Florida, but failing in others. The ACLU and gay rights activists, in concert, have attacked such views but without much success in Florida because the culture war rhetoric about the threat to the family and morality has had greater popular appeal there than individual rights. Cohabitation is not a hugely contentious issue in contemporary Florida, but it is also wrong to categorize the law as entirely symbolic, with no real effects, since the criminal law is a cornerstone for laws that justify other forms of discrimination against cohabitation.

THREE

Welfare Rights

Cohabitation was and is more common among interracial couples and the poor than among other demographic groups. Indeed, it has often been considered poor people's marriage because it is more flexible than formal matrimony, separating a couple's coresidence from considerations of support and division of property. Many poor couples are not self-supporting, however, instead turning to the government for aid. In this situation, the state imposes standards and obligations, which in turn become means of regulating and punishing cohabitation. In chapter 2, I showed that after rules for racial classification ended, rules for punishing cohabitation persisted; in this chapter, the focus shifts to poverty. It is not that poor people, regardless of race, are the only couples punished for cohabitation, but that when cohabiting parties are not self-supporting, the public expects and is willing to impose a higher degree of punishment, including surveillance, than self-supporting couples would tolerate. An indignant welfare mother in Los Angeles put it succinctly, "When you're on welfare, you can't have too much male company."[1]

The state has intruded on the personal privacy of many cohabitors, middle class as well as poor, but the intrusions have been more massive and have persisted longer when they involve poor people who are dependent on public aid. Is there a man in the house? The midnight raid of the early 1960s was the single greatest infringement on the privacy rights of cohabitors in American history. It was a mass search for "a man in the house," targeting welfare mothers and their boyfriends in order to throw the mother off the welfare rolls and to impose specific civil or criminal punishments on the woman and her boyfriend. In a midnight raid, social workers, sometimes accompanied by a sheriff's deputy, would enter the apartment of a mother on welfare, sometimes in the middle of the night or at 6:30 a.m. on Sunday.

The woman invariably was Hispanic or black, like the majority of welfare recipients at the time. Once in the home, the investigators, one at the front door, another stationed at the back, checked the closet, opened drawers in the bedroom, inspected the ashtrays for cigar butts, examined the bathroom sink for evidence of a man's hair or razor blades, and peeked under the bed. The amount and quality of the food and the number of beer bottles in a refrigerator constituted proof that a man was living there.[2] A welfare mother who lived in a southeast neighborhood of Washington, DC, told a reporter after a home visit in 1965, "You're not a free person. When you have to live like this, you're like somebody in prison."[3]

Actually, the midnight raid was only one of the ways that the welfare system punished cohabitation. Others included charges not only of cohabitation but also of adultery, fornication, or welfare fraud; those brought before the law could be put on probation or sentenced to a three-month jail term. In some counties, welfare applicants were required to sign a "chastity pledge" indicating that they would not allow "male callers" into their home and would not meet them elsewhere under "improper conditions." Some welfare agencies and judges imposed a marriage cure on welfare cohabitors, forcing welfare mothers who were on probation for having committed the crime of welfare fraud to get married or else return to their jail cells. In contrast, district attorneys generally were not interested in making couples marry; instead, they preferred to impose "a family law of the poor," transforming boyfriends into stepfathers without legal marriage, forcing such men to assume obligations of support, which, according to family law, were legally required only of married stepfathers. Finally, the welfare system punished cohabitation by privileging marriage. It originally did so simply by upholding the ideal of legal marriage and denying any public aid to cohabitors. As a result of legal victories for welfare mothers in the 1960s, cohabitation was permitted so long as the unmarried male partner contributed to the support of the woman and her children. However, reflecting the Christian Right's impact on welfare policy in the 1990s, welfare reform began to insist that the man should not only contribute to the woman's support but also marry her, as the government decided that legal marriage constituted the only permanent antipoverty program.[4]

Most of the welfare mothers active in the welfare rights movement that began in the 1960s were black and deeply influenced by the ideas and tactics of the civil rights movement. In addition to seeking a guaranteed annual income and various constitutional rights they wanted to be treated with dignity while receiving public assistance. The welfare rights movement was also a movement for sexual freedom because welfare mothers insisted on their right to have sexual relationships, without having to endure prying questions from social workers.

Although privacy was not a right stipulated in the Constitution, during the 1960s the US Supreme Court under Chief Justice Earl Warren discovered a right to privacy implied in the Bill of Rights and other constitutional amendments and enlarged the legal rights of welfare recipients. The Court's definition of the right to privacy was still quite limited; it did not extend this right to cohabitors. It was liberal state supreme courts, not the Warren Court, that claimed that welfare recipients had a constitutional right to privacy. In fact, although the US Supreme Court in the late 1960s and early 1970s issued rulings that ended midnight raids and explicit punishment of cohabitors on welfare, it also ruled that welfare recipients did not have a right to privacy.

The welfare rights movement failed to secure this right for welfare recipients; in fact, the other rights it seems to have established during its heyday have been whittled away. Nowhere is there a greater denial of the reality that cohabitation is here to stay than in the continuing punishment of cohabitation in contemporary American welfare policy. By the middle of the 1970s, the welfare rights movement had disappeared. Welfare mothers were less mobilized, antipoverty lawyers were fewer in number and less adequately funded, and the number of antipoverty class-action lawsuits had dwindled. The backlash against the sexual revolution was not always distinct from the backlash against welfare, as when white parents opposed sex education in the schools and busing as liberal plots that imposed a new morality. More importantly, the backlash was tied to the rise of conservatism, which ended up dethroning liberalism in American politics, law, and policy.

Although the stigma attached to cohabitation has decreased, the stigma attached to welfare has not. Receipt of welfare remains shameful, but cohabitation on welfare rarely rises to the top of the list of shameful acts. The "deadbeat dad" may be exactly the same individual as the live-in boyfriend, but he is being castigated for not paying child support, rather than for living with a woman on welfare. Similarly, when Ronald Reagan attacked the "welfare queen" as part of his unsuccessful campaign for the presidency in 1976, he was decrying welfare fraud rather than living together. Cohabitation is mentioned in antiwelfare discourse less as an immoral activity than as an adult practice that is harmful to children. Still, two punishments for cohabitation have been resurrected by welfare reform since 1996: marital privileging through policies that promote marriage and discourage cohabitation and surveillance of women on welfare to detect cohabiting boyfriends. Thus, although cohabitation is fairly common, government policy is to promote legal marriage of mothers on welfare and place limits on welfare eligibility.

Midnight Searches

Public welfare programs not only provide money or in-kind assistance to the needy but impose sexual, marital, childbearing, and child-rearing tests on eligibility for aid. Since public money is being given to support the poor, the question inevitably arises of who is deserving of assistance. In 1968, nineteen states and the District of Columbia had a substitute-father regulation that held a man who lived with a welfare mother responsible for the support of her children.[5] Finding a "suitable father" was a means of limiting eligibility for welfare; if there was "a man in the house" who was deemed a suitable father, he could be required to support the child. The way to prove that there was a suitable father was to show that a man had a sexual relationship with the child's mother. The man did not have to be actually living in the home or even providing funds; he could appear at the woman's place only intermittently, but by the rules of several states so long as he was having sex with the mother, he was a suitable father. In these rules, there was no attempt to make the suitable father marry a welfare recipient. The point was to find such a man and thereby eliminate the woman and her children from the welfare rolls—and sometimes, initiate further punishments against one or both of the adults. On the question of whether suitable-father rules reinforced a double standard among the poor that held women to a sexual criterion not required of men, the answer is yes. The woman was on welfare to begin with and had more to lose if the welfare department determined that she was living with a man. Moreover, one of the severe penalties she faced was loss of custody of her children. Nonetheless, if a man in the house was found, he and the woman on public aid could both be charged with welfare fraud, and the man might face additional charges of nonsupport. A boyfriend could also be threatened with prosecution for cohabitation as a means of getting him to admit paternity; he could be threatened with jail if he did not move out of his girlfriend's apartment in public housing.[6]

The welfare department imposed a standard of support on men in quite varied living situations. At one end of the spectrum was a man in a common-law marriage who was the biological father of the children in the home; the woman had adopted the man's name, and the couple had been living together for many years. At the other end of the spectrum was a man who stayed over on Saturday night and was not the biological father of any of the woman's children. Determining the duration of a relationship that met a minimum standard to be considered cohabitation provided a lot of room for interpretation. Many a man, even one who was not the biological father of a woman's children, could be designated as a suitable father. Cohabitation among the poor was often ill defined: it might be a live-in relationship or a visiting one; the couple might be together seven nights a week or a few nights per month. Some men were still maintaining sexual relationships with previous partners; they might have several homes where they lived on a temporary basis or stayed a night at a time in a kind of cyclical rotation. Suitable fathers were generally not fiancés; it was more likely that cohabitation was short-lived and serial, and that after one relationship ended, another began. What the man contributed to the support of the woman and her children also varied from occasionally providing money to bringing a gift once in awhile.

There was a huge class gap in cohabitation: in 1960, based on retrospective surveys of national samples, about 5 percent of couples with less than a high school education born between 1928 and 1932 were cohabiting, as compared with about 1 percent of college-educated couples. (The question about cohabitation used the term *living together*, not *common-law marriage*, although in 1960, popular parlance did not actually distinguish the two consistently.) Cohabitation was fairly common among the poor after women lost their eligibility for welfare. In 1960, Florida eliminated several thousand women from welfare for having children out of wedlock. A survey of the women thus removed found that about 5 percent of them were living with their boyfriends. In fact, poor women were more likely to live with their boyfriends than the general population—both while they were on welfare and if they had been thrown off of it.[7]

The welfare department learned there was a man in the house from anonymous calls from neighbors, landlords, relatives of the woman who did not like her boyfriend, jealous girlfriends, boyfriends who wanted to retaliate against women who had spurned them, or caseworkers on home visits who spied a man's jacket in the closet or shoes under the bed.[8] The mayor's office received anonymous complaints about mothers on welfare who had "continued intimacy" with a boyfriend and the father of the children, which were in turn referred to the welfare department. Some complainants were women holding low-wage jobs who resented welfare recipients. Welfare mothers who strictly conformed to the rules snitched on those who did not.[9] One welfare recipient told a social work professor that "if the person isn't guilty, then they shouldn't care when the worker comes."[10] Fraud investigators often parked outside a woman's apartment, watching who entered and left. A man carrying a bag of groceries into a house was sufficient proof of cohabitation. In East Harlem, an investigator climbed a tree at two in the morning to peer into the apartment in a housing project.[11] Every welfare department had its own procedures, and some caseworkers drew the line at questioning children, while others freely asked them, "Do any men visit your mother?"[12]

The way to prove there was a suitable father present was to find a man in a woman's apartment. In some cities, the social worker turned over her suspicions to a fraud investigator; in others, she accompanied the investigator on the midnight raid. Fraud units might be composed of the police, social workers, sheriff's deputies, or special investigators within the welfare department. In 1947, Maine was the first state to establish a special unit to investigate welfare fraud. By 1962, seven other states and eighteen large cities also had special fraud-investigation units. Fraud investigators were mainly white men, often former private detectives, police officers, or military intelligence agents. Although southern cities and rural counties had suitable-father rules, they generally did not have funding for special fraud units; they terminated women on welfare mainly for bearing children out of wedlock, which was determined from perusing birth certificates.[13]

In the 1960s, black migration to northern and western cities as well as Hispanic patterns of informal marriage led to public demands for crackdowns on welfare fraud. In a 1961 Gallup survey, half of the general public thought that unwed mothers on welfare should be thrown off the rolls. The question was not asked about cohabitors, but one can assume that the ordinary person believed that women who were living with their boyfriends should not receive public aid. The citizen at large, not just district attorneys, favored the midnight raid as a means of finding the live-in boyfriend and approved of prosecuting both the woman and her partner for welfare fraud. Perception of fraud undermined belief in welfare programs; therefore, government administrators felt that they had to show taxpayers that they were making a determined effort to find welfare cheaters. Thus, the headline of a 1960 article in the *Modesto Bee* revealed the function of the fraud investigation in shoring up public support for the program: "Investigators Hold Down Cost of Aid to Needy Children Program."[14] Caseworkers in Philadelphia were conducting raids in the middle of the night to detect welfare fraud in the late 1950s. The practice was similar to that in California in the early 1960s, and thus, California did not invent the midnight raid.[15]

Operation Bed Check, a mass visitation in Oakland in January of 1963, attracted more attention from the press than the raids in the other California counties in previous years because it targeted hundreds rather than merely dozens of homes in a single night sweep and the women on the search list were selected at random, not because they were suspected of fraud. The raid was also conducted by social workers rather than fraud investigators because of the number of personnel needed for the operation.[16] Because of the power of unions, civil liberties advocates, and nascent welfare rights organizations in Berkeley and San Francisco in 1963, what was acceptable in Tulare County or the San Joaquin Valley was considered a violation of constitutional rights in the Bay Area.

Benny Parrish, a twenty-eight-year-old Oakland social worker refused to participate in Operation Bed Check, denouncing it as "Gestapo-like practices."[17] Parrish wore thick glasses and was partially blind; a graduate of the University of California at Berkeley, he had been trained by Saul Alinsky in community organizing. Alinsky had been coming to California since the late 1940s and had helped to organize the Community Services Organization (CSO), a civil rights and labor organization for Hispanics. The Alameda County welfare director said to Parrish, "As you well know, the ANC [Aid to Needy Children] Program is under public fire. Something needs to be done in a dramatic way to prove the point . . . that the vast majority of these people are legitimately on the program."[18] After a week anguishing, Parrish told his supervisor, "This I cannot do."[19] Parrish saw the raids as an invasion of welfare recipients' privacy, which degraded both them and him, undermining his identity as a professional.[20] The county welfare department insisted that although conducting searches was not part of Parrish's job, it was not unreasonable to ask him to go on them and fired him for refusing.

In 1963, California's liberal Democratic establishment took on the midnight raid. Pat Brown, the governor of California, appointed Beverly Hills homemakers and law professors concerned about the rights of welfare recipients to the state welfare board that year. Both the NAACP and the CSO condemned the raids and pointed out that they targeted blacks and Hispanics. The Brown appointees on the state welfare board managed to outvote the district attorneys, predominantly men from agricultural counties, who saw the raids as a legitimate way of cutting down on "welfare chiseling." By July 1963, the state of California had banned the midnight raid. The National Association of Social Workers agreed with the ban and prominent law professors took up the cause, publishing influential articles denouncing midnight raids as a violation of a constitutional right to privacy.

Benny Parrish wanted to return to the job from which he had been fired—and the welfare rights movement sought a legal, not merely an administrative, victory in the banning of midnight raids. The American Civil Liberties Union (ACLU) helped Parrish sue his employers for firing him without sufficient cause. A district court in California affirmed his dismissal, agreeing with the state's argument that people on assistance waived their constitutional right to privacy. On appeal, however, the California Supreme Court, headed by an unabashed liberal, Chief Justice Mathew Tobriner (who would later pioneer legal approval of the concept of palimony), decided exactly the opposite, that welfare recipients did enjoy the constitutional right to freedom from unreasonable searches. Tobriner refuted the state's claim that a recipient "consented" to a search. He argued that because of the unequal power relationship between the investigator and the client, and because the client could be declared ineligible for welfare as a result of the search, there could be no real consent to a home inspection. An employee of the state, Tobriner's court held, had the right to refuse orders that were patently illegal. As a result of this California Supreme Court decision, Maryland and the city of Detroit outlawed midnight raids (of the nonmass kind), and in 1967 the Department of Health, Education, and Welfare (HEW) ordered states to desist from conducting them.[21]

Nonetheless, other conservatives (not just district attorneys) defended midnight raids as a legitimate tool for policing welfare fraud, and it was easy to see that the issue of welfare fraud was a covert reference to race by southern white congressmen who believed that the government should not subsidize what they believed to be immorality among blacks. The District of Columbia was a southern city experiencing a large wave of black migration. Of welfare recipients in the District of Columbia in the 1960s, 90 percent were African American. Those political and social conditions led the city to create the largest welfare fraud investigation unit in the country. As the chair of the Senate Appropriations Committee, Senator Robert Byrd of West Virginia (who had been a Klan member in the 1940s) denounced "welfare chiselers" and woman "breeders"; he did not make explicit the race of the chiselers and breeders, but he did not need to.[22] Byrd had a broader vision of morality than simply childbearing within legal marriage; he was the first nationally elected official to portray the immorality of both the "illicit paramour" and the home where he was living. He told reporters at his hearings, "These children would be better off if they were not living in homes where they are kicked around by the paramour, hear vile language and dirty jokes, and aren't given the care the mother should give them."[23] Byrd saw immorality in such environments as a justification for removal of children from the home.

The presence of cohabitation also justified surveillance and investigation in the District of Columbia. Byrd pressed the Department of Public Investigators in the district to find out how many welfare recipients were ineligible for aid, and after that he demanded a national follow-up study of the incidence of welfare fraud. As part of the initial study, the city hired fraud investigators who made as many as thirteen visits to the same residence to determine if a woman on welfare was ineligible—for example, because she had been "caught in illicit affairs."[24] In response to the Byrd-instigated crackdown, black mothers in welfare rights organizations, often living in DC housing projects, began to organize protests. They picketed the house of a welfare department administrator, arguing that they were forced to invade the man's privacy in order to dramatize the invasion of their own when their homes were searched without a warrant. The warrantless search, they argued, proved how coercive welfare was. They also claimed that investigators conducted these searches in retaliation for a woman's political activism; two welfare mothers sued the district to end the practice.[25]

Suitable Fathers

The state of Alabama probably had the strictest definition of the man-in-the-house rule and thus made the best target for a legal test of the constitutionality of such laws. In 1965, Sylvester Smith, a black mother in Selma, Alabama, had been disqualified from public aid because she had a lover who regularly stayed over on Saturday nights. She was not charged with fraud but was kicked off of welfare, and her male visitor was held responsible for supporting her and her children, even though he was not the children's biological father.[26] Sylvester Smith was poor and uneducated with a feisty personality and a keen sense of her rights and was unwilling to be bossed around by the "welfare ladies." She was a widow, mother of four, and grandmother who quit school by the ninth grade. Her husband, Judge Smith, with whom she had three children, had been killed in a fight over another woman. She had a fourth child with a man who deserted her and left for New York. Three years later, she began a sexual relationship with Willie Williams of Tyler, Alabama, a friend of her parents. Williams, who was employed doing manual labor, was living with his wife and eight of his nine children in Tyler. In 1966, Smith and two of her children and her granddaughter moved fifteen miles north to Selma, renting a three-room dilapidated shack in the middle of a red dirt field, with no indoor toilet but an outhouse. Smith's caseworker in Selma was more punitive than workers in the countryside and permanently reduced her check because of her occasional income from picking cotton and hoeing.[27] Smith wrote to President Lyndon Johnson complaining about the inadequacy of her government aid, especially since her thirteen-year-old daughter had been eliminated from welfare because she had given birth to a child out of wedlock. The letter to

LBJ was forwarded to the welfare office in Selma, which identified Smith as a troublemaker. The federal government never accepted any responsibility for the fact that a letter of complaint to the president was used as a reason for punishment.

The persecution of Sylvester Smith, the black welfare mother in *King v. Smith*, could be laid at the feet of the arch-segregationist George Wallace. Wallace ran for governor of Alabama on a platform of opposing federal intervention in states' rights and defending it in his inaugural when he endorsed "segregation now, segregation tomorrow, and segregation forever." Elected governor by a large margin and concerned that Aid to Families with Dependent Children (AFDC) was becoming "a black program," Wallace had appointed a law school friend of his brother as commissioner of public aid. In speaking tours throughout the state, Wallace had proclaimed, "If a man wants to play, then let him pay."[28] The state legislature hoped to abolish AFDC entirely, but Wallace wanted to retain the program because of the poor whites who qualified. Ruben King, Wallace's newly named commissioner of public welfare, who was charged with the task of eliminating blacks from welfare, pushed through suitable-father regulations, terminating about sixteen thousand children from the welfare rolls almost immediately, virtually all of them black.[29]

Civil rights workers had been coming to Selma since 1963 to register local blacks to vote. Because the county registration board rejected black applicants for trivial reasons, less than 1 percent of Selma's blacks were registered to vote even though the town was half black. In March 1965, civil rights demonstrators had planned to march fifty miles from Selma to the state capitol in Montgomery to protest the murder of a black civil rights worker. State troopers and sheriff's deputies on horses turned back the marchers at the Edmund Pettus Bridge in town, using billy clubs and tear gas. Dr. Martin Luther King sought national reinforcements; students, celebrities, and clergy from across the nation converged on Selma in response to King's call for a five-day march from Selma to Montgomery to dramatize the need for the passage of a national voting rights act.

Because local blacks had been arrested marching for their rights, it was easier for Sylvester Smith to stand up for hers. Smith contacted one of the recent arrivals in town, Donald Jelinek, a civil rights lawyer from New York who had come south during the Freedom Summer of 1964. Jelinek had been barred from litigating in Alabama courts because he was facing criminal charges for his civil rights work. He called Edward Sparer, known as "the father of welfare law" to ask him to take Smith's case. Sparer, head of the Center on Law and Social Policy in New York City, was a former Communist who left the party in 1956 over the Soviet invasion of Hungary. He believed that the law could be used as an instrument of social change on behalf of the poor and that antipoverty lawyers at his center should bring lawsuits in federal courts to establish national constitutional rights for welfare recipients. Among those rights, he believed, was a constitutional right to privacy and a right to be free from state-imposed tests of morality as a requirement for receiving welfare.

Martin Garbus, a long-haired thirty-three-year-old trial lawyer and codirector of the Center on Law and Social Policy with Sparer, was interested in taking on test cases that challenged the constitutionality of onerous welfare regulations. Preparing a "Brandeis brief" for this case, he did an extensive statistical survey of the number of families on welfare in Alabama and the suitable-father regulations of other states. In a footnote, Garbus argued that punishing cohabitation was not a legitimate government concern and that cohabitation should not be criminalized. But he buried the issue in his brief because he knew that the US Supreme Court would not agree with his view. Instead, he argued that substitute-father provisions were a violation of the equal protection clause of the Fourteenth Amendment because the rule had a disparate impact on African Americans.

As the case of McLaughlin and Hoffman had already shown, the civil rights movement placed a high premium on finding respectable plaintiffs. Almost by definition, litigants in suitable-father cases would not meet that standard—they were women who had children out of wedlock by multiple sexual partners, sometimes had affairs with married men, had daughters who were sexually active at a young age (implying lack of parental supervision), and often cheated the welfare system by hiding men's contributions to their households. Welfare rights lawyers thus put aside the standard of respectability in favor of finding the strictest, most punitive impositions of rules punishing immorality. What appealed to Garbus about Smith's case was that it was such an egregious example of suitable-father regulations. Alabama had identified as a suitable father a man who was not a cohabitor, was not the children's biological father, was not legally obligated to support the children, was not supporting the children, and was never caught visiting the woman and her children in her home. Since Williams was legally married to another woman, he could not have married Smith without getting a divorce or engaging in the crime of bigamy. Nor were there any elements of a common-law relationship between Williams and Smith, even if one could somehow ignore the existence of his legal wife. Smith had kept her own name and never presented herself to the public as Williams's wife.[30] In other words, the Smith-Williams relationship was totally devoid of the defining elements of a common-law marriage.

Prior to 1968, civil rights lawyers had been losing suitable-father cases in the courts. One suit reached a conservative federal judge who ruled that suitable-home provisions were entirely a matter of state discretion.[31] Sparer and Garbus's chances of overturning suitable-father regulations were dimming by the minute. They thought they had a better chance of success with a case from the Deep South because of the region's history of poverty and racial discrimination and the willingness of federal courts in the South, under the influence of the civil rights movement, to recognize arguments based on violations of the Fourteenth Amendment's clauses about equal protection or due process.

The state of Alabama argued that a man having sex with a woman had the legal obligation to support her and her children as if he was a lawfully married husband. In fact, the state made clear that a substitute father did not have to be a social stepfather, that is, he did not have to show "kindness and affection to the children."[32] If a man was having sex with a woman, Alabama claimed he was being "afforded the privileges of a husband," and because he was "like a husband," he was expected to support "his wife and children." The assumptions were that a woman exchanged sex for a man's provision of support, that he should pay for access to sex by supporting her children, and that he should provide cash assistance, regardless of his financial resources. The director of welfare in Alabama, echoing George Wallace's rhetoric, enunciated this principle directly in the state's brief: "It's like I have said so many times in speeches through this state that if a man wants to play, then let him pay, and if he has the pleasures of a husband, then he ought to have the responsibility of a husband."[33] Conversely, if a mother wanted to maintain her eligibility for welfare, sexual abstinence was expected—or even required of her.

King v. Smith (1968), the first US Supreme Court decision having to do with welfare rights, overthrew suitable-father rules and was a great, albeit temporary victory in beating back tests of morality for receipt of welfare.[34] As a result of the decision, about 750,000 children throughout the United States who had been eliminated because of suitable-father rules were restored to welfare rolls. The Court did not rule against Alabama on constitutional grounds, however, but instead chose more narrow reasons for overturning suitable-father regulations. An eight-vote majority argued that Alabama's substitute-father provision failed to conform to the Social Security Act. Alabama regulations violated the act, the Court's opinion stated, because that state had imposed a morals test rather than employing the federally mandated needs test for determining welfare eligibility. In addition, the Court argued that Alabama had erred in demanding support from a man who had no legal responsibility to support children—a man who could in no way be construed as a stepfather.

Although *King v. Smith* was a victory for welfare rights, it did not spell success for the cause of cohabitation. The Court's attitude toward the immorality of cohabitation had not changed from four years previously, when it recognized a state interest in regulating sexual morality in *McLaughlin v. Florida*. The same legal opinions were repeated, that the state had the right to regulate morality and that cohabitation was a form of immorality. Nor did the justices rule that a welfare recipient enjoyed a constitutional right to privacy. Instead, the opinion in *King* held that a state could not terminate assistance to needy children just because of the "immorality" of the parents. Children were not to be punished for what the Court still clearly regarded as the sins of the mother. As Chief Justice Earl Warren put it, "It is simply inconceivable . . . that Alabama is free to discourage immorality and illegitimacy by the device of absolute disqualification of needy children."[35]

The Court's decision led to hundreds of other successful lawsuits against state welfare administrators.[36] HEW issued a regulation that states could not simply assume a male cohabitor was contributing to a welfare family unless they could show that he was providing money on a regular basis. For Sylvester Smith, however, the victory was bittersweet: she had another child and again applied for welfare in Selma. The authorities asked her for the name of the father and his place of residence; she remained as obdurate as ever. Refusing to answer any inquiries into her personal life, she told the Selma caseworkers "to go to hell" and presumably she was disqualified again from receiving welfare.[37]

Man Assumed to Be a Responsible Spouse

Almost as soon as the Court decided *King v. Smith*, states devised ways of getting around it. Atypical though was the Michigan director of social services who simply insisted that he would deny aid to a woman having sex outside of marriage. In some states, local welfare officials ignored the Supreme Court's ruling. It was not surprising that officials in rural West Virginia paid no attention to it, but it is disconcerting to learn that a district attorney in Wisconsin, eleven years after the decision, admitted that his county still threatened to reduce a woman's welfare check if she was caught cohabiting. Nine northern and western states, including New Jersey, New York, and California, employed new rules that counted a boyfriend's income in determining a woman's eligibility for welfare. They did so even when the man was not the biological father and was not legally obligated to pay child support. The determination was not made solely at the welfare office, but also involved a "visit"—a caseworker who knew a man's income might dock a woman's check if she saw the man's shirt and trousers in the woman's apartment.[38] Moreover, although welfare officials were no longer allowed to deny a woman welfare because she was cohabiting, public housing officials could count a cohabitor's income as part of a woman's total resources in determining her rent. There was thus an incentive for a woman in public housing to hide a man from her neighbors, even if she risked eviction.

California's formal MARS (Man Assumed to Be a Responsible Spouse) regulation, in force beginning in 1961, was a less stringent form of suitable-father rule since the woman was not eliminated from welfare because she was cohabiting.[39] She was required to tell the welfare authorities if a man moved in with her; once she provided this information, her boyfriend's income was deducted from her check even if he was not the legal father of her children. Mainly California wanted to cut welfare spending, not stamp out cohabitation. California authorities were ambivalent about whether to encourage the man to remain and support the woman or to shoo him away. In one view, "the paramour" should be made to provide support; in the other, he was a "parasite" or "leech" who was living off the woman's welfare check and "such situations are poor for children."[40] Depending on which view held sway, the social worker for the family and the county district attorney decided whether to enforce the MARS regulation against the man.[41]

MARS rules permitted welfare officials to go to court to enforce child support orders or criminally prosecute the male partner. In reality, however, district attorneys knew they would have difficulty persuading judges to order child support against men who had no legal responsibility to pay it. Nor did the state really need to make the man pay, since his presence led to an automatic deduction in the amount of the woman's check. Other mothers were simply denied welfare on the grounds that they had a male partner who provided sufficient income; and some of those who did not report a cohabitor were prosecuted for welfare fraud. There does not appear to have been a consistent pattern across the country because the administration of welfare depended on local practice.[42]

For more than seven years, California welfare mothers, with the assistance of lawyers from the ACLU, brought suits against MARS regulations with little success. In 1970, antipoverty lawyers in Berkeley were finally able to overturn a MARS determination in the US Supreme Court case of *Lewis v.*

Martin (1970). Among the plaintiffs were Margaret Percy and her daughter Cleo in San Mateo. Melvin Jones was not Cleo's biological father, and the couple did not consider themselves to have entered into a common-law marriage. Jones covered the costs of the couple's housing but had loans and credit card debt that amounted to more than his monthly income. He was willing to help Percy and her daughter on an emergency basis but did not want to assume responsibility for their support. Percy applied for welfare just before the *King v. Smith* decision but was turned down because of MARS rules. Antipoverty lawyers in Berkeley encouraged her to reapply because, they concluded, *King v. Smith* had struck down California MARS regulations. When Percy did so, county social workers denied her request again, claiming that she was living with a man responsible for her support. Upset that she had no money to care for her daughter, Percy tried to kill herself by slashing her wrists and throat. She survived, and she and Jones parted; Percy took her daughter out of California to live with her parents, and she gave up on trying to secure welfare from the state of California.[43]

The case reached the US Supreme Court as a class-action lawsuit on behalf of Percy and several other welfare mothers in the Bay Area. The Court, in yet another victory for welfare rights, held that a cohabitor who was not the biological father of the woman's children did not have a legal obligation to support a welfare family and his income could not be counted in deciding the size of the family's welfare grant.[44] In a sense, the ruling was a high point for the sexual freedom of the poor because it removed the government from economic interference with cohabitation. The MARS regulation, the court ruled, was a modern manifestation of the Poor Law: special legal rules for poor men converted them into stepfathers when they did not in fact have a legal obligation to support.[45] As a result of rulings in *King v. Smith* and *Lewis v. Martin*, welfare mothers were permitted to cohabit. The number of cohabitors on welfare rose, to about 6 percent in one study of welfare mothers in 1987 and 17 percent in another (the latter study comprised mainly of women in their twenties, who were more likely have a live-in partner, since cohabitation is generally higher among younger age groups).[46]

Liberal popular culture, even into the mid-1970s, echoed the welfare rights movement's critique of public aid. Black artists, in combination with a left-leaning Hollywood director, saw an opening to reach a public demanding law and order. A film directed by John Berry, a blacklisted director who had spent the 1950s and 1960s in France, tried to explain to taxpayers how welfare dehumanized its recipients. *Claudine* (1974) starred Diahann Carroll as a trim, fit, thirty-six-year-old old mother of six on welfare who falls in love with Roop, a twice-divorced garbage man (played by James

Earl Jones) who is in arrears on his child-support payments. Combining romance (including some nude scenes of Jones) with the laugh lines expected in a television situation comedy, *Claudine* was the first and so far only major motion picture to offer a sympathetic portrayal of a welfare cheat. It does not actually depict cohabitation on welfare, however. In the film, Roop never moves in with Claudine, partly because her Harlem apartment is shown as small and crowded, and partly because he is portrayed as resentful of the New York eligibility rules that would dock her welfare checks by the amount of his pay. The film made the political points that the welfare system bred deception and cheating and that, although the public thought of women on welfare as "ignorant black bitches living like a queen on welfare," they were actually dignified, svelte mothers who were concerned about their children but still wanted to have a sex life. The "itinerant paramour" turns out to be a man who wants to act as a father, and, at the urging of Claudine's children, in the last scene of the film actually marries her in a small ceremony held in her apartment. Since the movie portrays Harlem in the mid-1970s, there are plenty of welfare eligibility checks during which Roop has to hide in Claudine's closet, until a young white caseworker discovers him and he is forced to confront her.

The last gasp of Supreme Court liberalism, a critique of a state welfare policy we would now call marriage promotion, came four years after Earl Warren had retired as chief justice. The US Supreme Court in *New Jersey Welfare Rights Organization et al. v. Cahill* (1972) held that the government could not promote marriage by establishing a two-tier welfare benefit system that rewarded legally married couples as against others. Critics of welfare had often charged that the program encouraged fathers to desert their families or live apart from them to enable the mother and children to qualify for aid. In response to this criticism, states and the federal government were experimenting with welfare programs for married couples. New Jersey established a program called Assistance to Families of the Working Poor. As a state rather than federal program, Assistance to Families did not run afoul of constitutional rulings governing the AFDC program. The New Jersey program provided aid to families in which there was at least one dependent child and "two adults of the opposite sex" who were "ceremonially married to each other." Thus, the program excluded cohabitors, heterosexual and homosexual, and children of unmarried mothers. The heterosexist bias of the program was never stated; the rationale for denying aid to cohabiting couples was the stereotype that had justified midnight raids in the 1960s, that "mothers and paramours would live it up and drink it up and the children would never see the money."[47]

A federal district judge upheld the New Jersey program on the grounds that it promoted marriage and family stability. The New Jersey Welfare Rights Organization appealed the case to the US Supreme Court. The belief that the state should promote marriage and punish immorality was too strong to confront directly by asserting that cohabitors had a right not to marry or that the state was discriminating against cohabitors by providing enhanced benefits to married couples. Instead, the welfare rights attorneys harkened back to the "needy children" arguments so effective in *King v. Smith*. They argued that New Jersey's program discriminated against poor illegitimate children in New Jersey while granting benefits to children whose parents were legally married. Agreeing with the New Jersey Welfare Rights Organization, the US Supreme Court in *New Jersey Welfare Rights Organization et al. v. Cahill* held that the New Jersey program was unconstitutional, a denial of equal protection under the law to children born out of wedlock. The ruling did not state that children should not be punished for the sins of their parents although it implied as much.

The dissent in the case foreshadowed more conservative judicial attitudes: Justice William Rehnquist argued that the program was fair and laudatory, a view that by the 1990s would become the prevailing one. Rehnquist wanted to reverse the rights revolution of the Warren Court. Unlike most other judges who saw themselves as protectors of children, Rehnquist regarded himself as a defender of legal marriage. He claimed that the New Jersey legislature should be able to establish a specific program to reward "ceremonial marriage," which was threatened with "dissolution due to the economic vicissitudes of modern life." Sensing that cohabitation was one of the many unfortunate legacies of the 1960s, he further argued that the legislature did not have to extend aid "to 'communes' as well."[48]

With conservative Nixon appointees like Rehnquist exerting increasing influence, the US Supreme Court began to throw out more class-action welfare suits on jurisdictional grounds, claiming the plaintiff had no right to sue. The Court began to show more respect for the authority of the state in some of the cases it did decide. Among the most important was making clear that the unannounced visit to a recipient's home by a caseworker was constitutional—a permissible search quite different from the midnight raid. *Wyman v. James* (1971) ended claims that welfare searches were violations of constitutional rights; instead, the decision in the case regarded such searches as necessary protection for determining eligibility for aid. Barbara James, a single mother in the Bronx, had refused to allow a caseworker to search her home to determine if she was eligible for welfare. She said that she would furnish the necessary protection for taxpayers the welfare department sought, but she refused to have a visitor inspect her home. Welfare rules stated that if an applicant for aid refused consent to a search, she could be declared ineligible for welfare. The US Supreme Court offered a long list of reasons why the search of James's apartment was reasonable (and should not even be called a "search," but instead a "visit"). The decision emphasized that the visit was announced in advance, took place during business hours, was conducted by a social worker rather than the police, and any penalties that resulted from it were violations of civil rather than criminal law.

Thus, the era of welfare rights established through the courts ended and a new, more conservative era began. The Supreme Court was responding to public opinion, which was growing increasingly hostile to welfare and to black recipients of public assistance. To buy social peace during a time of urban riots and welfare activism, public aid officials had allowed rolls to grow. Budgets ballooned and the public increasingly saw the program as disproportionately serving poor African Americans. The number of recipients on ADC rose from 3.1 million in 1960 to 4.4. million five years later, then to 6.1 million in 1968, and, after a short but painful recession in the early 1970s, reached 10.8 million in 1974. Newspaper and television coverage of welfare reinforced the racial distinction between the "deserving" and the "undeserving" poor. The white poor on welfare were portrayed in a neutral manner, whereas articles about waste and abuse of the system invariably featured black welfare recipients. Poor, lazy, immoral—the refrain was as old as the Elizabeth Poor Law. Ronald Reagan in 1976 received wide applause for his denunciation of a "welfare queen" who drove a Cadillac and used eighty aliases. Liberals had made it an article of faith that cheating on welfare was minimal; conservatives took the position that deliberate deception was extensive and that welfare queens were defrauding the government of tens of thousands of dollars. It was unstated but assumed that a welfare queen was an African American woman; that was simply taken as a given. By the 1980s, states had slashed their budgets for antipoverty legal aid programs, organizations of recipients had dwindled, and President Reagan was appointing more judges hostile to welfare rights. Still, there was no wholesale return to midnight searches; instead, states were spending their welfare funds on technology to ferret out fraud: computerized matching, fingerprinting of recipients, and photo identification cards for recipients of aid. Many welfare departments verified income in their offices, not through home visits.[49]

Despite the computerization of public assistance, fraud investigations usually included home visits, even though eligibility determinations—the once-over at the beginning—might be made from the inspection of paper documents. Door-to-door detective work was still an essential additional element of investigation. Politicians, as before, bowed to public furor over "welfare chiselers" in establishing special fraud units. By the middle of the 1970s, many welfare departments and district attorneys were discarding Warren Court rulings. Warrantless searches of the homes of recipients were justified as necessary to detect fraud in the federally funded food stamp program. Ruling in a lawsuit brought by the ACLU, a federal judge decided that the practice was unacceptable in Seattle, but in a different case, a federal judge ruled it permissible in Milwaukee. One law professor, who threw up his hands at reconciling the differences among decisions in various jurisdictions, noted the "fine line between a permissible home visit and an unconstitutional search." What seemed to bother a district court judge in Chicago was a black man dressed only in pajama bottoms who answered the door at 9:30 a.m. and his partner, a welfare mother in her nightgown who slammed the door on the investigator. Noting facts like these, the judge saw great merit in a home investigation "to ensure proper use of funds entrusted from the public."[50]

Getting tough on violent criminals and local drug dealers and granting freedom to district attorneys to devise local solutions led to the return of the midnight raid in two California counties in the 1990s. California had the largest population on welfare of any state, the greatest incentive to find a way to reduce its rolls, and apparently a sense of desperation. The new California rationale for the mass raid was not to ferret out cohabitors but instead to clear out drug dealers and violent criminals from a downtown apartment complex. Local authorities decided to stage an early morning mass raid on an apartment complex in Vallejo, using minor charges of welfare fraud as a way to arrest drug dealers. During the raid, the police knocked down doors of innocent people in the middle of the night. The ACLU successfully sued the county on behalf of several residents in the complex, and the raids were ended.[51]

Other California counties were resorting to a more wholesale approach to eliminating welfare fraud through the unannounced search. The lawyer Amy Mulzer writes, "Unable to alter eligibility levels without jeopardizing their caseload reduction credit—and eager to reduce their caseloads—states are employing a different brand of verification extremism, aimed not at rooting out fraud but at discouraging claimants from applying in the first place."[52] In devising Project 100% in 1997 (referring to checking the eligibility of 100 percent of all applicants for welfare), San Diego applied the unannounced home visit to what had become an in-office procedure, the verification of eligibility for welfare. In San Diego, applicants for welfare were given a ten-day window during which, they were told, an investigator would visit their home. The district attorney in San Diego admitted that the main reason for the search was to find live-in boyfriends. In 2002, investigators in San Diego made 14,600 home visits; in 2006, applications for aid were down, and the number of home visits had been reduced to two thousand. Still, the number of investigations was much greater than any other county welfare department had ever conducted. In New York City in 1964, the welfare commissioner claimed there were about 360 unannounced visits—thus, in San Diego in 2006, there were more than five times as many home visits in a city one-sixth the size of New York. Moreover, as part of the aggressive San Diego approach, women were prosecuted for fraud even when an abusive boyfriend did not share his earnings or refused to allow her to report it, a clear violation of the Supreme Court's decision in *Lewis v. Martin*.[53]

Judges more concerned about the rights of the taxpayer than the constitutional rights of the welfare recipient approved the San Diego home searches.[54] The US Supreme Court refused to consider the ACLU's appeal of this case and let stand the ruling of a California judge that applicants for welfare did not deserve the same level of privacy "even within the sanctity of the home" as the self-supporting did.[55] Whereas in 1971, the unannounced home visit had been permitted so long as there was no snooping, a quarter of a century later, snooping was being allowed. Thus, cohabitors on welfare in contemporary America do not enjoy the guarantees of liberty the welfare rights movement sought to enshrine in law; they have diminished rights to privacy not because they are cohabitors, but because they are recipients of public aid.

Marriage Promotion

Marriage promotion, initially attempted in state programs such as those of New Jersey in the 1970s, returned slowly, first in state experiments to curb teen pregnancy, and then nationwide in the 1996 overhaul of the welfare program. Although marriage promotion was most clearly associated with conservatives, many liberal adherents wanted to make sure that fathers were held responsible for child support. President Clinton's original proposals for welfare reform took a conservative turn with the 1994 election of Republican majorities in the House and the Senate. The public, as had long been the case, was concerned that welfare encouraged out-of-wedlock childbearing and wanted welfare recipients to be required to hold paying jobs and government to continue its commitment to ferreting out welfare fraud.

Temporary Assistance for Needy Families (TANF), as the welfare reform bill of 1996 was called, explicitly offered marriage as a solution to poverty.

Why promote legal marriage rather than simply imposing the common-law obligation of support, as had been done previously? Government marriage-promotion programs expressed the Christian Rights' ideal of a return to patriarchy. Conservatives who advocated what they termed "responsible fatherhood" believed that fathers should play a distinct but specifically masculine role in the lives of their children above and beyond that of simply being a breadwinner and specifically held that boys needed male role models in order to grow up to be responsible fathers themselves. Conservative think thanks provided specific policy ideas for marriage promotion and funded influential intellectuals of similar persuasion who argued that poverty was ultimately a moral problem, the problem of out-of-wedlock childbearing. Indeed, the percentage of births that were out of wedlock was climbing: in 1984, it was 15 percent among whites, 30 percent among Hispanics, and 51 percent among blacks. By 2010, the rate was 28 percent among whites, 50 percent among Hispanics, and 70 percent among African Americans. The growth of childbearing outside of marriage was not a uniquely American phenomenon but instead was occurring throughout the developed world. Greater personal freedom, the decline in sexual stigma—the disappearance of the word *illegitimacy* and the phrase *living in sin*—and the demise of the shotgun marriage led to increased incidence everywhere. But in the United States, rising rates of incarceration among minority men, the loss of secure jobs for poorly educated men, white and black, and the somewhat greater economic possibilities for women simply surviving on their own contributed as well. Although birth control was widely available, many of these out-of-wedlock pregnancies were the result of infrequent or inconsistent use of birth control.

As a result of welfare reform in 1996, several of the morality tests for welfare eliminated by the Warren Court returned. Under TANF, each state, no longer bound by federal law, was free to design its own rules for welfare eligibility; thus, states were allowed to depart from Supreme Court rulings of the late 1960s and early 1970s. California as well as five other states found a way around the anti-MARS ruling in *Lewis v. Martin*. Oklahoma reinstated MARS entirely, requiring that the cohabitor's income had to be included in determining eligibility for aid. Eight states restored a version of the New Jersey Assistance to the Families of Working Poor, offering an economic bonus to married couples on welfare and, thus, creating the type of two-tiered welfare system that the Supreme Court had declared unconstitutional in *New Jersey Welfare Rights Organization et al. v. Cahill et al.* in 1973. West

Virginia, for example, provided a bonus of one hundred dollars per month if cohabiting couples on welfare legally married.

During the presidency of George W. Bush, marriage promotion became an integral part of welfare policy. The Deficit Reduction Act of 2005 provides federal funding of $150 million per year for five years for marriage promotion, despite federal cutbacks in funding for welfare overall. The word *Healthy* in the program name, Healthy Family Initiative, was designed to placate groups concerned about domestic violence, who believed that promoting marriage at all costs could encourage victims of abuse to remain in a marriage. In some of the programs, federal funds were being used to encourage couples to marry and to warn women of the dangers of cohabitation. In a sense, the program was federal funding for lay or nonprofessional marital counseling, which had previously been largely reserved for the white middle class. The ideas were the same, however: that "relationships" involved work and that the woman would have to bear most of the responsibility for that work.[56]

In 1999, well before the Bush administration promoted the concept nationwide, Oklahoma pioneered one of the most extensive Healthy Marriage initiatives, not because the state's cohabitation rates were especially high, but because its divorce rates were the highest in the nation and the Republican governor, Frank Keating, and his constituents believed that a Bible Belt state such as Oklahoma should enforce morality. One Washington, DC reporter visited Oklahoma City to observe a marriage-promotion program there, following several black women from Sooner Haven housing project as they participated in a three-day Healthy Marriage seminar. Mainly poor black women who were divorced or had never married attended a seminar offered by a pastor at a local Baptist church; most had been unable to encourage their boyfriends to attend. The workshop materials offered some information about cohabitation; it was not described as a sin, but instead as a bad bargain for women. Other programs were far more subtle and taught couples communication skills, never mentioning the word marriage.

Many sex education programs reinforced federal policy to promote legal marriage. The federal government provided an additional $100 million for abstinence-only sex education programs in schools, an effort to encourage sexual morality among American youths, as well as women on welfare. The law in many states forbade teachers from providing birth control information and required them to encourage abstinence. Although an elaboration of the welfare program, such initiatives were also a historic first for anticohabitation, the first time fear of cohabitation was explicitly taught in the public schools. One survey in 2005 found that about a quarter of high school students said they had received abstinence-only sex education in school. The enabling federal legislation for these programs specified that a program must teach that "sex outside of marriage is likely to be psychologically and physically harmful" and that "a mutually faithful monogamous relationship in the context of marriage is the expected standard of human [sexual] activity." Designed to refute the belief, common among young people, that cohabitation prior to marriage is a good dress rehearsal for marriage, one abstinence-only curriculum taught, for example, that "outside of marriage, sex can be dangerous," and that "when couples live together outside of marriage, the relationships are 'weaker,' more violent, less [equal], and more likely to lead to divorce."[57]

Abstinence education did not, in fact, lead to abstinence nor did it stop the young from cohabiting, but there was greater hope that marriage promotion among the poor might lead to lasting marriage. Studies show that there was no difference in the cohabitation rates of women who lived in states with post-TANF punitive welfare policies and those who lived in less punitive ones.[58] The reason there was no difference was that women of limited means did not make personal and family decisions based on attending classes or workshops or on small differences in the size of cash grants. Like the rest of society, they idealized marriage as capstone experience, but they believed that they needed to postpone marrying until they found the right man who had a steady and secure job. A prospective male who used or sold drugs, had a drinking problem, was violent, was headed for prison, or was still sleeping with "his baby's mama" did not make an ideal marriage candidate. Welfare mothers who did marry often ended up disappointed and divorced; their marriages were often plagued by problems of infidelity, drug abuse, alcoholism, repeated incarceration, financial woes, and domestic violence. Some women were involved with men who were legally married to someone else, and other women did not make the best marriage material themselves, since they had drug or alcohol problems of their own.[59]

If the backlash against the 1960s has not succeeded in slowing the sexual revolution, either in the general population or among those living in poverty, it has been more successful in the domain of social welfare policy. Cohabitation prior to a wedding is now the norm, but the message of society is that cohabiting parents should get married. The public disapproves of revolving door cohabitation, which leads to the birth of children from multiple partners. Despite the willingness of Sylvester Smith to challenge the welfare authorities in Selma, welfare mothers today do not enjoy a right to privacy or a right to make sexual choices on their own and, thus, privacy rights for cohabitors differ by race and class. Cohabitors on welfare waive their rights to privacy as recipients of what is regarded as "public charity." The lawyer Kaaryn Gustafson writes, "In the end, the Fourth Amendment's protections from search and guarantee of privacy in the home do not appear to apply to welfare recipients."[60]

Thus, although cohabitation has become more acceptable and is legally permitted among welfare mothers, women on welfare are subjected to surveillance to find out if they are cohabiting, and the official policy of the government is to promote legal marriage.[61] The government is committed in deed, not just in words, to the belief that poverty can be reduced by the government walking the welfare mother down the aisle. What is new about marriage promotion is that it is funded by the federal government and being offered by ministers, high school teachers, and community organizations, and advertised on public buses and subway cars. It merges and reflects two distinct fears of the 1970s: anxiety about the increasing incidence of minority women on welfare bearing children out of wedlock and the threat posed by family instability for children and the moral decline of the American nation. In welfare reform and abstinence-only education, the backlash of the 1970s continues, but in a new, federally funded form.

FOUR

Coed Facing Expulsion, 1968

In March 1968, the *New York Times* fashion, furnishings, family, and food reporter Judy Klemesrud interviewed three young unmarried couples in Manhattan for an article entitled "An Arrangement: Living Together for Convenience, Security, Sex."[1] The colon in the headline indicated that *an arrangement* was alternative nomenclature for *living together*. "Susan," a twenty-year-old Barnard College sophomore described in the piece had an arrangement with Peter, a Columbia junior of the same age. They had been together for two years and had flown to Puerto Rico, where Susan secured an abortion, then illegal in New York. No longer taking birth control pills, Susan, according to the article, was attempting to get pregnant. Klemesrud mentioned the process whereby Susan had been granted permission from Barnard to move out of the dorm. A close friend of Susan's, a young married woman, listed a job as a live-in babysitter with the college employment bureau, for which Susan applied.[2]

Klemesrud had promised to conceal the identities of those she interviewed but seems not to have tried very hard. It was easy to figure out that Susan was the twenty-year-old Barnard sophomore Linda LeClair who had a boyfriend named Peter Behr. Barnard was in the midst of a $7.5 million fund-raising campaign when the Klemesrud article appeared. A Barnard dean called LeClair into her office and said to her, "Please tell us this person in this news story is not you, because the alumnae have been writing in." Refusing to accept the opening to save herself, LeClair told the dean, "It is."[3] The dean then informed LeClair that she was faced with "a suspension issue."

At Barnard, the judicial council, consisting of faculty, students, and administrators, had disciplinary authority over students, although the president had veto power over their decisions. LeClair demanded an open

hearing of the council and requested time to prepare a defense. She testified and examined witnesses at several meetings of the council, which
decreed a slap-on-the-wrist punishment that included deprivation of snack
bar privileges.[4] However, the president of the college, exercising her power
to overrule the council, did not let the matter die; she threatened LeClair
with suspension. She eventually offered LeClair reentry to school, provided
LeClair promised to abide by the college's housing rules. Exhausted by a
season of student protest during the spring of 1968 and disillusioned with
Barnard, LeClair declined the offer—and never returned to graduate.

College student cohabitation, 1968 style, was different from the cohabitation of interracial couples in the South or a boyfriend visiting a welfare
mother. Behr and LeClair were childless, living together on a regular basis,
not claiming to be legally married, and not intending marriage. But LeClair's
cohabitation cannot be separated from the zeitgeist of the 1960s. Activists
did not simply reside together in the 1960s; they lived in communes (or
in LeClair's case, several of them), based on their commitment to sharing,
antimaterialism, critique of traditional gender roles, and rejection of the
nuclear family. The couple's commune was actually a crash pad, with six
mattresses on the floor in a bedroom so that friends and fellow student
activists could stay for a night, a week, or a month.

Those born after World War II, sometimes dubbed "the NOW generation," formed the largest distinct cohort in American history; changes in
their lives had an enormous impact on American society. The baby boomers
used the term *generation* as a call to arms and believed they had a different
(better) sense of morality than the generation of their parents, prizing, as
they did, openness and honesty in sexual matters and believing that sexual
practices were a matter of personal choice. The great gulf in values, as well
as conflict with and disapproval from parents and college authorities, was
dubbed the "generation gap." Administrators in the older cohort were referred to as "the authorities," and the point of 1960s protest was to challenge authority, because it could not be trusted to do what was right.

College students had been demonstrating and signing petitions against
the punishment of students suspended for cohabiting since 1962 (at Cornell), but for the first time, their arrangements made the front page of the
New York Times. It seemed obvious that college men favored the sexual revolution and had much to gain from the new freedom among their female
peers. The reason articles kept referring to "sex and the college girl" was that
in 1962, Helen Gurley Brown, the editor-in-chief of *Cosmopolitan* magazine,
had written in her bestselling book *Sex and the Single Girl* that sexual freedom, including an apartment of her own, was part of the life of an unmar-

ried woman (usually a secretary), but Brown had not discussed mores on campus. LeClair was the rare instance of a coed demanding sexual freedom, not in the language of sex, but in the language of rights. It was April 1968 when she did so, four months into a year that shook the world to its core.[5]

The "Gray Lady," as the most prestigious newspaper in the nation was often called, had more personal reasons for its interest in off-campus housing rules at a local women's college. The mother of the paper's publisher did not much like the new sociological approach evident in the paper's women's pages. Iphigene Sulzberger, Barnard class of 1914, had been on the board of trustees at Barnard for twenty-seven years. Her granddaughter had graduated from Barnard in 1965, and her grandson, a student in Columbia's College of General Studies, was cohabiting with his girlfriend, though he hid it from his mother, father, and grandmother.[6] Sulzberger, age seventy-five at the time, told her son Arthur (called Punch) that she did not understand why the *Times* was endorsing "loose living."[7] Charlotte Curtis had taken over the women's page at the paper several years earlier with the intent of covering the social trends of the 1960s, even if the topics had previously been taboo. It was Curtis and her personal style of popular sociology that encouraged Klemesrud to feign social science, with a survey of twenty couples, boiled down to excerpts from interviews with three. Sulzberger wrote her son an angry letter: "What are those girls on the Women's Page trying to do to the reputation of *The Times* and Barnard College?" She added that she thought "premarital affairs are nothing new, but they are not a desirable way of life. . . . If we have a family page, let's stick to the subject."[8] Equally unnerving to her was that the couple had no plans to marry, because they regarded marriage as "too serious a step," yet they were planning to have a child out of wedlock. It was rumored that Sulzberger wanted Barnard to expel LeClair, presumably in order to defend sexual morality on campus by showing other Barnard women what could happen to them if they disobeyed the unwritten rules about virginity and marriage.

The LeClair affair was part protest, part media kerfuffle, an important episode in the cohabitation side of the sexual revolution. After LeClair, the deluge: in the subsequent few years, curfews imposed on women college students disappeared, and many universities and colleges established coed dorms. More college health services were making birth control available to unmarried as well as married women. By 1970, the state of New York had legalized abortion, and three years after that, the US Supreme Court declared abortion a constitutional right. In the next few years, women undergraduates at other campuses engaged in further battles to remove housing restrictions affecting them. By 1972, Barnard had recognized its first campus lesbian association. More fundamentally, LeClair's case was a significant opening shot in the women's liberation movement, identifying sexual issues as political and marking changes in the relations between generations and between the sexes.

LeClair had both supporters on campus and many detractors in the general public; the fact that there were two well-defined sides, with little room in the middle, reflects an originating moment of polarization over the sexual revolution. LeClair led a campus protest that became a symbol of the youth culture, the sexual revolution, and the decline of the double standard—a change that many adults perceived as immoral and dangerous precisely because it was about young women, not young men. Stanley Cohen defines a moral panic as "threats to societal values and interests . . . presented in a stylized and stereotypical fashion by the media."[9] The *New York Times* and other newspapers reflected the sense of genuine fear that "promiscuity was running rampant on the college campus." LeClair was more threatening than Connie Hoffman and Sylvester Smith because of her race, class, age, and gender and because she was agitating against sexual rules in a year of cascading national protest and tragedy.

The Discovery of Cohabitation on Campus

Newsweek reported about college student cohabitation in 1965, calling it *unstructured relations*, although the magazine acknowledged that college administrations used the term *student cohabitation*. The *Newsweek* article was accompanied by a photo of a college student couple holding hands, with their backs to the camera. There were two major reasons that the students did not want to reveal their faces: they did not want their parents or relatives to know, and at some schools, they could be referred to the disciplinary committee for living together. The *Newsweek* writer gave details about the relationships of three "typical" couples from the University of Chicago, UCLA, and the University of California at Berkeley. The article used first names or fictitious names, apparently because *Newsweek* was unable to find students who would pose for the camera or allow their names to appear in the magazine. The reporter interviewed three psychiatrists who claimed to be experts on the phenomenon; their attitudes varied from the positive to advising counseling for students who experienced trauma from cohabiting. *Newsweek* gave the last word to an associate dean at Berkeley whose view was closer to the latter. He repeated the oft-stated view that a girl cheapened her reputation and her marriageability by cohabiting ("Why buy the cow when you can get the milk for free?"). He was quoted as saying, "A girl is sometimes hard put to explain what happened when the next fellow comes along."[10]

Some historians like to claim that the 1960s revolution was more about openness and sexual frankness than about changes in sexual practice. After all, Kinsey's sexual surveys had demonstrated that in the decades prior to the 1960s, a substantial number of American women had engaged in sex before marriage. Actually, Kinsey showed that a substantial number of women had had "engagement sex," that is, sex with a man they intended to marry. Many of the surveys of sex among college students in the late 1960s found a fundamentally different world. To be sure, the more conservative the school, the more likely that the sex was engagement sex. But overall, the "virginity rate" had declined; young women on campus no longer thought it was immoral to have sex prior to marriage with a man they did not necessarily intend to marry.

The one Barnard faculty member interested in the question surveyed Columbia men, not Barnard undergraduates. What she found, naturally enough, was that there were few virgins among Columbia men, and those few felt quite embarrassed. Many Columbia undergraduates were living with their girlfriends in off-campus apartments. In the spring of 1968, LeClair and Behr conducted their own survey of Barnard students, which determined that fully one-quarter of the student body had lived in apartments off campus with their boyfriends. As to the world outside of Morningside Heights, suffice it to say that the late-1960s sexual revolution on campus was decidedly about sex and the college girl. The baby boom daughters who entered college in the 1960s were raised in a world that distinguished between the "nice girl" and the "bad girl." Even nice girls had been listening to rock and roll, however, including the question the Shirelles raised in 1960, "Will you love me tomorrow?" Many, deciding that he would not, engaged in "sexual brinkmanship": petting and oral sex without having heterosexual intercourse, what one of them had called "the TVA—the Technical Virgins Association."[11]

By reducing the chance of unwanted pregnancy and offering what was perceived as 100 percent effective contraception, the pill decreased one of the great fears about premarital sex, that it could lead to pregnancy and from there to nonmarital childbearing, which for white middle-class girls was still highly stigmatized and appeared likely to require them to drop out of school. The pill made it less risky to cohabit; even if a couple was having sex on a regular basis, the woman had no reason to worry that she would become pregnant. By 1967, 45 percent of college health services prescribed the pill for college students.[12] Barnard was not among them. Instead, Barnard students gave one another the names of gynecologists willing to prescribe the pill for unmarried women. They went to a clinic in New York and "said we're Mrs. So-and-so." But the sexual revolution had already arrived; Barnard students were dissatisfied with the hypocrisy of pretending to be married when they were not. An editorial in the *Barnard Bulletin* in 1967 called for an end to a charade that forced a Barnard girl "to go 'underground' for a prescription."[13]

Young People in Love

Linda LeClair's father was the assistant vice president of the Nashua Bank and Trust Company in charge of installment loans and the chair of the local school board. Her mother had worked in a piston-grinding factory during World War II and then became a homemaker active in the Hudson Community Church, where LeClair attended Sunday school, sang in the church choir, and belonged to the youth group. Her grandfather, who had a farm near Hudson, New Hampshire, was a Quaker who taught at a Friends school and thought of himself as a man of honesty and integrity; LeClair came to her honesty via family background, not simply 1960s inclinations. Her grandfather was her role model as to how to be open and truthful.[14] In high school, she was the associate editor of the yearbook, was active in the French club, the theater group, and the ski club, and was vice president of the local 4-H. A National Merit Scholar, she applied to two highly selective colleges in the Northeast, Radcliffe and Barnard. When she did not get into Radcliffe, it was settled that she would go to Barnard.[15]

Leaving home and going away to college was a kind of declaration of sexual independence in the 1960s. When LeClair left Hudson for Barnard at age eighteen in 1965, she thought herself free "to do what I want."[16] She was rooming at Barnard's Helen Reid Hall, and Behr was living at Columbia's Hartley Hall. Sometimes she wore lipstick, but she used no other makeup. She had gotten rid of her short bouffant hairdo from high school; like virtually all the other white students at the time, she had "long hippie hair."[17] She and Behr did not dress like flower children but instead looked respectable and well groomed. Behr was clean shaven: he had no beard or mustache. They met at a mixer when they were both eighteen. They fell in love, and he wrote her long love letters and poetry. She listened while he played his recording of *West Side Story* ("Somewhere we'll find a new way of living . . . Somehow, Someday, Somewhere!"). She was the first girl he had ever slept with. LeClair liked to say that her "first real" sexual encounter was with Peter, although there had been another serious boyfriend before him.[18]

They were the loving couple of nonmarriage, sharing a sense of adventure, belief in pacifism, and interest in studying sociology and humanistic psychology.

Behr was the perfect boyfriend for an idealistic college girl of eighteen. He was a highly intelligent "nice Jewish boy" who, though not sexually experienced, was committed to monogamy and deeply romantic. Social scientists would find that college males who cohabited were more likely to think of themselves as liberated from traditional gender roles and to be somewhat less managerial and competitive. Such young men tended to be warmer and more supportive than other male college students. Behr's father was a concentration camp survivor, a Berliner and a secular Jew who had no religious inclinations. He supported Martin Luther King in the late 1950s and liked to read *I. F. Stone's Weekly* and the *Carolina Israelite*. Behr's parents, who traveled in European intellectual circles, were acquainted with Jean-Paul Sartre and Simone de Beauvoir. The French existentialist couple remained Behr's model for a relationship between a man and woman based on equality.[19] He had grown up in an unfashionable neighborhood of row houses in Middle Village, Queens. His family background—intellectual, liberal, middle-class, urban, and Jewish—fit perfectly that of the student protest generation at Columbia 1968. Behr was not in revolt against the ideals of his parents but instead acting in accordance with what they had taught him.[20]

Martha Peterson, the newly appointed president of Barnard College, with her white hair, conservative suits, and unflappable manner, looked and acted the part of a Seven Sisters college president. In actuality, however, she had been born on the Kansas wheat farm of her Danish grandfather in 1916 and was not a daughter of privilege. Her widowed mother had supported the family by becoming a clerk at a Salina hardware store.[21] Peterson had enrolled at the University of Kansas during the Depression with the goal of becoming a high school mathematics teacher. She moved up the academic ladder at Kansas as the assistant dean and then dean and became a dean of women at the University of Wisconsin in 1956. While living in Madison, she finished a doctoral degree in educational counseling and psychology at the University of Kansas.[22] The unanimous choice of the Barnard trustees for president, the fifty-one-year-old-year-old Peterson had won out over 133 other candidates. Her partner was a distinguished woman doctor at Madison who took a year's sabbatical leave from her position to accompany Peterson to Barnard in 1967. Peterson understood nontraditional sexual lives but believed that if one practiced them, it was best to be very discreet—openness and honesty could decimate a career; she represented precisely the opposite point of view about the separation of public and private from LeClair—one had two selves, a double life, a lesbian wore a mask to protect herself from persecution.[23] Peterson's administrative experience was entirely at large coeducational universities in the Midwest. Wisconsin had already abolished curfews for juniors and seniors and, like Columbia, was a hotbed of protest. But she was now in the world of upper-class alumnae who hosted teas in their spacious apartments overlooking Central Park, and in her first year as president, she sought to reassure Sulzberger and the other members of the board of trustees that she would not turn Barnard into another Madison.

As a Seven Sisters liberal arts college of eighteen hundred women students across the street from all-male Columbia College, Barnard was supposed to be a protector of its female students from predatory men lurking in the bushes at night and the moral corruption of urban life. Indeed, women's colleges in general were slow to change, holding on more firmly than other types of colleges to their role as protectors and guardians of their students, standing "in the place of the parent," *in loco parentis*. As a small college in the midst of the most cosmopolitan city in the nation, however, Barnard could never fulfill its promise of supervision. Within walking distance of the Columbia and Barnard campuses were coffee shops, jazz clubs, bars, bookstores, and for inexpensive assignations, the Paris Hotel at West End Avenue and Ninety-Seventh Street. Barnard had a two-thirds female faculty who nurtured the intellects of young women and might on occasion be quite cosmopolitan themselves. The undergrads would have been insulted had anyone assumed that they were attending college to find husbands.

The college housing rules were more liberal at the men's school, Columbia College, than at the women's school across the street. Columbia students still had housing rules, but there were fewer of them than at Barnard. They had no curfews or sign-in and sign-out procedures. After the first year, undergraduate men were allowed to live off campus. By 1963, men could have female visitors in the dorm on Sunday afternoons, but the door had to be open the width of a book—thus, the common use of the matchbook to keep the door technically ajar.

Barnard, by contrast, had a full panoply of rules, beginning with elaborate sign-in and sign-out procedures. Male visitors had to be signed in and out of the dorm at the front desk. Women students also had to sign in and out whenever they left the dorm, even if they were merely going to meals. To sign out, a student filled out a little green slip, providing her place of destination and her expected time of return and filed it under the first letter of her last name in a large narrow wooden box; when she returned to the dorm, she dated her card. Dorm visitation hours for a male guests were three hours on Sunday afternoons; with a visitor in the room, at least three of the couple's four feet had to be touching the floor at all times.[24] The college had curfew hours during the week and on the weekend: a watchman locked the doors at 1:30 a.m. during the week and at 2:30 a.m. on the weekend. A girl who checked in even five minutes past the curfew could be grounded. Barnard administrators also believed that students needed a mother figure to counsel and watch over them; therefore, a housemother acted as a live-in counselor to students.[25]

Barnard had different rules for commuter students (who constituted two-thirds of the student body) than for the nonresidents of New York City, who lived in the dorms. By 1962, the college had liberalized rules for commuter students to allow them to choose where to live, so long as they had parental permission.[26] The stricter rules for noncommuters were designed to reassure parents of girls from outside of New York City that their daughters were safe and protected. Seniors, students older than twenty-one, and married students were permitted to live off campus; other nonresident students were not. All students living off campus had to file a form indicating they had parental permission to do so.[27]

Barnard students had always found ways to get around the rules. On Thanksgiving weekend, girls and their boyfriends checked into the Statler Hilton. Students made fun of the required health course offered by the college doctor who taught the class to abstain from sex before marriage or risk damage to their mental health. Some students took to signing out of the dorm as "Charles Baudelaire" or gave another fictitious name. They treated this procedure playfully because they felt that if they were not regarded as adults, they were justified in making fun of the rules.[28]

Barnard administrators, who knew infractions were common, accepted the reality that living in New York City offered many opportunities for sexual freedom. Girls who stepped over an invisible line were quietly asked to leave; the one clear line was, not living off campus, but rather living in the dorms and being seen to be engaged in sex with another woman. In 1963, a Columbia student, training his binoculars on the dorm room of Barnard College students, reported to a resident supervisor at Barnard that he saw two women roommates having sex. The supervisor then notified Barnard administrators, after which the girls were expelled. Even though there are no documented examples of female informants to the administration, girls monitored each others' heterosexual behavior, condemning those who were not "nice girls." "Watch out for her, she's the school slut," one undergraduate was told. The distinction between the nice girl and the bad girl had not entirely disappeared by the spring of 1968, but the LeClair protest was about to show that it was losing its force. [29]

Punishment and Protest at Barnard

Barnard classes were much more difficult than those at Albarine High School, and in the fall of 1965, her first semester in college, LeClair was put on academic probation. She withdrew from Barnard in the middle of her second semester due to illness. That summer, she and Behr found summer jobs in Provincetown; she was a chambermaid, and he was a dishwasher. Apartments in Provincetown were expensive, and they ended up living together as a way to reduce their cost of housing. LeClair told her parents that she was living with Behr, and although they did not approve, and kept referring to cohabitation as "the thing you are doing," they did not try to stop her. Behr's mother knew and approved of cohabiting but did not personally like LeClair.[30]

By the fall of 1966, LeClair was still on leave from Barnard, and the couple were living together in an apartment at 410 West 110th Street. LeClair was also pregnant; Rabbi A. Bruce Goldman, the "radical rabbi" at Columbia, provided abortion counseling, and students at Barnard furnished abortionists' names. Women's organizations joined physicians in pressing for the repeal of the New York abortion laws, but the only legal abortions available were therapeutic ones, hard to come by. An abortion in Puerto Rico was illegal, expensive (between five and eight hundred dollars), and not necessarily safe. Nonetheless, many East Coast college students went off for "the San Juan weekend" because the airfare was cheap and the procedure was quick. In 1965, about ten thousand women from the US mainland flew to Puerto Rico for abortions.[31] The couple used money that Behr had inherited after his father's death to pay for the procedure.

The abortion experience shaped LeClair's view that there were many aspects of women's sexuality that unfairly disadvantaged women. By 1970, women engaged in speak-outs revealing that they had had abortions. Before that, it was extremely rare for a woman undergraduate to mention the subject of abortion, yet LeClair did so in her interview with Judy Klemesrud in March 1968 (she certainly believed that she was speaking in confidence, however).[32] She became more frank after she decided not to return to Barnard a couple of months later, telling a *Life* reporter that in her freshman year she knew six girls in the dorm who were pregnant; five girls had had abortions, and the sixth had given her baby up for adoption and committed suicide.[33] She brought up abortion again in talking to a *Times* reporter in

September 1968. In referring to the position of President Peterson, she said, "She is aware of the needs of the students, aware that lots of people have become pregnant, that lots of people have abortions, aware that recognizing sexual intercourse would cause embarrassment to the ladies that give money to the college."[34]

If one could say that the illegality of abortion radicalized LeClair, so did the Vietnam War. LeClair and Behr were political activists deeply involved in resistance to the draft. A national antidraft organization, the Resistance, named after movements opposed to Nazi occupation of Europe during World War II, not only organized draft-card burnings but also pioneered new techniques of protest, always nonviolent.[35] LeClair staffed a table with antiwar literature in front of Low Library. The Resistance collected draft cards among men facing military conscription who sought to protest the draft and the war. The young people who formed the backbone of Resistance tended to have more anarchist and existentialist roots than their roughly similar counterparts in the student New Left. Peter Behr was a pacifist who liked to sign his letters "yours respectfully in peace" and who wore a peace button. He refused to register for the Selective Service when he turned eighteen and also refused to carry a draft card. These acts were punishable by a five-year term in prison and a ten-thousand-dollar fine. On their mimeograph machine in their Spanish Harlem apartment, the couple printed draft resistance literature, which they handed out at the New York City induction center at 39 Whitehall Street as part of the daily protests to shut down the center.[36]

They also attended meetings of the Columbia branch of SDS (Students for a Democratic Society), although they were not very vocal members of their chapter. SDS was the advance guard of antiwar activism on campus. The members of SDS had different views about tactics and strategy from those of the Resistance, but also believed in noncooperation with the draft and bearing witness to one's principles by taking risky actions. SDS was, above all else, an organization of students, and in its founding statement in 1962, it emphasized that students had the right to control their own lives. Among its early protests, seen as necessary to building a student constituency for larger projects, SDS on many campuses led protests against *in loco parentis*.

Close observers of the 1960s usually distinguish between hippies in the counterculture and the "politicos" who protested against the Vietnam War and believed they were engaged in making radical change in American politics as well as culture. Some of the participants of the day, such as LeClair and Behr, easily bridged this divide. The common denominator was not simply sex, drugs, rock and roll, *and* living in communes; it was also an idealistic belief in a new world of peace and love and in the creation of an alternative, free society that would replace a militaristic and materialist one over which they had no control.

In their second summer together, LeClair and Behr hitchhiked across the country to San Francisco, staying in communes along the way where they were welcomed not merely as overnight guests but as fellow utopians. Hitchhiking was by definition countercultural "because it was so footloose and fancy free."[37] Hassled by the police throughout their journey west, Behr was arrested and jailed in Kansas when he was asked for his draft card and was unable to produce it.[38] They were headed for Haight-Ashbury, a seedy neighborhood near San Francisco State University where communes were taking over large Victorian houses. Scott McKenzie's "San Francisco (Be Sure to Wear Some Flowers in Your Hair)" explained the dress code as well as the hip destination for the summer of 1967. About one hundred thousand flower children wannabes, many of them teen runaways, trekked there to participate in the Summer of Love—the celebration of free sex, free food, free clothes, and free rock concerts. Interracial couples, nudists, bisexuals, threesomes, and the occasional orgy were as common as the distinctive smell of marijuana and the acid trip. At the crash pads of the Diggers, visitors from New York could sleep on a mattress, along with lots of others. The Diggers, not just the media, had invited the young to their city for a Summer of Love. The Diggers were anarchists, former members of the San Francisco Mime Troupe, who tripped on LSD and began serving free food from their communal kitchen in Golden Gate Park.[39] Now most famous for their slogan for creative anarchy, "Do your own thing," they also ran a Free Bakery in the basement of an Episcopal church in the Haight. LeClair and Behr helped bake bread in coffee cans, which was then given away free.[40]

When they returned to New York City in the fall of 1967, Behr and LeClair moved into another apartment/commune.[41] They also wanted to make some easy money and were willing to attend six sessions sponsored by Manhattan psychiatrist who was writing an article about cohabitation for *Redbook* magazine and offered to pay five hundred dollars for their story. The psychiatrist was sympathetic to cohabitors but had decided that living together was not a threat to the institution of marriage but instead a phase prior to wedlock likely to become more prominent as the young postponed marriage. LeClair and Behr were the most political and most self-aware of those attending the sessions and did not fit the psychiatrist's assumptions because they were opposed to marriage and had a feminist critique of the institution of marriage as oppressive to women. For other couples, living together was something they did; for LeClair and Behr, cohabitation was principled living, based on anarchist and egalitarian principles. They saw themselves as too young to get married but also believed that in the ideal male/female relationship, the couple were friends and intellectual equals who never married—like Sartre and de Beauvoir.

In the sessions with the psychiatrist, they mentioned sex less often than they mentioned love, honesty, and self-disclosure. In living together, two people revealed their true selves to each other, they said, part of the process of truly getting to know another person. This generation believed that their parents had played stifling roles that led to a denial of their true selves; only by shedding these roles could young people live an authentic life. LeClair said, "I think that living with someone comes from a desire to really know him. There was a woman in my town who once told me that she'd been married for forty years and never really knew her husband. Well, under those circumstances, what's the point of being together?" After a year of living together, their relationship looked like an alternative to marriage. They were monogamous and eventually planning to have children together, although they had not made a lifelong commitment to each other. Moreover, they were clear that they were not a common-law couple: they were not holding themselves out as married, and they did not think of themselves as married.[42]

Behr and LeClair, who saw marriage as tethering a couple to traditional gender roles, believed they were engaged in creating an egalitarian relationship. They split the household chores (although he did more of the cooking), and they shared all expenses.[43] Behr told the psychiatrist that marriage encouraged traditional gender roles and that these roles consisted of a woman being the homemaker and a man the provider. LeClair indicated that she associated traditional marriage with yelling and conflict. She said to the psychiatrist, "What we are doing is different because marrying, to a great extent, is to adopt a status, to take on the roles that wives and husbands play. And a lot of people get married because they want the role. The girl might want security; and the guy might want someone he can come home and yell at."[44] It was not just the roles that made marriage empty; they saw cohabitation as spontaneous, but legal marriage as scripted and hollow.

By March 1968, Behr became the first Columbia College student to refuse induction into the army as a way "to challenge the legitimacy of the draft."[45] The army was calling draft resistors for induction in 1968. The resistor had to show up in a room full of conscripts and tell the army that he would refuse to be drafted; refusing to be inducted was a crime punishable with a prison term.[46] A dramatic confrontation with authority, a form of civil

disobedience, refusing to be drafted was also an act of great personal courage. About sixty protestors, largely from draft resistance groups, stood by
Behr at the Fort Hamilton army induction center in Brooklyn. The Klemesrud article appeared in the *New York Times* while Behr, who was recovering
from pneumonia, was facing the choice of jail or going to Canada.[47]

Instead of confronting the war makers, the couple now worked together
to confront the administrators of Barnard College, employing the skills and
rhetoric of the draft resistance movement and student protest against college housing rules. In the spring of 1968, protest against the student housing code on campus, including rules that restricted women more than men,
had been occurring since the late 1950s. Some students were protesting
rules that governed living off campus or supervised students off campus, not
simply on-campus regulations and restrictions. The previous year, LeClair's
good friend Jan Howell Marx, a graduate student in medieval comparative
literature who was active in the draft resistance movement, had led an undergraduate protest at Stanford demanding that women be allowed to live
off campus.[48]

LeClair began her protest at Barnard by writing a letter to the student
newspaper explaining why she was fighting her suspension. Her statement
combined a brief passage about equal rights for women with arguments
supporting student rights. About equal rights for women, she wrote, "Barnard College was founded on the principle of equality between men and
women. If women are able, intelligent people, why must we be supervised
and curfewed?" Her main argument, however, was that undergraduates
were adults who had the right to decide where they should live.

LeClair and Behr proceeded to gather information to show how widely
the rules were flouted. They revealed that many Barnard students wanted to
live off campus, often with their boyfriends, and they regarded dissembling
on a housing form as "a little white lie."[49] Lying on the housing form was,
of course, a continuation of lying about cohabitation, one of the main ways
people responded to the stigma of cohabitation. She and Behr circulated
a questionnaire that asked Barnard students if they, too, had violated the
off-campus housing rules. Within twenty-four hours, four hundred students
had returned the questionnaires. Three out of four said that they had, and
virtually all the respondents believed that the regulations were unfair. Many
felt that the two different sets of rules, one at Barnard and the other at Columbia, proved that "the double standard still exists today."[50]

Behr and LeClair applied the strategy of students with deferments turning in their draft cards to the protest against Barnard housing rules and em-

ployed the language of civil disobedience common in much 1960s protest, including draft resistance. Sixty students signed their name to a statement that read "I am a student of Barnard College and I have violated the Barnard Housing Regulations. . . . In the interest of fairness I request that an investigation like LeClair's be made of my disobedience."[51] Holding picket signs, thirty-five Barnard and Columbia students marched in front of the library in support of LeClair in a demonstration apparently organized by members of SDS.[52] A student committee circulated a petition asking for a review of the housing rules.

The judicial council met in the middle of April to hear LeClair's defense and then adjourned until a second meeting when she could call witnesses and examine them. The meeting was not open to the press, but the room was packed with 250 students and assorted faculty who applauded when LeClair's witnesses spoke. Behr sat beside LeClair at the proceedings. Close to tears, LeClair read an opening statement asserting her right as an adult to live wherever she chose. When committee members asked her questions, she rose from her chair to answer them. Although her lawyers were present, LeClair conducted her own cross-examination of Elizabeth Meyers, the housing director. Meyers was forced to admit that had LeClair's family lived less than fifty miles from campus she would have been allowed to live off campus. Meyers also acknowledged that there were no prohibitions against living off campus for Columbia undergraduates other than freshmen.[53] The two antiwar clergy on campus, Reverend William Starr and Rabbi A. Bruce Goldman, both testified. Starr told the council that it was unrealistic for colleges to try to protect the virginity of their students and that the housing rules were "ridiculous." Rabbi Bruce, as he was known, a reform rabbi and the chaplain for Jewish students, made clear that he thought LeClair and Behr had a meaningful relationship.[54] He said he did not support cohabitation but believed that the housing rules would not stop couples from living together but merely make them feel guilty about it.[55] Both Goldman and Starr omitted the crucial detail that when LeClair was applying for readmission to Barnard and living with Peter, the couple visited the clergymen, who told them to lie on the housing form. Since LeClair's dishonesty on the housing form became a major issue for her critics, the unwillingness of these two men to accept responsibility for encouraging telling falsehoods among youths is a striking silence in the record.

Much of LeClair's language about rights was framed in generational and familial terms. Like other students protesting campus housing rules, LeClair claimed that the rules treated her as a child rather than an adult and were hopelessly out of date. She said of Barnard's housing rules that the administration was "bound by antiquated and ridiculous rules. They are not acting in loco parentis but in loco grand parentis."[56] LeClair was not asserting her right to cohabit or her right to privacy but rather her right to live where she chose. She said to the judicial council, "Although I am old enough by law to marry without my parent's consent, support myself, which I am doing, live anywhere I want, without parental control, I am not old enough, according to Barnard, to live outside the dorm except as a domestic." She insisted that Barnard did not have right to "control [students'] personal lives": its function should be education of students, not control of their behavior.[57] She argued that "students should have a right to do what they wish, and set their own curfews and hours."[58] In language that echoed the draft resistance movement, she concluded, "I have disregarded a regulation which I believe to be unjust."[59]

LeClair clearly had had the judicial council's votes all along, since it consisted of students, two professors (including the feminist literature professor Kate Millet, who was a member of the New York branch of the National Organization for Women, or NOW) and two administrators. The council decided to punish LeClair very lightly by denying her privileges to the campus cafeteria and snack bar; it also called for an overhaul of campus housing regulations.

The television reporters who set up on the lawn at Barnard were gleeful at finding a real live story about "sex on campus." The judicial council decision was page one news not only in the *New York Times* but also in the *Milwaukee Journal*, the *Long Beach Press Telegram*, the *El Paso Herald Post*, the *Bryan (Ohio) Times*, and the *Idaho State Journal*.[60] In response to the widespread press coverage, Barnard received about 350 letters from alumnae, with about two hundred in favor of expelling LeClair. Alumnae who did not condemn LeClair as immoral mainly argued that she should be punished for lying and violating the college's housing rules. Recent graduates of Barnard and current students were her main supporters. The president's office also received more than two hundred phone calls and almost the same number of letters from members of the general public who wanted LeClair expelled. Many letters were written by women living in exclusive suburbs such as Glencoe, Illinois, or Valley Stream, New York. A New York City woman hand wrote on flowered personal stationery that "for a student to advertise to the world that she is a pig is disgraceful."[61] An anonymous writer wanted to tell LeClair, "You are only a cheap tramp and if I was you I'd jump into the Hudson river and forget to come up for the third time and take all the rest of your college girls like you along for the dip. You are a disgrace to the human race and if your parents continue supporting you I guess they are no better than you."[62]

So great was the press coverage of "the affair" that Barnard coeds were the recipients of "courtesy stigma." Thus, a man on the Long Island Railroad came up to a Barnard sophomore wearing her college sweatshirt and uttered "a vulgar remark." National magazines such as *Time* published hostile letters from the general public, which interestingly enough, depicted LeClair as a threat not to the sexual but rather to the gender order. Hariette Wagner of Northbrook, Illinois, responded to a photo of the Behr/LeClair commune published in the magazine. She wrote, "I don't know what kind of student Linda LeClair is or what kind of mistress she makes, but judging from the picture of her apartment, she makes one lousy housekeeper. Doesn't Barnard College have a Home Economics Department?"[63] Behr did not get off entirely scot-free, indicating that in the public mind, cohabitation by the college boy was not truly acceptable. One letter read, "Linda LeClair is NOTHING but a common whore and you a common PIMP!"[64] Liberal clergy such as Rabbi Goldman and Reverend Starr were also singled out for corrupting the young. To the authors of letters to Barnard the rabbi and the Episcopalian minister had disgraced "their respective religions by condoning WHAT AMOUNTS TO PROSTITUTION."[65]

The tone of press and television coverage vacillated between point/counterpoint, titillation, and condemnation. The *Today* show came closest to the first stance in a four- part series on college student cohabitation, with the now obligatory college psychiatrist opining on whether the behavior was normal and whether it damaged the woman's psyche. The editorial writer for *New York Times* thought LeClair was let off too easily, and editorials in the *Denver Post* and *Portland Press Herald* denounced her.[66] The conservative columnist William F. Buckley, who titled his column, "Linda's Crusade," recognized a fundamentally moral conflict. He termed LeClair "a pathetic little girl" unconcerned about lying, since she said she considered it "silly" to be worried about "a false entry" on a housing form. Buckley denounced LeClair because she was challenging the institution of marriage. He labeled her sexually promiscuous and did not have much respect for Barnard administrators either, who, he believed, were abdicating their role as moral guardians of youth.[67] He wrote, "In an age in which the playboy philosophy is taken seriously, a windy testimonial to the sovereign right of all human appetites, it isn't surprising that the LeClairs of this world should multiply like rabbits whose morals they imitate." The columnist Harriet Van Horne offered more subtle condemnation, indicating that the sexual revolution was acceptable so long as it was discreet. Van Horne believed that the pill was a boon to women but thought that the Columbia/Barnard couple, by ripping "away the veils of privacy," had shown "that some people are simply not adult at 20." The liberal columnist and Brandeis University professor Max Lerner parroted the view of many Barnard alumnae, that LeClair had lied and thus violated a necessary code of personal honesty.[68]

Different observers saw in the LeClair scandal the outlines of their own perspective on the world since this was, after all, a symbolic struggle, with varied opinions about what the symbol was. Feminists, scarcely evident on editorial pages in 1968, regarded the case as proof of the double standard. Conservatives such as Buckley feared moral collapse. Black leaders perceived racial hypocrisy. Roy Wilkins, the head of the NAACP who also wrote a newspaper column, believed that whites were engaging in hypocrisy in denouncing the immorality of welfare mothers. He argued that the reason white society wanted to stigmatize LeClair was so that it could prove that white people did not engage in the same form of sexual immorality as black people.[69]

The official rules of the university gave the president the ultimate power to accept or reject the decision of the judicial council. Pressured by negative publicity, angry alumnae, and presumably the board of trustees, Peterson was unwilling to accept the council's light punishment and felt she had to publicize the action she was taking. As soon as she received the council's decision, Peterson shot off a letter to LeClair indicating that she, not the judicial council, made disciplinary decisions and that she had the right to veto the council's ruling. Peterson was clearly angry with LeClair ("no useful purpose can be served by your continued enrollment in Barnard College"), but she was still seeking more information. She said she was shocked that LeClair had lied on a college housing form and annoyed that the council had not taken lying seriously, asking LeClair to explain "the importance of integrity among individuals in a college community." Peterson indicated that if LeClair did not reply to the letter by May 3, she could be expelled automatically.[70]

Peterson's letter opened the way for press interviews with Ethelyn and Paul LeClair (and provided their town of residence, previously concealed). The interviews with her parents added the important dimension of generation gap, particularly father/daughter conflict, to the story. In Hudson, people did not openly discuss sex and did not think other people should either. The LeClairs made the mistake of inviting various reporters and photographers into their home when they came to the door. Paul LeClair did most of the talking, and Ethelyn LeClair dabbed her eyes with a handkerchief. But after initially being willing to talk, they became overwhelmed. When Ethelyn LeClair picked up the phone, she told a reporter, "Why don't you people just leave us alone?"[71] Paul LeClair made the front page of the *New York Post* when he said that he was no longer willing to support his daughter, although he backed off repeating that in talking to the *New York Times*.[72]

When it became clear that Peterson was unwilling to accept the council's decision, Barnard students invited practiced feminist orators to generate excitement for the cause. For the first time, self-defined feminists spoke out opposing prohibitions against cohabitation as a denial of women's personal rights and demanded changes in the rules that punished it. The New York branch of NOW had in mind a broadening of the students' call for health prescriptions for the pill to other issues such as the establishment of university-run day care and equalizing of the Barnard and Columbia housing rules.[73] NOW membership included several Barnard women faculty; the administration had warned Barnard and Columbia NOW members not to interfere in the LeClair case. Nevertheless, Florynce ("Flo") Kennedy, an African American Columbia Law school graduate, New York NOW member, and flamboyant civil rights lawyer who opposed the Vietnam War, and Ti-Grace Atkinson, the president of New York NOW—both fiery orators— spoke at a meeting on LeClair's behalf. Kennedy wanted to confront the authorities by organizing a referendum opposing Peterson and urging noncooperation with a housing reform committee appointed by the president.[74]

In the spring of 1968, protest was merging with the unexpected, the inexplicable, and the tragic. The Tet offensive by the Vietcong in January was taken as proof that the Vietnam War was unwinnable. In March, LBJ announced that he would not run for reelection, and Eugene McCarthy and Robert Kennedy entered the Democratic presidential primaries. Martin Luther King was assassinated on the balcony of the Lorraine Motel in Memphis in April. As news reached Harlem of King's murder, the police in Harlem shot live ammunition in the air to stop looters from absconding with televisions and stereos from appliance stores. Standing on a Harlem street corner, it was possible to hear collective wailing.

Campus protest that spring was cascading at Barnard and Columbia into longer, more dramatic acts of civil disobedience. Students from both Barnard and Columbia occupied Columbia campus buildings for days in protest against a university unit engaged in military research and the plans to build a Columbia gym that encroached on city parkland shared by Columbia and Harlem. After several days of mediation, the president of Columbia decided to call the police. A thousand city officers with nightsticks in hand dragged off students in paddy wagons. LeClair and Behr were among those arrested for refusing to vacate a building on the Columbia campus.[75]

Days later at Barnard, Peterson was threatening to overturn the slap on the wrist punishment of LeClair the judicial council had ordered. Two hundred Barnard students held a rally on the campus lawn on May 11, protesting Peterson's letter to LeClair, her threat to expel LeClair, and her decision to overrule the judicial council. Peterson was changing her political calculation as the problems at Columbia escalated to the point of a bloody confrontation because Columbia's president had not known how to correctly defuse the situation. Barnard students engaged in a sit-in at Peterson's office, bringing with them a referendum, signed by fully half of the Barnard student body, that "deplored" Peterson's decision to overrule the judicial council. Students threatened to stay in Peterson's office until she agreed to abide by the judicial council's decision. Peterson decided to reverse her position "in light of the past turmoil" and affirm a judgment reached in a body that included representatives of students. LeClair would not be suspended, Peterson declared, provided that she had passing grades at the end of the semester. From reading *Time* magazine, Peterson would have known that LeClair had stopped attending classes by early April and therefore did not have passing grades. If LeClair dropped out without being formally expelled or if she failed her classes, Peterson's problem would go away.[76]

By the third week in May, the students had scattered. With other friends from the Resistance, LeClair and Behr left the city for one of the most famous communes on the East Coast, Total Loss Farm in Guilford, Vermont. The burned-out activists at the farm were turning on each other, however: the couple left weeks after they arrived, hitchhiking to the West Coast. During the summer, Peterson sent LeClair a letter telling her that she could return to Barnard in the fall if she behaved "in an appropriate manner."[77]

By the end of the summer, LeClair and Behr had returned to their apartment in Spanish Harlem. Peter told Linda that he had decided to return to school; she had always assumed that he was dropping out.[78] She and Peter no longer seemed to share the same outlook, and they split up. He refused induction into the military, graduated from Columbia, and avoided going to jail by emigrating to British Columbia, where many of the former student activists settled. Eventually, he became a massage therapist.[79] LeClair dropped out of Barnard and moved back to New Hampshire where she became an antinuclear activist; years later, she was able to complete her undergraduate degree at SUNY, Albany. She said of her parents, "We've always been close. They were not happy about that period at all, but we were never out of a relationship."[80] In 2009, she was living in Concord, New Hampshire, the mother of two grown daughters, and serving as executive director of NARAL Pro-Choice New Hampshire.

The New Left and SDS believed that "confrontation with the authorities" involved challenging everyone from military recruiters on campus to administrators enforcing college housing rules. Only a small percentage of college youths baked bread for the Diggers, faced down the Army at the Pentagon, occupied a university building, recuperated at the most famous commune in Vermont, and hitchhiked across the country. Living on the barricades, bearing witness required, as they liked to say, being true to one's self. In writing and speaking in her defense, LeClair was breaking the code of silence about student cohabitation, frankly referring to "sexual intercourse." Rather than merely trying to get around the rules, LeClair taught that the sexual revolution required a young woman to confront administrators, whom she called "the authorities," speaking up for her rights, and claiming that Peterson and others treated college students as if they were children.

The intensity of the press and public reaction to LeClair was a sign that the decline of the double standard on the college campus had provoked moral panic. If sexual morality was the cornerstone of the nation, then the sexual revolution at universities revealed the extent to which America was under attack. Martha Peterson's reaction was a product of the pressure she felt from influential Barnard alumnae of an older generation, who correctly perceived the beginnings of a "culture war," an assault on their values. Iphigene Sulzberger had understood correctly that LeClair was opposing the ideal of sexual respectability and "reputation." Peter Behr had only a walk-on part in this national psychodrama, however, because it was the "defiant girl," a girl from a decent and privileged background who was upsetting the moral order and the domestic role of women, and riling the *New York Times*.

Admitting that she was having sex off campus, challenging a college's housing rules, having her photo plastered on the front page of the newspapers, getting her parents and even her younger brother involved in what was dubbed "a scandal" in the press—all took their toll. As LeClair recalled years later, "I got burned out. I really did. I was just this farm kid from New Hampshire."[81] In 2008, she returned to the campus of her youth to speak at a fortieth-anniversary commemoration of the protests at Barnard and Columbia. Briefly recounting her story to an audience, some of whom belonged to a younger generation, she described what she called a process of objectification—or stigmatization—by which she was made into "the sex girl." She said of her experience in 1968, "It's still shameful after all these years."[82]

Being fodder for the tabloids conveyed to LeClair the stigma of cohabitation, a shaming that was personally wounding; to join the Diggers or SDS did not shield her from parental disapproval or from being demeaned in the press. The *New York Daily News* communicated to the world a deeply discrediting label ("free love Portia"). In 1985, LeClair told a *Chicago Tribune* reporter who had tracked her down, "With all the media stuff, in a strange way my name took on its own life. I didn't feel it was my name anymore. It was over there. Everyone knew something about Linda LeClair that wasn't me."[83] Unprepared to see her "love trial" on the front page, or to become the butt of a joke on the Johnny Carson show or of a demeaning limerick recited by the Barnard faculty, and forced to confront the pain her scandal had caused her brother and her parents, LeClair made an important choice: to change her name.

FIVE

From Sheboygan to Madison

When the sexual revolution arrived in small towns in the Midwest and the South, local authorities were shocked and fought back, sometimes martyring a hapless soul caught between the old and new morality. Even within the same state, attitudes toward cohabitation and enforcement of anticohabitation statutes could vary widely. While students were protesting in Madison, Wisconsin, the authorities in nearby Sheboygan were invoking the criminal law to defend their community against the perceived assault on their sexual and family values. This chapter focuses on the battle between conservative reaction to cohabitation and campus liberalism in Madison and the major cities of Wisconsin. In a process halting and ragged, most states eliminated their laws criminalizing cohabitation in the 1970s because of bipartisan penal reform and the impact of the sexual revolution. Wisconsin was not among the states to decriminalize cohabitation in that decade because of the power of the right wing in the culture war. The ordeal of a cohabiting couple had almost no statewide impact. Instead, the decriminalization effort was fueled, first, by bipartisan liberal reform of the criminal law, then followed by pressure group politics, in which the major pressure group was not cohabitors but the gay civil rights movement aligned with other liberal groups.

Although the last arrest for cohabitation in Florida occurred in 1969, arrests and prosecutions continued in other states (in New Mexico and Virginia until 1976, in Wisconsin until 1978, in North Carolina until 2003). In Florida and other states, criminal laws against cohabitation have been used to justify laws and policies that discriminated against cohabitors. The existence of laws against cohabitation have permitted discrimination by employers, landlords, professional licensing boards, and judges making decisions about child custody or, in the case of Michael Schiavo in Florida, guardianship of a spouse. The illegality of cohabitation has even been used as leverage in divorce proceedings and as a means to make fathers pay child support. Ministers have referred to the illegality of cohabitation to persuade couples to get married. It is not simply that a man and woman have occasionally been arrested by the police for cohabitation; cohabitation has also been punished by the border patrol, the military, school boards, and parole departments. Officers of the law were expected to live a moral life. Thus, police chiefs have ordered vice squads and bureaus of internal affairs to stake out the apartments of men on the force thought to be living with someone outside of marriage, who were then charged with cohabitation, tried by police review boards, and, if found guilty, dismissed from their jobs.[1]

This chapter shows that laws against cohabitation have been enforced but selectively, lives have sometimes been destroyed, and the general public has been divided (mainly along secular/religious, cosmopolitan/parochial lines) on whether the effort is worthwhile. This chapter also traces the politics of decriminalization through various phases, from broad nonpartisan penal reform to gay mobilization against Anita Bryant to explicit repeal of anticohabitation statutes. The major opposition to decriminalization has come from the Christian Right, which has been able either to delay repeal or to stop it entirely in a few states. Blocking repeal of such laws certainly constitutes evidence of a culture war over cohabitation, but a war in which cohabitation was still a relatively minor part of larger skirmishes over sexuality and the family.

Criminal Laws Punishing Cohabitation

In 1972, cohabitation was a crime in twenty-eight states and a few cities, such as Lawrence, Kansas, Bend and Culver, Oregon, and Milwaukee, Wisconsin. There had been separate laws making interracial cohabitation a crime, but these were declared unconstitutional by the US Supreme Court in 1964. Other statutes outlawed cohabitation by specific groups or under specific circumstances. In 1973, twenty-three states prohibited cohabitation by parolees. As these laws were administered, women prisoners often felt that they had to meet higher standards than men did to prove they were not living in sin.[2] Moreover, in questioning probationers, judges often imposed the marriage cure, requiring criminals either to cease cohabiting, get married, or go to jail.[3] There were also specific laws against false hotel and motel registration, that is, deceptively signing the register as husband and wife, which was punishable as a misdemeanor.[4]

The military, which had its own code of criminal justice, punished unlawful cohabitation with a court-martial and up to one year in jail; sixteen courts-martial for this crime reached the military appellate courts between 1951 and 1972. Of course, the military had an easier method of preventing cohabitation since only married military personnel were permitted to live off base. Like civilian authorities, the military enforced this regulation selectively. Military police tended to look the other way when a serviceman was living off base with a woman in Korea or Japan, but they believed the respectability of the armed services was damaged when a man in uniform was staying with a woman in the United States—say, in Boise, Idaho.[5]

Among the twenty-eight states that criminalized cohabitation in 1972, eight were in the Midwest and another eight were in the South, reflecting the regional strongholds of opposition to the sexual revolution and homosexual rights. Five of the midwestern states that criminalized cohabitation (Illinois, Indiana, Iowa, Michigan, and Wisconsin) were contiguous: legislators tended to be influenced by the laws and judicial opinions of their neighbors The rationale for criminalizing cohabitation was rarely stated in the statute itself, except for the one from Illinois, which justified criminalization as necessary for the "protection of the institution of marriage and normal family relationships from sexual conduct which tends to destroy them."[6] The statutes were worded in a variety of ways. Cohabitors could be punished for fornication, adultery, or the crime of cohabitation. Although there were laws punishing lewdness, the lewd and lascivious cohabitation statutes were separate, and "one act of single lewdness" would not be enough to constitute cohabitation. According to these laws, the actual crime could be living together in adultery or fornication, living in a state of cohabitation, living together in open and notorious adultery, or cohabitating together as husband and wife without being married. Some states required proof of intercourse to bring a charge of lewd and lascivious cohabitation, others simply stated the offense as living together, and still others defined it as living together if there was proof that the couple was having intercourse. Even if the statute did not explicitly declare that cohabitation was a crime of heterosexuals, it was understood as such; the charge of sodomy was applied to homosexuals (primarily gay men) who were living together or were caught in public engaging in or soliciting homosexual acts.

These statutes usually assumed a certain duration of the relationship and common residence and foreclosed a rationale of common-law marriage. The Indiana Supreme Court in the 1930s held out the standard that a couple had to live together for "some period of time" in the "manner of a husband and wife" to be guilty of cohabitation.[7] Still, a man and woman could be charged with cohabitation (or disorderly conduct) even if they were merely spending the weekend together. On the whole, the courts were deliberately vague on the definition of cohabitation. Such charges could be made in conjunction with claiming welfare fraud. Complaints to police often originated from an annoyed neighbor or ex-spouse. But they were also a tool used by district attorneys who wanted to secure plea bargains to lesser charges or who were intent on demonstrating to the public that they were taking a strong stand against immorality. The crime of lewd and lascivious cohabitation was often punishable with a fine of three hundred to one thousand dollars and/or with a prison term of six months to three years.[8]

Many cohabitors fought back against arrests and firings in the 1970s. A few women successfully sued on the grounds of sex discrimination because they, not their boyfriends, had been fired. A number of men were arrested for cohabitation as well as dismissed from their jobs, and they also sued.[9] A scorecard of cases would probably reveal as many losers as winners, however. Despite the fact that the US Supreme Court had broken new ground in recognizing a constitutional right to privacy for married couples and concerning abortion, the Court's general reluctance to get ahead of public opinion caused it, for the most part, to dodge the issue of whether cohabitors also had a right to privacy under the US Constitution. The court merely affirmed its earlier views in *McLaughlin* that the state had the right to police morality. Some state courts, similarly reluctant to buck dominant views, sidestepped the issue entirely, leaving it to the people's elected representatives to resolve.

The initial wave of decriminalization of cohabitation in state law resulted from a slightly different kind of postwar liberalism than that of the Warren Court. Between 1951 and 1962, the lawyers and judges who composed the American Law Institute, headquartered in Philadelphia, drafted a model penal code to replace the diverse, patchwork criminal codes of the states. The new code decriminalized sodomy as well as adultery, fornication, and cohabitation. The ALI also provided an elaborate philosophical rationale for decriminalization, based on its views of the proper role of the state, the concept of privacy, US pluralism, and marriage promotion. In reaching its conclusion, it relied heavily on statistical evidence from Alfred Kinsey that showed that extramarital and premarital sex were common, as well as on Kinsey's claim that one out of every ten American men had had some homosexual experience. The ALI argued that the state had a responsibility to protect people from physical danger but should leave moral regulation to "spiritual authorities." Indeed, it saw no point in regulating morality because human sexual behavior was extremely difficult to change through legal sanctions. They argued that it was far preferable for the law to reflect the actual state of sexual practices. The ALI emphasized the distinction between private and public, holding that the state should not intervene in sexual relationships between consenting adults that took place "in private," usually meaning in the home, or, more broadly, out of public view. ALI's pluralism argument was that American society consisted of people who held differing views of sexual morality, and therefore, no single standard of morality existed. Because this was so, the ALI claimed, if the authorities tried to enforce morality, they would end up enforcing the morality of only one segment of the population.[10] Reflecting these views, the model penal code rejected the idea that the state could promote marriage through the use of the criminal law. It did not take the radical position that the state had no interest in promoting marriage but, instead, claimed that punishment of adult consensual behavior that took place in private was an unwieldy and ultimately ineffective tool for marriage promotion.

ALI's approach turned out to be highly influential. State legislatures appointed commissions to revise state criminal codes, and these commissions spent many years overhauling the penal codes, not under the guise of decriminalizing cohabitation but rather as part of a bipartisan effort by legal experts to modernize state law. Thus, in a single package, a state's laws against bestiality, cohabitation, adultery, and sodomy might be eliminated. Other state legislatures, however, unpacked the category of consensual sex between adults, leading to the decoupling of the decriminalization of sodomy from that of cohabitation. Hence, in 1961, Illinois decriminalized consensual sodomy, which it considered flouting morals in public, but retained its criminal law against cohabitation. In fact, the law against cohabitation was used to deny child custody to a woman whose "public" cohabitation consisted merely of telling her neighbors that her boyfriend was moving in.[11]

Wisconsin and the Beginning of the Culture Wars

In 1967, penal code reform failed to pass in Wisconsin, and through the 1970s and early 1980s, Wisconsin state law lagged far behind the growth of cohabitation. The fight continued in the state legislature for sixteen years before Wisconsin finally repealed its criminal law against cohabitation in 1983. The legislative battle in Wisconsin was the beginning of the end and the end of the beginning. It signaled the end of bipartisan legal reform eliminating laws against cohabitation and the beginning of the culture wars contest about them, pitting the cry for sexual freedom and personal privacy against the defense of family and morality.

Motel owners outside of Madison were still posting the state laws against cohabitation in the rooms of their establishments. Even as late as 1978, the criminal law against cohabitation was still being enforced in many counties in Wisconsin, ruining lives. In the college town of Madison, there was quite a bit of tolerance and acceptance of cohabitation, but considerably less (or none at all) in nearby Sheboygan.

Among those whose lives were destroyed were James Decko and Judy Sampson. In 1970, the Sheboygan Police Department staked out an apartment and arrested Sampson and Decko for cohabitation, and the school department, which employed Decko as a park supervisor, gave him the choice of resigning or being fired; he chose to resign. Stigma, surveillance, and enforcement of the criminal law against cohabitation worked together in Sheboygan. Decko's arrest and the surrounding publicity grew out of moral panic. The press, school board, and public in Sheboygan were fearful because an "authority" such as Decko, who was supposed to be in charge of enforcing traditional morality and setting a positive example for the city's young people, was instead engaged in the new morality. Stigma in Sheboygan involved being literally expelled from the town, cast out and shunned as a sinner. Moral panic also led to aftershocks, namely, denunciation and negative publicity about Sheboygan itself. After they had been forced to leave Sheboygan, Decko and Sampson brought a lawsuit challenging the constitutionality of Wisconsin's law against cohabitation. Their suit, *Wisconsin v. Decko*, reached the US Supreme Court in 1971 but was remanded to a lower court in Wisconsin. Although preliminary hearings were held, the case never came to trial.

The Greatest Little Town in the World

Sheboygan took pride in being the cohabitation arrest capitol of the United States in the 1970s. In 1972, Bob Abbey, a town resident of Sheboygan, said, "Sheboygan, Wisconsin, has enforced its laws and ordinances regarding the moral conduct of the people within its jurisdiction to a greater extent than any similar government body in the nation. I say thank the Lord."[12]

Under the headline "Sheboygan vs. New York," in 1968, the *Wall Street Journal* contrasted criminal arrests in the two cities as evidence of the difference between cosmopolitanism and small-town puritanism. In New York City, over a fifty-year period there had been two prosecutions for adultery, none for fornication, and none for cohabitation. In Sheboygan, in 1967 alone there were thirty-five arrests for adultery, eleven for fornication, twenty-seven for lewd and lascivious cohabitation, four for bigamy, and one for sexual perversion. The reporter interviewed Sheboygan's police chief, Oakley Frank, who defended his town's record, explaining that that most of the arrests were made because neighbors complained to the police. Frank said, "We have high principled people who find this kind of conduct abhorrent."[13] The article noted that district attorneys throughout the nation had resuscitated "archaic sex laws" to prosecute welfare mothers, SDS members, and drug sellers. The reporter interviewed that exemplar of cosmopolitan sexual attitudes Hugh Hefner of *Playboy*, who informed him about the many statutes still on the books that punished adultery and fornication. The reporter also spoke to Gerald Mueller, a law professor at New York University and the author of ALI's model penal code. Mueller repeated *Playboy*'s explanation for the persistence of such laws, telling the reporter, "It's our heritage of Puritanism. . . . In the United States, we're virtually alone in punishing these crimes."[14] The *Sheboygan Press* reprinted the *Wall Street Journal* story in its entirety, not in the least embarrassed by the town's residents being seen as sexual puritans. The headline, "'Most Arrests Made' for Sex Law Offenses in Smaller Cities," indicated civic pride that Sheboygan was actively policing morality.[15]

One month later a reporter from the London tabloid *People*, having read the *Journal* article, showed up in town and stayed three days to query local residents, including the police chief. The reporter told the *Sheboygan Press* that he was going to tell his readers that Sheboygan was a typical midwestern town, enforcing a law criminalizing cohabitation that was on the books in Wisconsin. Chief Frank, pleased by the attention he received from the visiting Englishman, arrived at his office on a Sunday morning to be interviewed. The tabloid reporter flattered the locals by telling them, "You probably have far less promiscuity than the big cities . . . since everybody knows each other." After he returned home to London, he filed a story that appeared under the headline "Sheboygan: Town of Peeping Toms."[16]

A legal history of family law, published in 2011, states that "few modern-day couples have faced a sheriff's pounding on their door in the middle of the night demanding to see a marriage license." The Playboy Foundation funded a survey of 426 chief prosecutors. They turned up a whopping 3,241 prosecutions for fornication and cohabitation during the years 1968–72. The survey underscored the *Wall Street Journal* article that prosecutors, especially in the Bible Belt, were bringing such charges against interracial couples, minorities, and welfare mothers and their boyfriends. In 1978, a law professor at the University of Wisconsin surveyed every county in Wisconsin and found that there had been ninety prosecutions for cohabitation in the state during the period 1973–78. In most counties of Wisconsin, there were none—none in Milwaukee or Madison, and one district attorney indicated that he himself was living with someone![17] Some counties were bent on prosecution, however. In three counties, there were five to nine prosecutions; in one, there were ten; in another, twenty; and in Sheboygan, thirty-five. Both studies found great variation, with some prosecutors bringing cohabitors to court quite frequently. Most cohabitors convicted of cohabitation paid a small fine, but a few were serving jail terms. In fact, the law professor did not detect the full extent to which the law was being enforced in Wisconsin because she did not examine the police department in Milwaukee. The police chief there had been unable to persuade the district attorney to prosecute any of his officers for the crime of cohabitation, but he had ordered his vice squad and the bureau of internal affairs to stake out the residences of those on the force, who were then brought before the city's police board on charges of cohabitation. By the early 1980s, officers who had been fired had successfully sued and were reinstated with back pay, but not before the Milwaukee public learned about dozens of stakeouts of the apartments of police officers.[18]

Arrests for cohabitation in Wisconsin were a long-standing tradition: the criminal law was enacted in 1837, when Wisconsin was still a territory. In frontier Wisconsin, such charges were brought against French fur traders taking Indian wives according to the "custom of the country." The couples were brought into court, and if they legally married, charges were dropped; if they refused to marry, they were fined. But Wisconsin law was also used to police morality, irrespective of race or ethnicity. In Sauk County or Green Bay, there were more prosecutions of illicit cohabitation per capita in the nineteenth century than in the 1970s. In that sense, Wisconsin was not as repressive in the 1970s as it had been a century earlier. But in a state shaken by urban riots and campus protest at Madison, the public was demanding law and order: an occasional arrest for cohabitation seemed an appropriate way to prove the authorities were trying to quell unrest.[19]

Sheboygan

Great waves of European immigration in the nineteenth and early twentieth centuries had populated Sheboygan, and some Mexican immigrant workers who came to pick crops in the summer stayed and settled. Sheboygan had a reputation as a white-only town, and many blacks steered clear or were encouraged to do so by realtors, homeowners, and landlords who found ways to skirt fair-housing laws. Sheboygan was known as the city of the four Cs: chairs (manufactured there), cheese (made in the cheese factories), children, and churches (more than eighty of them). Cohabitation was decidedly not one of the Cs. The town had a large working class, who usually owned their own homes and were employed in local factories opposite residential neighborhoods. There was a small group of business owners and professionals, and at the top of Sheboygan society was the manufacturing elite of factory owners and their families, often active in philanthropy and Wisconsin politics.

The town of Sheboygan, with a population of forty-eight thousand in 1970, was a compact collection of neighborhoods in a state that had a law punishing lewd and lascivious cohabitation. Cohabitors often pretended to be married in order to be able to rent from landlords who refused to accept unmarried couples as tenants. The German-Americans of Wisconsin were known for their thriftiness; many who settled in Sheboygan had converted their homes to include rooms to let, so rental income could be used to help pay the mortgage. Some of the more prosperous also owned houses that they rented out. Nestled at the intersection of three rivers, the town itself was relatively compact and houses were built fairly close to one another. People knew their neighbors, and gossip traveled quickly at parks, taverns, bowling alleys, churches, and grocery stores.

Many in Sheboygan believed that outsiders did not share the town's values—the English journalist had made fun of Sheboygan, and Chief Frank was known to arrest hippies, drunken bikers, and sun-seeking young people who frequented downtown bars during the summer. Next to Sheboygan was the factory village of Kohler, a planned community of company buildings and worker housing where the Kohler Company produced bathtubs, sinks, and toilets. The Kohler strike, which lasted from 1954 to 1965, increased the feeling that the village of Kohler and the nearby town of Sheboygan were beset by violence (one man died in the strike) and by scabs brought in from the outside. The strike not only generated suspicion toward outsiders but also heightened the feeling that Sheboygan's way of life was under assault.

The 1970 bombing of the Army Mathematics Research Center at the University of Wisconsin–Madison, which killed one and injured three people, and the numerous disruptive student protests at Madison were enough to convince residents of Sheboygan that the SDS was a Communist plot, or at least a Communist front. Sheboygan residents were appalled and frightened by terrorism in Madison, since not all of the unrest could be attributed to youth who attended the university from outside of the state. Tucked away north of Milwaukee, Sheboygan was driving distance from Madison as well as Milwaukee and Chicago but geographically quite separate, and it sought to maintain that distance, even if it meant closing down the Bratwurst Festival, which attracted one hundred thousand visitors for one day each August until it was abolished in 1967.[20]

In Sheboygan, residents were aware of the morals revolution among their own young and shared the sense of moral panic of Iphigene Sulzberger and the outraged adults who wrote to Martha Peterson at Barnard. By 1971, it was clear that youths in revolt were not simply college kids living away from home, but also high school students rebelling while still housed under the parental roof. Sheboygan residents, confronting the generation gap and protestors at campuses in Madison or Oshkosh, were worrying about their own children. The children of the town's county court judge were having wild parties in the loft of his garage. An underground newspaper published in Milwaukee was circulating in town. Sheboygan high school students were protesting the Vietnam War, and young men were burning their draft cards. Students at one of the two local high schools, charging voter fraud in student elections, staged a sit-in at the principal's office. They were expelled, but with the help of the ACLU, they sued successfully to be reinstated. One of the protestors ran away from home and was living at the high school. Sheboygan residents struck back at the hippies, the druggies, and the porn sellers; hippies were arrested for vagrancy, potheads were busted for possession of marijuana, and local newsdealers selling the underground newspaper were issued a warning but not arrested so long as they agreed to cease distributing it.[21]

Decko and Sampson

In 1964, James Decko, his wife, Mary, and their baby daughter, Kathleen, moved to Sheboygan from Olympia, Washington, where he had been physical director of the local YMCA. They were members of the 1960s generation who had married young and started a family right away. Jim and Mary quickly stepped into the gender roles laid out for husbands and wives of the middle class. He was only twenty-four when they moved to Sheboygan, but already a father and family man who wanted to make a career out of his athletic abilities, outgoing personality, and managerial skills.[22] Mary became a homemaker and civic volunteer and at age twenty-two had a second child, Julia, born in 1965. Jim Decko's world was athletics; when he wasn't supervising athletics, he was engaged in sports, playing on the men's tennis team, and becoming a linebacker on the semiprofessional Sheboygan Redwings football team.[23]

After two years as a recreation supervisor in Sheboygan, James Decko was promoted to head of the recreation department, overseeing more than two hundred part-time employees.[24] An administrator employed by the school board, he was a member of the civic elite, joining the local Rotary Club. As chair of the town's United Way drive, he encouraged his employees to contribute. Active in professional associations, he became treasurer of the Wisconsin Park and Recreation Association.[25] An accomplished public speaker, he was called on to serve as master of ceremonies at a town talent show.[26]

Citing the rationale that many of the recreational facilities were located in school buildings or on school grounds, the Sheboygan Board of Education rather than the parks department oversaw the recreation department and employed its director. Decko's job involved planning, organizing, and arranging the youth, adult, and senior citizen clubs and recreational activities from learn-to-swim programs to touch football leagues to children's theater programs. He coordinated programming with the YMCA, arranged bus trips to the Milwaukee Zoo and nature hikes, and scheduled use of park and school facilities and the ice rink. He often appeared at public forums, moderating panel discussions and answering questions about the programs of his department. Favoring a military model of management, he liked to give orders to his employees, which he expected them to carry out. When they did not follow his orders, he would say, "You did this wrong."[27]

By 1969, his marriage was crumbling, and he began an affair with Martha Judy Sampson, a young divorcée. Sampson had grown up on a farm in Iowa and married a local boy, a basketball coach and high school teacher, when she was eighteen. The following year she had given birth to a daughter, but soon after that she started taking classes at Upper Iowa College where she was a honors student. In college, she had an affair with her art teacher, who was a married man. In 1969, she took her four-year-old daughter with her to Reno, where she obtained a divorce and was granted sole custody of her daughter. She moved to Sheboygan, where she took a job as an elementary school art teacher, perhaps because she had some family in town; her grandfather had been a wealthy chair manufacturer in Sheboygan. Then she became a bookkeeper at the Sheboygan art center and worked weekends as a cocktail waitress at a local nightclub. It turns out that wife swapping was not something occurring only in exclusive suburbs. In 1970, it was an idea that Judy Sampson embraced. She met Jim Decko; he left his wife for her, and they planned to marry after his divorce became final. Jim's friends told him that he was asking for trouble if he moved in with Judy Sampson, but he ignored them.[28]

Decko and Sampson found a small Victorian house within walking distance of downtown and Jim's office but moved from there to another apartment building, perhaps by June 1970, where they signed the lease in the name of "Mr. and Mrs. James Decko." They probably had to do so in order to rent an apartment together. Some of the neighbors knew that they were not married and liked them, but a police captain's sister who lived down the hall was suspicious and called the police. By August 1970, two police officers were driving by the house periodically throughout the night. They noted that Decko's "blue Ford, license R-96 240," was parked on the street outside throughout the night. Police reports noted when the apartment lights were turned on and off.[29] The police issued Decko a warning. Was he staying in the apartment overnight? Where did he sleep in the apartment? Decko asked them if he could visit Sampson. They said yes, so long as he left by midnight or one in the morning. He moved out, but still stayed over at Sampson's apartment on weekends. He asked friends to drop him off at the apartment so that he did not have to park his car in front. Police surveillance continued, and in September 1970, Decko and Sampson were issued a summons to appear in court on charges of having committed lewd and lascivious cohabitation.

If he was discreet, not actually living in the apartment, and no longer parking his car in front of the apartment building, why was Jim Decko arrested? Apparently, the police captain's sister did not want cohabitors as neighbors. She was not just any constituent, but a citizen with a powerful relative in the police department. Even after the summons, Jim Decko still thought he had room to maneuver. He talked to Chief Frank and told him that he wanted to keep his name out of the papers and settle out of court. Frank said that his superiors had encouraged him to prosecute and that if he failed to do so, his department would be held accountable. Frank's view was that Decko had chosen to ignore a warning he had been given and therefore did not deserve a third chance. Frank, a Sheboygan native, had served in the military during World War II and returned home to join the Sheboygan police force as a patrolman after the war. A stocky man with graying hair, he had been chief of police for seven years. Frank easily sensed that the new morality of the sixties was disrupting life in the town he loved.[30]

The school board, which found out immediately about Decko's arrest, told him he could either resign or be fired on grounds of moral turpitude; he chose to quit. Teachers, school board employees, librarians, and police were expected to be role models and held to a high standard of morality.

Adopting a defiant attitude in his letter of resignation, Decko wrote, "Because of ancient and archaic laws I am guilty of a misdemeanor which the Board of Education will have no sympathy with."[31] Decko's use of the word *laws* rather than *law* is appropriate since Wisconsin had a law punishing cohabitation as well as another law allowing school boards to dismiss employees for immoral conduct.

Decko resigned on a Friday and went away for the weekend. On Monday morning, he returned to find his picture on the front page of the *Sheboygan Press*. The similarity between the *New York Times* coverage of LeClair and the *Sheboygan Free Press*'s coverage of Decko was that both stories were front page news, including a photograph, although Decko's story did not receive the same kind of national attention as LeClair's. Arrests for morals offenses, not uncommon in Sheboygan, were a regular feature of the paper, but buried in a small article on page three or four. For the Decko arrest, the paper reproduced a head shot of Decko in his plaid suit under the front page headline, "'Rec' Director, Decko, Resigns."[32] Printing Decko's photo was a public shaming and a message to get out of town. Judy Sampson was also fired from her job, but her dismissal was never mentioned in the paper, and her photo was not published.

Jim Decko contacted a young lawyer with whom he attended Milwaukee Bucks games, Peter Bjork. Bjork took on Decko and Sampson as clients on a pro bono basis because they had no money to pay his fees. Bjork hoped that he could settle the matter quietly. He asked the Sheboygan County district attorney, Lance Jones, to drop the charge. Jones, the youngest district attorney in Wisconsin history, was a twenty-six-year-old graduate of the University of Wisconsin and its law school. He came from a wealthy family in Kohler and was living with his parents. He had run for district attorney on the Republican ticket in 1968 and lost badly. When the winner resigned his post to return to a private law practice, the Republican governor appointed him to serve out the rest of his opponent's two-year term. Lance Jones was intent on winning the election for district attorney on his own and was also considering running for higher office after that. Speaking out against radical campus protest, which he had witnessed in Madison, he told junior high school students that "the full force of public disapproval" should be turned on conduct that "openly flouts and undermines a system of law and order about 200 years old."[33] Previously, Jones had shown some leniency in the prosecution of cohabitation cases.[34] In 1969, he had reduced most charges involving consensual sex to charges of disorderly conduct.[35] In this case, however, he decided to pursue full prosecution because he was intent on showing that he enforced law and order, no matter who was involved.

Prosecuting Decko, he thought, would give him favorable publicity and help his political career.[36]

A week after Decko and Sampson received the summons, Bjork appeared in court for a pretrial hearing. Feeling persecuted, Decko and Sampson had left town. Before departing, Judy Sampson had mailed a letter to the *Sheboygan Press*. She excoriated the police captain's sister and the prying neighbors as "crucifiers" who had snooped on her and Jim, fearful "of their own inadequacies," and she denounced the school board as well for forcing Jim to resign. Her capitalization of "PROGRESSIVE" versus "PRIMITIVE" underscored her understanding of the culture war that was dividing cosmopolitan cities from small towns. She wrote, "Laws like these exist all over the United States but for the past 25 years, they have been ignored (at least in the PROGRESSIVE cities)." She expressed outrage at the stakeout of their apartment for two months. She and Jim, she wrote, were ready to leave, "for Sheboygan is not the kind of city I care to live in or, for that matter, ever return to." She added, "I was told that Sheboygan was conservative but this surpasses my wildest conceptions. Sheboygan is not conservative; it is PRIMITIVE."[37]

The stigma against cohabitation was even stronger in Sheboygan in 1971 than at Barnard in 1968, but in both places, revelation of cohabitation was a "public scandal," because cohabitation was seen as an affront to public decency and a threat to the institution of marriage. It seems likely that most Sheboygan residents approved of the school board's actions and the publicity the case received. One local resident, Ellen Smith, wrote to the paper to denounce Judy Sampson and point out that cohabitors like Sampson and Decko were few in number and a decided minority in Sheboygan. Smith chastised the couple for disregarding the laws laid down in the Bible. She added that she thought it especially immoral "for people in public positions, leaders, teachers" to cohabit. Smith strongly defended the police with several exclamation points: "Detectives are paid to uphold the law! That is what they were doing!!" The town did not regret that Decko and Sampson had left, she claimed. She closed her letter by noting that "Sheboygan has lost very little, we shall live on moralistically."[38]

Decko and Sampson left Sheboygan for the big city, Chicago, and then Los Angeles. While they were living together in Los Angeles, Bjork urged them to challenge Wisconsin's law against lewd and lascivious cohabitation. He was willing to take the case all the way to the US Supreme Court. They agreed to the lawsuit, recognizing that they were subjecting themselves to further publicity about their case, just when they had finally escaped prying neighbors by moving to liberal Los Angeles. Bjork contacted the Playboy Foundation in Chicago, which provided some funding for his legal fees.

Hugh Hefner had already made clear to the *Wall Street Journal* three years earlier that he opposed laws such as Wisconsin's: his foundation and the Wisconsin ACLU became involved in this case.

In March 1971, Bjork filed a legal brief in Sheboygan County Court arguing for a dismissal of the charges against Decko and Sampson on several grounds. One was that the Wisconsin statute violated the constitutional protection of the right of privacy. Bjork further claimed that Wisconsin law deprived Decko and Sampson of their right to freedom of association, guaranteed by the First Amendment. As was common for a defense against a criminal law of this kind, Bjork claimed that the vagueness of the statute lay in its wording referring to "circumstances that implied sexual intercourse" when it was impossible to prove what those circumstances were.[39] The charge of vagueness was a standard one of criminal defense lawyers who noted that the police and citizens could not discern the rule of law sufficiently well to figure out what criminal conduct was.

The force of small-town morality depended on surveillance of neighbors and the interlocking power of the police, the newspapers, and the courts. The judge who heard the case was a lifelong Sheboygan resident and the son of a famous Sheboygan family. As a district attorney, he had also prosecuted some cases of adultery, fornication, and lascivious conduct, but he claimed that the increase in morals prosecutions came about after he left the district attorney's office.[40] To Judge Buchen, who ruled on Bjork's brief in August 1971, Wisconsin's law against cohabitation was a valid means of protecting the morals and general welfare of Sheboygan. He believed that if Decko and Sampson wanted to challenge Wisconsin's law, they should lobby the state legislature, not petition the court. He decidedly did not agree with the ALI that cohabitation did not cause any harm. He regarded Decko and Sampson as examples of the kind of people who were swept up in the sexual revolution and did not understand the injuries they were inflicting on others and on morality. Buchen insisted that the Wisconsin statute was constitutional and that the law was very clear, not at all vague as Bjork had claimed. Decko and Sampson had "cohabited" by pretending to be husband and wife, claiming to their landlady on Erie Avenue that they were Mr. and Mrs. Decko. Their cohabitation met the legal definition of "open" because "it was known in the community." The judge conveniently omitted the facts that Decko and Sampson had not appeared together in public and that the main reason their cohabitation was known was that their neighbor had complained, which led to the police staking out their apartment.

The stigma of cohabitation plagued Decko even in Los Angeles where no one cared if he was living with Sampson. Once he had given orders to his employees like a military commander; now he had lost not only his job but also his standing in the world. He was unable to find work, and it is unclear whether Sampson was employed. He applied for jobs as a recreation director, but the prospective employers called Sheboygan to check on his references and immediately eliminated him from further consideration. The criminal charge of cohabitation, even though not a conviction, was enough to blacklist Decko from gaining employment as a recreation supervisor even in liberal Los Angeles. Eventually, he took a job as a sales clerk, but lost it because he cashed a customer's bad check; he found work as a night guard at a factory. Depressed, one night he drove to a town an hour from Los Angeles, parked in a lot, and slashed his wrists. The police found him bleeding and brought him back to Sampson in Los Angeles. Willing to commit himself to a mental hospital, he stayed there only a few days. Forlorn, he swallowed a bottle of tranquilizers, and the police found him unconscious on a beach. This time he refused to check himself into a mental hospital.

Sampson and Decko parted. He headed for his parents' home in Perrysburg, Ohio, and she found a job teaching school in Mount Carroll, Illinois. He again tried to find work as a recreation director, but employers checked his references with the board of education in Sheboygan and decided not to hire him.[41] Eventually, he found work as a manager of a Penney's store in Toledo but could not shake off his depression over the loss of his former life, the end of his marriage, his separation from his children, and from Sampson. After a party on Halloween night in 1971, he ripped a gas stove from the wall, slashed his wrists, and swallowed a bottle of tranquilizers. His friends in Sheboygan urged him to get professional help, but he refused. Ever more despondent, he was fired by Penney's for lack of initiative.

The trial of Decko and Sampson was scheduled for December 1, 1971, in Judge Buchen's courtroom in Sheboygan. The day before the trial, Decko drove to Mount Carroll to see Judy. He had a .22-caliber revolver with him, and he seems to have threatened her, perhaps contemplating a murder/suicide. He had no intention of driving to Sheboygan to attend the trial.[42] After he left Judy's apartment, he parked his car at the city sewage plant, walked to Point Rock Park, and fired one shot into the air, perhaps testing whether anyone would intervene, perhaps not finding his courage at first. He walked another mile, fired a second and fatal shot, and fell face down on top of his revolver. Judy Sampson called the police, who trudged through the park to find Decko's body in the snow the next morning.[43]

Perhaps the *Sheboygan Press* was too embarrassed to report the death on its front page; it printed a lengthy story, but on the back page and without a photograph. After Jim Decko's death, the trial was canceled, and Lance

Jones dismissed the charges against Judy Sampson. Mary Decko remarried and had a child with her new husband. Judy Sampson eventually remarried as well.

But Peter Bjork wanted the world to know the stigma and suffering Sheboygan had inflicted on his client. He wrote a letter to *Playboy*, published in April 1972, railing against the residents of Sheboygan who were "only interested in extracting their pound of flesh from James Decko."[44] Decko's death was precisely the kind of story of sexual puritanism *Playboy* was eager to tell, of how hypocritical, moralistic people in a small, parochial town of Peeping Toms hounded a good man to death and how laws against cohabitation, vestiges of sexual repression, were being enforced in Sheboygans all across America. The magazine wanted to prove that the *Playboy* philosophy had not yet won and that there were many legal battles yet to be fought. *Playboy* attacked "those in this country who think that puritanism is no longer an important issue and that the anti-sexual laws it has inspired are mere curiosities to be joked about. Tragedies such as this, however, show that Puritanism is still a destructive force in the land."[45] *Playboy* had it right. Stigma attacks self-esteem; Jim Decko had lost all the bases of his identity. He had not been prone to depression before he was fired; he was not the only cohabitor who became suicidal, and it seems likely that had he found a new job in Los Angeles similar to his old one, he could have rebuilt his life.

Playboy sent Richard Rhodes, a journalist who often wrote essays for the magazine, to Sheboygan to investigate the hounding of Jim Decko. Rhodes's own mother had killed herself a year after he was born, and he knew the suffering that suicide wrought. Although raised in the Midwest, he had graduated from Yale; yet he loved the heartland and was fascinated by its landscape and people. Rhodes arrived in Sheboygan during the winter, checked into a motel, and began calling for interviews. Judge Buchen portrayed himself as a liberal who had to bow to the will of the voters. Oakley Frank, wary because of his interview with the London tabloid reporter, told Rhodes that Sheboygan was characterized unfairly in the press when many other towns also arrested people for cohabitation. Buchen and Frank blamed the tragedy on Lance Jones, who refused to speak to Rhodes. The Rhodes article in *Playboy* tells a distinctly masculine side of the story of cohabitation, focusing on James Decko but not saying much about Judy Sampson. Jim Decko emerges as protagonist, the sole tragic victim, and a man whose violence was entirely directed inward.[46]

"Sex and Sin in Sheboygan" by Richard Rhodes appeared in the August 1972 issue of *Playboy*, with a subtitle that read "Richard Rhodes Reveals the Cruelty of American Sex Laws." The cover of the magazine showed two candy mint hearts, broken open by a gavel. Rhodes was eloquent in his denunciation of Sheboygan, indignant in his defense of the right to privacy. He wrote, "A law that butts into private lives and sunders them with public humiliation is squalid enough, but Wisconsin's lewd and lascivious law is even more squalid, because it isn't really designed to stop cohabitation. It is designed to spare the sensibilities of neighbors who might better the spare their sensibilities simply by minding their own business."[47]

After the Rhodes article appeared, reporters, radio talk show hosts, and television crews from Green Bay and Milwaukee descended upon Sheboygan to make fun of it, just as the tabloid reporter from London had done four years earlier. At a news conference, Lance Jones insisted that the police had responded to complaints from neighbors and did not initiate investigations on their own. He quickly turned the subject from Sampson and Decko to a more general defense of the criminalization of cohabitation. It was a standard one at the time: that cohabitation led to children born out of wedlock and thus children were the "tragic victims" of cohabiting relationships. His reasoning was not clearly stated, but apparently he was arguing that cohabiting relationships were unstable and therefore contributed to father absence, and father absence deprived children of a masculine role model, which was essential for a child's development. According to Jones, "The children born of these illicit unions will never know a father or benefit from the strong, loving, and guiding hand of a father image in the home. . . . Who will be able to stand up or step forth and say that illicit living arrangement will have no adverse psychological import on the children?"[48]

Repealing Laws against Cohabitation

Peter Bjork was never able to challenge the constitutionality of Wisconsin's law against cohabitation. The majority of the justices of the US Supreme Court, in carving out a constitutionally protected right of privacy, made it clear that they did not intend to put an end to anticohabitation laws and other forms of morals legislation; in fact, they believed that criminal laws against cohabitation were constitutional. In essence, they were engaged in marital privileging, in expanding constitutional rights for married couples, but not providing them for others, such as homosexuals or cohabitors, straight or gay. Lawyers who argued the case for the legalization of birth control also claimed that the law should be able to criminalize cohabitation both to promote morality and to reduce the birth of illegitimate children. States should be able to punish cohabitation, they claimed, so long as they did not interfere with the privacy rights of married couples.

In *Griswold v. Connecticut* (1965), the court accepted these arguments, ruling only that married couples had a constitutionally protected right to marital privacy. In subsequent cases, the court recognized a right of marital and sexual privacy in specific domains, such as abortion, contraception, the right to bear children, and the right to raise children as parents saw fit. In concurring with the majority in *Griswold*, Justice Arthur Goldberg argued that the state had an interest in upholding morality. He wrote that "the state of Connecticut does have statutes, the constitutionality of which is beyond doubt, which prohibit fornication." As if to reassure the public about the essentially conservative nature of the court's decision in *Griswold*, Goldberg added, "it should be said of the court's holding today [in *Griswold*] that it in no way interferes with a State's proper regulation of sexual promiscuity or misconduct."[49] Other landmark decisions about the right of privacy similarly held to a narrow view of its meaning. Legal briefs in favor of the legalization of abortion in *Roe v. Wade* (1973) argued that the state did not have to regulate sexual behavior by criminalizing abortion since criminal laws against cohabitation already did so.[50]

Between 1978 and 1983, the US Supreme Court refused to hear three cases involving cohabitors.[51] In two of the three, the Court's failure to hear the case let stand the punishment of cohabitors. In the third, the failure to hear the case let stand a lower court judge's decision, that cohabitors did have a constitutional right to privacy—a confusing situation in Michigan because the state retained its criminal law against cohabitation. Thus, it appears that the US Supreme Court wanted to stay out of the way as lower courts debated the issue.

With the Supreme Court steering clear of the question of the constitutionality of laws against cohabitation, and many state courts saying the matter was best left up to the people's elected representatives, city councils and state legislators began to consider repeal of the laws. The city councils in Lawrence, Kansas, and Bend and Culver, Oregon, repealed their bans on cohabitation in the 1970s because they wanted to make clear that their communities did not consider cohabitation a crime. Most states repealed their laws in the same decade as well, not because they wanted to show acceptance of cohabitation but instead as part of penal code revision. To the extent that cohabitation was mentioned, it was argued that the law could not be enforced because cohabitation was so common and that nonenforceable laws led to disrespect for the rule of law.

By 1975, California was considering penal code reform as well. The closeness of the vote to repeal California's consensual sex crimes in 1975 made it evident for the first time that repeal of a law against sodomy or cohabitation would be controversial because decriminalization had come to be seen as "a homosexual rights bill." After Watergate, a Democrat was elected governor of California, and the number of Democrats elected to the state assembly increased, making it possible to pass the legislation. The fact that gays were organized in the state and the Democratic governor backed the legislation was significant to the winning margin of one vote.[52]

NUMBER OF STATES WITH CRIMINAL LAWS
AGAINST LEWD AND LASCIVIOUS COHABITATION[53]

1968	30
1972	28
1979	16
1985	13
1986	11
1996	10
2011	5

Madison

What started out as simply one more state effort to modernize its penal code came to a screeching halt in a conservative-dominated Republican state legislature in Wisconsin. In 1967, Lloyd Barbee, a liberal black legislator and civil rights activist from Milwaukee, introduced the first bill to reform Wisconsin's state penal code, and, as part of that reform, to repeal the state's criminal law against cohabitation. His bill was defeated. Three years later, Governor Patrick Lucey appointed a forty-member Citizen's Study Committee on Offender Rehabilitation to look into court reform and judicial salaries; the committee broadened its agenda to include reform of the criminal law. A University of Wisconsin criminologist testifying before the task force repeated a standard argument in model penal code reform, that repealing all laws that "regulate personal morality" would free the courts to prosecute crimes against persons and property. He also made the familiar claim of the ALI, that laws that regulate the private consensual behavior of adults give the police too much discretion to decide on questions of morality.[54]

Influenced by the criminologist and the ALI's report, the majority of the committee had concluded that laws criminalizing cohabitation, gambling, and possession of marijuana clogged the courts. The committee also came out in favor of no-fault divorce, a subject the ALI had never considered. In 1970, however, the bombing in Madison shook state legislators; they read the ALI report not as modernization of the penal code but as toleration of the hippies and radical activists in the state capitol. "Legalize Pot, Abolish Some Sex Crimes," read the headline in the *Daily Tribune* in Wisconsin Rapids.[55] Corporate Wisconsin was also opposed to decriminalization; the vice president of Johnson Wax Company in Racine thought it an "outrage to come here and discuss reforms relating to our state court system and then go ahead and legalize adultery."[56] A poll of state legislators showed that they were opposed to the proposed legal changes by a margin of two to one.

With decriminalization of cohabitation bogged down in the state legislature, leadership for repeal passed to a new generation, born out of struggles against the Vietnam War and in favor of gay liberation. David Clarenbach was Jewish, had protested against the Vietnam War, and had fought for civil rights. He was a closeted homosexual both because his mother did not approve of homosexuality and because he wanted to run for higher office and believed that openness about homosexuality would hurt his chances for election in rural parts of his electoral district. Clarenbach had a family background of activism. His mother was a college professor and founder of the National Organization for Women, and his father took part in the civil rights movement. First elected to the county board of supervisors when he was eighteen, Clarenbach won a seat in the state legislature when he was twenty-one. Representing his student constituency in Madison, he flung back at the state legislature a more radical formulation of establishment legal reform in 1975. He introduced a bill that would also have permitted same-sex marriage and legalization of marijuana, prostitution, and abortion, reduced the age of consent from eighteen to fourteen, and lowered the penalty for incest with a child to a misdemeanor. The bill was buried in committee. Clarenbach later claimed that he had introduced a radical bill at first in order to make his subsequent legislation appear tame in comparison.[57]

Anita Bryant's success in a 1977 campaign to get voters to repeal ordinances prohibiting discrimination against gays in Dade County and elsewhere mobilized gays in Wisconsin because they saw her movement as taking away their rights. Their major concerns were passage of a statewide civil rights bill based on sexual orientation and decriminalization of sodomy; decriminalization of cohabitation was folded into the category of decriminalizing sex activities between consenting adults. Clarenbach built a previously unheard-of religious coalition at the time, which included liberal Protestant clergy, Jews, the state Baptist Convention, and even the Roman Catholic Church in support of the Wisconsin civil rights bill for homosexuals. As a member of the ACLU, Clarenbach had no trouble persuading others in the organization that decriminalization of consensual adult sex was an issue of the right to privacy. Women in the state legislature were upset that welfare mothers in Waukesha who refused to name the father of their children were being singled out for prosecution on charges of fornication. Witnesses testifying before the state committee considering repeal of sex crime laws invoked Decko's suicide. State legislators, presented with statistics about the prosecution of cohabitors in the state, had to admit that the law was still being enforced.[58] Privately, they were willing to concede that if they were voting their conscience, they would vote to repeal.

The two bills actually advanced together; test votes on decriminalization of sex acts that were narrowly defeated were used to identify wavering legislators who might vote for gay civil rights, and the success of civil rights for homosexuals seemed logically to require decriminalization of homosexual conduct. Clarenbach faced opposition from the New Right both in the state and outside of it. An innovation was that the Right was using talk radio commentators to encourage listeners to write letters to their state legislators. One minister from Eau Claire stated, "If God condemns it, we ought not to court it." Religious conservatives were distributing warnings about "the tragedy of San Francisco," while others raised the specter of out-of-wedlock births, abortion, and venereal disease.[59] Clarenbach had always enjoyed the support of Democrats in both houses of the state legislature; successive close votes made it possible for fence-sitting Republicans to favor legislation that he defined as a matter of antidiscrimination, the right to privacy, and remedying selective enforcement of the law.

Culture Wars and the Republican Family-Values Agenda

By the mid- to late 1970s, penal code reform had been completed in most states, and it was no longer possible to bury repeal of the criminal law against cohabitation within an effort to modernize the state's penal code. Thereafter, state legislators had to debate openly repeal of laws against sodomy, sodomy and cohabitation combined, and eventually cohabitation. The legislative battles were almost uniformly between conservatives and liberals, and in these battles, gay rights and same-sex marriage were consistently visible after the 1975 vote in California. There was also a religious geography of the states that still criminalized cohabitation: they tended to have politically influential religious groups: the Southern Baptist Convention, the Church of Jesus Christ of Latter-Day Saints, or the Roman Catholic Church. But it took so long to remove these laws because legislators did not want to appear to be condoning immorality.

Proponents of decriminalizing cohabitation won four major state victories between 2001 and 2007 (New Mexico, Arizona, North Dakota, and North Carolina). By this time, cohabitation was the issue in and of itself, not part of general effort to decriminalize sex crimes. The arrest (but not prosecution) in New Mexico of a cohabiting couple in 2001 provided enough proof to the state legislature there that the law was still being enforced to secure the votes for repeal. In neighboring Arizona, however, the law was rarely enforced, and there had been no case reported in the press; the legislative fight in that state had dragged on for twenty-six years. A gay lawyer who led the American Association for Single Persons helped to assist the repeal effort in Arizona; this was the first example of a cohabitors' organization being involved in the repeal effort. A unique element of Arizona politics was that a Republican legislator from Sun City, with its large population of elderly who were living together, led the fight.[60] In 2001, Janet Hull, the governor of Arizona, signed a bill to repeal the state's law against "open and notorious cohabitation" despite public opposition. She explained that she was signing the legislation because keeping such laws on the books "teaches the lesson that laws are made to be broken."[61]

Similarly, in North Dakota, the lengthy fight (fourteen years) lined up conservative Republicans defending the family against liberal Democrats who claimed that the anticohabitation law was unenforceable and made the state a laughingstock. Once again, there was no case in which the law was enforced. Because the North Dakota fight occurred subsequent to the emergence of marriage promotion in welfare reform, opponents tended to cite social science evidence about the negative consequences of cohabitation that appeared in marriage-promotion workshops. Thus, advocates for retaining the law against cohabitation argued that living together increased the chances of divorce, led to domestic violence, and was harmful for women and children. However, in North Dakota, unlike many other states, homosexual rights and gay marriage were never mentioned. Advocates of repeal described the adverse impact of laws prohibiting cohabitation on college students and especially on elderly couples who had not married in order to keep a veterans' pension check. Finally, a liberal Democrat from Fargo, citing the plight of seniors living together, received a sympathetic hearing, and North Dakota finally decriminalized cohabitation in 2007.[62]

The thirteen-year campaign to eliminate the law in North Carolina ricocheted through the courts as well as the state legislature. Gays in North Carolina had opposed the anticohabitation law in North Carolina as early as 1994, but had been checkmated by fundamentalist Christian ministers.

The deciding factor in North Carolina was that there was a case where the law had been enforced. A sheriff threatened to dismiss his dispatcher for cohabitating, but she chose to quit and challenge his policy. The ACLU brought suit on her behalf and was able to prove that the law was being enforced in North Carolina, not simply through secondary enforcement against the dispatcher but through arrests and convictions. The ACLU collected criminal statistics to show that between 1997 and 2003, thirty-six people had been brought before local courts for cohabitation, and seven had been convicted. In 2006, a state superior court then struck down the statute as a violation of the right to privacy. The next year, the state legislature repealed the law.

The constitutionality of the anticohabitation statutes in the five states that still have them is dubious, but they are still on the books as of this writing. There are efforts to repeal in some of these states, invariably opposed by Christian family organizations. But the arguments of the Right have been updated to take advantage of opposition to same-sex marriage. The Christian Right now claims that repealing laws against cohabitation would help pave the way for same-sex marriage.[63]

A new form of liberalism, insisting that the state should not interfere with private sexual conduct between adults, was used to counter the idea that the state should promote marriage. The model penal code that reflected such principles led to the decriminalization of cohabitation in many states in the 1960s and 1970s and was very successful precisely because the rights of cohabitors or gays were rarely discussed. Instead, legal experts, the major advocates for reform, framed the issue as the modernization of the criminal law. Not to be confused were efforts in the states versus those in the Supreme Court. When it came to cohabitation, the US Supreme Court created a two-tiered right of privacy, with the more controversial subjects, cohabitation and homosexuality, omitted from the expanded zone of privacy they recognized.

By 1975, however, the battle at the state level was no longer about modernizing criminal law but about the sexual revolution, namely, gay rights. In this period, cohabitation was part of general reform to repeal laws against consensual sex acts, which often included sodomy. The question is not whether the law lagged behind reality, but the geography and ideology of the opposition. The Christian Right took a stand first in city and state politics and then on the national scene, with cohabitation a relatively minor issue in comparison with the battle against homosexual civil rights. The politics of state repeal subsequent to 1975 depended on the strength of opposition to gay rights, the nature of the liberal coalition, and the leadership of an individual Democratic state legislator. In Wisconsin, the winning coalition consisted of gays, college students, many religious groups, and women's rights organizations, with some Republican state legislators providing the margin of victory. In some states, such as Arizona and North Dakota, the political power of the elderly—or at least rhetoric about them—led to success. In a few states such as New Mexico and North Carolina, there was a current case that proved that the law was still being enforced. Conservatives were aware that the law had failed to stop the growth of cohabitation; the point of retaining a criminal law against cohabitation was to promote marriage by restigmatizing cohabitation, making cohabitors feel that they should not be open about their practice. The implicit argument of conservatives was that no one was actually hurt by the criminalization of cohabitation and that individuals did have a right to privacy in their own homes. But they believed that the criminal law should be used to send an entirely symbolic message that the state believed in a single standard of morality, derived from religion, and that as part of that moral standard, the state should promote legal marriage. In that sense, then, the last stand in favor of the criminalization of cohabitation was part of marriage promotion, indicating the persistence of belief that the state could not simply uphold or favor the institution of marriage but also had to punish the alternative to it.

SIX

Alternative Lifestyle

In 1972, the psychologist Eleanor Macklin, an assistant professor at Cornell University, and a married mother of two, became the first sex expert to publish a scholarly article on cohabitation. Macklin discussed cohabitation as part of the general trend, the sexual revolution among college students. She developed the topic as a legitimate one for study, convening researchers at conferences, at Cornell, and publishing the *Cohabitation Research Newsletter*, whose subscribers included social scientists in the United States, Belgium, Scotland, and Sweden. When Macklin began her research, it was still generally believed, despite the LeClair protest, that college students rarely lived together. Before social scientists began studying cohabitation, the major experts on the subject had been psychiatrists, who were divided in their views but relied on qualitative data from interviews or anecdotes about life on campus. Macklin, in conducting several small-scale qualitative and quantitative surveys, was trying to decrease the stigma attached to college student cohabitation by showing that such behavior was not only common but also had few ill effects on the participants.

Macklin held entirely favorable attitudes toward the sexual revolution and cohabitation. By the late 1970s, other social scientists, studying cohabitation, reported more negative results. They included both cultural conservatives and scholars who might otherwise have been favorably disposed toward the sexual revolution but who simply added cohabitors to their sampled population without distinguishing the effects of cohabitation per se from the effects of socioeconomic status and cultural stressors—which resulted in a more unfavorable portrait of cohabitation. There were two fundamental reasons for the change in the tone of the research: scholars began to study cohabitors other than college students, which led to a conflation of the effects of the short duration of cohabitation with the fact that cohabitation is more common at the lower end of the social scale, where family problems are numerous; and in the backlash against the sexual revolution in academia, and in society at large, cohabitation came to be seen as a threat to the American family.

By the 1970s, *alternative lifestyle* had replaced *counterculture* as the term denoting what the students sometimes called "shacking arrangements" and what the sociologist Robert Whitehurst referred to as "unmalias," unmarried liaisons. Macklin not only adopted the new terminology but was part of a group of academics who legitimated the study of alternative lifestyles. When the term *alternative lifestyle* first appeared in 1968, it referred to protest against the Vietnam War, communes, and the counterculture. In the early 1970s, the term also included the sexual revolution among the married middle class, especially mate swapping and group marriage. As these behaviors came to be condemned as "adultery" by the end of the decade, the ambit of *alternative lifestyles* shrank, referring primarily to straight cohabitation and same-sex relationships.[1]

Social scientists sought to influence public debate about the family and certainly had a major impact on the discussion about welfare policy. But when it came to acceptance of alternative lifestyles, the experts invited to national conferences tended to represent the more conservative side of academe, either those not interested in the subject at all (because it did not have to do with poverty and unemployment, their real concerns) or those who believed that cohabitation posed a threat to the survival of the family. By the late 1970s, whether couples living together could be accepted as a form of family was debated at government-sponsored conclaves, part of three regional meetings comprising the White House Conference on Families—a debate that reflected the huge gap between the views of liberals and those of conservatives.

The separate worlds of academe and conferences open to the public rarely converged. Nonetheless, a few relatively obscure academic sex researchers moved closer to the perspective of the Christian Right, even as the Christian Right used the liberal stance of early 1970s sex researchers as a rallying point to whip up public outrage they could channel into political action. President Jimmy Carter sought to bridge the gap between liberalism and the Christian Right, combining a conservative moral stance on cohabitation and abortion with an acknowledgment of liberalism's view of preserving the right to privacy and not using the power of the state to enforce morality. However, the White House Conference on Families made clear that Carter's bridging of these two points of view had not succeeded, and Christian evangelicals perceived they could not be comfortable within the Democratic Party.

By the late 1970s, feminists and advocates of gay civil rights, important constituencies of the Democratic Party, sought positive recognition of the pluralism of American families through an expanded definition of what constituted the family. Conservatives, by contrast, upheld the belief that the state should enforce morality by exclusion of homosexual or straight cohabiting couples from the definition of the family. It appeared at first that Jimmy Carter, a Christian evangelical from the South, could appeal to social conservatives because he believed that cohabitation was living in sin and that the government had to do more to promote legal marriage. Whatever his private views, it was nonetheless the case that the stalwarts in the Democratic Party upheld a more expansive definition of the family and were supporters of feminism and gay rights. By 1980, a loud and inconclusive debate about the definition of the family at the White House Conference on the Family, initiated by Carter, showed that the Democrats stood for acceptance of alternative lifestyles and that the Republicans did not. Cohabitation was not a very visible or threatening issue, but it was understood by all to belong within the larger category of alternative lifestyles.

Studying Cornell Undergraduates

Eleanor Macklin's story is the adult equivalent of Linda LeClair's, bringing the stigma of cohabitation into the 1970s. In both cases, the events occurred on the campus of a prestigious East Coast institution of higher learning. A woman speaking to the press publicizes the secret that students are living together. Campus administrators are inundated by irate letters and phone calls from those who think that cohabitation is sinful and immoral. An outspoken and articulate feminist, ignoring public scorn, is disowned—in this case, not by her father but by her department and university. The phenomenon was the same (college student cohabitation), but the arena of moral judgment in this case was not student housing rules but a decision about tenure. Macklin had not actually lived with someone outside of marriage; she suffered from "courtesy stigma," being condemned not for cohabiting but for being an expert who approved of it.

Macklin's father was a gentleman tobacco farmer from a Maryland family that traced its roots to colonial times, and her mother, a Radcliffe graduate, was a nurse. After graduating from Oberlin in 1953, Macklin earned a master's degree in student personnel administration at Cornell. She married a Cornell graduate student in psychology who held a teaching position in the psychology department. By 1959, she had entered the PhD program in educational psychology and had given birth to her first child; in 1963, she became a lecturer at Cornell, and her second child was born four years after that. She first began teaching a course on adolescence in 1963 in her home department, psychology. By 1969, she was offering the same course, Adolescent Development in Modern Society, in the Department of Human Ecology, in Cornell's College of Agriculture. After receiving her PhD, she remained a non-tenure-track lecturer, a status common among academic women at the time. The Department of Human Ecology had formerly been the home economics department at Cornell; many of those affiliated with the department were "agricultural specialists" who engaged in outreach programs with the public in both upstate New York cities and in rural areas of the state. After working many years in various departments at Cornell, Macklin finished her PhD in 1973 in educational psychology, writing her dissertation evaluating a program designed to help poor black children learn to read.[2]

Macklin was tall and thin, had medium-length hair, and wore conservative sheath dresses and odd-shaped glasses—she was not a hippie and did not look like one. Instead, she was a popular, empathic, and charismatic lecturer, sometimes called Ellie by her students. She had a group photo of herself taken with her class the first day of each semester. Despite an enrollment of a hundred, she knew every student by name. She lectured to the large group once a week; the other sessions of the class involved field placements in public schools, tutoring, or juvenile probation programs.

Macklin became interested in student cohabitation as a result of teaching her course about adolescence. Each year she asked student volunteers to describe to the class the emotional and ethical issues that arose in their lives as they came of age sexually. From these student presentations, she learned that the sexual revolution had arrived on the Cornell campus. In the early 1960s, coeds anguished about whether to remain a virgin. By 1969, they were trying to decide whether to move in with a boyfriend; some were cohabiting, either by staying over or moving into their partners' dormitory rooms, or by sharing their partners' quarters in fraternity houses or off-campus apartments. Women students commonly left most of their belongings in the dorm or at a sorority house while they lived with their boyfriends, who usually had male roommates. The roommates, even if displaced by the girlfriend, accepted the situation without complaint.

By 1971, when Macklin began her research, cohabitation had become more chic among young celebrities. Every woman's magazine had published an article about the new trend of living together. When gossip columnists in the 1940s reported that stars were living together, they were forced to get married (thus, the wedding of Ava Gardner and jazz artist Artie Shaw in 1945). In the 1970s, openly living together had come to Hollywood. Michael Douglas was sharing a house with Brenda Vaccaro, Jacqueline Bisset with actor Michael Sarrazin. When Barbara Hershey and David Carradine were asked how they would deal with the stigma of illegitimacy if they had a child, they replied that the stigma would disappear by the time their children grew up.[3]

In terms of feminism, Barnard was probably a few years ahead of Cornell simply because of the presence of radical feminists like Millett and Ti-Grace Atkinson and the history of the LeClair protest. But women's liberation demonstrations broke out at Cornell in 1970. The first women's studies course was offered to a large and eager student body the same year. Dorms were coed; the university health service was prescribing the pill; gay students were coming out and forming their own homophile organizations; the elderly house mothers had been replaced by dorm residents, who were mainly graduate students, and not even first-year students were required to live in the dormitories. In Ithaca, a large number of undergraduates were living off campus in a residential area called College Town.[4]

By this time, women's liberationists on campus were critical of traditional roles for women in marriage but also critical of the sexual revolution as a revolution on men's terms. They saw marriage as an oppressive institution for women, and some believed that the only way to be liberated was to never marry and never have children. In cohabitation, they were looking for equal sharing of the household tasks and separate financial accounts. They sang along to the anthems of independence of female long-haired folksingers. Joni Mitchell defended her arrangement with her boyfriend Graham Nash in a clearly autobiographical song, "My Old Man." Later, there was also the black R&B sound. On the popular television program, *Soul Train*, often referred to as a black *American Bandstand*, the queen of Philadelphia Soul, Barbara Mason, warbled her hit single, "Shackin' Up" (1975). Although the neighbors disapproved of cohabitation and called her dirty, she intoned, "Mmm, hmm, living together / perfectly happy, yeah / my man and me."[5]

Macklin's specific topic of interest was cohabitation, but her scholarly community consisted of family scholars who studied, endorsed, and often engaged in alternative lifestyles. In 1971, she delivered her first preliminary research at the Groves Conference on Marriage and the Family, an annual elite group of professional family studies researchers, which that year was devoted to the theme of "alternative families." The audience at the Groves conference was amazed that so many students were living together and encouraged Macklin to do more research.[6] In 1974, she published an article, "Going Very Steady," in *Psychology Today*, a magazine that popularized academic research.[7] Members of the college student generation wrote to the magazine that they were delighted to learn that they were normal, wishing only that they "could send a copy to my parents, who unfortunately are among your 30% strongly disapprove category."[8] The older generation thought that cohabitation was "living in sin" and that Cornell, like Barnard, was running a "bawdy house." Writers of the letters differed in whether they castigated Macklin herself as a whore or as a "sick, frustrated sex-starved, evil old woman getting your kicks in advocating such immoral actions."[9]

A new element in the angry letters to Macklin, related perhaps to gay liberation or to legislative efforts to repeal sodomy and anticohabitation laws, was the association of cohabitation with homosexuality. One unsigned letter read, "PHD Eleanor Macklin who are you to ruin our childrens [sic] lives? I could gladly choke that silly face, weak mouth. Any one looking and listening to you would know you weren't fit to teach a dog, let alone our children. It seems that colleges are full of such trash as you. You are only there for the pay check. We sent our most darling innocent child to Madison University. He learned to be a homosexual . . . signed heartbroken."[10]

Quite a few of the letter writers were devout Christians who perceived Macklin as a handmaiden of immorality. Thus one man wrote to her, "May God have mercy on your filthy soul. But I doubt it."[11] For whatever reason, there was more explicit racism in the hate mail Macklin received than in that sent to Barnard, even though black power and race riots were more palpable in 1968 than in 1972. Nonetheless, unsigned letters regretted that "it is so easy these days to return to animalistic trends, such as exist in great abundance among the Zulus and the Arabs and the India people and others too, who cohabitate forever without restraints of any kind." An unsigned postcard, received in response to newspaper coverage prior to the publication of the *Psychology Today* article, was printed in pencil. It read, "Baby I is comin down soon I'll let you blow me I is afraid you have VD but a blow job by you is OK by me I will pay 50 cents I want you whity [sic] I is a nigger baby."[12]

Initially at least, research on cohabitation was the academic wing of both the feminist and sexual revolutions; while posing as objective and neutral, scholarly researchers investigating cohabitation expressed approval of it and of women's newly found sexual independence. The college professors who studied cohabitation tended to be nontenured academics who believed that the major purpose of sex was pleasure.[13] The sexual pleasure they advocated was based on emotional intimacy in what were termed "meaningful relationships"—they did not favor anonymous, impersonal sexual encounters. Macklin wrote, "in most cases, living together seems to be a natural component of a strong, affectionate 'dating' relationship—a living out of what used to be called 'going steady.' The relationship may grow in time to become something more, but in the meantime it is to be enjoyed and experienced because it is pleasurable in and of itself."[14] The father of alternative lifestyles thought was the psychologist Abraham Maslow, who published *Toward a Psychology of Being* at the height of the counterculture. To Maslow individuals who were motivated by the need to realize their full, self-actualized potential were superior to those who were simply trying to meet their basic needs. Maslow and the popularizers of his ideas emphasized the importance of innovative therapies and programs to help an individual reach intimacy and personal growth, along with autonomy, "self-actualization, openness, and exploration."[15] Such ideas legitimized, even justified, cohabitation not simply as countercultural but as realizing selfhood, a growth experience.

The question was whether cohabitation was good or bad, and Macklin and the researchers listed in the *Cohabitation Research Newsletter* answered that it was good. A second question was one of measurement, of how to define cohabitation. The legal definition required a minimum duration and that the couple could not be legally married. Macklin recognized that there were many types of cohabitation, although her main focus was on heterosexual childless cohabitation among college students. For Macklin, the minimum duration of the relationship was the college semester, defined even more specifically as a couple spending four or more nights together over a three-month period. One of her key findings was that there was no definable beginning to a cohabiting relationship. In querying students about why they decided to cohabit, she found that they did not really initiate living together on a specific date, but simply drifted into it, the result of a "gradual, often unconscious, escalation of emotional and physical involvement."[16]

Although fully aware that some lesbian and gay male students also lived together, she believed that the process of coming out as a homosexual to one's self, friends, family, and other students was the most important feature of gay sexuality, not the actual living arrangement of a same-sex couple. Macklin was always a supporter of gay liberation and became an AIDS researcher in the 1980s. She thought that viewing the purpose of sex as

pleasure rather than procreation would eventually lead to societal acceptance of homosexuality. She forthrightly told the Binghamton Rotary Club
in a 1971 address about the sexual revolution that "if you separate procreation from the sex act . . . and you put an emphasis on relations between
human beings, you can soon get led to the question of whether it is possible to have an affectionate relationship with members of the same sex,
and whether a sexual relationship should develop as an extension of that
relationship."[17] Macklin further contributed to gay liberation by using the
term "heterosexual cohabitation" in her article titles, which implied that she
understood that cohabitation was not limited to straight couples.

Cohabitation was a new subject of inquiry in academia but seemed to
belong in the home economic departments because such researchers studied marriage and the family. Macklin's academic home was the Department
of Human Ecology, founded in 1903. Home economics originally began
hiring extension specialists around World War I. These specialists taught
farm women about nutrition, budgeting, planting vegetable gardens, and
helping to prevent infant morality. As home economics became an established field, the extension faculty often disseminated new ideas from psychology and the other social sciences to the wider public in urban as well
as rural areas. By the 1960s, for example, Macklin was working in the area
of prevention of juvenile delinquency with black youth living in Ithaca. In
a bid to become more professional and prestigious, more men were hired
in human ecology who engaged in research rather than the combination
of research and public outreach that had characterized the field in its early
days. Female chairs of the department were replaced by men, but the graduate students remained largely female. Even during Macklin's years in the
department, about four out of five students were female. But in an effort
to rebrand itself as the study of family in relationship to multiple contexts
rather than a woman's field, the department had adopted the name of human ecology in 1969.[18]

Believing in tolerance and the positive elements of the sexual revolution, Macklin saw herself engaged in outreach, trying to bridge the gap
between the generations. She wanted to soften the attitude of the World War
II generation and plead for sympathy and compassion, since parents needed
"help if they are to understand and to react without alarm, recrimination,
and rejection."[19] Speaking to groups of parents during Cornell's orientation
program for first-year undergraduates, she informed them that the sexual
revolution was now part of campus life. She told them, "We must have faith
in our children and not cut ourselves off from them." Student cohabitation,
she explained, was not primarily about sex, claiming instead it was about

"getting to know another as a whole person and the emphasis on sharing as openly and as completely as possible with that person."[20] She wanted the Binghamton Rotary Club to understand that the older generation had failed. She told them, "I think we have to recognize that we parents have not been the best role models for healthy sexuality, and we haven't done the best jobs in our own marriage. . . . The young people are wise in trying to form new kinds of relationships."[21]

Macklin did a small survey of parents of juniors and learned that most of them disapproved of their sons and daughters cohabiting. She found that the majority of parents considered cohabitation sinful, imprudent, or "emotionally unhealthy." No parents would recommend that their children cohabit. The producers of *60 Minutes* sought to interview Cornell cohabitors and their parents, with Macklin as their sympathetic expert on the subject. They wanted to find students whose parents knew their children were living together and approved of their doing so. Some parents who initially indicated their willingness withdrew when the camera crew arrived at Cornell.[22]

Macklin found that parents tried to stop their children from cohabiting but did not go into detail about the matter. If students could lie to their parents, the older generation also had a powerful response at hand. In 1972 an anonymous "Mom and Dad" replied to their daughter's letter that she was moving into an apartment with her boyfriend, Tony, the second semester of her senior year. The mother wanted to underscore the financial consequences of her daughter's action. She wrote, "We do want you to be able to retain your good grades and graduate when you planned, and hope that you will reconsider what you proposed in your letter so that we will want to put you through this last quarter. Of course you realize that would be impossible if you should go through with it." She layered on guilt on top of threat: "How about Tony's sweet mother, the one who mailed the violin to you? Are you a girl whom he would like to take home to meet his mother? Would she condone such an arrangement? Is he considering her feelings?"[23]

At the height of the generation gap American television not only sided with the parents but also believed they would be successful in imposing marriage on rebellious cohabitors. The first television sitcom to include a segment about cohabitation was in 1969. In *Love American Style* a young student couple was living together in an off-campus apartment, with both of their names penciled in the mailbox nameplate. The girl even wanted to protest against the local bank that denied the couple a car loan because they were not married. Having found out that their daughter was living with her boyfriend, her parents burst into the apartment. Although the outraged father wanted to take his daughter home immediately, the mother hoped to convince the couple to have a "nice simple" wedding. The daughter objected to being forced to marry on feminist grounds, but her boyfriend was persuaded. He eventually reveals to his girlfriend that on their vacation trip to Mexico four months ago they had actually been married by the town clerk. On their way out of the apartment building, the parents stopped to change the nameplate on the mailbox to "Mr. and Mrs. Hurst."[24]

Why had the generation gap persisted and when did it begin to dissipate? Because there was no other student confrontation subsequent to LeClair, it might at first appear that the *New York Times* had fully aired the subject. But in fact, the conflict continued on television, in letters to Dear Abby, and in correspondence, phone calls, and home visits between college-age children and their parents. Parental disapproval did not stop the trend: in fact, census household figures indicate that the number of cohabiting households quadrupled in the 1970s. By the end of the decade many parents, while still disapproving of cohabitation, no longer issued threats. One mother wrote to an advice columnist in 1978, "It was a shock to us when we first learned of it. But we considered all the angles and while we don't condone this lifestyle we have given our love and good wishes."[25] *Three's a Crowd* (1984–85), the first television sitcom about a cohabiting couple (rather than a single episode in a series), was merely announcing a truce in generational conflict. The "you and me together" were much older and childless, but the boyfriend had lied to his parents and his dowdy, grey-haired aunt, not telling them he is sharing his apartment in Los Angeles, with the girl of his dreams, and her father so disapproves of the relationship that he moves nearby in order to break it up. The ostensible motive for cohabitation is that the girlfriend, a perky airline stewardess, does not want to marry because of her parents' divorce.

Prior to Macklin's research, journalists had simply guessed the incidence of college student cohabitation. In 1966, *Newsweek* interviewed a dean who estimated that there were fifty couples living together among Cornell students. Interviewed by the *New York Times* the same year, Cornell students put the number at 150. Nine years later, Macklin's figure was twenty-four times the *New York Times* estimate. Although there was a substantial increase in cohabitation in the intervening years, it seems likely that both the Cornell students and the dean had reason to vastly underestimate the extent of student cohabitation in the mid-1960s.[26] The dean did not want to alarm parents of current and prospective students, and the undergraduates sought to shield their fellow students from the kind of inquiry so wounding to LeClair. Macklin not only reported that one-third of Cornell students had cohabited but also found that even more would do so if they located a willing partner. As the organizer of the *Cohabitation Research Newsletter,* she also compiled figures from other surveys about the incidence of cohabitation on other campuses. To be sure, few of the colleges were in the South or were historically black or Catholic schools, where traditionalism and religious belief were stronger and living together was not permitted by college rules and/or more stigmatized. Assembling rates of cohabitation from seven universities and colleges extending from California State University at Northridge to CUNY, Macklin found that cohabitation was more common at coed schools with coed dormitories, twenty-four-hour visitation policies in the dorms, and liberal rules permitting students to live off campus.[27]

Gays were not the only cohabitors invisible in the early research. The remarried, the elderly, cohabitors raising children, serial cohabitors, and the poor were all missing from these studies. The early focus on college students gave inordinate attention to one particular style of cohabitation—that among liberal, not very religious, countercultural, childless, mainly white, and economically privileged couples who often smoked pot and protested the Vietnam War and who were living together on a temporary basis, not long term, often not by themselves but in a place that included other students as well. A few of the students, like LeClair and Behr, opposed the institution of marriage, but most saw cohabitation as part of the process of college dating. They eventually intended to marry but not necessarily the person with whom they were living; they were postponing marriage while they pursued their education. At that time, it was common to generalize about human behavior based on experiments using college students. Most studies in social psychology and the social sciences employed student samples. College students were an easily available population who could be handed questionnaires to fill out and were more willing to admit to cohabiting than many other populations were. It was much more expensive to contact the general population, and the public had less reason to respond. Thus, it was not until the late 1970s that researchers began to study cohabitation beyond the campus.

Macklin continued to develop new research studies related to the sex lives of Cornell undergraduates, despite the hostile calls and letters. She began a new project, called "Intimacy and the Capacity to Develop Intimacy," after she found that at Cornell liberal arts and home economics students were eight times as likely as engineering students to cohabit.[28] She received permission for a more detailed questionnaire among male engineering students and wrote up her findings in a preliminary memorandum, which the dean passed along to the director of advising and counseling in the College of Engineering. In October 1974, the incensed director, barely concealing his sexism within stereotypes of students by major, wrote to Macklin, "I am surprised at your closing paragraph, where you imply that engineering students are somewhat weird for retaining a standard that was totally acceptable not long ago. . . . In short, I resent, and I think engineering students resent, the value judgment you have imposed in the wording of your queries. On top of that, the reasons you cite for your observation do not deserve the time of day. They represent the sloppiest kind of scholarship, and have no more standing than the casual observation that Home Eckies are groupies who like to sleep around. . . . Nevertheless, I appreciate the data. But pray tell me, why are all the men in Arts and Sciences so insecure that they have to cohabit?"[29]

The Phil Donahue Show, like *60 Minutes*, covered current social trends, but the program was live, and Donahue allowed audience members to question guests on the show. Donahue was also known to be sympathetic to changing gender roles, and Macklin had every reason to believe she would be treated with respect by Donahue. Producers of the program flew her and two Cornell students, Pat and Clair, to Chicago to appear live on his program about "college morality." Even in 1975, Pat and Clair did not want to provide their last names, but they, along with Macklin, answered questions from Donahue's studio audience. Some of the members of the show's audience lambasted them as sinners. After she returned to Ithaca, Macklin received irate letters from Donahue's viewers. One wrote, "Is it worth eternal damnation just to bring your views into the open and contribute to the degeneration of the young people you have influence over?"[30] A woman in Westmont, Illinois, scolded Macklin who "as a mother and a teacher . . . should be trying to establish moral values instead of condoning and beaming your approval of two single kids living together."[31]

Notoriety was not a useful credential for an assistant professor being considered for tenure. The tenure system in academia not only considered the teaching and publication record of the candidate, but also evaluated the topic of inquiry. While Macklin was developing the subject of cohabitation as a legitimate field of study, her senior colleagues still held that it was not legitimate. At Cornell in 1975, cohabitation was still perceived as deviant, abnormal, and a threat to the institution of marriage. Times have changed at Cornell, and as I write, Cornell is probably the leading academic institution for the study of cohabitation.

At the end of February 1975, Macklin was considered but not hired for a tenure-track position in the Department of Human Development and Family Studies, where she had been teaching as a lecturer for six years. At the time, faculty women at Cornell were suing the university to upgrade their status on campus. Many women were teaching as lecturers, without the rank, status, and privileges of a tenure-track position. Under pressure from the federal government and women professors to hire more women faculty, Cornell considered hiring lecturers, most of whom were women, as assistant professors eligible for the coveted lifetime position of tenure. To hire an assistant professor, the department was required to conduct a national search. Macklin was one of the two finalists for a tenure-track position in adolescent development; the other candidate was a man teaching at another university.

In previous years, all members of the department, including the lower-status extension specialists and extension faculty, had been allowed to vote in hiring decisions. This was a common practice in a department that had evolved out of home economics. All the members of the department could vote, but the opinions of the tenured faculty, who secured grants for research and published scholarly articles in journals, carried the most weight. There was only one tenured woman in a faculty of fifteen. The tenured men tended to make their hiring decisions based on a candidate's record of publication, promise of a future research program, and ability to secure large grants.

The chair of the department, who was new to his position, reserved the right to make a final decision if he thought there was not enough support for a candidate to make an offer. The first vote at a faculty meeting was split evenly between Macklin and the outside candidate. Because the vote was a tie, it was decided to conduct a mail ballot, in which lecturers, extension specialists, instructors, and other faculty were asked to vote. Macklin won among the larger group, but the vote was split among the "professional faculty." By this time, student petitions and meetings with faculty forced the faculty to meet for a highly irregular "unannounced meeting" to figure out what the second vote, by mail ballot, meant.[32]

One hundred fifty of Macklin's students, outraged, organized a protest meeting at which they confronted the dean and the chair of the department. They disseminated a petition and lobbied for two weeks on Macklin's behalf. The students talked about a possible boycott of classes or a sit-in, but Macklin was unwilling to sue the university and did not want to fight her department. In 1975, students were more likely to talk about sit-ins than engage in them. Women faculty, clustered around the women's studies program, supported Macklin, as did the women extension specialists. Women in other departments sent letters of support, which were ignored because they were not members of the department. Moreover, some of these letter writers were untenured as well and also lost their own battles for tenure. The chair of Macklin's department told a student leader that protest only stiffened the resolve of the tenured faculty to vote against Macklin.[33] He then announced that the department had abandoned its search without making an offer, and Macklin was out of a job.

The campus protest in support of LeClair was much larger and more sustained than the one for Macklin, and the pickets and sit-in on behalf of LeClair occurred during the upsurge in campus unrest in the spring of 1968, which SDS helped to organize. Macklin discouraged students from protesting, telling them that there was no hope and that the tenured faculty would win. LeClair felt the force of stigma much more than Macklin did. Macklin did not feel disgraced; her sons and her husband supported her, as did many students and her women colleagues, and she was still a respected figure within her world of researchers who studied cohabitation and alternative lifestyles. In 1981, other faculty women brought a class-action lawsuit against Cornell for sex discrimination, hoping to include in the suit all women who had held academic appointments at Cornell between 1972 and 1980. As of 1980, only 6 percent of the tenured faculty at Cornell were women.[34] Macklin, who did not consider herself a social activist, chose not to participate in the lawsuit.[35] When I interviewed her at her summer home in Nova Scotia just before her seventieth birthday, her memories of Cornell were still quite painful, and she brushed aside tears as she talked about losing her job there.

What if anything did this hiring decision have to do with the stigma attached to cohabitation? None of the other professors in the department were engaged in sex research. Many of them did not believe in studies based on interviewing subjects. The department as well as the university administration had received angry letters about Macklin's investigations of cohabitation, some perhaps related to her recent appearance on *The Phil Donahue Show*.[36] The senior professors in the Department of Human Development and Family Studies did not conceal their beliefs that cohabitation was abnormal, even sinful.

Urie Bronfenbrenner, the most distinguished social scientist in the department, was a Russian Jew who had moved to the United States when he was six. He attended Cornell as an undergraduate and earned a PhD from the University of Michigan in 1942 before enlisting and serving in World War II. An eminent scholar of human development with a lengthy list of publications, he took pride in the fact that he was "communicating through articles, lectures, and discussions—the findings of developmental research to undergraduate students, the general public, and to decision makers both in the private and public sectors."[37] Bronfenbrenner called Macklin into his office and told her that he thought that cohabitation, along with excessive individualism and other aspects of the sexual revolution, was causing the breakdown of the family in the United States.[38] Furthermore, longitudinal studies of cohabitors had to be conducted, he argued, before any research could be published on the subject. A longitudinal study, Bronfenbrenner believed, would show negative consequences from cohabitation. However, faculty researchers were not expected to conduct longitudinal studies in 1975. Bronfenbrenner told Macklin that a trend had to exist for at least ten years. His requirement meant that she could not publish her results for another six years, a standard that was rarely applied in academic research.[39]

It appears that Bronfenbrenner, like many opponents of cohabitation, believed that cohabitation was a fad, that it would eventually go away. Given his attitudes, however, it seems unlikely that even after the ten-year mark had been reached, he would have approved of studying cohabitation. He made his personal attitudes public at various family forums across the country and in an interview with *Newsweek* two years later. Individualism had run rampant, he told the reporter, and feminism had been good for women, but America's children were suffering from parental neglect. He told a *Newsweek* reporter that he believed "that cohabitation is seriously weakening the family and undermining the sense of obligation in all our love and work relationships." He further stated that "society needs some kind of custom or institution in which people are committed to each other, no matter what. . . . In sleeping together you don't develop those commitments."[40]

Macklin's other major opponent was Henry Ricciuti. A full professor, he was a fifty-seven-year-old Catholic and a World War II veteran who had done his undergraduate and graduate training at Fordham, a Catholic university in New York City. He was well known and well connected in his academic field of early child development, but he did not make any major contribution to the several different research areas in which he worked. He wrote a letter to the student newspaper explaining that he opposed hiring Macklin because he had "reservations" about "her scholarly competence." He refused to say more, indicating it was unfair to Macklin to discuss her case in public.[41] After the second vote against her, Ricciuti asked Macklin to come to his office. He told her that the faculty had not hired her because they did not think she would receive tenure. He added that he thought cohabitation was a private matter and "not an appropriate area for inquiry."[42]

Professors in the department studied only "normal" human ecology, he told her, implying that cohabitation was not normal. Some of the faculty also charged that Macklin had "disseminated her research too quickly," meaning that they did not approve of the publication of her findings in *Psychology Today* and her appearance with the students on *The Phil Donahue Show*.[43]

In 1975, a sex researcher who generated hostile letters to the editor in the local paper did not have an easy time finding a new academic position. After losing her job at Cornell, Macklin applied to teach at the University of Minnesota, Kansas State University, and the University of Connecticut. She did not receive offers from any of these universities. At Kansas State, the dean came to her job talk and quizzed her about her personal attitude toward open marriage, then a popular subject because of the appearance of a book by the same title on the bestseller list. After digesting her answers, the dean told her, "Kansas is not ready for you," and she did not get the job. She taught in untenured positions at several universities, commuting from her home and family in Ithaca. In 1977, she secured a position at the University of Maryland but was denied tenure there, allegedly for lack of a sufficient record of publication. Eventually, she switched fields and became a marriage and sex therapist. She developed a program to train therapists at Syracuse University, where she ultimately became a tenured and then a full professor and where she remained until her retirement in 1998. By the early 1980s, she had given up doing cohabitation research because she found "being the center of controversy" exhausting.[44]

In 1980, Macklin's summary of research about alternative lifestyles appeared in the prestigious *Journal of Marriage and the Family*. She included under the umbrella of alternative lifestyle almost any sexual or family form other than a legally married couple with children in a monogamous family in which the husband was the male breadwinner. By that definition, the majority of American couples today have alternative lifestyles, since the dual-earner couple was then defined as alternative.[45] She heralded the arrival of these alternatives as an expression of "the continued evolutionary movement toward freedom of choice."[46]

Macklin published her last study of cohabitation in 1983, remaining entirely positive in her valedictory. She wrote, "Many of the concerns about nonmarital cohabitation have been put to rest during the past ten years. Societal experience, substantiated by research, has indicated that the benefits tend to outweigh, or at least balance, the costs, and that there are few deleterious effects. Participants tend to report cohabitation as having been a positive experience that they might well repeat another time, and later relationships do not seem to suffer."[47]

The Incidence of Cohabitation

The US Census Bureau contributed to removing the stigma of cohabitation by demonstrating that it was common and thus helping to define it as normal, but the bureau could not entirely escape the controversy about whether cohabitation was a social trend or an instance of immorality. Studies of the incidence of cohabitation based on census figures always made newspaper headlines because they were quoted to prove that cohabitation was not a fad and was not disappearing.

In 1977, Paul Glick and Arthur Norton of the US Census Bureau, two highly reputable demographers, published an article about the incidence of cohabitation in 1977. They gave the study of cohabitation the imprimatur of a federal agency and provided estimates of incidence based not on small student samples but on the entire population. Because of the smaller size of the gay population, they did not believe that they could also use census tabulations to estimate the incidence of homosexual cohabitation. A reporter interviewing them invented the term POSSLQ (persons of the opposite sex sharing living quarters) to describe their measure of heterosexual cohabitation.[48]

The census demographers were trying to determine the extent of a trend, even though the census and more frequent population surveys, called the Current Population Survey, did not ask a direct question about cohabitation. Not until 1990 did the Census Bureau consider inquiry about cohabitation neutral enough to pose the question in a national study of the entire American population. Before that, the bureau inferred relationships based on the marital status and relationship to the head of household reported in the decennial census and in Current Population Surveys. POSSLQ both overestimated and underestimated the extent of cohabitation. It overestimated it by including roommates, boarders, and servants who were not engaged in a sexual relationship as cohabitors; it underestimated cohabitation by omitting unmarried couples with children older than fifteen. Since the latter group was larger than former, the net effect was an underestimation of the extent of cohabitation. Although Glick and Norton were demographers who stayed out of the public eye and had no responsibility for the training of impressionable youth, they nonetheless received letters criticizing them for not calling the trend "shacking up." The letters were unsigned, but it was clear from the views expressed that the writers had religious affiliations.[49]

The academic study of cohabitation for its first few years was entirely positive. Macklin was announcing that the sexual revolution was here to stay and that cohabitation among college students was a healthy part of the process of dating. The sociologist Nancy Moore Clatworthy became the expert of choice, however, when a *Newsweek* reporter was looking for a respected academic scholar on cohabitation who was willing to suggest that living together was bad for women.[50] She claimed that the sexual revolution was a passing fad and that young women on campus were no longer choosing to cohabit. (It was invariably the case that those who said that cohabitation was a passing fad wanted it to go away.) She argued that genital herpes as well as the return of religious values was leading to a decline in cohabitation on campus. In 1975, Clatworthy had published an article that corroborated Macklin's view by stating that cohabitation was a stage in the dating process, concluding that it "appears to be serving some beneficial and useful purposes on the college campus for those individuals who do so."[51] By 1977, when she was interviewed for an article in *Seventeen* titled "The Case against Living Together," she had changed her mind.[52] Clatworthy said that she found cohabitors had less successful marriages, were more likely to divorce, and had relationships filled with conflict.

Clatworthy's research, which was based on a sample of one hundred, was never published and thus was never subjected to the process of peer review. There were several reasons Clatworthy was deemed an expert despite her slim research credentials. She was a tenured professor at a major research university (Ohio State); she was an apostate, who claimed to have changed her mind because of her findings, and she framed her critique in terms of antifeminism, that cohabitation was bad for women. At a time of women's liberation, a cautionary tale about the negative consequences of the sexual revolution for women was easier to absorb if told by a woman. She was also refuting the view that cohabitors were more egalitarian than married couples. She reported that women cohabitors felt they were dominated by their partners, they were unable to be themselves, and their partner did not share the household chores. Part conservatism, part moral panic, Clatworthy's comments combined fear of disease with biological explanations for the order of things. She told *Seventeen* that "biologically, and as demonstrated in nature, males are aggressive. Women can certainly be conditioned to be aggressive, but all too often, in living-together situations, I see women who do suffer as a result of being exploited by men. . . . You're much better off marrying than living together."[53]

Other studies of student cohabitors also reported that cohabitation was not the egalitarian relationship it claimed to be. Many women students, including Linda LeClair, wanted to avoid the trap of the traditional roles of breadwinner and housewife the institution of marriage seemed to create. They accepted the feminist view that the gender division of labor in marriage was one of the key sources of woman's oppression. Cohabitation was fairer for women since a boyfriend living with his girlfriend did not think of himself as a family provider, and the girlfriend did not see herself as a housewife. Cohabitation, it was thought, represented the chance to fashion egalitarian gender roles and divide chores fairly, not based on gender. By 1978, two separate surveys of college students reported that few students had achieved their ideals. Girlfriends were doing the cooking, cleaning, and grocery shopping, and their boyfriends were working on the car or taking out the garbage.[54]

By the late 1970s, cohabitation was associated with the social problem of drug abuse, in part because the federal government was funding survey research about the drug problem as cocaine abuse was spreading and becoming more visible to the middle class. Researchers received money from the federal government to find the causes and consequences of "illicit drug use," which, though poorly defined, included everything from marijuana use to heroin addiction.[55] Studies of college student cohabitors at Rutgers in the early 1970s found that they smoked pot on average about three times a week. Two researchers with federal funding concluded that cohabitors who smoked marijuana were part of the weakening of "norms regarding commitment to traditional roles" and traditional roles were a necessary part of being an adult.[56]

Researchers studying family violence provided additional refutation of Macklin's portrait of cohabitation as a healthy development. Initially, scholars thought of family violence as an outgrowth of patriarchy in the family, exhibited in patterns of control that reflected male dominance in a legally married couple. Murray Straus, a sociologist who pioneered in the study of family violence, made the connection to legal wedlock in his statement that the "marriage license was a hitting license."[57] Straus, who devised a set of survey questions to measure the incidence of family violence, and Kersti Yllo, a sociologist trained by Straus in his graduate program, compared thirty-seven cohabiting couples with the more than two thousand married couples previously studied. Women in cohabiting couples, they found, were much more likely to suffer severe violence (being punched, kicked, or attacked with a knife or gun) and were also more likely to hit their partners. Straus and Yllo did admit that well-educated cohabitors with high incomes and those who had been together a long time were a quite peaceful lot and that the high level of conflict among cohabitors may have been related to social class.[58] Instead of emphasizing that family violence was related to social class and that cohabitors tended to be poorer and less educated than the general population, however, they stressed that social isolation was the reason for the higher level of violence among cohabitors. Straus and Yllo claimed that cohabiting relationships were more violent because cohabitors were isolated from kin who could intervene. They characterized cohabitors as social isolates cut off from social support, abandoned, and unable "to cope with their problems." Because cohabitors were often lying to their parents about living together, they argued that cohabitors were less able to draw upon parents for help. Straus and Yllo also implied that cohabiting women accepted violence as proof of a man's love. To Straus and Yllo, legal marriage demonstrated each partner's belief in the ideal of undying romantic love, and since cohabitors did not have this proof that their partners loved them, they resorted to hitting "as a symbol of closeness and ownership in the absence of a license and label."[59]

A quarter of a century later, Catherine Kenney and Sara McLanahan, two sociologists who have analyzed levels of domestic violence among cohabiting and married couples, concluded instead that "selection effects" explain the lower level of violence among married couples. As a result of both higher rates of divorce among the most violent married couples and the propensity of the least violent couples to marry, they argued that the category of currently married couples includes people who, as a whole, are less prone to violence than the population.[60]

Other researchers wanted to know whether cohabitation served as an effective compatibility test for marriage, providing valuable information that a couple should not marry and leading the rest to more lasting unions because they had found the right person who met their standards. The argument that cohabitation was a training ground for a "healthier" or longer-lasting marriage had first appeared in the heyday of the companionate marriage ideal of the 1920s. Judge Ben Lindsey of the Denver Juvenile Court promoted the idea of "companionate relation," a special form of marriage for a childless couple in which it would be easy to obtain divorce simply by mutual consent.[61] The philosopher Bertrand Russell took the case for companionship one step further, arguing such a couple need not undergo a formal marriage. If parties did want to legally marry, he believed that they should have a sexual relationship first as a test of compatibility. In 1966, Margaret Mead resurrected the idea of companionate marriage (which she considered different from marriage that included parenting), arguing in *Redbook* that a childless couple in the first years of their marriage should be allowed to terminate their union easily. She believed that a couple should advance to parental marriage only after they succeeded in a trial marriage. Mead held that divorce from parental marriage should be more difficult to obtain because being raised by two parents was in the best interests of the child. Other popular writers in the late 1960s, such as Vance Packard, endorsed her ideas.[62]

In 1980, Alfred DeMaris, a graduate student at the University of Florida who was trained in demography, undertook the type of longitudinal study of cohabitors that Urie Bronfenbrenner had called for to find out if cohabitation increased divorce rates. Unlike Macklin's circle of researchers, DeMaris ventured outside the college campus and sent a questionnaire to the general population of Gainesville. DeMaris limited his group to whites because he believed that blacks had lower levels of marital satisfaction. He drew up a list of white married couples based on the Gainesville marriage records and mailed them questionnaires. His study appears venturesome at first because he was inquiring about cohabitation in Florida where cohabitation is still illegal. But it appears that the more important feature of his study was that it was conducted in Gainesville, a college town, among a mainly white, highly educated population.

DeMaris found that couples who had cohabited prior to marriage were less satisfied with their unions than those who had not and that formerly cohabiting women were especially discontented with their marriages. He concluded that cohabitors were "unconventional people," ambivalent about marriage, and that women who had lived with their boyfriends were feminists afraid to abandon their careers for more traditional and subordinate marital roles. He had difficulty in explaining a further result, that cohabitors who had married for a second time did not express dissatisfaction with these marriages.[63] He claimed that those who remarried (most of whom had been divorced) had adapted "to the norms of marriage and have demonstrated a commitment to matrimony by having entered into it at least once before."[64] But it was equally true that second timers had demonstrated lack of commitment to matrimony by getting divorced. Overall, Maris viewed cohabitors as part of the counterculture and was hard pressed to explain results that challenged his opinions.

With funding from the National Institute of Aging, two well-known family studies researchers, Alan Booth and David Johnson, tackled the question of whether cohabitation increased the chance of divorce. In the Booth and Johnson longitudinal study, couples who had cohabited for less than ten years were found to be more likely to get divorced than couples who had not. They also found that couples who had previously cohabited but had been married more than ten years were no more likely to get divorced than anyone else. They argued that if couples had stayed together for a decade, their prior history no longer shaped their marriage. Booth and Johnson seemed determined to believe that cohabitation was risky. Thus, they speculated that in a larger sample, they would be able to show that cohabitation led to divorce, no matter how many years a couple had been married. Their explanation of why cohabitors were prone to divorce was that they were social misfits or what they termed "poor marriage material," people who could not hold a steady job, were in trouble with the law, took drugs, ran up credit card debt, filed for bankruptcy, or had "personality problems."[65] Other researchers, echoing Bronfenbrenner's views, claimed that living together was risky because cohabitors brought to their marriages "an individualistic ethic."[66]

In *American Couples* (1983), two sociologists, Philip Blumstein and Pepper Schwartz, issued an ambivalent report about cohabitation, that it was a pathway not to stable marriage but to divorce but also that it was a more egalitarian arrangement than conventional marriage. Their research, although seemingly more inclusive since they interviewed lesbian and gay male couples, nonetheless confirmed the definition of cohabitation as heterosexual. Cohabitors were defined as heterosexuals; gay men and lesbians were considered as being in other types of relationships, even though the gay couples they interviewed were living together. Blumstein and Schwartz concluded that cohabitation was undesirable. Society and the law recognized marriage as an institution, but cohabitation was not an institution, and it would not become one, they believed, because cohabitation was an unpredictable, unstable arrangement fraught with possibilities for misunderstandings and lacking clear-cut norms, which meant that there was greater opportunity for conflict. They wrote, "There is often no basis for trust, no mutual cooperation, and no ability to plan." Couples who were living together needed to recognize "what an awesome task they have taken on."[67] Unlike Macklin and her circle of cohabitation researchers, Blumstein and Schwartz made no mention of the need to decriminalize cohabitation or equalize benefits available to cohabitors and married couples. Instead, they presented society as unwilling to accept cohabitation and assumed that reformers should not even try to change laws and social policies. At the same time, they also concluded that cohabitation did not impose the same expectations of traditional gender roles as marriage and that some women in such couples insisted on separate financial accounts as a symbol of their economic independence.

Thus, in the space of less than a decade, the scholarly verdict on cohabitation had gone from highly positive to negative, with the degree of negativity tempered by a bit of feminism of some of the researchers. Like the American public, many of the social scientists were also frightened by feminism, the sexual revolution, and any change in the family likely to contribute to divorce. But there were also empirical reasons for the more negative researchers' findings. The positive portrayal of cohabitation was based on small samples of college students and was part of a defense of alternative lifestyles. The negative portrayal was derived from larger samples of the general population and reflected the fact that cohabitation was more common among the less educated and poorer part of the population, whose relationships reflected the conflicts, lack of resources, and unstable familial backgrounds common to their lives.

The sociologist Julia Ericksen writes, "Sex researchers cannot avoid involvement in the ideological wars of the late twentieth century."[68] Cohabitation was central to both sides of the debate about the future of "the family" since it offered evidence about marriage, the sexual revolution, religion, morality, feminism, and the generation gap. Defining cohabitation as frequent and normal was essential in attacking the stigma attached to cohabitation. In fact, cohabitation came under attack precisely because it was becoming too common and therefore appeared to threaten the institution of marriage and offer women the fool's gold of liberation when what they needed most was commitment. The opponents of this trend then labeled cohabitors as social misfits and sought to show that they were isolated from society and perhaps even deserved their isolation.

The Carter Presidency

The backlash against the sexual revolution did not have one moment of origin but several. Public outcry against fraud in public aid generated special crackdowns on welfare cohabitors in the early 1960. Anger against race riots, black power, busing, and growing welfare rolls coincided with public anxiety about hippies, Vietnam War protestors, and the sexual revolution. The resignation of an American president, a shocking rise in the price of oil, and the combination of high inflation and high unemployment increased the desire to bring in new leaders untainted by Washington politics. The political activism of evangelical Christians was more often local than national, at least until the campaign of the first presidential candidate to publicly proclaim himself a born-again Christian. Sixty million Americans, who considered themselves born-again Christians, thought that Jimmy Carter was one of their own, a candidate who promised moral leadership for the nation. Jimmy Carter seemed to straddle polarized views about the sexual revolution: he was opposed to abortion, but in favor of abortion rights; he thought homosexuality was abnormal but also favored outlawing discrimination against homosexuals.

Carter, a one-term governor of Georgia, ran for president in 1976 as an outsider who would bring honesty and efficiency to a government racked by the scandal of Watergate. The specific instances of family decline Carter worried about were rising divorce rates, widespread delinquency, soaring rates of out-of-wedlock childbearing, and the spread of venereal disease, but he also pointed to the decline of the extended family, the rise of single parenting, alcohol and drug abuse, and suicide as additional factors undermining the family. In the 1960s, language about family breakdown was mainly rhetoric about black families, especially poor black families. Within the first six years of the 1970s, the divorce rate doubled, the number of households headed by women increased by one-third, and the rate of cohabitation grew by a factor of thirteen. To Carter, these changes signaled that the middle-class American family was "weakening" or "deteriorating." Carter campaigned on a pledge to restore "traditional values." At the 1976 convention of the National Conference of Catholic Charities, Carter promised that, if he was elected president, he would convene a White House conference on the family as a means of addressing "the steady erosion and weakening of our families." Carter was personally opposed to abortion and wanted to end federal funding for it, but also believed that, since abortion had been legalized by the Supreme Court, it should remain legal. The promise of the conference seemed a small strategic way of placating Catholic leadership.[69] Carter believed that federal government policies should promote marriage, that federal tax rates imposed a marriage penalty, and that welfare policies encouraged men to abandon their families so that their wives and children would qualify for welfare.[70]

Carter never used the term *alternative lifestyles* because he did not approve of them. After he was elected, Carter did not fire any staff members for cohabiting, but he engaged in his own version of the shotgun marriage. He confronted a high-level appointee who, he had learned, was living with his girlfriend. Carter asked him, "Do you two have plans for getting married?" The appointee replied, "Oh, certainly." Carter then asked, "When?" The man responded, "Well, we were thinking of getting married when the azaleas were in bloom." Carter responded, "Where I come from the azaleas are in bloom right now." The appointee married soon after this conversation.[71] Subsequently, a half-dozen male aides married belatedly and in apparent haste. One droll insider, noting the flurry of recent weddings, said, "It does seem to defy the laws of probability."[72]

In 1977, when the president talked about "living in sin," sophisticated employees in Washington, DC, thought he must be joking—but he was not.

Carter told employees at the Department of Housing and Urban Development that year.

> I think it's very important that all of us in Government not forget that no matter how dedicated we might be and how eager to perform well, that we need a stable family life to make us better servants of the people.
>
> So, those of you who are living in sin, I hope you'll get married. [Laughter] Those of you who have left your spouses, go back home. And those of you who don't remember your children's names, get reacquainted.
>
> But I think it's very important that we have stable family lives. And I am serious about that.[73]

The former first Lady Betty Ford and the liberal columnist Mary McGrory insisted that Carter had violated the bounds of privacy and should mind his own business. Those who wanted to stem the tide of cohabitation took heart from Carter's comment, which was used by realtors to argue in favor of legislation that would exclude unmarried couples from renting apartments.[74]

Carter made a campaign promise to address the threat to marriage and the family by hosting a White House Conference on the Family. Most White House conferences, usually on children rather than the family, were meetings for the social welfare establishment, with additional input from experts in academia. However, recent federal government conferences had been attracting social conservatives, especially conservative women opposed to feminism. Federal sponsorship of a national women's conference in Houston in 1977, which affirmed support for abortion and gay rights, led to the formation of a conservative profamily coalition who were opposed to government subsidy of a conference that espoused feminism. Conservative women leaders such as Phyllis Schlafly, Beverly LaHaye, and Connie Marshner defined "profamily" as opposition to the Equal Rights Amendment (ERA), gay rights, abortion, and sex education in the schools.

Planning for the White House conference kept being postponed. Personnel came and went (an African American divorced single mother was replaced as director of the conference by a married Catholic man), and some White House staffers secretly hoped that what promised to be a battle royal in the culture war would simply go away. The family policy establishment of academics and social welfare professionals had mainly focused on how poverty and unemployment affected the family. Since single-parent families met the standard definition of the family (a unit defined by blood, marriage, or adoption), the battle would not involve significant discussion about minority families or welfare. Thus, the fight was a secular/religious one, without class or race dimensions. Conservatives demanded that the conference explicitly define the family as two or more persons related by blood, marriage, and adoption. Gays, feminists, and some professional organizations such as the American Home Economics Association opposed that definition. As a compromise, the organizers changed the name of the conference from the White House Conference on *the Family* to *Families* but avoided adopting any explicit definition of the family.

States held meetings to elect delegations to the three regional events that would comprise the conference. In the more liberal states, gay men and lesbians who had children attended, demanding that "traditional families must acknowledge the existence of lesbian traditional families like mine."[75] In conservative New Hampshire, ministers opposed delegates who favored defining cohabitors, gay or straight, as a family, as did the first lady of Alabama, Bobbie James. Jo Ann Gasper, the author of *The Right Woman* newsletter, successfully defeated the liberal definition of the family proposed primarily by the public employees' union in Virginia. She succeeded in getting the delegates to define family as blood, marriage, adoption, or a covenantal caring relationship "which is not contrary to law or sound public morality."[76] Paul Weyrich of the First Congress Foundation debated a left-wing rabbi about the definition of the family at a planning conference. He indicated that he disagreed with the rabbi about calling "a couple of lesbians who are bringing up a child, calling a couple of roommates a family, calling a couple of fornicators a family. These are families . . . under your definition—garbage!! It is ludicrous to call acquaintances, neighbors, live-in types, and so on families."[77]

By the end of the three regional conclaves, the definition of the family had proved to be a subject about which there was no consensus. The West Coast regional meeting turned out to be not liberal enough to pass a resolution that defined the family to include same-sex couples and straight cohabitors. As one might expect, midwestern and southern delegates convening in Minneapolis reached the most conservative verdict, passing a resolution to define the family as "two or more persons related by blood, heterosexual marriage or adoption." The delegates from the East Coast, meeting in Baltimore, came the closest to adopting a resolution in favor of a definition that included cohabitors and gay couples, but their resolution lost by just two votes.

A dictionary definition of the family had turned into an exercise in politics and power. The definition of the family was both an abstract, philosophical, and religious debate as well as a measure of social acceptance of cohabitation and homosexuality. Was the US government ready to put a stamp of approval on alternative lifestyles? One side sought acceptance of same-sex couples and cohabitors as families; the other side carried signs that read, "There's only *one* true family structure."

No one was completely satisfied, but the conservatives who walked out of the meetings in Baltimore and Los Angeles were the most unhappy and believed that Carter was promoting "sinful lifestyles." Taking a personal stand against cohabitation and stating a belief that homosexuality was not "a normal sex relationship" was an insufficient conservative credential when Carter still supported specific policies and laws conservatives opposed, such as ratification of the ERA and the legality of abortion. Both Carter and his Republican opponent in 1980, Ronald Reagan, were personally opposed "to living in sin." But Republicans were better able to capitalize on fears about alternative lifestyles because they had a consistent policy of no—no to homosexual rights, abortion, the ERA, and sex education in the schools. As James Davison notes, the major result of the White House conference "was to further crystallize and politicize, on a national scale, differences of opinion over the nature, structure, and composition of the family."[78] The Republican strategist Paul Weyrich was correct when he said that the family was going to be to the New Right what Vietnam had been to the New Left: the means by which a fringe social movement entered the mainstream of American two-party politics. By 1980, war about the family had broken out, with the two political parties as enemy combatants. The national Democratic Party and its presidential candidates represented acceptance of alternative lifestyles, and the Republican party, which defined itself as the party defending family and morality, represented rejection.[79] Of course, the Democratic Party never claimed it was working on behalf of the rights of cohabitors. Nonetheless, cohabitation was an invisible part of the issues of gender and sexuality that were helping to polarize the two national political parties.

SEVEN

Palimony

They met on the movie set of *Ship of Fools* in 1964. He was forty, separated from his wife, and one of the stars of the film; she was thirty-one, divorced, and a stand-in. They had lunch, then cocktails, and then two weeks later they had sex in his dressing room on the Columbia lot. Michelle Triola moved in with the Hollywood tough guy par excellence Lee Marvin and lived with him for six years, from 1964 to 1970. They shared the two-bedroom Malibu beach house he rented, which he subsequently purchased in his own name. He divorced his wife but was not ready to marry again, although Michelle wanted to get married. Embarrassed by having to check into hotels as Miss Triola, Michelle called herself Mrs. Marvin and had credit cards in the name of Mrs. Lee Marvin; she legally changed her name to Marvin at her own initiative.[1] In 1970, Lee Marvin told his lawyers to evict Michelle from the Malibu house. He had abruptly legally married his long-lost high school sweetheart in Las Vegas and wanted to occupy the beach house with her. As a settlement, he agreed to pay Michelle Marvin $833 a month for five years, but he stopped making the payments after a year and a half.[2] Michelle Marvin approached a prominent Hollywood divorce lawyer, Marvin Mitchelson, because she was a tenant in an apartment building his mother owned. Mitchelson told her that in court she could win a great deal more than the restoration of her monthly payments. In discussing the case with the media, Mitchelson coined the term *palimony*, a combination of *pal* and *alimony*, to refer to the division of property and alimony-like support Michelle Marvin was seeking.

Marvin Mitchelson earned a seven-figure income from representing Hollywood wives suing their husbands for their share of community property and alimony. Around town, he drove one of his three Rolls Royces, kept the other two in the garage of his $5 million mansion, wore five-thousand-dollar hand-tailored suits, and was known to have a cocaine and Percodan habit. He outfitted his office in Century City with Persian rugs and a Jacuzzi. On the ceiling of the office was a lighted stained-glass replica of Botticelli's *Birth of Venus*. Dubbed "the paladin of paramours" by *Time* and "the sultan of split" by *People*, Mitchelson rose to fame as Hollywood's leading divorce lawyer by winning the first "million-dollar divorce"—of Pamela Mason from the British-born actor James Mason. Mitchelson was proud of his pro bono work, appearing before the US Supreme Court to win the right of representation for indigent clients. Because that kind of advocacy did not pay for the Rolls Royces, however, Mitchelson increasingly devoted his practice to Hollywood divorce cases. Cloaking himself in the mantle of feminism, he stated "that a woman who has lived exactly as a wife with everything but an $8 marriage license should have the same rights."[3] Subsequently eight women, including a palimony client, accused him of rape, although he was never convicted on any of the charges.[4]

In 1972, Michelle Marvin sued Lee Marvin for half his earnings and movie royalties. She lost her case in an appeals court, which ruled that contracts between cohabitors were unenforceable because, like prostitution, the relationship involved an exchange of money for sex. She appealed to the California Supreme Court. In *Marvin v. Marvin* (1976), the California Supreme Court formulated the new legal principle that cohabitors had the right to enforcement of the contracts they made with each other and envisioned new remedies of compensation for the vulnerable partner when such a relationship dissolved. They sent the case back to a trial court in Los Angeles to determine whether Lee and Michelle Marvin had entered into a valid contract and therefore he should be held in breach of contract. But as the case made its way through lower courts in Los Angeles, it became more difficult to prove that Michelle Marvin's situation conformed to the rules required to prove an implied or verbal contract. When the case finally came to an end in 1981, Michelle Marvin did not receive any money whatsoever from Lee Marvin. She had won a theoretical point in the state supreme court about the legal rights of cohabitors but did not see any practical benefit from that victory.

The *Marvin* legal case emerged in the early 1970s, precisely at the moment when cohabitation was becoming more open and visible in Hollywood and among young people. The extensive surveillance and punishment of cohabitation seemed to prove that what cohabitors really needed was to be left alone—the right of privacy, the right not to have to marry—so that they could pursue their relationships without being punished or spied upon.

Couples tend not to think about the financial and legal aspects of their relationship until it is about to end. However, the termination of long-term cohabitating relationships was generating a variety of legal suits involving child custody, alimony, and postrelationship support and division of assets. Moreover, gay and lesbian couples who had exchanged vows in nonlegal ceremonies were seeking the equivalent of divorce. After the legal demise of common-law marriage, it was mainly women in long-term cohabitations and the financially more vulnerable parties in a gay or lesbian relationship who stood to gain the most from having their day in court.

Prior to *Marvin*, there were no legal consequences to dissolution after cohabitation. Parties were free to walk away with whatever property was in their own name, and there were no continuing obligations. The California Supreme Court responded to the lack of rights and obligations by fashioning a contract approach to the dissolution of long-term cohabiting relationship. It did so as a liberal court, open to legal innovation and breaking with judicial precedent. In December of 1976, the California Supreme Court issued its landmark decision about a cohabitor's right to contract and remanded the case to the lower courts to figure out whether the facts of the case fit with the legal principles they had enunciated.

Mitchelson formulated his brief in precisely the language of the times, as a defense of the right of privacy of cohabitors, the right of nondiscrimination by marital status, and the recognition of cohabitation as a form of family. But Associate Justice Mathew Tobriner of the California Supreme Court deliberately avoided the language of family and the law surrounding it. He did not define cohabitors as a family but instead as two parties in an "intimate relationship," who should not be deprived of the rights to contract available to other unmarried persons merely because they had a sexual relationship. He had a choice between thinking about cohabitors as a family status versus thinking about them as two individuals living together who had the same legal rights as other unmarrieds; he chose the latter. *Marvin* thus represents private ordering of cohabitation rather than an attempt to update family law.

The *Marvin* decision by the California Supreme Court and the subsequent trial in a Los Angeles courtroom was a media sensation and led to many similar rulings in other states. Predictably, it generated a backlash, especially in the Midwest and the South. The best-known lawsuit that explicitly denied *Marvin* rights to a long-term cohabiting woman was *Hewitt v. Hewitt* (1979), which the press liked to call "a mini-Marvin case."[5] The Illinois Supreme Court as well as the Illinois legislature upheld the proposition that the state should discourage cohabitation because it threatened the institution of marriage and thereby threatened the nation. This chapter examines how and why cohabitors became defined as participants in "intimate relationships" who had the right to contract with each other; the conservative backlash against this legal framework, especially in Illinois; the adoption of the contractual framework in most states; and the failure of that framework to provide legal protection for vulnerable women and children in long-term cohabiting relationships.

Marvin was an attack on the state policy of punishing cohabitation and promoting marriage, an attack based on the liberal idea that law should accept social reality and should remain morally neutral toward new alternatives to the family that couples were choosing. The solution the court offered, freedom to contract, was obviously an improvement over no legal right to contract—it was innovative, creative, and offered legal options to both same-sex and opposite-sex cohabitors. Nonetheless, if the law is more than a symbolic statement and is expected to deliver just, efficient, and fair results, then the contract approach must be deemed a failure because it proved lengthy, expensive, and unworkable. Thus, the liberalism, feminism, and gay activism of the late 1970s was unable to formulate a viable legal framework for cohabitation. With that failure also ended the belief that private ordering of relationships rather than state-imposed laws or status was an effective legal response to the dissolution of long-term cohabitation.

Prior to the California Supreme Court's *Marvin* decision, cohabitors had been denied the right to make and enforce contracts with each other having to do with the terms of their relationship because cohabitation was seen as similar to prostitution. (They were allowed to make business contracts and partnerships, but not contracts that dealt with the terms of their relationship.) According to the law, a woman living with a man was participating in a "meretricious" relationship—a Latin word that meant similar to prostitution.[6] Since prostitution was a crime, it was illegal for those engaged in it to enter into a contract to provide sex. The California Supreme Court in *Marvin v. Marvin* rejected the notion that "the nonenforceability of agreements expressly providing for meretricious conduct rested upon the fact that such conduct, as the word suggests, pertained to and encompassed prostitution. To equate the nonmarital relationship of today to such a subject matter is to do violence to an accepted and wholly different practice."[7] Just because couples engaged in sex, the court argued, did not negate their right of contract with regard to the nonsexual aspects of the relationship such as sharing earnings, property, or expenses. The court held that the law should not "impose a standard based on alleged moral considerations that have apparently been widely abandoned by so many."[8] Nonetheless, it also ruled that it was important to distinguish between nonsexual services provided, which could be subject to contract, and the couple's sex life, about which no agreement, written or oral, could be made.

NUMBER OF STATES AND THE DISTRICT OF COLUMBIA
RECOGNIZING COMMON-LAW MARRIAGE

1850–79	18
1880–99	21
1900–1920	22
1921–40	17
1941–60	12
1961–80	12
1981–2000	13
2001–10	12

The contract approach to cohabitation was quite different from the common-law marriage tradition, although both were legal attempts to specify rules for nonformalized adult sexual relationships. Common-law marriage involved legal recognition of a marriage on the basis of various aspects of the couple's conduct without the requirements of formal marriage or registration of the union. The California Supreme Court could not claim that the Marvins had a common-law marriage because the state legislature had declared such marriages illegal in 1895. In fact, California was the first state in the nation to abolish common-law marriage through legislative rather than judicial means. The California legislature wanted to prevent fraud by a young "adventuress" scheming to get hold of a wealthy man's money. The decline of Victorianism—including the belief in the innocence and victimization of a deserving woman—made it easier to accept eliminating common-law marriage.[9] In other states, there were a variety of reasons, including this one, for the elimination of common-law marriage. Published divorce statistics for the first time set off a panic about rising divorce rates; the state had to act to defend the family. Eugenicists provided another scientific argument for abolition, criticizing common-law marriage because it thwarted state-imposed restrictions on the eligibility to marry.[10] About the time of World War I, another reason to favor abolishing common-law marriage was that it provided too easy a way to make a claim for publicly financed programs such as veterans' pensions and workmen's compensation. In the 1950s and early 1960s, two southern states, Mississippi and Florida, abolished common-law marriage because it was known as an informal form of African American marriage that could then be used by blacks to claim public benefits.[11] In more recent years, the most common reason for abolishing common-law marriage is once again the possibility that it might encourage fraud.

California set the trend in twentieth-century marriage law in other ways as well. In 1969, it became the first state in the union to institute no-fault divorce. In the fault system of divorce, the guilty party was punished by losing much of the couple's assets. The aim of no-fault divorce was to eliminate the blame and acrimony of divorce in imposing a judicial decision about the division of property, the award of alimony or child support, and custody of children. The philosophy behind no-fault divorce also reflected the decline of belief in state-imposed solutions to marital problems. Instead of the state dictating when a couple could divorce and for what reasons, no-fault allowed the parties themselves to make their own decision as to when to terminate their marriage. Although it appeared that no-fault bills were designed for legally married couples who sought a divorce, once it was enacted as law, such protection was also sought by cohabitors. Thus, a California Appellate Court applied no-fault divorce law in the case of a cohabiting woman from the Bay Area, Janet Forbes, originally from Canada, who had met Californian Paul Cary. They lived together for eight years and had four children. When the relationship ended, she took their two younger children with her and returned to Canada, and he kept the two older ones but continued to fight for the custody of all four children. Finally in 1973, a court resolved their custody dispute (the children remained where they were) and divided the couple's property in half, according to the principles of community property and no-fault divorce. The reasoning was that if the legislature was eliminating blame from determining family property rights, and if a long-term cohabitation relationship looked a lot like marriage, then concepts of guilt and innocence were outmoded, "where there be a legal marriage or not."[12]

The *Marvin* Decision

Other unmarried couples in California failed in their efforts to have no-fault principles applied to their breakups. The case of Janet Forbes came uncomfortably close to reintroducing the concept of common-law marriage, a concept California had abandoned seventy-nine years before. Meanwhile, other appellate court decisions in the state held that a cohabiting woman was not entitled to any legal relief. The California Supreme Court in *Marvin* wanted to reconcile conflicting recent legal decisions in the state and provide some kind of overarching legal principles to apply to a trend becoming more common by the day. The justices chose as their legal framework the law of contract, which seemed to have three advantages: first, it offered couples the freedom to figure out the terms of their relationship rather than forcing them into the rigid rules for the institution of marriage, which some of them had rejected; second, it seemed to conform to the feminism of the times, which called for explicit contracts even within the institution of marriage (as well as in prenuptial contracts); and finally, it was a legal standard well developed in the United States, a nation that prized individualism, private property, and free enterprise.[13]

The *Marvin* decision was the handiwork of a liberal Democratic jurist, an associate justice of the California Supreme Court, Mathew Tobriner, a seventy-two-year-old liberal activist appointed by his old friend, the Democratic Governor Pat Brown, to the court fourteen years earlier. The fact that the California Supreme Court was appointed rather than elected provided the justices with protection from public opinion. Tobriner was Jewish, a labor lawyer, and a New Dealer, who supported state funding of abortions for poor women, homosexual rights, affirmative action, and reduced penalties for possession of marijuana. He had already contributed to the legal rights of cohabitors by ruling in 1966 in the case involving the Oakland social worker Benny Parrish that midnight raids of the homes of welfare recipients were a violation of the constitutional ban on unreasonable searches and seizures.

Associate Justice Tobriner's liberalism combined his view that people should be able to be free from established rules and institutions with a belief that the state should not impose morality on it citizens. He was a judicial activist, who held that the law should fashion innovative solutions to new social problems and certainly not wait until the legislature figured out a way to do so. The view that the law should correspond to new social reality meant that he paid a lot of attention to statistics and trends. To Tobriner's critics, he was less a judge than a "legislative sociologist."[14]

He was also sympathetic to the underdog—in the case of the cohabiting relationship, usually the woman, because without the right of contract she was denied a share of property that she had helped to acquire during the relationship. The cause of the displaced homemaker was at that time an especially prominent one among feminist lawyers, who believed that the no-fault divorce revolution failed to adequately take into account the woman's in-kind contributions to the union. Tobriner's decision stated, "Unless it can be argued that a woman's service as cook, housekeeper, and housemaker are valueless, it would seem logical that if, when she contributes money to the purchase of property, her interest will be protected, then when she contributes her services in the home, her interest in property should be protected."[15] Tobriner borrowed freely from the friend of the court brief of Carol Burch, a law professor at the University of California at Davis, who wanted to protect the jilted woman abandoned by her male partner and considered it unfair when the man got all the property that had actually been acquired through mutual efforts.[16] She saw the *Marvin* decision as a "statement that all people are entitled . . . to fair and equitable treatment," although by *people* she really meant economically dependent women who had been abandoned by their lovers.[17] The friend of the court brief by two feminist lawyers, Herma Hill Kay and Carol Amyx, was even more expansive than Bruch's. They worried that as women devoted themselves to careers, men would simply abandon the idea of any long-term commitments. They were decidedly against the idea of pushing people into legal marriage when instead couples should be able to choose not to marry, an idea far in advance of anything Tobriner had in mind. At different times in their lives, they believed, people needed different relationships. Without citing any social science research, they declared cohabitation good for the mental health of the partner and good for the health of children. Emerging as it did at a high point for second-wave feminism, their brief was based on the assumption that for the lonely mother having a companion would make her happy and would therefore benefit her children.[18]

In 1976, the California Supreme Court sent *Marvin* back to a lower court to be tried under the implied contract principles it enunciated. Sixty witnesses testified during an eleven-week trial in Los Angeles (from January to April 1979) to determine whether there had been an implied contract. The reason so much testimony was required was because the Marvins did not have a written contract governing their relationship. Instead, the court had the power to inquire into whether an implied contract could be inferred from the behavior of the couple and the promises they made to each other. All the dishonesty and acrimony the courts had tried to eliminate via no-fault divorce resurfaced.[19] One Hollywood insider after another testified, including stunt men, producers, agents, gossip columnists, and accountants, along with over-the-hill celebrities such as Gene Kelly, Mel Tormé, and Trini Lopez. Michelle Marvin sought to prove her argument that Lee Marvin had made an express promise to take care of her, that she gave up her own career to help support his, and that she and Lee assumed collaborative roles in their relationship. Lee Marvin countered that he had not agreed to anything and told Michelle he did not believe in marriage because it gave a woman rights to community property. His lawyer tried to show that far from suffering from the relationship, Michelle Marvin had benefited from the fur coats, Mercedes, and foreign travel Lee Marvin had paid for. The witnesses described a real-life soap opera—infidelity, impotence, alcoholism, drug use, attempted suicide, two abortions, a miscarriage, an exciting breakup, and a night in jail, plus each side claiming that the other was a liar. Michelle Marvin testified that as a result of her second abortion, she was unable to bear children. Although mainly set in Malibu, the action also took place offshore in the South Pacific, Hawaii, coastal Mexico, London, Tokyo, and Tucson. Michelle Marvin took the stand for six days and Lee Marvin for four, with Michelle Marvin sobbing frequently and Lee Marvin looking grim. Mitchelson read love letters from Lee to Michelle Marvin written when he was in London for the filming of The Dirty Dozen. Among other things, the letters proved that Lee Marvin did not know how to spell. More important, Mitchelson sought to show that Lee Marvin truly loved Michelle and that she therefore had reason to expect to be provided for. In one of his expressions of enduring affection, Lee Marvin wrote, "Hey baby, hey baby, hey baby, hey baby, hey baby, hey baby."[20]

Michelle Marvin claimed that she gave up her career at Lee's request and then became a homemaker with the expectation that she would be taken care of for life. According to Michelle Marvin, on a sport fishing trip to San Blas, Mexico, Lee told her, "What I have is yours and what you have is mine."[21] When Gene Kelly offered her a singing part in the Broadway musical Flower Drum Song, she turned it down because Lee wanted her at his side. Kelly denied offering the part, and the crooner Mel Tormé testified that Michelle's singing voice was only "slightly better than average."[22] Michelle Marvin's alleged infidelity could also be used to impeach her testimony since she had sworn on the witness stand that she had never any sexual affairs while she was living with Lee.[23] Lee Marvin's attorneys called to the stand a mystery witness who refuted her statement. Lee had brought Michelle with him while he was filming Hell in the Pacific on the Micronesian island of Palau. A handsome young Peace Corps volunteer, who, with Lee Marvin's help became an actor, swore under oath that Michelle Marvin had had sex with him once a day for three months while on Palau—and occasional trysts in Los Angeles and Tucson, at her insistence, after that. When Marvin Mitchelson tried to even the score, the presiding judge ruled that evidence about the sexual affairs of Lee Marvin was inadmissible because such testimony would "merely demonstrate what he (Marvin) has been contending all along, that there was no contract."[24]

A contract was also implied from the idea that Michelle Marvin had performed housekeeping services and had a reasonable expectation that she would be compensated for them in the future, if the relationship dissolved. Thus, a decision so careful to avoid the word *family* ended up using traditional gender roles as part of the criteria to decide if the couple had an implied contract. To prove her case, Michelle Marvin had to demonstrate that her conduct implied a contract that involved housekeeping, cooking, and companionship in exchange for financial support. Mitchelson claimed that Michelle Marvin was upholding her part of the contract by engaging in "wifely behavior," as she waited on Lee and tried to sober him up. Known for her culinary expertise, she claimed that Lee showed her a recipe from a magazine and asked her, "Can you cook this?"[25] She told of putting out spreads for the crew of Lee's movies and making roasts. She even played the role of the long-suffering partner of an alcoholic, showing up at the set to sober him up and throwing hidden liquor bottles into the ocean.

The narratives of Michelle and Lee Marvin helped transform a trial about equitable remedy, the breach of an implicit contract, and the obscure doctrine of *quantum meruit* into a battle of the sexes in the final days when the Equal Rights Amendment was still being considered in state legislatures. The age-old battle was fought with a Hollywood supporting cast of several dozen and was designed to answer the question of whether the double standard was still alive. Many men were frightened by the prospect that a brief affair would end up as an assault on their finances, but the threat often seemed a broader one, related to feminism and the sexual liberation of women.

Many women in situations similar to Michelle Marvin's, unmarried and abandoned, supported her, if her fan mail is any guide. Several feminists recognized that *Marvin* was a critique of the double standard; her lawsuit claimed that it was possible for a woman to have a sexual relationship outside of marriage and still retain her legal rights to contract. Her treatment at court reinforced the view that a woman trusted a man only at her peril. The definition of a feminist was a woman willing to wear a T-shirt that read, "It's Michelle's Money, Too."[26] Gloria Steinem, who supported Michelle Marvin, engaged in hyperbole, predicting after the *Marvin* trial ended in 1979 that "women will now be far more likely to insist on a financial agreement in writing before they give up their careers or wash even one dish—and that's probably healthy. If this results in men complaining that women no longer believe the promises of romance, let them complain to the Lee Marvins."[27] The California women's rights attorney Gloria Allred, along with three other feminist supporters, walked hand in hand with Michelle Marvin down the hallway of the courthouse. Allred asserted that the press identified Lee Marvin by his occupation (actor), but identified Michelle Marvin by her sexual relationship: "live-in girlfriend," "mistress," and "former lover."[28] The ideal of the independent woman who refused alimony on grounds of principle was an entirely different kind of feminism, which made Michelle Marvin appear a throwback to an earlier age. Another feminist, the screenwriter Nora Ephron, who rejected the idea that Michelle Marvin was a wronged woman, seemed to belong in that camp. She believed that Michelle Marvin's behavior reinforced the notion "that a woman is a flimsy spineless child, a will-o-the wisp who can be swayed by the least little puff of smoke from a man."[29] Seeking to overcome the stereotype that she was an "old-fashioned gold digger," Michelle Marvin portrayed herself as a wronged woman, a crusader on behalf of woman's rights, and an advocate of the Equal Rights Amendment for women. At the end of the trial, she insisted, "I did it for all womankind," and several years later proudly proclaimed that she had become a feminist.[30]

Public attitudes toward Michelle Marvin split along lines of age and gender. The *San Francisco Chronicle*, recognizing the entertainment value of the trial, asked readers to call in their response to the question of whether "live-in lovers" should receive alimony. Among twelve thousand callers, the vote was two to one against; the overwhelming majority of the respondents were women, who seem to have come from the large pool of disapproving mothers. A middle-aged housewife told the *Chronicle* that "living together is immoral and doesn't deserve protection by the courts." A mother of three daughters thought Michelle Marvin needed to lose her suit so that living together did not appear attractive. A woman in South Lake Tahoe came right to the point: the case was "the ultimate expression of greed on the part of Miss Marvin."[31]

On television, both parties were objects of ridicule and even limericks. A skit on *The Tonight Show Starring Johnny Carson* presented the couple as Adam and Eve, with Eve demanding half of the community property. On *Saturday Night Live*, the laugh lines were set up as a "point, counterpoint" between the comedians Jane Curtin, taking a feminist stand, and Dan Ackroyd, posing as a station manager who told her that "bagged out, dried up, slunken meat like you and Michelle Triola know the rules." Curtin's arguments on behalf of Triola generated some applause, but Ackroyd's satire of sexism received the most guffaws. The butt of his humor was Michelle Marvin, who "had sex over 40 times with another man while living with Lee Marvin." But his major point was not that she was unfaithful but that she was both a prostitute and a gold digger, "a screeching, squealing rapacious swamp sow after Lee Marvin's three million dollars." Ackroyd's character proffered the view that women had to name their price in advance of sex so that "we can choose which two bit tarts and bargain basement sluts to shack up with."[32]

The editorial page of American newspapers reflected established and largely male verdicts on the trial as well as the conventional advice to "get it in writing." No editorial writer saw the results of the trial as a ringing affirmation of alternative lifestyles; the *Garden City Telegram* hoped that Lee and Michelle had learned their lesson that such relationships are risky. The *Pittsburgh Press* decided that the case proved that it was much better for couples to get married. The *Nevada Daily Mail* refused to consider the question of what arrangement was a better financial deal, but instead declared the decision tells us that "such conduct in the eyes of the law" is unacceptable. The hometown newspaper, the *Los Angeles Times*, regarded the suit as business news, assessing the possible legal liability among the stars in the entertainment industry.[33]

The more conservative the region, the more Michelle alone was excoriated. Thus in the *Atlanta Daily World*, she was seen as a gold digger who was allowed to sue because in California "nothing is too zany to dupe some."[34] But a *San Francisco Chronicle* editorial was more evenhanded, intoning that "the thoughtless, shrill and egotistical lives of these litigants as aired in court had begun to weigh upon the soul. They deserved each other, just as they deserved the shallow thrashings that marked their public set-to."[35]

Mitchelson decided against a jury trial because he did not "think a jury would go for it."[36] The decision was entirely left up to Los Angeles Superior Court judge Arthur Marshall, who ruled that there was neither an express nor an implied contract between Michelle and Lee Marvin and that she was not entitled to a share of his income or property. The judge claimed that Lee and Michelle Marvin had never made any verbal agreement to share household duties and income. Yet Judge Marshall wanted Michelle Marvin to receive something as a consolation prize since he knew she was subsisting on unemployment benefits. In the back of the judge's mind was the old common-law judicial attitude of shifting the burden of welfare from the taxpayers to Lee Marvin since he was wealthy and she was needy. The judge noted that Michelle Marvin's chances of resuming her singing career were "doubtful," and out of a sense of fairness, he awarded her $104,000, or two years' worth of the highest weekly salary she had earned as a singer. The award, the judge ruled, was for "rehabilitation purposes . . . to reeducate herself and to learn new, employable skills."

When Lee Marvin appealed the award of $104,000 in 1981, a California Appeals Court reversed Marshall's required payment to Michelle Marvin, finding no legal justification for it.[37] Why had Lee Marvin challenged what was a minimal sum for him, especially since he had to pay lawyer's fees for two years to achieve the victory? A 1966 comment he made, a year after he won his Oscar for *Cat Ballou*, provides a possible answer. He said, "The only thing in life that's really interesting is the contest."[38]

The *Marvin* Decision and Gay Rights

Because gays and lesbians were denied the right to marry and thus had fewer legal options than straight cohabitors, *Marvin* was actually more important to them. Tobriner, who was a supporter of homosexual rights, had carefully referred to "nonmarital partners" in his ruling, adopting gender-neutral language that left open the possibility that the partners could be either same sex or opposite sex. Precisely because *Marvin* used the framework of contract rights, it was a legal remedy available to gay and lesbian couples. The first victory in court for a gay or lesbian litigant was in San Diego in 1978.[39] Because of her written contract, Dee Richardson won a temporary support order from her partner, a local dentist. Same-sex palimony suits (lesbian suits were dubbed "galimony") also offered equal opportunity for scandal as *Marvin*, as when tennis star Billie Jean King's lover or the chauffeur, animal trainer, and partner of Liberace sued in court.

Among gays and lesbians, the right to contract was much wider than simply the right to divorce. There is no systematic study of the success rate of contracts for straight versus gay cohabitors, and probably none could be undertaken since it is impossible to know how many cases were settled out of court. On the whole, it appears that same-sex couples fared pretty much the same as opposite-sex couples, that verbal promises are rarely enough to prove a contract, and that judges infrequently order postrelationship support in exchange for years of homemaking services provided. The success of written contracts seems to vary with the state's overall attitude toward contract rights for cohabitors, rather than its attitude toward homosexuality. In fact, in Georgia, a contract of straight cohabitors was ruled illegal because cohabitation is illegal in the state, whereas a contract of a lesbian couple was accepted. The one area of prejudice is that some judges seize on and throw out initial contracts that referred to "my lover" and thus seemed to specify a "meretricious relationship." Once that language was removed, however, the results in such cases seem to have been much the same as in those involving heterosexual cohabitors.

The issue of contracts for same-sex couples now emerges more often as part of the debate about same-sex marriage. On the whole, the contract approach to relationship recognition has the same problems for same-sex as for opposite-sex couples—it's expensive, time consuming, and offers unpredictable results.[40]

The *Hewitt* Case

Among straight cohabitors, even in California, *Marvin* did not open the floodgates of litigation, and its impact was relatively short-lived.[41] In California, there was an initial flurry of palimony cases from about 1977 to 1982, and cases continued to be filed after that, but less frequently.[42] In California, where *Marvin* suits were most frequent, judges' decisions depended "upon the discretion, and perhaps the personal prejudices of the judge."[43] A Los Angeles Superior Court judge and author of a family law textbook offered his "sense . . . that it [*Marvin*] isn't really amounting to much since."[44] Most clients seem to have been deterred by the length of time these cases took—usually about five years—as well the expense. Attorney fees for the winning party had to be paid out of assets rather than the settlement the client won, as in divorce suits. Lawyers learned their lesson from Mitchelson not to take such cases on a contingency basis. A reputable lawyer would also tell clients that their chances of winning were slim.

After the California Supreme Court ruling, the state courts in New Jersey, Oregon, Minnesota, and Michigan adopted *Marvin* principles almost immediately (Oregon actually preceded the California decision). Georgia, Illinois, and Louisiana in the late 1970s did not; Mississippi, West Virginia, and Ohio in the 1990s explicitly rejected the *Marvin* approach.[45] The fact that cohabitation was a crime in four of these six states strengthened the case against recognizing a contract that involved it.

The most significant and widely cited explicit rejection of the *Marvin* decision was *Hewitt v. Hewitt* (1979). There was a sense of panic when Victoria Hewitt her palimony suit on appeal, with Cook County divorce attorneys predicting "a big foot in the door in Illinois" for *Marvin*-type cases. Republican legislators tried, but failed, to pass a bill that would prohibit couples from entering into implied contracts, even making the legislation retroactive to stop *Hewitt* in its tracks. An Illinois matrimonial lawyer explained that "we're a conservative state where the Catholic church has considerable influence."[46] Cohabitation was still against the law in Illinois, although the law was not enforced. The state had just passed divorce reform that retained fault provisions because it was believed that no-fault divorce would encourage marital breakup. As part of the divorce reform bill, Illinois had also adopted a punitive measure to eliminate alimony for any divorced woman who was cohabiting.[47]

Robert Hewitt and Victoria Neel met as undergraduates at Grinnell College in Grinnell, Iowa, in 1958. He was a husky football player on an athletic scholarship, and she was a diminutive blonde from an affluent Catholic family; they both lived in the dorms. By the spring of the second semester of her senior year, Victoria knew she was pregnant. The couple called their parents and announced that they had gotten married. At this time, it was not that unusual for cohabitors with Catholic parents to lie and tell parents they had eloped. Robert and Vicki had no ceremony, but Robert told Vicki that they didn't need one and he considered that he had married her.[48] They were both twenty years old. That summer they lived with his parents in Rockford, Illinois, and then moved in with her parents in Lake Forest. Her father, a wealthy dentist, helped pay for Robert Hewitt to attend dental school. Two of their three daughters were born while they were living with her family. In the late 1960s, after Bob Hewitt finished his training, they moved to Champaign, Illinois, where he became a children's dentist and oral surgeon. Vicki worked part-time as Bob's dental hygienist. She was paid a salary, which she deposited in the family account.[49] They joined the country club, had season tickets to University of Illinois football games, and lived in a seven-room ranch house that was larger but looked quite similar to James and Mary Decko's house in Sheboygan.[50]

In 1975, Robert Hewitt told Victoria that he had not loved her for some time and moved out. She had no money to pay the utility bills, and the electricity was almost turned off twice for failure to pay. Several months later, Bob showed up at the house to pick up "his things." The two started to fight, and he poured a bottle of liquor on her head. She locked the door to keep him out of the house, but he broke a windowpane and told her he would come into the house whenever he pleased. Frightened, she and the children fled. A couple of weeks before Christmas, the three girls learned that their parents were breaking up; the girls were brought to court as potential witnesses for their father, where for the first time they learned that they had been born out of wedlock. Vicki Hewitt sued for divorce, arguing she had been married in Iowa. Forced to admit that there had been no wedding ceremony, she fell back on the claim that she was a common-law wife, since Iowa recognized common-law marriage. But there was no proof that the couple had lived together in Iowa before moving to Illinois. Victoria Hewitt explained that she thought of herself as a lawful wife during fifteen years together with Bob Hewitt. She said, "I always introduced Bob as my husband because I truly believed he was. I don't lie. How could I bring him home to my parents if I believed we were living in sin? I'm the kind of person who comes to a complete halt at a stop sign. I can't lie. And he always introduced me as his wife."[51]

Champaign was a college town where students often lived together, and although Champaign was only a little larger than Sheboygan, it was far more cosmopolitan. But the judges of the circuit court often upheld the values of central Illinois small towns and farming communities, which still viewed cohabitation as a sin. To Harold Jensen, a circuit court judge in Champaign, Victoria Hewitt was a woman of ill repute who "wants 'shacking up'" to be "elevated to a formal legal status." Sensing the feminism in the *Marvin* decision, he wrote, "Whatever attractiveness the *Marvin* case may have in its appeal to the equalization of the sexes in light of the most [*sic*] daily radical new approach of California community standards and life reflected in that state's legislature and judiciary is lost upon a closer analysis of the case at hand against the backdrop of Illinois law and public policy." Illinois law and public policy, he added, encouraged "marriage, the major social institution of our society."

Judge Jensen thought that Victoria Hewitt's needs would be adequately cared for by receiving half of the proceeds from the sale of the student apartments she and Bob jointly owned and that she did not deserve half the proceeds from the sale of the family home or the right to remain there. The judge also ordered that Victoria Hewitt, as the loser in the case, should pay for Robert's legal fees. Robert Hewitt bought another house in the same suburban-style neighborhood of Champaign. Vicki Hewitt enrolled in nursing school in 1978. The family house was sold in 1981, and she and two of the three children moved out of town.[52] After the decision from the Champaign divorce court, Victoria Hewitt's children were receiving child support at about the standard amount for the time, but it was voluntary.[53] She was not entitled to any interest in Robert Hewitt's pension, a wife's rights to her husband's Social Security benefits, alimony, or any share of the proceeds from the sale of the family house.

In 1979, Victoria Hewitt appealed the circuit court decision to the Illinois Appellate Court. Judge Harold Trapp of the appellate court approved of the *Marvin* decision and quoted from it extensively. The judge used the *Marvin* decision to offer reasons for approving a divorce-like division of assets and alimony for Vicki Hewitt. But what really impressed him was that Vicki Hewitt was "respectable," and that the Hewitts had had a "stable family relationship" of "the most conventional sort." A suburban wife and mother like Vicki Hewitt, he believed, did not threaten the institution of marriage. The judge argued that Illinois rules sent the message that a man in the breakup of a live-in arrangement fared far better than a legally married man, and therefore the law was offering an incentive for men not to marry. After the appellate court ruled against him, Robert Hewitt hired a team of Chicago lawyers in addition to his Urbana attorney to bring an appeal to the Illinois Supreme Court. He also tried to win favor among his fellow men by telling them, "If the appellate court [decision] is upheld, you may learn if you're in bed with a woman for a few days, she's entitled to compensation."[54] Vicki Hewitt retained her original lawyer and probably did not have the money to add talent to her legal team.

The contrast between the politics of Justice Tobriner and Chief Justice Robert Underwood of the Illinois Supreme Court is proof of the maxim that the ideology of judges determined the outcome of decisions. The chief justice of the Illinois Supreme Court, Robert Underwood, was born and grew up in the college town of Bloomington, Illinois, and originally practiced law there. A conservative Republican, Underwood held that the law should try to stem immorality by protecting and preserving the institution of marriage and upholding enduring moral values. The law, he believed, should be used to punish those who had lived in sin and discourage others from doing so. Underwood's decision was exactly the opposite of the California Supreme Court's *Marvin* decision. He argued that there could be no implied contract in the Hewitt relationship because such a contract was based on providing sex in exchange for support and therefore was meretricious. The incident when Robert Hewitt smashed the glass of his house, broke in, and forced Victoria Hewitt and his children to flee in fear went unmentioned. What was the impact of cohabitation on the children? Underwood wanted to know. He asked in his decision, "What of the social and psychological effects upon them of that type of environment?"[55]

Underwood never expected that the Hewitt children would provide their own answer to his question. Totally hidden from the courts was the resentment and anger Bob Hewitt's daughters felt about the way their father had treated their mother. They saw the breakup not as a question of cohabitation but as a divorce suit, which harmed them and their the mother. They stood to lose as well because their family home was being sold and they were being forced to move. The two older Hewitt daughters, Wendy, twelve, and Victoria, eighteen, engaged in their own response to Underwood's decision, holding protest signs that read "Father of the Year" and "Dad, How could you do this?" outside their father's dental office in Champaign. They told reporters that they hoped their mother would appeal the decision. If the stigma of cohabitation was reinforced through the media, so, too, was the stigma of being a no-good dad.[56]

The state of Illinois today still does not recognize contractual rights of cohabitors in order to preserve and uphold the institution of marriage. Lawyers in the Land of Lincoln tell their cohabiting clients, gay and straight, that contracts are unenforceable in Illinois. Legal scholar Cynthia Grant Bowman is unsure whether a court in Illinois would decide the *Hewitt* case today in exactly the same manner as it did in 1980, but she does note that *Hewitt* "is still the law in the state (though it has been cited with decreasing frequency over the years.)"[57] Nonetheless, Illinois is one of six states that do not recognize contracts between cohabitors; the District of Columbia and twenty-five states do, although the rules they impose vary widely; that leaves nineteen states with no appellate case law to define the state's rules.

The Failure of the Contractual Approach in *Marvin*

There are several reasons why *Marvin* must be considered a judicial failure on the road toward the legal acceptance of cohabitation. Among them is that it offers highly variable results. Certainly rules of divorce vary by state, but there is no state in which divorce is not permitted. The legal map for cohabitors' contract rights is far more diverse and disconcerting for couples from one where their contract would be honored to another where it would not. Even in the majority of states where such contracts are enforceable, it has proved difficult to bring such a lawsuit and even more difficult to win. Despite what was supposed to be the basic message of *Marvin*, "to get it in writing," fewer than one-third of cohabitors in one study had legal contracts, and, if they did, most of the contracts involved pooling of resources, and made no provision for remedies upon termination of the relationship. Cohabitation agreements were "largely the province of the rich, the famous, the cynical and the once-burned."[58] Although some states refused to accept implied or verbal agreements as contracts, many did. Even if an implied contract was honored in theory, it was still hard to prove its existence. It was a "he said, she said" situation, a promise rarely made in front of witnesses. A judge could inquire into the circumstances of the couple to find out if there was an implied contract between them, but such inquiries were time consuming and the outcome ultimately depended on the prejudices of the judge. Moreover, the fact-finding inquiry was fraught with difficulty even for the most objective judge because couples rarely conceive of their relationship in contractual terms.[59] As one lawyer critical of the approach suggests, "a doctrine that directs courts to decide their disputes by looking for contract is unlikely to find one."[60] There are two other logical possibili-

ties for the legal recognition of cohabiting relationships other than promotion of marriage and no legal recognition of cohabitors' rights. First, a few
feminists in the United States and Canada favor abolition of legal marriage
and requiring all couples to draw up private contracts, putting all adult
relationships on an equal footing. Such a suggestion is accompanied by
the view that all social benefits should be based on individual entitlement
rather than family status, essentially a return to the situation prior to joint
income tax, medical coverage for dependents, and Social Security survivors'
benefits. If there are no relationships and no marriage, then there would
be no need for relationship contracts or for rules about the dissolution of
relationships. It is hard to decide whether the major objection to such a
proposal is that it is unfeasible or would prove hugely unpopular.

Second, most other developed countries do not rely on legal principles
of contract but instead impose a quasi-marital status on cohabitation—applying the approach of status rather than contract and thus bringing the law
closer to the old common-law standard. Countries such as Australia, New
Zealand, and Canada that have adopted such principles were responding
to rapid increases in cohabitation, often even more rapid than the United
States experienced. They were also cutting back on their welfare states, shifting the burden of public support onto the wealthier private party. Usually, a cohabiting couple was treated exactly the same as a marital couple
under rules for support (and sometimes for property division) after they
had cohabited for several years or had born a child together. Many of these
ascribed-status approaches also gave the cohabiting couple the right to opt
out of the provisions of the law through a private contract. The ascription
or status approach seemed to combine the liberalism of the recognition
of rights for those engaged in alternative lifestyles with the "family law of
the poor," imposing legal support obligations on the Lee Marvins and Bob
Hewitts of the relationship world. (In general, commentators think governments that use this approach seem to be motivated more by upholding
equality and tolerance than by saving the government money.)

Since making men pay was such a strong element of antiwelfare rhetoric
and child support enforcement in the United States since the 1960s, it at
first appears remarkable that American states with the exception of the states
of Washington and Nevada had not chosen the ascribed-status approach to
dissolution of cohabiting relationships.[61] The answer as to why they have
not done so appears twofold. First, American family law, even for the poor,
has explicitly rejected man-in-the-house and MARS (man assumed to be
responsible spouse) rules as an unfair application of the support rules of

family law. Second, the United States is committed to promoting legal marriage as social policy, which means not putting cohabitation on an equal legal footing with legal marriage.

The failure of Michelle Marvin to receive the rehabilitative alimony Judge Marshall awarded reveals sexual and gendered prejudices at work. The surge in women earning their own paychecks shrank the concept of alimony to a brief period of postrelationship retraining. One University of California lawyer, commenting on Judge Marshall's award of $104,000 to Michelle Marvin said, "I see no reason why Lee Marvin or any other non-relative should be made a patsy to save the California welfare department money."[62] However sympathetic the public might be toward the displaced homemaker, the sympathy did not extend to a woman who had lived in sin. To judges and the general public, homemaker services have economic value only if there is a marriage license.

The Significance of *Marvin*

To be sure, *Marvin* had cultural as well as legal significance, as the most publicized single case of cohabitation since LeClair. One linguist pronounced it a "wellspring of lexical creativity" since it led to the invention of the word *marvinizing* as a substitute for *cohabitation* and created a new term for cohabiting partner ("this is my marvin"). It is significant in American law as well since it represents an important instance of a cohabitor demanding legal rights. The plaintiffs in *Marvin*-type cases were mainly straight women, gay men, and lesbians who saw their demands as an extension of feminism and gay liberation. By attacking the idea that cohabitation was immoral, *Marvin* made a woman in a heterosexual couple or the more vulnerable party in a gay or lesbian couple into a rights-bearing citizen. Appearing on the steps of the courthouse was a sign of the decreasing stigma of cohabitation, but the continued characterization of the lawsuit as a "scandal" and the attack on her character Michelle Marvin endured in the courtroom took its toll.

But the most enduring significance of *Marvin* is that it left the glass much less than half filled. Before *Marvin*, cohabitors had no legal rights to sue each other at the termination of their relationship. Rights acquired are not the same as justice fulfilled, however. Cohabitors cannot use the same divorce procedures and property claims as married couples. Their relationships have fewer strings attached, but also fewer rights and obligations in legal proceedings against each other or third parties. By providing a contract rather than status remedy for the legal vulnerability of the weaker cohabiting party, *Marvin* offered an unworkable solution to dissolution of long-term cohabiting relationships. As Ann Laquer wrote, "with all of its celebrity, the Marvin decision stands more as a cultural icon than a legal watershed."[63]

Every legal advance for cohabitors is evaluated in terms of its impact on the institution of marriage—whether it weakens or strengthens marriage. There were too few palimony suits, and they proved too unworkable to constitute any threat to the institution of marriage. As the Swedish scholar Goran Lind writes, "There is no justification for maintaining that the legal effects of the Marvin doctrine constitute a principal alternative or threat against marriage" precisely because *Marvin* did not offer a very generous option for cohabitors.[64] It certainly makes sense not to cohabit in Illinois, but in fact, the unenforceability of contracts between cohabitors in the state appears to have done little to deter couples from living together. Most couples pay scant attention to legal rules in deciding whether to live together or whether to marry rather than cohabit.

Marvin and *Hewitt* are also significant as real-life examples of the effect of legal approaches on the lives of cohabitors. To ask whether a cohabiting couple would enjoy greater freedom under one or another approach presumes that the couple has a unity of interests. It is to protect one party against the other in the event of a dissolution of the relationship that legal rules are required. Should policy be designed to protect the weaker and more vulnerable parties and to impose fewer burdens on the public purse? But if those are indeed priorities, *Marvin* and *Hewitt* are case studies that prove that current legal approaches do not benefit the weaker party in a long-term cohabitation. The *Hewitt* case has the added advantage of providing evidence about the impact of such decisions on children. Although the Illinois Supreme Court held that cohabitation was harmful to children, the Hewitt daughters retorted that the law harmed them and their mother. Adult women fared badly in both cases. The more modern and less judgmental solution in *Marvin* offered no greater compensation than the moralistic defense of marriage in *Hewitt*. That many other countries adopt a third way, the ascription approach, suggests their greater acceptance of reality as well as their lesser faith in the principles of private contract. In essence, the ascription approach is a return to common-law marriage using different language as well as the prevailing wisdom of nineteenth-century judges, that the state should protect the weaker and more vulnerable party, precisely so that such parties do not make demands on the public purse.

Lee Marvin's agent said that the trial was good for the actor's career.[65] He died of a heart attack at age sixty-three in 1987, and the World War II veteran is buried in Arlington National Cemetery. Marvin Mitchelson, convicted of tax evasion, in 1996, went to a federal penitentiary, where he ran the prison law library and worked on appeals for fellow inmates. He emerged from his years of confinement considerably subdued, eventually resumed his law practice, and died in 2005. Michelle Marvin received a large advance from a publisher for her personal story, but she never wrote it. While working as a secretary for the William Morris Agency in Los Angeles, she met the comedian and recovering alcoholic Dick Van Dyke, who was a client of the agency. They began a relationship, probably in 1976, a year before the trial to determine whether she and Lee had an enforceable contract. In 1980, she was arrested for shoplifting two bras and three sweaters from Robinson's department store in Beverly Hills. She was fined $250 and placed on probation for six months; Mitchelson represented her.[66] Van Dyke gave her a small part in an episode of his TV series *Diagnosis Murder* in 1993. The credits listed her as Michelle Triola. The couple never married, but Mitchelson drew up a palimony agreement for them, and they remained together for thirty-three years, until she died at their Malibu home of lung cancer in October 2009 at the age of seventy-five. She always insisted on the historical significance of her fight for cohabitors' rights and her contribution to the cause of women's rights. But at the dinner table and in the press, she was referred to as a concubine, a jilted mistress, and a paramour, and the best Judge Marshall could do is call her a "longtime companion."

As the 1970s were ending, there were two rival solutions to the legal status of cohabitors, the conservative one of punishing cohabitation to promote marriage (as exemplified in *Hewitt*) and the liberal one of recognizing the cohabiting relationship using principles of contract law (as exemplified in *Marvin*). Liberalism was far preferable, but ironically resulted in a return to the mutual blaming involved in fault divorce while failing to provide a remedy for the more vulnerable party. Thus, even when a liberal court tried to use the law to keep pace with the reality of the growth of cohabitation, the proposed solution turned out to be unworkable.

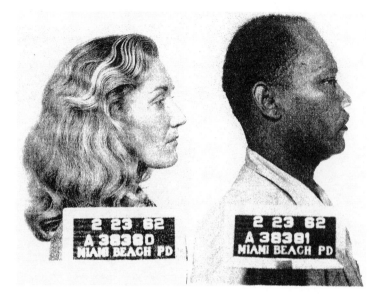

1. The Miami Beach police department took these booking photographs of Connie Hoffman and Dewey McLaughlin, who were arrested for the crime of being a "Negro man and white woman habitually living together in the nighttime" in April of 1962. Courtesy of Miami Beach Police Department.

2. Sylvester Smith held her granddaughter while her children and a nephew stood behind her at their house in Selma, Alabama, a few months after the US Supreme Court ruled in her favor, holding that she, her children, and granddaughter were unconstitutionally denied state welfare aid. Courtesy of Redux Pictures.

3. A Barnard College student signs out for the night as her date looks on,
Brooks Hall, ca. 1960. Courtesy of the Barnard College Archives.

4. A year after he began to live with Michelle Triola, Lee Marvin won an
Academy Award for best actor. Courtesy of Getty Images.

5. After the student protests at Columbia and Barnard ended in the spring of 1968, LeClair and Behr remained in New York City and posed on campus for a photographer from *Life* magazine. Courtesy of *Life, Inc.*/See Your World LLC.

6. When Yale law students Bill Clinton and Hillary Rodham took summer jobs in the Bay Area, they shared a small place near a park. Upon returning to Yale, they rented an apartment together close to campus.
Courtesy of the William J. Clinton Presidential Library.

7. Joni Mitchell's "My Old Man" was the first statement in favor of cohabitation in American popular music. The refrain in her song went, "we don't need no piece of paper from the city hall keeping us tried and true." Readers of *Rolling Stone* understood the song was autobiographical because the magazine revealed that Mitchell had recently purchased a house with British-born rock star Graham Nash.
Courtesy of Henry Diltz Photographs.

'Rec' Director, Decko, Resigns

, Charged Friday afternoon with a moral's offense, Sheboygan Director of Public Recreation James E. Decko has resigned.

His resignation, tendered shortly before 4 p.m. Friday after a warrant charging lewd and lascivious conduct was served on him, was accepted unanimously and without comment at a special meeting this morning of the Sheboygan Board of Education.

Decko, 30, head of the Department of Public Recreation the past four years, was divorced by his wife last month on grounds of cruel and inhuman treatment.

Friday he and Martha Judy Sampson, 23, a local elementary art instructor, were charged with "openly cohabitating" at an apartment at 2612 Erie Ave. from June 1-21 as Mr. and Mrs. James E. Decko.

They are scheduled to appear before Judge John G. Buchen on the charge at 9 a.m. next Friday.

In his letter of resignation, Decko wrote: "Because of ancient and archaic laws I am guilty of a misdemeanor which the Board of Education will have no sympathy with."

"It is with sadness that I submit my resignation to you as director of recreation.

"I have enjoyed working with you."

- The resignation was accepted, effective 5 p.m. Friday.

The department's second-in-command, Steve Stauber, will

James E. Decko

8. The *Sheboygan News* routinely published names and addresses of residents arrested for cohabitation, but on the inside of the paper and without a photo. James Decko's arrest for cohabitation and resignation from his job as park director was front-page news. Courtesy of *Sheboygan News*.

with sliding doors, new tubes, $175. Call 684-3967.

MAPLE DINING ROOM TABLE 60"x40" with 12" leaf. 4 spindle back chairs, one arm chair, $90. 443-1159.

MAYTAG GAS DRYER. 3 years old, coppertone, $125. Call 684-1304.

NEW 30" gas range, $125. New 30" electric automatic range, $185. New 14 cubic foot 2 door refrigerator, $195. All 3 are avocado. Cash and carry at Mobile Manner, Pittsfield-Lenox Road. Dial 442-6815.

RCA WHIRLPOOL REFRIGERATOR good condition $50. Gas grill, good condition, $50. 655-8126.

Rock Maple Bedroom Set
Double bed,
bureau, mirror
chest of drawers,
night stand.

TOP QUALITY
442-2426 after 5:30

RUGS, REMNANTS, ends of rolls. Quality carpets at reasonable prices. Shea's Rugs and Upholstery, 186 Wahconah St. Dial 447-7048.

SALE ON RUG REMNANTS. Save 40 to 50%. New England Furniture, 117 Fourth Street.

SCISSORS SHARPENED 99c
WILLIAMS SEWING CENTER
Downtown Pittsfield. 442-1401

One extra large room semi-private bath $90 monthly. Call owner 1—243-9709.

ONE ROOM FOR RENT. 711 Tyler Street, near GE. Clean, reasonable. Gentlemen only. Apply Mr. Monette, Apartment 2. 499-1229.

ONE ROOM FOR RENT. 771 Tyler Street, near GE. Clean, reasonable. Gentlemen only. Apply Mr. Monette, Apartment 2. 499-1229.

PRIVATE ROOMS. Parking, all utilities. Dial 443-0673 or 443-1212.

Mobilehome Rentals 108

MOBILEHOME on Pittsfield-Lenox Road. 1 bedroom, security required, no unmarried couples, $120 monthly. 499-3281.

Apartment Rentals 115

BROWN STREET, 68. 3 rooms, heat, hot water, electricity, stove and refrigerator, second floor rear, no pets, $120 a month. COWELL REALTY, 442-3913.

BURBANK STREET, 89. First floor 4 room apartment. Does not include heat or electric. $125 month. 447-7757.

CENTRAL, large room efficiency, modern 3 rooms. Tyler Street. References, security. 443-0167.

COLONIAL GARDENS. Luxurious 1

September 3 till June. $350 plus ties and security.

MARCIL REALTY
443-6641 or 442-0415

Office Space

AGGIE BANK
North Street, individual or and professional suites.
RUFFER REALTORS, 445-5641

CHOICE PROFESSIONAL South Street. 1100 sq. ft., ground air conditioned, parking. Dial

PLEASANT TWO ROOM SUITE on second floor corner and West Housatonic Streets. mately 450 sq. ft., low rent parking. Dial 445-4597 morning

PROFESSIONAL SPACE AVAILABLE For rent in West Stockbridge tion. There are now availab for lawyers, doctors, account surance companies in newly buildings on Main Street, W bridge Associates, Box 1 Stockbridge, Mass. 01266. 413—232-7044, 413—232-7077.

THREE ROOM SUITE. Pan carpeted. Also single offices. Street. SECUNDA REALTY.

3 ROOM SUITE, North Street First National Store. Reason Available July 1. Dial 445-4589

9. It is still not against the law to discriminate against cohabitors in housing. Most typical advertisements making discrimination explicit appeared in classified advertisements from owners who lived on the premises or rented out mobile homes and did not want tenants who fit the stereotype of "trailer trash." Courtesy of *Berkshire Eagle*.

Oct. 3-9, 1978
Section 10

CHICAGO TRIBUNE
TV WEEK

'ALL'S FAIR'

10. Known for sitcoms involving characters engaged in culture war, TV producer
Norman Lear made *All's Fair* (1976–1977) about a May-December romance
between a middle-aged, conservative, sexist columnist and a young,
feminist photographer. Halfway into the series' one-season run,
Bernadette Peters's character moved into the townhouse
of the columnist, portrayed by Richard Crenna.

"Look, it's nothing to be ashamed of.
We chose to get married before living together."

11. In this cartoon published in 1975, cohabitation, not legal marriage, was portrayed as the norm for the sophisticated readers of *New Woman*, a popular magazine targeted at feminists. Courtesy of Joseph Farris.

"WE BOUGHT AN APARTMENT TOGETHER.
MAYBE WE'LL GET MARRIED.
MAYBE WE WON'T.
ANYWAY, IT'S A GOOD INVESTMENT."

12. A large apartment complex in Rosslyn, Virginia, River Place explicitly marketed apartments for cohabitors in this advertisement in the *Washington Post* in 1982. After being told that cohabitation was illegal in Virginia, they decided to pull the ad. Courtesy of River Place.

13. In 1982, Scott Thorsen, an animal trainer and chauffeur for Liberace, sued for
$110 million in palimony, claiming that he and Liberace had an implicit contract
for his support in the event of a breakup. The lawsuit publicly outed Liberace,
who had always denied he was gay. But Thorsen lost his suit and
four years later accepted a $95,000 settlement.

14. New York City mayor Michael Bloomberg attending a celebrity fund-raiser with
Diana Taylor and Robert DeNiro and his wife. Bloomberg was the first major
politician who was an "open cohabitor," since he was living at his Upper East
Side townhouse with Diana Taylor. Although sometimes referred to as
a "gal pal" or "girlfriend" of Bloomberg, Taylor was also called the
"First Lady of New York City" by the time Bloomberg was
sworn in as mayor.

15. By 2005, the US government was spending $5 million a year for marriage-promotion advertisements displayed on buses and subways. The fine print on this ad, appearing on the L train between Brooklyn and Manhattan read "engagement ring, wedding ring, snoring. . . . Find marriage and relationship tools to help you along your path to happily ever after."

EIGHT

Mothers on Trial

In March of 1980, the CBS weekly news program *60 Minutes* aired a segment about a divorced mother, Jacqueline Jarrett, age thirty-eight, of Mount Prospect, Illinois. Jarrett had lost custody of her three daughters to her ex-husband who charged that his ex-wife was providing his daughters with an immoral upbringing because her boyfriend, Wayne Hammon, had moved in with her. In December of 1979, Illinois judges had ruled in the husband's favor and removed the girls from the custody of their mother. At her lawyer's suggestion, Jacqueline Jarrett was seeking favorable publicity in order to persuade the US Supreme Court to hear an appeal of her case. Both Jarrett and her ex-husband Walter were willing to be interviewed on *60 Minutes* to present their point of view. Morley Safer asked the ex-husband, "Do you regard the manner in which Jacqueline lives, your ex-wife lives, as living in sin?" Walter Jarrett answered. "I would consider that to be so, for me, yes."[1] Safer turned to Jacqueline Jarrett and asked her if there was anything she would like to tell the justices of the US Supreme Court. Looking into the camera she pleaded, "Give me my children back." The camera crew finished filming, and Jacqueline Jarrett burst into tears.[2]

She did not get her wish; in 1980, the US Supreme Court declined to hear her case. After the refusal of the Court to hear her appeal, a subdued Jackie Jarrett was interviewed on a Chicago television program. She now said, "Knowing what I know . . . that I would have lost my children, Wayne wouldn't live with me." She added, "Wayne and I would do anything if it would get the kids back. . . . If getting married would guarantee getting my children back, I would get married."[3] Occurring in the midst of the divorce wars, her case pitted judicial defense of family values against her definition of her household, which included her boyfriend and her daughters, as a family. Most cohabitors had warded off threats to modification of child custody by undergoing the marriage cure, by marrying their boyfriends. Jacqueline Jarrett had initially asserted her right not to do have to do so and still retain custody of her daughters. The taming of Jackie Jarrett was a courtroom battle of the culture wars, feminism versus family values, in which family values won.

In addition to college student housing rules, child custody was the other area of cohabitation that required disciplinary authorities to come to grips with the changing role of women, from straight divorced mothers with a live-in boyfriend to lesbian mothers with a resident partner. Wives fleeing unhappy marriages saw themselves as taking back their lives. Divorced mothers were clearly engaged in a largely invisible fight for women's sexual freedom, and by the middle of the 1980s, it seemed that they were winning. First, they had to sustain several losses before going on to victory, including in the courts of the state of Illinois. Illinois was the only northern state that had not ratified the Equal Rights Amendment (ERA), was one of only two states that—in order to defend the family—did not permit no-fault divorce, and was home to the leading opponent of the ERA, Phyllis Schlafly. The court had issued a double-barreled barrage against cohabitation that year, first ruling in September against Victoria Hewitt in finding that in Illinois contract rights between cohabitors were unenforceable (see chapter 7) and then in December denying child custody to Jacqueline Jarrett.

Between 1976 and 1980, the culture wars had spread from local hot spots such as Dade County, Florida, to national conferences, politics, and film. The New Right strategist Paul Weyrich, who had made known his opposition to defining cohabitors as a family, had coined a new term for a political action group of evangelical Christians: the Moral Majority. They insisted that there was a moral consensus in the country that should be enforced by politicians and the courts. The very fact that politicians and courts had departed from this goal was, in their view, partially responsible for the breakdown of the American family. Ideological conservatives broadened their political power by joining forces with the Religious Right in opposition to feminism. Conservative Christian women believed God had called them to defend the family. In July 1980, the Republican Party platform affirmed "our belief in the traditional role and values of the family in our society." As the defeat of the ERA loomed, it appeared that the backlash was growing. Disapproval of cohabitation seemed not to be confined to the Christian Right since Jimmy Carter had already made clear that he was opposed to it and encouraged federal employees to stop living together and get married (see chapter 6).

The *Jarrett* case was not only the most publicized case of a cohabiting mother but also the most (and as far as one can tell, the only) politicized case of cohabitation. The Democratic candidate for state supreme court had ruled in favor of Jackie Jarrett on appeal. Child custody decisions rarely surfaced in elections. But the Republican candidate for state supreme court believed that he had found a political issue that would resonate with the public mood. In Illinois, judges were elected; the justices who ruled against Jacqueline Jarrett were Republicans, and those who voted for her were Democrats. The subject of "open fornication" became a matter of debate between the Republican and Democratic candidate for justice of the Illinois Supreme Court in 1980, with the Republican candidate condemning his Democratic opponent as "immoral" because he had ruled in favor of Jacqueline Jarrett in appellate court. The Republican judicial candidate thought that he could use cohabitation to his advantage; he insisted that Cook County voters wanted a judge who decided cases based on morality. The election was highly partisan. While the nation turned rightward with the election of Ronald Reagan, Jimmy Carter carried Cook County, and the judge who believed that Jackie Jarrett should retain custody won a position on the state supreme court (and eventually became its chief justice).

By 1983, with a slightly different composition of justices, the Illinois Supreme Court reversed itself and claimed that it had never ruled that cohabitation was an absolute bar to custody. The *Jarrett* case was like a fever of family values, and the fever seems to have broken for most northern states, with the exception of Michigan, where cohabitation is still illegal, and, up to 1989, in Rhode Island. State by state, judges were making fewer moral pronouncements against cohabitation from the bench, apparently acceding to the reality of cohabitation among both divorced parents. The gap between reality and law was closing, at least as it concerned child custody, in fact, more so in child custody than in other areas of law, precisely because the courts were overwhelmed by the prevalence of cohabitation. Nonetheless, to this day in a few Mormon-dominated and a handful of southern states, judges still condemn immorality, and, if not ordering a change of custody because of cohabitation, will still order cessation of alimony or a ban on overnight visitation because of it.

Prejudice against gay and lesbian parents was declining by the 1980s, but was so much more virulent than that against cohabiting straight parents to begin with, the outrages so much more common, that the legal battles had to be more organized within the gay community and the assistance of academic experts and outside legal organizations was virtually required to win. In the 1970s, gay male and lesbian parents—mostly lesbian mothers—were for the first time revealing their sexual identity and fighting to hold onto child custody against a straight parent. Many lesbians, divorced mothers who had been granted child custody, risked forfeiting their children if they came out. They often lost child custody and had limited visitation rights, such as not being allowed to have their children with them in the house if they had a roommate, even if not a lover. Lesbian and gay parents not only faced far greater prejudice than straight cohabiting parents, but initially enjoyed far less success in the courts. They made their struggles into a cause for the entire gay community, contacted scholarly experts to testify on their behalf, and solicited friend of the court briefs from gay rights organizations. For gay and lesbian parents, securing child custody from the courts was part of the first phase in the struggle for the recognition of gay relationships, an initial stage on the road to domestic-partner statutes and recognition of the legal right to marry.

Legal Standards and Practice in Disputed Divorce

Family law was statute law, passed by the states, with the state trial court judges who heard these cases having broad latitude in arriving at their decisions. Judges relied on (or more literally referred to) state laws and general standards in making their decisions. Judicial and legislative preference for the father or mother as the custodial parent underwent huge swings of the pendulum over the course of a couple of centuries. From the colonial period through the mid-nineteenth century, fathers had an absolute right to custody of their children, not because children were considered paternal property but because it was believed that fathers provided the best moral guidance. By the 1840s, the common-law presumption in favor of fathers could be modified if the children were very young ("of tender years"). The idea was that young children (younger than six) needed to be breast-fed and required a mother's love—provided the mother was a moral woman. In a sense, judges came to believe that maternal love trumped paternal guidance, perhaps because what they emphasized most about fathers was not their moral leadership but their status as breadwinners who must provide support. Maternal custody was in the best interests of the child, judges claimed. The women's movement of the 1970s, insisting upon equality between men and women in the family as well as society, had a profound impact on child custody standards. Gradually, the best interests of the child became the prevailing standard, with most states passing legislation that formally adopted a gender-neutral version of this standard in the 1970s.[4]

Cohabitation entered into divorce settlements in several ways, as a bargaining chip for the noncohabiting parent prior to the divorce, or in a modification of custody after a judge had already made a decision (the situation with the Jarretts), or having to do with alimony or visitation for the noncustodial parent.[5] Punishing cohabitation in a divorce case usually affected the mother more than the father because she was the parent most likely to have custody and thus most in danger of losing it because of cohabitation; most fathers did not have custody but were granted visitation. Charges and countercharges emerged subsequent to divorce as part of an ongoing struggle between divorced parents. Simply because the wife had fewer economic resources to sustain a legal battle, it made sense that more of these cohabitation suits arose at the husband's initiative and involved a cohabiting wife. The common pattern was that the boyfriend was living with the mother or was staying over several nights a week. An ex-husband noticed the boyfriend at his wife's place and hired a private detective, or the wife, like Jackie Jarrett, informed her ex that her boyfriend was moving in. On occasion, a woman had become pregnant by her "paramour," and her pregnancy became a symbol of immorality and "illegitimacy." A father might tell a trial court judge that he thinks his son should not "be living with his mother when she is living in sin."[6] Wives as well as husbands were also using the threat of a custody fight or a restriction on visitation as a means of controlling each other's sex lives. Thus, for example, a former husband felt that he had the right to tell his ex-wife how to live. Occasionally, a father, who gained possession of a child under his visitation rights, refused to return the child to the mother because of her cohabitation and then brought suit for custody.

Custody conflicts were rare among the poor primarily because few poor fathers wanted responsibility for a child. Moreover, a contested custody case was an expensive conflict to engage in. Thus, former partners like the Jarretts who were willing to take their fight all the way to the US Supreme Court were quite rare. In most cases, the couple contemplating divorce settled the matter out of court, if for no other reason than that the cost of legal fees was so high. A matrimonial lawyer, who charged by the hour, usually billed about three thousand dollars and up in the typical disputed child custody case at the time of *Jarrett*. Therefore, parents tended to compromise; only about one in ten divorces involving children ever went to trial, and of those only a small group of disputes was appealed.[7] *Jarrett v. Jarrett* was not a disputed divorce, but instead a suit for the modification of child custody filed on the grounds that circumstances had fundamentally altered since the divorce.

Whatever way one looked at it, the courts were clogged with several million divorce suits in the 1970s. The divorce rate reached an all-time high in the late 1970s—an indication of the difficulties men and women had in adjusting to the rising expectations and different understandings of marriage created by feminism, the growth of women's employment, and the sexual revolution. More of these divorcing couples had children, who were then being exposed to cohabitation. The courts were also filled with cases involving cohabitation because fathers were fighting back against the automatic assumption that the mother should be given preference in child custody. While father's rights cases generally involved legally married men, the US Supreme Court in *Stanley v. Illinois* (1973) recognized that men did not have to legally marry in order to claim legal rights to visitation and custody of their children. The number of such custody disputes was relatively small, but definitely rising. For example, disputed child custody cases in Minnesota rose from 5 percent of divorces in 1970 to 14 percent in 1979.[8] Fathers were taking a more active, even aggressive role in seeking custody of children after a divorce.[9] They were forming associations such as ADAM (the American Divorce Association for Men), the Second Wives Coalition, and Fathers United for Rights to press for their claims to child custody. Fathers believed divorce laws discriminated against men. Such fathers were not only bringing more appeals but also were succeeding more often, although the figures about their rate of success vary widely from a high of 51 percent in one study in the 1980s to a figure closer to 20 percent in research conducted in the next decade.[10] Perhaps the odds were highly variable, and a father was never quite sure whether to believe he had a good chance of winning, which is why a lawyer's advice was so central.

Trial court judges in their role as moral guardians of the community not only denounced sin from the bench but also imposed rules of sexual behavior. A good lawyer advised his or her client not to cohabit prior to the custody decision, and, in cases of modification of custody, to remove the boyfriend from the home or marry him.[11] They coached female clients to testify that they had been morally wrong to live with a man. Moreover, a mother did herself no good if her boyfriend moved out right before the trial and she was forced to admit on the stand that she had kicked him out on her lawyer's advice, not because of any genuine moral awakening.[12] Judges were also very punitive toward visitation. Some judges did not believe the girlfriend or boyfriend should be present when the child was visiting. Judge

Francis William Lanam of the Superior Court of San Mateo County denied Anne Holman, a divorced mother, visitation with her children in 1980. His Q&A with Holman provides evidence of the kind of moral acquiescence required of a chastened mother.

Q. You don't think it would be appropriate to confine your relationship to the daytime or to some premises away from your own home if you are going to have extramarital relationships considering the benefit of the children.

A. Yes.

Q. So if you are allowed custody of the children, then this would be one of the understandings you will agree to?

A. Yes.

Q. No more over-night visitation unless you are married, and if you are going to take some relationship, then it should be on some other premises?

A. Uh-huh. I understand what you are saying.[13]

Attitudes toward the Cohabiting Mother

The taming of the cohabiting mother was actually a familiar trope in fiction and film by the time of the *Jarrett* case. The understanding of cohabitation as sin and the cohabiting mother as marked with a scarlet letter *A* underlay popular attitudes and judicial thinking. Harold Robbins translated popular attitudes into trashy melodrama when he wrote *When Love Has Gone* (1962), subsequently made into an Academy Award–nominated film in 1964 in which Bette Davis played the disapproving grandmother and Susan Hayward her wayward divorced daughter who had taken a live-in lover. Davis's most memorable line in the film was "somewhere along the line the world has lost all of its standards and all of its tastes." Robbins liked to paste together celebrity gossip to create his novels, and in the case of *Love*, he took his story from the celebrated murder trial of Cheryl Crane, the fourteen-year-old daughter of the Hollywood star Lana Turner. Turner had fallen in love with a minor Los Angeles mobster, Johnny Stompanato, who liked to show off his chest hair and abs by wearing his shirts open to the waist. She had recently settled into a Coldwater Canyon mansion, and Stompanato had moved in. Cheryl heard her mother screaming, grabbed a kitchen knife, opened the door of her mother's bedroom and inadvertently thrust the knife into Stompanato's chest, killing him instantly. The Hollywood rumor mill whispered that Lana Turner herself had murdered her lover and allowed her daughter to stand trial because a minor would never be sentenced to prison for homicide. If it was possible, Robbins's novel increased the melodrama of the murder trial. Robbins also changed the details slightly, so that the cohabiting mother became a sculptress with an insatiable sexual appetite whose first husband divorced her when he caught her in bed with another man. Robbins added an Oedipal twist in which the mother and her teenage daughter are both having sexual affairs with the live-in lover; distraught over her daughter's rejection, the mother, like Tolstoy's Anna Karenina, committed suicide. In real life, the Stompanato murder was declared a justifiable homicide, and Crane was made a ward of state and sent to a home for problem girls. In 1958, when the Cheryl Crane murder trial grabbed the headlines, it was easy to conclude that a mother's promiscuity led to the ruin of her daughter and a man's death.[14]

The cultural anxiety about the sexually liberated divorced mother continued unabated through the next two decades. Almost as if she followed the Jarrett case, Sue Miller's first novel, *The Good Mother* (1986), took cohabitation one step further, by portraying the situation of two divorced parents, both of whom were cohabiting after they split up. Her novel, which sold 1.2 million copies, was adapted to the screen the next year in a film starring Diane Keaton and Liam Neeson.[15] In the *Good Mother*, Anna Dunlap, a divorced piano teacher living in Cambridge, Massachusetts, with her young daughter, finds happiness with a new lover. For a brief period, she, the new man in her life, and her four-year-old daughter, Molly, seem to have become a new kind of perfect family. But Anna Dunlap's life is shattered when her ex-husband calls her to say that he is keeping custody of their daughter and taking her to court. On one occasion, it appears the live-in boyfriend had allowed the little girl to touch his penis. Even though the father in the novel had lived with his girlfriend before remarrying, the courts considered his remarriage proof that he could provide a more suitable living environment. The mother does little to fight her husband in court and instead blames herself for the loss of custody of her daughter.

The *Jarrett* Case

Jarrett v. Jarrett seemed to be not only a real-life version of these novels and films but also the story behind the doubling of the divorce rate between 1966 and 1980; a pretty housewife who married relatively young and lacks a sense of self undergoes a divorce, finds a job, and meets a new sensitive man. On *60 Minutes*, Jarrett described her "three-year nightmare" of a custody battle with her ex-husband, Walter, a chemist and former Army Reservist whom she had married in a Catholic church in Niles, Illinois, when she was twenty and he was twenty-six. The next year she had given birth to the first of her three daughters, who were born within the space of five years. The fact that the girls were being raised Catholic entered the arguments made by Walter Jarrett's lawyers. The girls' religious and moral education was not neglected, but it was highly contradictory. Their mother was dropping them off at CCD (Confraternity of Christian Doctrine) classes on Saturday, and their father was taking them to Mass on Saturday night or Sunday morning. But Walter Jarrett believed that his ex-wife was violating the teachings of the church, which held that fornication was "a mortal sin."[16]

Walter Jarrett had his anchor in his faith, but Jackie was changing. She grew up in the suburbs of Chicago, the daughter of an alcoholic mother and a long-suffering father who was a tool-and-die maker. After graduating from high school, she took a job as a secretary at a chemical company, where she met Walter. After they married, she quit her job and became a full-time homemaker and mother of three girls. In her late twenties, she discovered that she felt unfulfilled. She stopped bleaching her hair blonde and reverted back to her natural hair color, dark brown. Although she was seeing a therapist and beginning to take college courses, she was still unhappy. Discovering that her relationship with Walter was "paternal," she "realized she did not want a father any more."[17] As part of her divorce, she was awarded custody of their three daughters, then ages twelve, ten, and seven. A coworker at the office where she worked as a secretary introduced her to Wayne Hammon, a quality-control manager for a chemical company. He was a lanky divorcé seven years younger than she, with thick glasses, a moustache, a heavy black beard, and sideburns. Four months after the divorce, Jarrett informed her husband that she was selling some of the furniture to make room for Wayne's things. She asked her daughters if it was all right if Wayne lived with them. They told her that they were not "overly enthused" and asked if she was getting married. She told them she wasn't planning to marry, but they offered no objections. Wayne moved in and was soon paying the girls' allowances and helping them with their homework.

Conservative judges perceived cohabitation as a threat to marriage, morality, and the family and were quick to discern in Jackie Jarrett's doubts about the benefits of matrimony a feminist critique of the institution of marriage. The initial lawyer for Jackie Jarrett and Wayne Hammon should have warned them not to hold hands in the courtroom of Judge Marion E. Burks, a conservative Republican and former state legislator whose reputation had been somewhat tarnished by corruption charges brought against the insurance company he headed. Jarrett took the stand and explained why she chose not to marry. She was afraid of getting divorced for a second time, having only been divorced from Walter Jarrett for four months when Wayne began to live with her. She said, "I just wasn't ready to remarry, and I certainly didn't want a forced marriage."[18] Wayne had also been divorced for three years and was not ready to remarry either. Jackie Jarrett was also trying to provide stability for her daughters. In her divorce agreement, she was required to sell the house six months after remarrying and divide the net proceeds with her ex-husband or sell when the youngest child turned nineteen. The girls wanted to remain in their home, and she and Wayne did not have the money to buy the house or move to another one in Mount Prospect. Jacqueline Jarrett made matters worse by telling the court, "I don't believe a marriage license makes a relationship between two people. It's [sic] doesn't guarantee anything." Wayne Hammon further testified that he saw "no moral wrong in living with Jackie." He explained that he told the children it was "morally proper" to live with Jackie so long as they two loved each other, and he further indicated that he and Jackie had no intentions to marry.[19]

Jackie Jarrett had been lulled into a false complacency by lawyers who counseled her that she could retain custody of her daughters without making Wayne move out. In order to alter custody once it had been awarded, it had to be shown that there was a significant change in circumstances since the decision had been made. Her initial attorneys told her that the legal standard in Illinois was that the husband had to show that the children were suffering current harm for the court to order a modification of custody. They reassured her that a judge would not take away the children but would at most order Wayne to move out or tell her to get married. In fact, what her lawyers were telling her was standard practice in many states, but not in Illinois. Judge Burks was clearly offended by Jarrett and Hammon using the word *moral*, and he used it as well to justify a change of custody for the "moral and spiritual well-being and development" of the girls. Jackie Jarrett's lawyer put no expert witnesses on the stand, and the girls were not questioned. After only forty-five minutes, Judge Burks ruled against Jacqueline Jarrett and ordered the children removed to Walter's custody. (She was still allowed visitation of the girls, which meant that they had dinner with her and Wayne on Tuesday nights and slept there on Friday nights.) After the ruling, Jacqueline Jarrett broke down in the courtroom and collapsed. Walter Jarrett was upset enough to offer a deal after the hearing, that if Wayne moved out, he would not follow through on taking custody of the girls. Apparently, Jacqueline Jarrett refused the offer, after which the parents proceeded to the three-judge Illinois Appellate Court. Jackie Jarrett calculated (rightly) that she could win on appeal, without having to force Wayne to move out or marry her.

The appellate court reversed Burks's decision, ruling that he had failed to show that Jackie Jarrett's daughters suffered any harm because their mother was living with Wayne Hammon. The appellate court judge Seymour Simon in a concurring opinion wrote that he thought that Burks had decided the case not on the basis of the best interests of the children but rather on his own moral opposition to cohabitation.

Walter Jarrett responded by taking the case to the Illinois Supreme Court, which ruled against Jackie Jarrett for two main reasons. The first was that Illinois, like Wisconsin next door, had a law making open and notorious cohabitation a crime. Jarrett was never arrested for committing the crime of open and notorious cohabitation because, unlike in Wisconsin, in Illinois the law was never enforced. What made her behavior "open and notorious" was that she had informed Walter, the neighbors, and the members of her sewing circle that she and Wayne were living together. The Illinois Supreme Court, as a bastion of traditional family values, ruled that engaging in the act of open and notorious cohabitation, even while not being charged with a Class B misdemeanor, not only violated the moral standards of the community "but also encourages others to violate those standards, and debases public morality." By engaging in what constituted criminal conduct, Jackie Jarrett sent the message to her daughters that she may "contravene statutorily declared standards of conduct." The second reason for the Court's decision was that Illinois law held that judges could modify custody in the first two years after a divorce if they had "reason to believe that the child's present environment may endanger seriously his physical, moral or emotional health." At the same time, the law also said that judges should weigh the removal of the child as against "the harm likely to be caused by a change of environment."[20]

If the decision was a reflection of backlash against feminism, the debate about the decision reflected attitudes about feminism among the public and on the editorial pages of newspapers. Feminists saw Jacqueline Jarrett as a heroine because she fought so hard to keep her daughters, framed her fight in terms of women's rights, and had a critique of traditional marriage. Divorced mothers appear to have been on her side, as in the instance of a New Jersey woman who wrote that her "mother's heart is with you." But there were many other women who believed that Jarrett was immoral and that if she really cared about her children, she would have gotten married. Phyllis Schlafly, who was leading the Stop ERA campaign to defeat ratification of the ERA in the Illinois legislature, denounced Jarrett as an immoral mother and supported the election of judges who would rule against sin.[21]

Jacqueline Jarrett was treated far better by editorial writers outside the state of Illinois. It was to be expected that editorials in the *Los Angeles Times* or the *Boston Globe* would defend her on the grounds that cohabitation among divorced mothers was a reality of contemporary life and would sharply criticize judges for "capricious, arbitrary, and punitive" thinking in custody decisions. But the *Kokomo Tribune* in Indiana also came to her defense because the editorial board thought that the new family in which she was raising her daughters might "well be healthier and happier" than a conflict-ridden home of married parents "where bitterness, hatred, intolerance and abuse abide."[22]

The most influential newspaper in Illinois, however, not only backed the Illinois Supreme Court's decision but saw itself in a role in many ways similar to that of the courts, as a guardian of public morality. To the *Chicago Tribune*, Jackie Jarrett was a stubborn woman who refused to marry Wayne Hammon or evict him from her home so that she could keep custody of her children. The paper's editorial board approved of the state supreme court's decision denying Jarrett custody because it "expressed moral standards of the state." They saw the case as an issue of marriage promotion, of whether the state should promote marriage and morality. The *Tribune*'s editorial argued that it was far preferable for a court to say "that marriage matters" rather than "saying that marriage does not matter."[23]

As it turns out, the voters in Cook County did not agree with the *Tribune*'s editorial stance. The justices of the Illinois Supreme Court were elected, rather than appointed, from various districts in the state; Cook County elected three justices. The recently vacated state supreme court seat for Cook County was popularly considered the Polish-American seat on the state supreme court. The Republican candidate, Robert Sklodowski, was pro-life, wanted to close down *Playboy* magazine, and hoped to make the *Jarrett* case a major issue in his campaign. His Democratic opponent was Seymour Simon, the Mathew Tobriner of Illinois, a Jew and New Dealer, a former Chicago alderman noted for his independence of the Daley machine. For the first time, the courtesy stigma about cohabitation extended to a judge, a longtime married man, because he had ruled in favor of a cohabiting mother retaining child custody. Sklodowski called Simon immoral and antifamily and said that Simon's concurring opinion in the appellate court (discussed earlier in this chapter) showed that Simon "has condoned Mrs. Jarrett's actions of openly living with a lover." Simon countered by claiming that his "opponent is trying to make the first Supreme Court election in history turn on the subject of fornication."[24] Jackie Jarrett was so upset by the attention to her private life that she begged the candidates not to discuss her case. She told a reporter, "I wish they'd stop and think how the people feel, especially the children."[25] The Democrats carried Cook County in 1980, but Simon ran ahead of Jimmy Carter at the top of the ticket, which he attributed to public reaction against his opponent's personal attacks on him.[26]

Illinois Supreme Court Changes Its Mind

Four years after *Jarrett*, the justices of the Illinois Supreme Court reversed themselves. But even before 1983, appellate court justices were backing away from *Jarrett* because they considered it too harsh or unenforceable. In 1983, the Illinois Supreme Court ruled on a disputed custody case in which the father had two successive live-in girlfriends, the second of whom became his third wife. The court held that a father's sexual relationship with a woman was insufficient reason to modify his custody of his son. In *In re Marriage of Thompson*, the court decided that "the *Jarrett* case does not establish a conclusive presumption that, because a custodial parent cohabits with a member of the opposite sex, the child is harmed. No such presumption exists in this State."[27] Headlines in the *Herald* of Mount Prospect, Illinois, conveyed the change in attitudes. In 1979, the newspaper was not sure what to think about the Jarrett family; its headline about the case asked, "Is Live-In Custody Harmful?" Four years later, the paper's headline on the 1983 *Thompson* decision read, "Ruling Means Sex Life Won't Cost Parent Child Custody."[28] On this case, the *Chicago Tribune* had no opinion.

The reversal of *Jarrett* was all the more remarkable because Thompson was an unsavory character; he was a truck driver with a reputation for dishonesty. One witness testified that he "took various salvage items" from his job, and he had admitted to forging the couple's IRS refund check. An Illinois Appellate Court judge described him as "a patent bully who will use any means to obtain his way."[29] After his second wife, Kathryn Allen, learned that he had been sleeping with "a female business associate," possibly a woman at the trucking company, she left him, taking their three-year-old son, Daniel, with her to her parents' home. She stayed with her parents briefly before moving into a battered women's shelter in Saginaw, Michigan. While her husband went to the Illinois courts, which granted him temporary custody of Daniel, she gained temporary custody in a Michigan court. Her husband wanted his son and hired a detective to track Kathryn down. He kidnapped Daniel as he was walking on a street in Saginaw with his mother, taking him back to the small town in southern Illinois where he had been living. Thompson had met a woman with two children who was staying over on weekends, but she broke up with him when she found out that he was not faithful. When he learned that this former girlfriend had been called to testify at his custody hearing, he showed up at her door unannounced and reminded her that he had taken nude photographs of her. Threatened and fearful, she called the police. In spite of all this, court documents stated that, after a rocky initial period, the boy's physical care while he lived with his father was excellent.

John Thompson had kidnapped his son when he was about three and still in diapers. It appeared that the local woman who provided day care, not Thompson, did the toilet training and that one reason John Thompson was so happy to have a live-in girlfriend is because she changed Daniel's diapers. In custody cases, the father's girlfriend was always portrayed as a substitute mother and homemaker: she cooked and did the laundry, thus providing the father with unpaid child care and housekeeping services.[30] If a "live-in companion" had her own young child, "that too might be considered a plus" because then the father's child had a playmate.[31]

The Illinois Supreme Court seems to have backed away from *Jarrett* both because of Simon's election to the court and because the justices perceived the *Jarrett* decision as too punitive. They were unwilling to impose as harsh a standard on the fathers who appeared before them as on mothers, and thus, it appears, the relatively dramatic reversal in legal decisions occurred because the court heard cases involving cohabiting fathers—and because Seymour Simon had ascended to the court. Between 1979 and 1983, the only change in the membership of the Illinois Supreme Court was the election of Seymour Simon. He did not write the *Thompson* opinion, but he was a vote in favor of it. The court was reluctant to apply the *Jarrett* standard to a cohabiting father. In this case, the double standard led to change that brought benefits for women as well as for men.

Changing Judicial Views in State Courts

Across the country, trial court judges were changing their minds about removing children from cohabiting parents, although with less dramatic reversals in court opinions. One reason they were doing so was that their courtrooms were filled with divorced parents who had live-in boyfriends or girlfriends. One possibility, as in *The Good Mother*, was to choose the cohabiting parent who was the quickest to remarry. The other, of course, was to abandon the idea of punishment, when there were two parties engaged in the same behavior. Trial court judges were also changing their opinions because more of them were younger than fifty, divorced, women, or had cohabited themselves. It was very uncommon to find a woman judge who wanted to punish a mother for cohabiting, especially because the typical woman judge thought it very important to treat men and women equally. The younger generation of judges, much like the younger generation as a whole, tended to regard morality as a matter of personal freedom or personal privacy. As a result, trial court judges tread more lightly. One Denver County Domestic Relations Court magistrate, who considered himself less old-fashioned, explained his views: "I used to be very hung up on the fact that a parent was living with a boy or girlfriend, but now this does not enter anymore in my considerations."[32] Finally, even religious judges who thought cohabitation was sinful had come to believe that the state should remain neutral because the moral consensus of society had broken down. In the words of one Massachusetts Appellate Court appointee, "judges should avoid making moral judgments on the lifestyles of proposed custodial parents." A study of one hundred appellate court decisions each year from 1920, 1960, and 1990 found that "moral fitness" was a stated reason for change of custody in a little less than one-third of the decisions in 1920 and 1960. By 1990, only about one in ten of the appellate court decisions mentioned it.[33]

Still, there is the puzzling matter of why trial court judges in divorce cases were keeping pace with reality more than judges deciding palimony cases. A cohabitor had reason to be confused by the courts of Illinois: cohabitation was acceptable by 1983, even for gay and lesbian couples, but a palimony contract was not (see chapter 7). If it was simply a matter of the frequency of cohabitation in Illinois, then judicial opinions in both matters should have changed. The more likely explanation is that trial court judges listened to thousands of divorce suits of cohabiting parents, whereas in the equity courts where contract matters were disputed, judges rarely heard more than one or two legal cases pressing the right to a palimony contract.

In this broad liberalization of attitudes and rulings in the mid-1980s, gay liberation was also good for the rights of straight cohabitors, even though attitudes toward the gay or lesbian cohabiting parent were much harsher than those toward the straight parent with a live-in partner. In a disputed child custody case involving a lesbian mother in Sacramento in 1976, a California Appellate Court asserted the "nexus" standard for deciding what was in the best interests of the child. Homosexuality (or cohabitation) would be held against the parent only if there were a clear nexus (that is, relationship) between the parent's cohabitation and harmful effects on the child. There had to be proof that the parent's cohabitation would harm the child in order for cohabitation to be used as a factor in denying cohabitation or visitation. In this new standard, the parent seeking a modification of custody had to show that the child was suffering an immediate observable "harm" from the other parent's cohabitation, such as poor school performance, being upset, or bed-wetting, before custody could be modified. Rulings employing the nexus standard seemed to vary as to whether it was up to the complaining parent to prove that the child was harmed or for the custodial parent to show that the child was not.

The nexus standard was new and favorable toward the gay, lesbian, or straight cohabiting parent, but it was still being administered by trial court judges who had great discretion in reaching their decision. Attorneys for gay and lesbian parents suspected that judges had learned to couch their denials of custody in less overtly prejudiced terms. One gay rights attorney recalled an Ohio case, for example, in which the children were seen outside during the winter not wearing their coats, which was taken as proof that the mother was not providing an adequate standard of care. In so many of these cases, who was to say what problems a child suffered because of parental conflict prior to divorce as opposed to difficulty adjusting to the parent's new friend? If a little boy was hyperactive while he was living with his mother and her fiancé but improved when he went to live with his father, cohabitation was adduced as the source of his problem.[34] A Florida judge took away custody of a four-year-old girl whose mother had moved to Canada to live with a man whom she expected to marry. The evidence of harm was that the little girl was "anxious" and missed her father in Florida.[35] A Utah trial court judge decided that the "moral development" of two girls, ages four and eight, was harmed because they lied to him when he interviewed them in his chambers. Their mother had a boyfriend who was not living with her but was staying over during the weekends and some weeknights; the couple subsequently married. Apparently coached by the mother, the girls said that on the weekends the boyfriend was sleeping on the couch. Afraid of being taken from their mother, they lied in order to be able to stay with her.[36] As in the other cases adducing "harm," the children were not asked which parent they preferred to live with. One study by a law professor found that in sixty-three appellate court cases that used the nexus standard in the 1980s, 60 percent of the parents kept the child, a high rate of success. Fathers were 100 percent successful (six out of six), whereas mothers' rate of success was 56 percent (thirty-three out of fifty-seven). The study concluded that judges felt freer to make attributions of harm about mothers whom they believed to be (more) immoral, dishonest, or desperate.[37]

Despite the decided shift in attitudes and rulings by the mid-1980s, the victory was incomplete for two major reasons. First, there was considerably more prejudice against gay and lesbian than straight cohabiting parents, and their success in keeping custody was uncertain. Second, trial, appellate, and supreme court judges in Mormon-dominated and some southern states continued to hold on to the principle of moral condemnation of cohabitation, among straight couples and gay or lesbian parents. These two reasons were related, and thus, many of the adverse decisions against lesbian and gay parents were issued by judges in Mormon-dominated or southern states.

Although the first lesbian mother custody lawsuit appeared in the courts in the late 1960s, such cases were becoming much more common in the 1970s, as lesbian mothers were facing loss of custody after they came out; gay fathers were less likely to seek custody when they came out but were often denied visitation by their ex-wives. Daniel Rivers detects a shift in attitudes by the mid-1980s, with more judges deciding that homosexuality in and of itself was not a reason for denial of child custody and did not prove that the parent was unfit. Many of the fears about gay and lesbian cohabiting parents were the same as those about straight cohabiting parents, that the living situation was immoral for the child, that the child was being raised to become a cohabitor or a homosexual, and that the child would suffer from stigma from neighbors or children at school and should be protected from these harsh opinions by being raised by the other parent. Because of the idea that homosexuality was so polluting, judges applied special rules in order to cordon it off as a means of protecting the child. Thus, the child could not be present when a gay person appeared in the home, could not be taken to a place where gays gathered, and could not accompany the parent to meetings of any gay organization or Gay Pride parade. Some judges even tried to partition the space of the father's home. Thus, a Virginia court allowed a gay father to retain joint legal custody of his child so long as he and his partner did not share the same bed or bedroom.[38] Because of attitudes like these, friendly expert witnesses were an absolute necessity in gay or lesbian parent custody cases to provide scientific expertise to persuade the judge. Gay legal defense fund organizations argued these cases, lesbian mothers formed their own legal defense groups, and ACLU lawyers also often joined these suits. Denial of gay or lesbian parents' custody rights was not simply a personal tragedy but a social cause and a building block for the development of broader rights to adoption and legal marriage.[39]

Homophobic judges were surprisingly frank in admitting their prejudices. Most research on the decision making of judges relied on administering questionnaires, asking them to fill out surveys about their hypothetical response to specific living situations for the child or parental conduct. Among heterosexual parents, judges said they selected the parent who had remarried over the one who lived alone, and they preferred both to the co-habiting parent.[40] They also admitted that parental homosexuality was a factor in their decision making, irrespective of the parent's living arrangement. Homosexuality always ranked as "more inappropriate" than heterosexual cohabitation, but by exactly by how much varied from survey to survey. One law professor concluded in 1988, "the vast majority of the decisions of the past fifteen years still regard homosexuality as cause to deny custody to a parent and severely to restrict visitation, even to the extent of prohibiting the child from attending religious services with the parent at a church where a large proportion of the congregation is homosexual, attending social activities in which homosexuals are present, or attending gay activist meetings."[41]

The other major reason for the incomplete victory for cohabiting parents by the mid-1980s was that judges in Mormon-dominated regions, border states like Missouri, and many states of the South still believed that they were moral guardians of the religious views of the community.[42] In much of the Bible Belt adultery, sex "out of wedlock," cohabitation, and homosexuality, irrespective of the gay person's living arrangements, was still considered sinful.[43] Many matrimonial lawyers in the South refused to take a custody case if the parent had a live-in lover because they knew such a client had no hope of winning. A lawyer warned a client that even if she married her live-in boyfriend or asked him to move out, a judge could still remove children from her because he considered her immoral and would regard a last-minute marriage as a ruse to fool the court.[44] Several Kentucky Circuit Court judges, when interviewed in the 1980s, said that the mother's having a "live-in companion" was proof of "deficient moral character." A Georgia mother whose second husband had stayed overnight a few nights at her trailer four months before they married lost custody because she was held to be morally unfit and had engaged in what was a crime in the state.[45] Even after Peggy Bagents married her lover, a Louisiana trial court ruled that "her moral values" had not changed and she did not exhibit "a desire to reform."[46] A Virginia trial court judge admitted that "it would just shock [his] conscience" to allow children to visit their mother in Arizona since she was living with her boyfriend.[47] For many judges in the South, mothers and fathers could be immoral, but for different reasons. Adultery and prostitution were evidence of immorality in mothers, whereas higher up on the list of a father's sins were rape or failure to provide.

There was clearly an association between the prevalence of cohabitation in the state and judicial decision making. I tested this proposition by looking at the relationship between state appellate court decisions restricting a

Table 8.1 Appellate court decisions reversing custody or visitation and percentage of unmarried households by state in 2000

State	Year of last restrictive decision	Unmarried partner households, 2000 (%)
California	n/a	10.4
Massachusetts	n/a	9.9
New Jersey	1974	8.5
Illinois	1981	8.5
Connecticut	1981	9.2
Louisiana	1983	9.4
Nebraska	1983	7.6
Rhode Island	1989	10.5
Missouri	1989	8.9
South Carolina	1997	8.3
Alabama	2002	6.1
Idaho	2004	7.5
Arkansas	2005	6.7
Virginia	2007	8.1
National average		9.1

Sources: For appellate court decisions, see June Carbone and Naomi Cahn, "Judging Families," University of Missouri Kansas City Law Review, 77, no. 2 (Winter 2008): 267–305; US Census Bureau, "Married-Couple and Unmarried-Partner Households," http://www.census.gov/prod/2003pubs/ censr-5.pdf (July 2, 2010).
Note: n/a = not applicable.

parent's custody or visitation rights and the percentage of the population co-habiting in the state (see table 8.1). I chose the last date I could find involving the decision of a state appellate court issuing such a ruling (modifying custody or limiting visitation for cohabitors), with respect to rights of either straight or gay and lesbian parents. The first time the US census provided state statistics about the prevalence of cohabitation was 2000. These show the number of unmarried partner households (of all sexual orientations) as a percentage of all households. Courts that played a progressive leadership role—the homes of judicial activism—were California and Massachusetts, where the cohabitation revolution occurred relatively early and was more common than in the nation as a whole. Holdout states had large numbers of Mormons or were in the South.[48]

It is no coincidence that the largest number of custody cases involving gay parents occurred in Arkansas, where the state legislature had passed a bill banning adoption by straight or gay cohabiting couples.[49] Bill Clinton found that it took considerable charm to offset the influence of the Moral Majority in the state, which continually wanted to pass new legislation punishing couples who lived together. From the trial court to the state supreme court, Arkansas judges condemned cohabitation. An appeals court in Arkansas in 2001 that held that cohabitation "has never been condoned in Arkansas, is contrary to the public policy of promoting a stable environment for children, and may of itself constitute a material change in circumstances warranting a change of custody."[50]

In this particular case, the law was catching up with the rising rate of cohabitation. Judges were taking their cues from society's disapproval of cohabitation and from their personal views; society's disapproval was declining, and many judges were reconsidering their perspectives. Not enough judges upheld the tenets of the Moral Majority. Even those who believed that cohabitation was sinful often stated that they should not impose their own morality on couples who appeared before them. As a result, the sexual revolution was becoming a family revolution, and with that revolution, there was a decline in the double standard and homophobia. Family law was catching up with reality sometime in the middle of the 1980s, except in religious regions of the country, where there remained less of a reality for the courts to catch up with and thus more active support for judges to conduct the culture war from the bench.

Many players were active in achieving this result, which reflected the interaction between feminism and the increasing sexual liberalism of the Democratic Party. Jackie Jarrett forced the law to confront the existence of cohabitation as a new form of family by taking her case all the way to the Supreme Court and generating publicity for a new social trend. Seymour Simon was elected to the Illinois Supreme Court, and with him more judges on all levels who accepted the important tenet of liberalism that the law should remain morally neutral and not intervene to enforce morality, especially when moral consensus was changing. Liberal Democratic judges were very good for the rights of cohabitors; so was the elevation to the court of more women and more lawyers who had cohabited themselves. Two lawyers, June Carbone and Naomi Cahn, hail judicial acceptance of the belief that law should not enforce morality because they think such an attitude is less divisive and polarizing and leads to more public faith in the courts.

There is an amicable coda to Jackie Jarrett's case. She and Wayne Hammon legally married in 1983, and the girls insisted that their preference was to live with both their parents. Walter and Jackie worked out an arrangement so that the girls alternated every three months living with each parent.[51]

NINE

Get Married or Move Out

Twice a student couple lost an apartment because "we didn't want to sign a lease Mr. and Mrs."[1] In most states it is perfectly legal for a property management company to refuse to rent apartments or houses to unmarried couples. The civil rights movement successfully pressed for the passage of a national fair housing law in 1968 designed to end racial discrimination in housing. The idea of equal access to housing spread to the protection of many other groups, including women, families with small children, and the disabled. Nonetheless, cohabitors are among the classes of people least protected by fair housing laws, and discrimination is defended on the grounds that the state should be able to favor marriage, punish cohabitation, and send the message that the law is not intended "to promulgate promiscuity." In many areas of law, the right to privacy is an effective legal way of countering the defense of discrimination. When it comes to housing, defense of traditional morality trumps the right to privacy. The fight is the standard one between the old and new morality, but it is conducted in terms of space: an apartment, a neighborhood, or even an entire town off limits to the unwed. British cultural geographer Don Mitchell writes, "Geography is structured in fights—culture wars—over inclusion and exclusion, over the making or shaping of boundaries around race, gender, ethnicity, and sexuality, and over defining who constitutes part of the group. Geography is structured precisely by the question: who has the right to space?"[2]

There was no fight so long as cohabitation could be concealed, which meant that many couples chose to lie in order to secure an apartment or a home. Straight cohabitors claimed to be married; upon occasion a gay male couple put out the story that they were uncle and nephew. When college students ventured outside of student neighborhoods to find a cheaper place to live, they bought wedding rings to wear when they met the landlord. A riskier strategy was for one partner to lease the apartment and the other to move in later. Concealment, of course, did not always work: a couple could lie and claim that they were married, but if they were found out, they could be denied the rental or asked to move out. Some landlords were not fooled and asked to see a marriage certificate. Even more intrusive was the approach of a landlord in College Park, Pennsylvania, who, when he found out a couple was not married, demanded that they call their parents and receive their permission to live together before he would allow them to sign the lease.[3]

Only two studies have tried to measure the extent of housing discrimination against straight cohabitors, both concerning discrimination in rental housing. In 1977, a college student group in Orlando sent two sets of checkers to seventy apartment complexes; one straight student couple posing as married, the others posing as unmarried. Given the Florida criminal law against cohabitation, and many instances of housing discrimination against cohabitants in the state, it is surprising that the students posing as unmarried encountered only one rental agent who refused them; one of the managers was even living with someone himself. Nonetheless, they also met an agent who told them it was company policy to deny cohabitors, but "we're not really checking." Another coached them in the basic strategy of concealment: "Come in as Mr. and Mrs. because what they don't know won't hurt them." In 1984, a Sacramento fair housing bureau in 1984 sent out three anonymous couples to check on housing bias; one married, one gay male couple, and one straight couple. The "testers" were assigned the task of trying to rent a one-bedroom apartment. Landlords denied rentals to one-third of gay couples and one-tenth of all cohabiting straight couples; none of the straight married couples were refused a place to live.[4] It seems highly doubtful that in Sacramento, where bias against cohabitors was illegal according to state law, there would have been more housing bias than in Orlando, where cohabitation was still a criminal offense. The likely explanation for the difference is that if Orlando apartment complexes accepted students, they did not differentiate between unmarried and married ones.

It might at first appear that landlords and realtors had no economic incentive to bar cohabitors because they were restricting their pool of potential buyers and tenants. But while discrimination made no economic sense, it was based on morality and stigma, stereotypes about cohabitors, and wholesale condemnation of "living in sin." In the early 1970s, cohabitation was still thought of as part of the counterculture, "wild parties, drugs, all that stuff." Landlords who believed that flower children made untidy tenants, worried that they would turn an apartment into a crash pad, and thought they were dirty did not rent to them. Hippies, it was believed, were bad for property values.[5] At the same time, public housing authorities banned live-in boyfriends from the premises, fearing gang violence and drug sales. Landlords did not want to rent to unmarried couples because, they claimed, couples often split up and the partner who stayed did not have enough money to pay the rent. Some owners of very large blocks of rental apartments discriminated against both homosexuals and unmarried couples, considering them sinners. Another fear was of middle-aged flight: that other tenants would leave rather than having to live next to unmarried partners. Those occupants who did not want to move sometimes voiced their moral objections. A manager of garden apartments in Prince George County, Maryland, testified that "many tenants get very angry with us for renting to unmarried people. They wonder if we don't care about the morals of their children."[6] The laws criminalizing cohabitation served as additional justification for not leasing to cohabitors since landlords claimed that in providing such housing, they were abetting a violation of the state's criminal law. Of all these rationales and arguments, by far the most common was that cohabitors were immoral, engaging in sexual conduct that affronted religious values, threatened the family, and endangered children.

Although landlords' policy against "overnight guests" disappeared by the end of the 1960s, a rather large number of legal devices for restriction of cohabitors remained, ranging from restrictive covenants to occupancy restrictions in leases to requirement of town registration for cohabitors, but not married couples.[7] But the two major methods of discrimination against cohabitors were covert discrimination under the guise of family-only zoning ordinances and overt discrimination: landlords or property owners who stated that they rented (or sold) only to married couples or checked whether prospective tenants were married. In a few cases, the two forms of discrimination were related, as in judicial rulings that held that family-only zoning did not constitute a form of marital discrimination. Certainly, considering cohabitors not to be a family was one major means of discriminating against them in both home ownership and rental housing, but it was not the only one.[8]

Housing discrimination against cohabitors is an important instance of the law lagging very far behind the reality of the unmarried couple next door.[9] Of course, the law consists of many features, some of which directly contradict one another. In general, it can be said that discrimination against unmarried couples in one area served as justification for denial of protection or rights in other areas. Thus, a state such as Illinois that criminalized cohabitation and did not enforce contracts between cohabitors used those two principles to justify housing discrimination. In 1990, dredging up the denial of property rights to Vicki Hewitt and the loss of child custody to Jackie Jarrett, an Elgin County Appellate Court, in adjudicating a complaint of two different unmarried couples who had both been refused units in apartment complexes in Wheaton, decided that landlords in Illinois had a right to deny housing to unmarried couples. At the time, open and notorious cohabitation was still a crime in the state. The judges argued that couples who admitted they were living together were being "open and notorious" and thus were engaging in a criminal act. Moreover, the court also decided that the fact that Illinois law did not enforce palimony contracts showed that the state was in favor of preserving marriage by punishing cohabitation.[10] Could Seymour Simon, the protector of the rights of the unmarried in the Illinois Supreme Court, not help them? Unfortunately, he had stepped down from the court two years earlier, and the new state supreme court refused to hear this case upon appeal. In many other states, criminal laws against cohabitation had been removed, and contracts between cohabitors were enforceable. But even in many of those states, housing bias against cohabitors was still not considered a form of marital status discrimination.

No state legislature has expressly protected cohabitors from discrimination in the housing market, which certainly reflects the absence of a social movement by cohabitors. The idea is not popular, and there is little demand for such legislation. Individual unwed couples do complain about discrimination to fair housing commissions and upon occasion bring a case to court; they do not, however, lobby city councils or state legislatures for legislation to remove bias against them. Despite suffering from even more extensive discrimination in housing, ironically, gays are better protected from discrimination in city and state ordinances than straight cohabitors. (To be sure, neither group is protected at the federal level.) As a result of gay activism, more than sixty cities outlaw discrimination based on sexual orientation in housing; only a handful of counties ban discrimination against unmarried straight cohabitors. A few college towns and an occasional state legislature considered bills to outlaw housing discrimination against both groups, but the bills failed largely due to homophobia. From the perspective of gay activists, adding the cause of unmarried straight couples to their own did nothing to help them—and it seems to have been jettisoned accordingly.[11]

This chapter shows that housing discrimination is strongly rooted in the belief that cohabitation is sinful and that the state must protect marriage and the family and enforce morality, and the view that a landlord should be able to tell a couple to get married if they want a place to live. It thus demonstrates that the key overriding bias against cohabitors is a moral one applied to space, above and beyond the social categories of race, class, and sexual orientation. That the power of the state to enforce morality so often outweighs recognition of multiple definitions of the family, diverse views about sexual morality, and the principle of housing antidiscrimination is highly revealing about what constitutes acceptable public prejudice. Bias against families with children, the pregnant, and the disabled is now considered housing discrimination, but prejudice against unmarried straight couples living together is not.

Fights over space began in the early 1970s, as hippies and college students living together were beginning to move into family neighborhoods or were denied rentals by landlords who believed that cohabitation was sinful. Human rights commissions in college towns debated banning discrimination against unmarried couples, but never had the votes to do so. By the middle of the 1970s, cohabitation was far more widespread, among, for example, the engaged and the recently divorced. It was the purchase of a new place, which both parties would occupy, that made discrimination visible. By the middle of the 1970s, cohabitors began to complain of housing bias, using newly passed laws that prohibited marital status discrimination, mostly without success. Religious landlords, sometimes supported by the residents of the small towns where they lived, began to fight back against charges of discrimination, more often winning than losing. Today, cohabitors have no federal protection from housing discrimination, and state protection varies, with the state of California and many cities within it offering the most, outlawing bias against cohabitors not by statute but in court decisions, and most Rocky Mountain and southern states offering none whatsoever. The absence of cases in the state courts of these regions is proof of the acceptability of discrimination.

By definition, housing discrimination enforces stigma since it is a spatial form of exclusion. The people with master's degrees, PhDs, and law degrees whose stories are recounted in this chapter did not break down in tears; they either married, and thus were allowed to remain in their homes, or they found other places to live. They had no difficulty securing suitable housing; the issue was their citizenship rights, whether they were denied equal access to housing because they were unmarried couples. High social status and friends, employers, and relatives who accepted living together insulated these people from being harmed by their experience; they were not called names by the other side either. Other couples dropped their lawsuits because they were not willing to accept the adverse publicity. Some of the less well situated also pressed on in the courts; when they were denounced as "fornicators" by the attorneys of religious landlords, they felt hurt. When they lost in court, they tended to say that they did not want to live among people who did not want them anyway.[12]

Zoning by Morality

Zoning laws are a tool for enforcing legal marriage by keeping cohabitors out of family neighborhoods. During the first suburban boom of the 1920s, zoning ordinances were used to create single-family residential districts, separated from stores, hospitals, schools, and factories. In 1926, the US Supreme Court upheld the legal basis for municipal zoning as a legitimate exercise of a city's "police power." Municipalities were thus free to carve out separate residential, business, and industrial zones, with the idea of preserving the best space for married couples raising children. The US Supreme Court ruled that it was up to a challenger to prove that a town's zoning ordinance did not have a reasonable and substantial relation to public health, safety, morals, or the general welfare.

Many of these early zoning ordinances created single-family zones but took a functional rather than a formal view of what constituted a family. The earliest zoning ordinances regulated the number of people in a dwelling unit rather than actually trying to define the family. There was little unanimity about what constituted a family in these ordinances, in part because many judges were sympathetic to property owners who took in lodgers in order to pay the rent. Because the terms *family* or *single family* usually were not spelled out, cases reaching courts required a judicial definition of the family. Thus, it is difficult to find any distinctive pattern to the state court rulings on what constituted a family up to the 1970s; in general, courts were inclined to think that priests or nuns, nurses, or missionaries living together constituted a family and that lodgers might be part of one. By the 1970s, courts in liberal states such as California and New York had differing views on whether a couple or group of college students constituted a family. If there was one common theme, it was that judges did not think fraternities and sororities constituted families, and they usually considered them bad for neighborhoods.

In the 1970s, small elite towns with a substantial number of large older homes enacted zoning ordinances to screen out hippie communes. Belle Terre, New York, was a small village on the northern tip of Long Island whose seven hundred residents lived mostly in very large Tudor-style homes. The village of Belle Terre restricted all land use in the town to single-family dwellings, and the town's zoning ordinance defined the family as a unit consisting of people related by blood, marriage, or adoption and up to two unrelated adults. The significance of *Village of Belle Terre v. Boraas*, a US Supreme Court case in 1972, was that it upheld as constitutional the use of a definition of the family as a device to exclude communes.[13] A dentist and his wife rented a house in Belle Terre to six undergraduates, five men and one woman, from the State University of New York at Stony Brook. The students and their landlords argued that the city's zoning ordinance interfered with their right of privacy and their right to personal associations of their own choosing. The students argued that "it is of no rightful concern to villagers whether the residents are married or unmarried." About a year before the Supreme Court applied the concept of privacy to a woman's constitutional right to secure an abortion, the Court decided in this case that privacy had nothing at all to do with questions related to housing. Thus, in the opinion for the majority, Justice William O. Douglas held that "the police power is not confined to elimination of filth, stench and unhealthy places. It is ample to lay out zones where family values, youth values and the blessings of quiet seclusion and clean air make the area a sanctuary for people." Douglas stated that Belle Terre did not intend to discriminate against cohabitors, because the ordinance permitted the residence of two unrelated adults. As usual, Thurgood Marshall dissented. He thought that a municipality could validly restrict the number of people who could occupy a home, but could not consider whether the occupants were "Negro or white, Catholic or Jew, Republican or Democrat, married or unmarried."[14] His view did not prevail, and as a result of the Court's decision, several communities enacted anti-commune zoning ordinances.[15]

In 1974, the Supreme Court defended family zoning in a second housing case, while also broadening the definition of family to include a larger group than simply a married couple and their children. East Cleveland, a black working-class community adjacent to Cleveland, had passed its own distinctive version of a family-only zoning ordinance in order to limit traffic congestion and curb overcrowding in the public schools. The East Cleveland ordinance defined family as including the head of household, the spouse, parents, one married child, and the married child's children. By this definition of family, cohabitors would have been excluded, but the Supreme Court decision ignored that question entirely. Ruth Moore was an elderly African American grandmother with arthritis; one of her married sons and his son were living her, as well as her divorced son and his boy. Housing officials in East Cleveland told Ruth Moore that the housing ordinance required that one of her grandsons would have to move out; she refused and was convicted of violating the local ordinance but never served her sentence of five days in jail because she immediately appealed the decision. The US Supreme Court ruled in her favor, holding that the nation had a family tradition that included "uncles, aunts, cousins, and especially grandchildren sharing a household along with parents and children."[16] East Cleveland was allowed to engage in family-based zoning (and, by implication, to exclude unmarried cohabitors), so long as the definition of the family included the extended family.

The most restrictive forms of family zoning involved defining the family as a housekeeping unit consisting of members united by blood, marriage, or adoption—no exceptions allowed. Exclusive upper-class suburbs were the first to employ this definition and remain the last to hang on to it; snobbishness was a national principle, not confined to any particular region of the country. The stigma attached to cohabitation was implied rather than explicit in these ordinances. Cohabitors were perceived as people of "loose morals" who, by example, taught the young that they did not have to marry to have sex and threatened the family atmosphere of the community. Other ordinances permitted occupancy by a family as well as two unrelated adults to allow for domestic servants, caretakers of the elderly, and possible guests as members of family households. For example, Oyster Bay, New York, allowed families (related by blood, marriage, or adoption) and two unrelated adults older than age sixty-two because the town recognized that many of the elderly could not maintain a home on their own and were forced to take in a roommate.[17] Usually the number of unrelated adults was limited to two or three.

In the 1960s, small towns, not intentionally aiming to exclude cohabitors, adopted zoning ordinances with the most restrictive definition of the family: a unit defined by blood, marriage, or adoption. When the middle-class suburb of Des Plaines, Illinois, added such a restriction in 1960, it was aiming to stop multistory apartment buildings and boardinghouses. In 1966, Greeley, Colorado, passed a blood, marriage, or adoption zoning ordinance to keep student couples from encroaching on family neighborhoods. Summer resorts also adopted these laws because they wanted to keep out drunken students and noisy weekend parties. Towns on the New Jersey shore filled with large Victorian shingled houses very close together on the beach were inundated with rowdy young men and their cars, girlfriends, and kegs of beer. Spring Lake Heights, Manasquam, Brielle, and Sea Girt, New Jersey, upscale towns frequented by elderly couples and families with young children, all responded by enacting zoning ordinances that defined a family as a unit of "kinship, blood, marriage, or adoption."[18]

Exclusivity was the same as exclusion, and thus, small suburbs where the lots were large and the homes very expensive were the most common zones of restriction. A student of urban planning, Marsha Ritzdorf, examined the Seattle-Everett, Washington, area in the early 1980s. One town had no zoning, but thirty communities had adopted family definitions in their municipal ordinances, several since the 1950s, and many had substantially revised them between 1960 and 1982. Most town ordinances restricted zoning to families, plus several unrelated adults; the communities that adopted the definition of family as restricted to those related by blood, marriage, or adoption were wealthy suburbs, with the exception of the city of Everett (population fifty thousand). The posh suburbs were quite tiny, with populations as small as three hundred or as large as forty-two hundred. The residents of Forest Park, Washington, vocally defended the single-family character of their town, but many other residents were unaware of the town's housing rules. Clerks in such places knew there were cohabitors violating the ordinances but did not enforce the rules.[19] When Ritzdorf replicated her study in 1994, she found that the number of municipal ordinances restricting cohabitors with children had actually increased to 10 percent of all municipalities she surveyed.[20] Towns were enacting new family-only restrictions because social conservatives had gained political power and sought to exercise their clout on the local zoning board to promote family values.[21]

Living Together in Ladue

Ritzdorf did not find any cohabiting couples who had been evicted from their homes in these towns; to find cases in which the zoning law was enforced not once but several times, one has to examine a similar sort of town but in a far more conservative state. The adjective *snooty* so often preceded the name of Ladue, Missouri, that it seemed as though it must have been a street, adjacent to Picardy Lane or Oak Bend. *Private* was another word often attached to Ladue, from the private lanes to the four country clubs, two private schools, and innumerable squash clubs, stables, and racquet clubs. In the 1980s, Ladue had the highest median income of any suburb in the metro St. Louis area and was the fourth richest suburb in the United States. The town had very few public facilities, but those few were excellent; Ladue spent lavishly on its public schools, which were widely regarded as among the best in the country. Tax and real estate lawyers, physicians, commodity traders, bank executives, home builders, and corporate executives who mainly voted Republican lined up to live there. Very few blacks, Hispanics, or poor people of any race resided in Ladue; the town was 1 percent Hispanic and 1 percent black in the 1980s. Nonetheless, Ladue was not entirely isolated from the sexual revolution, since William Masters and Virginia Johnson (the most renowned sexologists of their day, who ran a sexual dysfunction lab in St. Louis) invited celebrities to their home in Ladue for therapy so that they did not have to check into a hotel or risk being observed entering their lab.[22]

An unsuspecting middle-aged couple, Terry Jones and Joan Horn, bought a house in Ladue in 1982. Both were divorced, had children from their previous marriages, and were interested in progressive Democratic politics. After his divorce, Terry Jones lived with his son in an apartment near Washington University; he had sole custody of his son, and he wanted a house near the university and close to his son's school. Joan Horn's daughter Kara was in junior high school, and her five other children were in college or graduate school and living at home or returning frequently. One of Joan Horn's sons had committed suicide, and she was looking for a new home that had no unpleasant memories attached to it. She and Terry Jones wanted to buy a house with a large number of bedrooms in their price range: 8570 Colonial Lane in Ladue met their requirements. The seller did not inform them about Ladue's family-only zoning ordinance and may not have known of its existence.[23]

At age forty-eight, Joan Kelly Horn's wavy hair had turned white; she was tall, thin, distinguished looking, and dressed conservatively. Terry Jones, age forty-three, was balding and bespectacled, had a mustache and a beard, and looked like the tenured college professor he was. Horn had married young and dropped out of college to have children, but went back to school to complete college and get a master's degree. She had worked as a contract officer for the St. Louis County Housing Authority and, with Jones, started her own survey research and polling firm, often working with school districts or doing polling on behalf of Democratic candidates. Jones was a political scientist, the dean of the liberal arts college at the University of Missouri–St. Louis who also had hosted a program about Missouri politics on local public radio.

Two years after Horn and Jones had moved to Ladue, a policeman knocked at their door and asked to see their marriage certificate. He handed them a summons, charging them with violating ordinance 1175, which prohibited persons who did not meet Ladue's definition of a family from owning a house in town.[24] The town sued Horn and Jones, and they countersued, claiming that they had a constitutional right to privacy. It was relatively easy for them to go to court because they had several friends who were prominent lawyers with the ACLU. The ACLU paid the costs for the lawsuit, and Horn did much of the legal research.

When charges were brought regarding violations of zoning ordinances, most likely it was because a neighbor had complained. When the two-story garrisons, all the same, were built in the early 1950s, it was assumed that all the homeowners were legally married, but new people were moving into Colonial Lane. Jones and Horn never found out who had called the police, but it may might have been the retired neighbor a couple of houses away. Joan Horn's daughter was dating a football player with the St. Louis Cardinals who was African American. He visited their home on the weekends and played touch football on the front lawn, which was easy for the neighbors to observe.[25] In other suburbs as well, cohabitation complaints arose because a black man appeared in an entirely white neighborhood.[26] Neighbors may have been agitated by the presence of blacks, white cohabitors, or both, bothered by immorality, threats to the value of their property, and their way of life.

Most of the residents of Colonial Lane defended Horn and Jones privately, but the only one who did so publicly was an endocrinologist down the street who employed Horn's daughter as a babysitter. He wrote a letter to the St. Louis Post-Dispatch vouching for Horn and Jones and displaying a flash of anger at some of the other residents on Colonial Lane. He wrote, "If it turns out that it was one of my neighbors who brought this matter to an issue, it is he I would like to see removed from the neighborhood."[27] The woman next door told the press "the ordinance itself is embarrassing."[28] An anonymous neighbor erroneously claimed that Jones and Horn knew about the ordinance, broke the law, and thus were deserving of punishment.[29] There was never any support for a petition to the zoning commission or the mayor, partly because people in Ladue valued privacy and partly because they accepted the decisions of the longtime mayor, Edith Spink, who believed that the town should be able to exclude unmarried couples.

Cohabitors in Ladue, resorting to the standard tactic of lying about their marital status, had reason to fear. When the police received complaints from neighbors, they did enforce the ordinance. Between 1982 and 1984, there had been six complaints to the town about people violating the zoning ordinance. Judging from the names of the accused parties, it appears that cohabitors were heterosexual male or female students or gay male or lesbian couples; there was also a husband and wife with a boarder who were charged with violating the ordinance. Five of the six complaints about violations of the single-family ordinance were brought against people living in

Dwyer Place, an area near the highway consisting of small, mostly two-bedroom houses. Colonial Lane was a more expensive area than Dwyer Place, although both were "Lower Ladue," east of Interstate 170 and close to the grocery store and shopping.[30] The *St. Louis Post-Dispatch* hinted at possible class bias in the summons against Horn and Jones when it suggested "if the couples were prominent members of a local country club, would the city have exercised its discretion and not prosecuted—particularly on the basis of an anonymous tip?"[31]

In large cities, the press played the role of cosmopolitans, denouncing bigotry and the punishment of an upstanding and committed couple. There was no mistaking the fact that the *Post-Dispatch* enjoyed contrasting the sophisticated ethics of the city and the outdated morality of the ruling elite in Ladue. Jones and Horn had never tried to seek publicity; in fact, it was the *Post-Dispatch* that broke the story. One of the reporters for the paper had been a student of Terry Jones at the University of Missouri–St. Louis. While leafing through court actions at the district court, she came across their case against Ladue. The *Post-Dispatch* made the lawsuit front-page news and devoted editorials to denouncing Ladue when Horn and Jones lost at the district and appellate court levels. The headline of the first editorial ridiculed the town ("La-De-Dah in La-De-Due"), and the second conveyed their attitude in one word, "Shame." What made the story unusual and interesting was that it concerned a very respectable middle-aged couple living in a two- story suburban home somewhat larger than that of their neighbors; in fact, it was a college dean, not one of his students, who was threatened with eviction.[32]

Like the Decko case, this one involved the local press and police, but unlike the Decko case, there was no police stakeout of their home. Horn and Jones did not receive any hate mail, and although they were threatened with having to sell their house, they ended up not being cast out. They were never called sinners, and they personally experienced no shunning as a result of their lawsuit. Instead, Joan Horn and Terry Jones were "bemused" by Ladue's ordinance, and their children thought the situation was "funny." Terry Jones's mother enjoyed the idea that her son had become a celebrity. The chancellor of the University of Missouri–St. Louis told Terry Jones "not to worry about it." Since their ACLU lawyers did not believe that publicity would help their case and Jones and Horn wanted to safeguard their privacy, not win their case through the media, they turned down requests to appear on television. In the academic world of the University of Missouri–St. Louis, a dean of students who was "shacking up" was considered cool.

Most of their daughter's friends at Ladue Horton Watkins High School told her they thought the town antediluvian. Because the facts were not in dispute, Horn and Jones were not deposed; they did not have to take the stand at a trial and therefore were not asked the kind of personal questions Jackie Jarrett and Wayne Hammon had had to answer.[33]

The city argued that it was following a US Supreme Court precedent in *Belle Terre v. Boraas*, which allowed municipalities to employ definitions of family to restrict zoning. It refuted the view that Horn and Jones were a family. According to the Circuit Court of St. Louis, one aspect of a family is that "certain of its inherent attributes arise from the legal relation of the family members."[34] The circuit court ordered that either Horn or Jones move out of the house within ninety days. The couple appealed the case to the state appellate court, which unanimously ruled against them. Although the decision was mainly devoted to the question of a locality's right to zone, the court also offered its own statement about the importance of government in defending the institution of marriage. Thus, in the opinion of the Missouri Court of Appeals, "there is no doubt that there is a governmental interest in marriage and in preserving the integrity of the biological or legal family. There is no concomitant governmental interest in keeping together a group of unrelated persons, no how matter how closely they simulate a family."[35]

After they lost in district court, Joan Horn and Terry Jones decided to get married. Because their union was now legal, the town of Ladue dropped its objection to their residence. The Missouri Supreme Court refused to consider their lawsuit because they no longer had legal standing to sue. Joan Horn had not married Terry Jones when they moved to Ladue because Terry's income would have invalidated her children's applications for college financial aid. When her youngest son was in his senior year of college in 1987, however, the issue of financial aid had become moot. Moreover, Joan Horn was thinking about running for Congress, and she realized that she needed to be married to present herself as a convincing candidate. She won her congressional race in 1990 by an exceedingly close margin, and lost her seat by less than fifty votes two years later. Horn and Jones separated in 1996 and divorced in 1999; he has subsequently remarried.

After Horn and Jones sold their house, Ladue modified its ordinance in 1998 and now defines a family as two unrelated persons or as a unit defined by blood, marriage, or adoption.[36] The law is not currently being enforced in Ladue, but it nonetheless sends an informal message to straight, lesbian, and gay couples. In a recent posting to a website, a lesbian couple explained their decision not to buy a house in Ladue. A realtor informed them of the ordinance and reassured them that it is no longer enforced, but they decided against living in Ladue because they did not feel welcome there and did not want to have to take the time to have to challenge the ordinance.[37]

The most significant legal and political battle against these ordinances occurred in Denver, a large city that nonetheless engaged in suburban-style zoning; unlike in Ladue, in Denver unwed couples won. In 1989, Denver was the one major city in the United States with a zoning ordinance that defined the family narrowly. After a fourteen-year fight in the courts, the Denver City Council finally removed the ordinance. The "living in sin" law, as it was commonly called, was first enacted in the 1950s and grew out of a fear that black families composed of a number of unrelated adults might move into preferred, almost entirely white, neighborhoods. By the time the ordinance was revised in 1963, Denver homeowners were mainly concerned that large Victorian houses were being converted into group homes and hippie communes.[38] The Colorado Supreme Court upheld the ordinance in 1974; fourteen years later, the same court refused to hear a challenge to the law and remanded the lawsuit of two Denver cohabitors to a trial court in Denver.[39]

Although Denver was a city of five hundred thousand, the purpose of the zoning ordinance was quite similar to Ladue's: to cordon off the affluent area near the country clubs for the traditional single family. The city also derived extra revenue from charging each unrelated couple in other neighborhoods twenty dollars a year for a room and boarding permit. One of the first women elected to the Denver City Council, Cathy Donohue, tried without success to get the ordinance repealed; church groups, homeowner associations, and neighborhood residents opposed her. Realtors worried that if Denver changed its law, families with young children would move out. Because there was so much support for the ordinance, it took two meetings and two separate votes of the city council in 1989 to repeal it by the slimmest of margins.[40]

After the victory in Denver, cohabitors brought suit against less restrictive ordinances that excluded cohabiting couples and their children. Black Jack, Missouri, had to be threatened with state litigation by the ACLU several times in order to change its housing ordinance. In 2006, Black Jack decided not to contest a threatened law suit and changed its rule for obtaining a housing occupancy permit to allow an unmarried couple with children so long as the children were the biological children of both parents. Two years later, the town denied a housing occupancy permit to a woman, her three children from a previous relationship, and her boyfriend because they did not constitute a family. When threatened by another lawsuit, Black Jack decided to further liberalize its housing ordinance. In many other suburbs, restrictive zoning ordinances are still on the books, but not enforced, and the most restrictive ones can be found, as before, in small, tony suburbs. For example, Huntleigh, Missouri, a town of 305, a tiny Ladue, had a zoning ordinance that defines a family as "one or more persons related by blood or marriage" living as a single housekeeping unit. There were six suburbs in northeast Ohio that employed a similar definition of family and another thirteen prohibited cohabitors with children. Because Illinois law permits family-based zoning, it is not just the exclusive and older lakefront suburbs such as Winnetka and Kenilworth that restrict single-family zoning to units related by blood, marriage, or adoption. A newer, equally pricey suburb to the west, Barrington Hills, has a five-acre minimum lot size and a restrictive definition of the family, as does the smaller contiguous village of North Barrington. In Illinois towns with restrictive zoning tend to be contiguous, enlarging their physical perimeter of posh embattlement against the pluralistic world outside their borders.[41] Thus, at present, the housing situation can be characterized as the three nos: no awareness of discrimination, no enforcement of the rules, and no pressure to remove restrictions—a unique combination of lack of citizenship rights with lack of awareness of the denial of those rights.

Fair Housing Laws

Cohabitor's federal protections against housing discrimination are very slim: they apply only to discrimination in credit and in public housing. The main legislation against housing discrimination, the Fair Housing Act of 1968, does not prohibit discrimination against unmarried couples or homosexuals. Twenty-one states and the District of Columbia have laws barring marital status discrimination; thus, the majority of states do not prohibit discrimination on the basis of marital status. The culture war, as always, is regional: no southern state bars discrimination by marital status, and only two Rocky Mountain states (Colorado and Montana) do. As a result of favorable court decisions, marital status discrimination also applies to cohabitors in five states, explicitly does not apply in ten others, and has not been tested in the rest. Thirteen states have passed fair housing laws prohibiting discrimination based on sexual orientation.[42] The difference in state court rulings has to do with a limited versus broad understanding of marital status discrimination. In the limited view, marital status is an attribute of an individual—a person is single, married, widowed, or divorced. In this view, since cohabitors are not discriminated against because they are single, they do not suffer from marital status discrimination. The broader definition of marital status discrimination recognizes that discrimination involves denial of rights to a couple, not simply an individual. Thus, if a landlord decides not to rent to a couple when she learns that they are not married, she is discriminating against them in comparison with a married couple. This view not only recognizes that marital status has to do with couples rather than individuals but also apprehends that unwed couples are being measured against the norm of the married couple and found wanting.

College towns and the largest metropolises in the North and West began to pass fair housing laws that barred discrimination based on marital status in the early 1970s. Feminist groups succeeded at the state level in securing passage of fair housing laws that banned discrimination based on marital status; the main purpose of such laws was to remove housing bias against single women or divorced mothers with children; upon occasion women legislators also brought up specific bills to bar discrimination in housing against unmarried couples, but their bills were defeated.[43] What constituted marital status discrimination? No state legislature intended to bar discrimination against cohabiting couples; in fact, in three states, Oregon, Connecticut, and Colorado, state law explicitly exempted discrimination against cohabitors, arguing that landlords should be able to bar unmarried couples based on religious objections to cohabitation.

In 1976, Arthur Emil of New York City became the first cohabitor to sue for denial of housing on the grounds of a state's legislation banning marital status discrimination. Emil was a multimillionaire Manhattan real estate developer with a friend who was one of the most distinguished constitutional law authorities in the country. One of the most prestigious buildings in Manhattan, at 79 East Seventy-Ninth Street, had about sixteen apartments fronting Park Avenue. Its co-op board reviewed the application of Emil, who had signed a purchase agreement with a seller in the building. Emil, age fifty-one, had graduated from Yale College and Columbia Law School, had made his money from real estate development in the city, and was president of a nearby co-op. A shareholder in the building, sympathetic to Emil, told him that he had been turned down because he indicated on his application that he intended to live in the apartment with his partner and her daughter. The Upper West Side on the other side of Central Park was perceived as the neighborhood for wealthy Jews; some of the co-ops and condos on the Upper East Side were known to be Gentile-only, accepting at most one or two Jews. Emil believed that anti-Semitism was also a factor in the co-op denial. He sued for marital status discrimination, and his case was tried in the Supreme Court of New York (unlike in most states, the trial-level court of general jurisdiction in New York is called the supreme court). The court dismissed his complaint, arguing that the law did not cover marital status discrimination. Emil took his case to the state court of appeals, which decided against him on a technicality, that he had failed to file a complaint with the State Division of Human Rights first before taking his case to court.[44]

Another complaint, from a legally savvy aggrieved tenant in Manhattan, was just a matter of time. Four years after Emil, another Manhattan lawyer sued on grounds of marital status discrimination in housing, once again losing. Julia Weiss, age fifty, was a divorced mother with two grown children who, three years after her husband moved out of her apartment, invited Jack Wertheimer to live with her. Because of rent control laws, landlords in New York City had an economic incentive to discriminate against unmarried households, straight or gay. Milton Coleman, the manager for Hudson View Properties, had told the building staff at 310 West Seventy-Second Street to inform him whenever any nontenant moved into the building. Coleman was not concerned about policing morality but instead wanted to be able to remove an apartment from rent control in order to charge tenants market rates. Weiss was paying the phenomenally low rent of $550 a month for a five-room apartment that Coleman could list for $1,300 a month if he evicted her. According to law, he had the right to evict her immediately, cancel her lease, and offer her thirty days to leave, which he did. The actual restriction was closer to family-only zoning than simple discrimination: the standard lease form limited occupancy to a tenant and his or her immediate family, with family defined by blood, marriage, or adoption. The question was whether such a lease occupancy restriction constituted marital status discrimination. Not surprisingly, a civil court judge ruled that social mores had changed and that bias against cohabitors was a form of marital status discrimination.[45] The state court of appeals argued that the case had nothing to do with marital status discrimination but had to be decided on principles of family-based zoning. The lease limited occupancy to tenants and their families. The court argued that Weiss had not claimed that she and Wertheimer were a family and that, according to the legal definition, a boyfriend was not a family member because he was not related to her by blood, marriage, or adoption.

The decision frightened both straight and gay couples in New York City, many of whom called lawyers, inquiring whether their landlords could evict them. Gay couples had long been concerned about the provisions of landlord leases. Seeking their own solution to the denial of family status, some had engaged in adoptions: one partner formally adopted the other to meet the legal definition of a family. Within a month, the state legislature acted to counter the court's decision. The major reason for such swift action was gay and tenant activism, since a tenants' organization had a full-time lobbyist in Albany.[46] The "roommate law" the New York legislature passed allowed a "roommate" to remain in the apartment in the event that the tenant of the lease vacated. It also provided that tenants did not have to gain the landlords' permission to have partners, or roommates, live with them. The roommate law opened the floodgates to many more discrimination lawsuits by gay and straight cohabitors. Many litigants succeeded, especially in administrative agencies and lower courts in New York City. Although the New York legislature remedied the problem of housing discrimination in New York, it did not actually change the state's fair housing law, which does not prohibit discrimination against straight cohabitors.[47]

More recently, religious landlords have sued, protesting cohabitors' complaints of marital status discrimination. The landlord/tenant dispute could also become a small town's defense of its way of life, as unmarried couples tried to find a place to live in a small midwestern town. Attorneys argued against renting to "fornicators" not only to discourage sin and encourage marriage but also to "reduce the risk of sexually transmitted disease [and] of adding more unwed mothers and children to county, state, and federal welfare rolls."[48] Religious landlords racked up a considerable number of favorable rulings from state court judges concerned that cohabitation represented the downfall of civilization and a threat to the family. Their most recent success was in the Supreme Court of North Dakota in 2001, which held that a religious landlord was exempt from the state's fair housing provision against marital status discrimination. However, the decision actually led the state legislature to abolish the state's statute criminalizing cohabitation. The pace of these landlord suits seems to have slowed after a US Supreme Court decision in 1997 that ruled that religious claims could not be used as an excuse for exemption from civil rights laws.[49]

State policy promoting marriage is not simply a symbolic statement of values, since it undergirds and justifies housing discrimination against cohabitors. In the name of defending the institution of marriage, the law is allowing landlords to enforce morality. Cohabitors are denied equal access to housing because of the landlord's religious beliefs, class exclusivity, and the ideal that the state should promote marriage. In a country that is as rights conscious as the United States, with so many protections against discrimination, cohabitors' lack of legal protection against housing discrimination is strong evidence that discrimination against unmarried couples is an acceptable form of exclusion and is considered beneficial to society because it imposes the marriage cure. Ironically, in the area of housing, there are legal safeguards for the poor in public housing that are not available elsewhere. The law takes the position that it is up to an unmarried couple to find someone to sell or rent to them who can accept their lifestyle, not that it is the responsibility of the government to treat them fairly and respect their privacy. One young woman, denied a garden apartment by religious landlords in Illinois, stated her shock: "I can't believe we aren't protected. . . . I can't believe the state of Illinois would do this to us. This floors and upsets me."[50]

TEN

Domestic Partnerships

Despite various government health coverage programs, most Americans receive health care coverage through an employer. These benefits used to be filtered through marital status. To secure health insurance for one's partner, one needed to be married. Married couples enjoyed privileges denied to the nonmarried, straight or gay. Once the stigma of cohabitation had declined, it became easier for cohabitors to demand these benefits as a matter of their workplace rights. Gay men in unions and as city employees pressed for the extension of these benefits to their partners. Two small advocacy organizations for singles (Unmarried America and American Association for Single People), established in the 1990s, joined the effort a decade after the initial battles had been won. Later on, a loose alliance developed between the straight elderly and gay advocates for domestic partnership status. But the movement was led largely by gays. Because the cause of cohabitation was so dependent on gay activism, it was also dependent on gays defining their situation as similar to cohabitation—an alternative lifestyle. When gay activists instead began to seek the right to legal marriage, the movement for domestic partnership changed, from a vanguard development within gay liberation to a consolation prize offered instead of state recognition of same-sex marriage. So long as some states were continuing to offer domestic partnership registration, cohabitors benefited. But in a rhetorical sense, the emphasis was on the right to marry rather than approaching the issue as the right to marry and the right not to be forced to marry. Moreover, on the whole, advocates of same-sex marriage pointed out that marriage bestowed privileges, but did not attack the idea; instead, they simply insisted that they should not be denied the privilege bestowed on straight married couples.[1]

Legal marriage was an important symbolic prize to the civil rights and gay rights activists. In both these social movements, marriage was a symbol of full civil rights, and rights as domestic partners was for many simply a way station on the road to securing legal marriage. As the prospect for legal marriage appeared more likely, domestic partnership came to be defined as a consolation prize, a sign of disrespect for same-sex couples who sought the ultimate civil right, the right to marry. The closer gay civil rights came to achieving the legal goal of same-sex marriage, the harder it was to claim that cohabitation and legal marriage were both valid options for different people or at different stages of life. Domestic partnership was presented as a legal status that, at best, same-sex couples choose only when the right to marry is not available to them. As the legal scholar Ariela Dubler writes, "The focus of advocates of gay rights on the right to marry will continue to marginalize those individuals—gay and straight—who want to organize their sexual and intimate lives outside of marriage."[2]

This chapter traces the origins and developments of domestic partnership as an employee benefit and then as a form of "relationship recognition" by city and state government. The concept of domestic partnership reflects gay activists' initial ambivalence about whether to critique the institution of marriage or seek to advance the cause of same-sex marriage. After the tragic deaths caused by AIDS in the gay community, more and more gays wanted the financial and personal security symbolized by legal marriage. As a result of a surprise court victory for proponents of same-sex marriage in Hawaii in 1993, opponents grew alarmed about the prospect of same-sex marriage and passed legislation at the federal and state levels to try to stop it. All aspects of domestic partnership became defined in the shadow of the battle for same-sex marriage. There were both advances and retreats in this latest demand for sexual citizenship rights, ushering in a new phase in the culture wars. The opposition of the Christian Right to gay civil rights in the form of legalized same-sex marriage contributed to ballot measures that threatened domestic partner benefits in many states.

Cohabitation was caught in the crossfire between gay civil rights activists and their opponents in the Christian Right. Cohabitors were voters, too, although not mobilized as a group, but county-level voting data does show much less support for same-sex marriage bans in counties with high numbers of cohabitors. Public opinion among the rest of the population was growing ever more favorable toward same-sex marriage, but the Christian Right's opposition depended less on public attitudes than on turning out its supporters at the polls in record numbers. Gay rights issues are divisive, so divisive that the backlash generated spillovers into laws and policies affecting cohabitors. Cohabitation could benefit or lose, depending on the state of play between gay activists and the conservative backlash. Law and policy not only lagged behind public opinion in this crucial area but also reflected the ability of the Christian Right to galvanize public fears and hatreds.[3]

Domestic partnership certainly moved cohabitation closer to being an "institution" with attendant rights, but the rights secured were in no way equivalent to those of legal marriage. In 1981, domestic partnership began as a collective bargaining demand by gay union members for employee benefits and became a highly complicated—in fact, virtually inexplicable— patchwork system of new family law, which benefited gays, straights, and sometimes both. No employee enjoyed such benefits in 1982; by 2010, one-quarter of cohabitors at companies that offered health care benefits could cover their partners.[4] In 1985, West Hollywood, California, became the first American city to offer registration for domestic partners; by 2004, 105 cities offered it; in 1982, there was no such thing as statewide domestic partnership benefits and registration; by 2010, seven states and the District of Columbia offered this legal status.

The workplace benefits aspect of the larger movement for domestic partnership grew out of the distinctive system for providing health care in the United States. In the United States, health insurance coverage is provided through a public/private system, with coverage through employers backed up by a separate government system for veterans, the elderly, and the poor, and by purchase of private insurance.[5] In this public/private system, many people fell through the cracks and had no coverage whatsoever. Employers used marriage as the principle in deciding who received certain fringe benefits, the most important of which was health care coverage. The married employee could gain benefits for a spouse and perhaps dependent children; the unmarried employee was the sole recipient of benefits. The workplace system sounded better than it was, since many employers did not provide such coverage. This system of benefits has often been criticized for perpetuating an outmoded model of the husband as breadwinner with his wife and children as his dependents. But it should also be criticized for privileging the legally married and straight people who possess the legal right to marry.

The "relationship recognition" component of the domestic partnership movement was slightly different from the demand for benefits. It was a method of licensing relationships by a city, a county, or later a state, but one different from marriage. It began simply enough as the bureaucratic proof necessary to qualify for the employer's domestic partner benefits. A person who was married could be asked to produce a marriage certificate, but what kind of certificate might a domestic partner be asked to supply? First, private employers and then cities (especially in California) began systems of registration for domestic partners. Some gay couples wanted relationship recognition, even when they had no goal of securing benefits, which revealed their desire for legal marriage. On Valentine's Day 1992, thousands of same-sex couples dressed in bridal gowns or tuxedos showed up to register as domestic partners at San Francisco's city hall and participated in a mass interreligious ceremony. By then it was already clear that domestic partner recognition had come to mean the first step on the road to legal same-sex marriage.[6]

Cohabitation was always perceived as a threat to the institution of marriage; at the White House Conference on Families in 1980, conservatives made it clear that they believed that same-sex marriage and straight cohabitation were both endangering the traditional family. The first opponent of city ordinances that recognized domestic partnerships was the Roman Catholic Church, which stated its opposition to these measures in precisely these terms. Within a few years, conservative Christian groups joined Catholics opposed to domestic partnership laws, to protect the American family.[7] They organized ballot initiatives and occasional boycotts of companies that offered domestic partnership benefits, and spoke out against it on religious radio programs. Eventually, the same groups became the backbone of opposition to same-sex marriage.

Origins of Domestic Partnership Benefits

The domestic partnership movement, which scored its first success in 1982, developed quite slowly during the rest of the decade. It succeeded first mainly in the two major gay population centers, New York City and the San Francisco Bay Area.[8] The *Village Voice*, a weekly newspaper serving the free-thinking community of Greenwich Village, was the first private employer to provide employee health benefits for the partners (called "spouse equivalents") of both gay workers and straight cohabitors in 1982. In 1984, Berkeley, California, became the first US city to enact a domestic partner policy for city and school district employees; it provided health and dental insurance coverage for the partners of city employees the next year. By 1990, the movement had scored limited success, mainly among municipal employers, especially in California, where gay groups were able to exert political pressure.[9]

Despite the gay activism that it took to create domestic partnerships, straight cohabitors initially benefited more from domestic partnership benefits at work than gay men and lesbians did. In 1994, Hewitt Consulting, a benefits firm in suburban Chicago, estimated that two-thirds of the couples electing domestic partners coverage at work were straight. All major employers that provided coverage reported the same disparity. In Berkeley, about 80 percent of the covered domestic partners were heterosexuals; at the *Village Voice* by 1990, half of the covered workers were straight.[10] There were several reasons for this result. First, more cohabitors were straight than were gay. Second, many gay couples were dual earners, and both partners in the couple already had coverage at work. Meanwhile, some employees chose to remain in the closet rather than come out at work.[11] At the same time, most of the couples who registered with cities as domestic partners were gay men and lesbians. They registered even when there were no benefits involved because they wanted their relationship recognized; some accepted domestic partner registration as the closest thing to marriage available to them.[12]

Why were gay men and lesbians interested in domestic partnership benefits at all, given the emphasis on same-sex marriage in the 1970s and the desire for marriage evident in the popularity of these registration ceremonies? Why not simply press for rights as married couples? Even in the 1970s, some gays had defined themselves as "spouses," using the language of marriage to describe their relationships. Some exchanged rings or bracelets and held their own nuptial ceremonies; a few showed up at the courthouse and were allowed to marry; others were stopped from doing so and took their cases to court, where they invariably lost. National gay organizations, which were just beginning to be formed in the 1970s, played no part in these lawsuits because they did not perceive marriage as a priority of the movement.[13] Nonetheless, the occasional wedding or court case was enough to infuriate some state legislators. Between 1974 and 1977, a total of fifteen states, most in the South and the West, including California, enacted legislation to ban same-sex marriage.[14]

Although gay newspapers and magazines featured cover stories about couples who wanted to wed, on the whole, gay activists were opposed to marriage and believed that gay people should not want to get married. The gay men's liberation movement embraced the ideal of having multiple sex partners or short-term encounters, not long-term, committed relationships with a single partner, and saw the recognition of sex, in public or private, as part of a less shameful, more honest acceptance of human sexuality. Carl Wittman could not have been more blunt when he wrote in *A Gay Manifesto* that "traditional marriage is a rotten, oppressive institution" and that "liberation for gay people is defining for ourselves how and with whom we live, instead of measuring our relationship in comparison to straight ones, with straight values."[15] Meeting in convention in Chicago in 1972, the National Coalition of Gay Organizations adopted a platform that state governments should repeal "all legislative provisions that restrict the sex or number of persons entering into a marriage unit; and the extension of legal benefits to all persons who cohabit regardless of sex or numbers."[16] Leaders of the movement dismissed gay couples who wanted to tie the knot. Activists in Illinois in the mid-1970s thought nondiscrimination legislation was the highest priority and criticized a lesbian couple who got themselves arrested at the Cook County marriage bureau "for grandstanding and taking the wrong tack on a low-priority issue within the gay liberation movement."[17] Opposition to legal marriage was especially strong among lesbian activists, who more often valued committed relationships with a single partner but nonetheless denounced marriage as a patriarchal institution designed by men to control women. They tended to emphasize the right of women not to have to marry so as not to be forced to become economically dependent on a man. The gay liberation movement had several priorities, and marriage was not one of them. It wanted to end persecution by the police, who were charging gay men and lesbians with the crime of sodomy, and to remove homosexuality as an illness from the Diagnostic and Statistical Manual of Mental Disorders. Lesbian mothers sought to retain custody of their children after divorce, even when their ex-husbands claimed in court that they were unfit mothers.

Domestic partnership did not tackle all the privileges of married couples, but instead concentrated on the most important of them, health insurance for a partner through one's employer.[18] Ironically, at a time when radical students like Behr and LeClair were so critical of the institution of marriage, the privileges it offered were more valuable to the average couple than ever before. Although private industry developed a system of social benefits for workers by the 1920s, for the most part, only the individual employee was covered. During and immediately after the end of World War II, however, companies, restricted from offering higher wages by wage and price controls, turned to offering fringe benefits as a form of incentive for labor. Large employers began providing formal health care plans to employees and their families, although the extent of coverage was quite limited. In the 1960s and 1970s, the number of employers offering these family benefits grew. Legislators amended the federal tax code so that employers were able to deduct their contributions to employee health care coverage; similarly, they changed the tax law so that the employee did not pay tax on health care benefits for him- or herself and for spouses (and dependents).[19]

District 65–United Auto Workers Writers, Editors, and Clerical Workers Union, which included gay shop stewards, achieved the first significant victory for domestic partnership in 1982, largely because it was a union that included among its organizers 1960s activists. After graduating from Brandeis University with a degree in biology in 1968, Jeff Weinstein moved to San Diego to attend graduate school in English and American literature. When he came out in 1969, he was the first and only openly gay person on campus. As a member of the Radical Coalition, he organized and spoke at rallies against the Vietnam War. Off campus he belonged to a consciousness-raising group that met weekly, consisting of other antiwar activists, feminists, United Farm Worker supporters, and advocates of gay liberation.[20] After dropping out of graduate school, he moved back to New York, where he had grown up. He joined the socialist/feminist New American Movement and became a freelance writer for the *Village Voice*. The rock critic of the paper and his girlfriend, who chose not to marry because of their bohemian and feminist beliefs, were unofficially receiving partner health coverage at the paper, as were several other straight couples. In 1978, Weinstein was invited to attend a meeting of the newly organized union, which had a gay and lesbian caucus. Why can't the health plan cover same-sex couples? someone asked Kitty Krupat, a lesbian within the caucus and a union organizer. She said she did not know the answer. Weinstein had a personal, not merely an abstract, interest in the question since his partner had no health insurance coverage.[21]

By 1982, Weinstein had become a full-time employee of the *Voice*, the author of the Eating Around column in the paper, and the elected union shop steward of District 65–United Auto Workers. He liked to say that ideas like domestic partnership "floated in the air" at a "gay bar when, disco, sweat and cigarette smoke evaporating from our bodies, we batted around scenarios for our future."[22] When their contract expired, the union was threatening to strike; the negotiating team for the union consisted of gay and straight workers. Gay organizers sought to appeal to liberal-minded straights by arguing that gay couples and straight cohabitors stood to benefit equally from changing the rules for employer-provided health coverage. Weinstein claimed that a written policy "would be good for nongay couples too—it would put into words what had been past practice."[23] He was trying to build a coalition, and his argument was not about same-sex marriage, but instead about equal pay for equal work. Since management was not offering much of a wage increase, the benefit for domestic partners yielded "goodwill."[24] Bert Pogebrin, the lawyer for management in the labor negotiations, a Red diaper baby and the husband of the feminist writer Letty Pogebrin,

came up with the infelicitous term *spouse equivalent* for a person who qualified for this benefit.

When the movement went from the *Village Voice* to the West Coast, domestic partnership became a political demand of city government by gay
activists.[25] Tom Brougham, a 1960s radical who had joined the Gay Liberation Front in its early years, had applied for domestic partner benefits from
his employer, the city of Berkeley, where he worked as an accountant clerk,
but his request was denied. His partner, Barry Warren, had sought benefits
for himself and Brougham from his employer, the University of California. The university's personnel department told him that his relationship
with Brougham was not legally recognized and therefore he was not eligible
for benefits, and that giving benefits to gays would require providing them
to straight cohabitors, which the university did not want to do because it
would be too expensive. After they had been turned down by the city of
Berkeley and the University of California, Brougham and Warren had to
shelve their demands temporarily.[26]

Meanwhile Harry Britt, a former Methodist minister, postal carrier, and
night auditor at the Miyako Hotel in San Francisco, was inspired by hearing Brougham explain Berkeley's hoped-for domestic partnership plan at
a meeting of gay student unions. The San Francisco gay community had
become more focused on claiming political rights after Dan White, smarting
from public political humiliation, in November 1978 assassinated Harvey
Milk, the first openly gay man to win political office in California as a member of the San Francisco Board of Supervisors (the equivalent of the city
council), and George Moscone, the city's mayor. Britt wanted to make use
of public sympathy after Milk's assassination to extend rights and benefits
for San Francisco's public employees. Britt, working with a gay lawyer at the
ACLU, came up with a domestic partnership ordinance.[27] The plan called
for equal visitation rights at local jails and hospitals for all city residents
who registered as domestic partners and provided city workers with a day
off from work to attend a funeral. (The latter had become an issue because a
gay man was suing his employer for denying him a day of paid bereavement
leave for attending the funeral of his lover, who had committed suicide.)
The proposal in San Francisco was that domestic partners would be eligible
to purchase the low-cost health insurance the city offered to married couples for the modest cost of about fifty dollars a month. Some provisions of
their plan appeared to be specific, and others were quite broad. One section
stated that "whenever the City and County of San Francisco uses marriage
as a factor in making any decision . . . it shall use domestic partnership in
the same way."[28]

In Britt's initiative, the argument for domestic partnership bridged the difference between advocating for the right to marry and insisting on the right not to have to marry by "singles" whose alternative lifestyles were deserving of recognition.[29] Britt claimed that same-sex couples deserved the right to marry because "we are cheated out of the benefits that are given" to married couples, but he also asserted that, as singles, "gay people and unmarried heterosexuals" were denied "the fundamental right to love and happiness." The relationships of singles were "not frivolous," he argued, since singles also wanted "a way to provide for people they love."[30] Mayor Dianne Feinstein opposed the idea of domestic partnerships because she thought the measure overly broad and potentially costly, and the Catholic archbishop of San Francisco opposed it. He had sent Feinstein a letter saying that the measure was "severely inimical to marriage and the family." Feinstein vetoed the bill and wrote to Britt telling him "that San Francisco should not be called upon to voyage into the unknown in terms of setting precedent for the entire nation for partnerships that may be fleeting and totally vacant of a mutual sense of responsibility or caring [which] is I believe, putting too much strain on our social fabric."[31] About two hundred gay protestors assembled at City Hall and hung a "Dump Dianne" banner. About fifty of them marched to St. Mary's Cathedral to protest the Catholic Church's opposition to the proposed law. Despite the demonstrations, Feinstein successfully fought a recall organized because of this and other issues.[32]

In Berkeley in 1979, the organization of gay voters helped elect Gus Newport, an African American and a former community organizer who was sympathetic to the cause of domestic partnership. He worked with Brougham in contacting a local Catholic priest in Berkeley who favored the idea of domestic partner benefits. Brougham figured out that he could neutralize the bad press the idea had received in San Francisco where the newspapers had called the measure "the live-in lover's law." He came up with the more neutral name, *domestic partnership*, which was descriptive but nonsexual. Brougham later recalled, "We wanted to emphasize the humdrum living together routine. Those were exciting times. We sort of invented the vocabulary step by step and expanded the consciousness step by step."[33] Gays in San Francisco and Berkeley had organized their own organizations within the structure of the Democratic Party. The East Bay Gay and Lesbian Democratic Club, which Brougham helped start, testified before the hearings of the Human Relations and Welfare Committee of the city of Berkeley in 1984, fleshing out the terms of the debate for the next twenty years. Were domestic partner benefits designed to remedy the inability of gays to marry?

Should they instead overcome the privileging of marriage in benefits? And should employers recognize many alternative family relationships or simply privilege ones of a committed and sexual nature?[34]

Still their proposal was turned down by the Berkeley City Council in 1983. Brougham turned to the Berkeley School District, which had a disabled lesbian activist as a board member; she was able to persuade the district to extend domestic partnership benefits to its employees in 1984. The East Bay Gay and Lesbian Democratic Club then campaigned on behalf of a different slate of candidates for the Berkeley City Council who were prepared to vote for the idea. The new council, elected with the gay vote, enacted the measure in 1984, which provided school district and city employees with domestic partnership benefits. In 1985, the gay enclave of West Hollywood, a small independent municipality surrounded by Los Angeles, went a step farther, offering a licenses for domestic partnerships to residents of the city.[35]

On the whole, as domestic partnership spread from one California city or university town to the next, it remained an alternative to marriage. There were a number of interesting legal innovations gay activists were proposing, including second partner adoption, in which the older adult partner legally adopted the younger party, thus making the partner a dependent for the purposes of filing as a head of household on the federal and state income tax returns and qualifying for various benefits at work.[36] Adoption was certainly an innovative model of family, which had as its purpose taking advantage of favorable tax rates for heads of household and employee benefit plans that covered dependents. But symbolically it defined one partner as the "child" of the other, a denial of the adult nature of their relationship, and could not provide the kind of dignity, ritual, and symbolic recognition of the relationship that many couples sought.

For the most part, domestic partnership was the idea of a benefit for an unmarried couple, but individual localities, beginning in the college town of Madison, Wisconsin, also enacted broader definitions of the family ("any two people in a relationship of mutual support") and for various reasons. In Madison, the reason was to offer benefits to the large student population that might live in communes; in Washington, DC, a city with a large African American population, often not living in married couples, local politicians sought to benefit black extended families. In Salt Lake City, the mayor adopted an "adult designee" benefit for a couple and an individual's children as a means of trying to avoid state law that prohibited state recognition of any relationships other than legal marriage and to steer clear of local opposition to benefits for gays. The federal government's sick leave policy allowed employees to define their own family members, even if those family members did not live together: for "any individual related by blood or affinity whose close association with the employee is the equivalent of a family relationship."

Then a "virulent mysterious disease" began to snuff out the lives of gay men and enhanced the appeal of monogamous legally recognized relationships. The gay legal scholar David Chambers argues that AIDS made gay men and lesbians more aware of "the domesticity" and "mutual interdependence" of long-term relationships. As early as 1982, an openly gay doctor argued that if society really wanted to prevent AIDS, it would allow gays to establish committed relationships including the most committed of them all, legal marriage. AIDS not only made visible the concept of stigma but also revealed how many parents there were who rejected their sons, who did not want them to come home to die, who stepped in to make medical decisions on behalf of a son, ignoring his partner, or who, while estranged during life, showed up after the son's death to claim the body. Many an obituary did not mention the cause of death or a partner of a man in the prime of life who died mysteriously; the partner was often not invited to attend the funeral. What was an attorney supposed to say to a new client who explained his situation thus? "My lover has just died. His parents are at the door. They want to take our plants, our art collection, our couch. Do I have to let them into our home?"[37]

Activists also invoked the personal tragedy of Sharon Kowalski and Karen Thompson to make the case for legal marriage for lesbians. They were a closeted lesbian couple in St. Cloud, Minnesota, who owned a house together and entered into a commitment ceremony, unbeknownst to their parents. In 1983, Kowalski was in a car hit by a drunk driver, suffered brain damage, and was paralyzed. Her conservative, antigay father refused to believe that his daughter was a lesbian and took control over her medical decision making, gaining legal guardianship and refusing to allow Thompson to visit. For nine years, Thompson fought in the courts and led a nationwide movement to bring Kowalski back to their home. After three unsuccessful attempts in Minnesota courts, in 1991, Thompson finally won guardianship rights to care for Kowalski. Thompson claimed that she and Kowalski would have been protected if the two of them had signed a durable power of attorney. But their story was also used to argue that legal marriage would be the simplest, most automatic way for a gay or lesbian couple to protect their rights against homophobic relatives and insensitive hospital staff.[38]

A massive protest in Washington, DC, in 1987 was the first national evidence that the lesbian and gay movement had embraced the demand for same-sex marriage. In that year, after so many had known and mourned people who had died of AIDS, one hundred thousand protestors assembled in Washington, DC, for an entire week of protests. They massed in the capitol, demanding a governmental response to the AIDS crisis and protesting the Supreme Court decision the previous year in *Bowers v. Hardwick*, which denied the constitutional right of privacy to gays and continued to define sodomy, even if conducted in private, as a crime. Karen Thompson, hailed as a lesbian hero, explained to the crowd that "if we had been a man and woman, this would not have happened to me." The Reverend Troy Perry had flown in from Los Angeles to preside over a mass wedding ceremony in front of the IRS building, in which about two thousand couples exchanged vows.[39] Couples who had just said "I do" told reporters they were protesting the absence of Social Security survivor rights and not being able to file a joint tax return. But since the protest was occurring during the height of the AIDS tragedy, the practical advantages of legal marriage were merging with the meanings of hope and joy, validation by relatives, and secular and sacred celebration.

In 1991, a model of gay-only partnership benefits at work emerged at Montefiore Hospital in the Bronx and Lotus Corporation in Cambridge, Massachusetts, representing both a more conservative and cheaper innovation for large public and private companies. Gay employees at private, nonunionized corporations other than the havens of bohemianism such as the *Village Voice* had been unsuccessful in pressing employee benefit offices to provide their partners with health coverage. They had taken their complaints to courts and had usually failed. Judges told them that if they wanted their rights, they would have to lobby the state legislature. By the early 1990s, gay groups at work were demanding that employers, not simply the state legislature, had to remedy their situation. Montefiore was the prestigious teaching hospital for Albert Einstein College of Medicine in the Bronx. When Dr. Katherine O'Hanlan, a resident oncologist, was told by the benefits office in 1989 that state laws did not require coverage of her life partner, her department chair urged her to bring the issue to the faculty senate of the medical college. They unanimously endorsed a resolution to provide coverage to domestic partners of the same or opposite sexes. But the personnel department of the hospital turned her down. It said that it was discriminating against her based on her marital status (single), which was perfectly legal, not on the basis of her sexual orientation. The question of what kind of discrimination O'Hanlan faced was a philosophical one that had been posed in Berkeley eight years earlier. Was she in fact discriminated against because she was single or because she was a gay person who was not allowed to marry? Although the answer may indeed may have been both, in the corporate setting, discrimination based on sexual orientation was the more effective answer because gays were more organized, more conscious of discrimination, and more successful in winning state and local ordinances against discrimination and because their claim for fairness appeared "more just" since they were denied the legal right to marry.

Dr. O'Hanlan took her case to William Rubenstein of the ACLU Gay and Lesbian Rights Project, who worked out a confidential settlement with the hospital. When a second couple threatened to sue, Montefiore decided to change its policy in 1991. Montefiore was self-insured, meaning that it was paying for the extra cost of medical coverage out of its own budget. If the medical center didn't have to cover unmarried opposite-sex couples, it saved money. Rubenstein understood that accepting gay-only coverage was a political compromise, but because Montefiore was the largest private employer of the time to adopt domestic partner benefits, he declared victory. He told reporters that "although this is not equal treatment for unmarried heterosexual couples, and their [Montefiore's] policy is not perfect, it is a huge step in the right direction."[40] Straight couples at Montefiore did not protest the decision, even though one has to assume that there were many of them who would have benefited from being able to secure health coverage for their partners.

Six months later, Lotus Development Corporation of Cambridge, Massachusetts, a computer software company, announced a similar policy.[41] Montefiore was actually a larger employer than Lotus, but Lotus was a publicly traded corporation and received far more press coverage for its decision than the hospital in the Bronx did. Major corporations knew their gay and straight cohabiting employees wanted health coverage, but, as an executive recruiter explained, "no corporation wants the grief of being a pioneer in this area."[42] In 1987, Margie Bleichman, a software engineer at Lotus, filled out her personnel forms and put down her partner's name in her application for health insurance coverage. She recalled, "I was politely told that the insurance company wouldn't allow it."[43] Bleichman and two other lesbian employees organized the Lotus Extended Benefits Group. They proposed that Lotus's health coverage should include the employee and another person of his or her own choosing. Russ Campanello, vice president for human resources, was supportive of the idea of domestic partnership benefits, but rejected the Extended Benefits Group's proposal to cover significant others, apparently not without considerable debate, out of fear that employees would nominate their sickest friend for coverage.[44] To Lotus's executives, gay employees had a more just claim for benefits than straight cohabitors because they were denied the right to marry. In establishing a system of registration for benefits, Lotus saw itself as "providing a parallel process to getting married."[45] If gays were able to marry legally, so far as Lotus was concerned, domestic partnership benefits would be unnecessary.[46]

The company hesitated several years before adopting a domestic partnership policy because its insurance carrier feared the cost of covering partners with AIDS. Campanello became convinced that the fear was unjustified based on the experience of California cities that offered such benefits; he found that premium costs in California municipalities rarely rose more than 3 percent after these benefits were established.[47] Eventually, Lotus decided to pay the cost for health claims itself, and its stop-loss insurance carrier assumed the cost of health claims for partners only in catastrophic cases.

Thus Lotus's executives were not surprised by threatening phone calls, returned shredded software disks, and customers who told them "You people are supporting Satan" and vowed never to use Lotus software again. They seemed to have been taken aback, however, when the company's internal e-mail system was overloaded with messages. Unlike at Montefiore, at Lotus there were many straight cohabitors who were upset that they could not secure coverage for their partners. Although some employees thought that company policy should not recognize homosexual relationships, most were bothered by the fact that such an innovative employer had not offered benefits to straight cohabitors. As was true in many workplaces, engaged cohabitating couples on the route to being married wanted to take advantage of benefits for married couples. A young marketing specialist who had just married said, "It would have been nice to have those benefits during my courtship." Another employee criticized the idea of promoting marriage (or compensating for the denial of it) through benefits. He wrote, "The policy discriminates against heterosexuals who choose not to marry. If you choose to buy into the married model, you can get your spouse insured. If you don't buy in, you suffer."[48] As in the Montefiore case, William Rubenstein of the ACLU hailed the victory at Lotus, but another gay rights attorney, Ivy Young, panned it. She told a reporter the day the company announced its decision, "I applaud Lotus' action, but it leaves out a big segment of people who are also affected by family policies that are 50 years behind the reality."[49] Lotus (now part of IBM) has retained the corporate model of domestic partner benefits: domestic partner benefits are still offered only to gays.

While corporate employers took domestic partnership in a new direction, state legislatures were seeking to balance the older vision of benefits for alternative families with the newer emphasis on rectifying discrimination against gays. State domestic partnership law in California illustrated the result, a new political compromise of domestic partnership for "gays, lesbians, and seniors." The initiative for domestic partnership at the state level in California began in 1994 with Life AIDS, an advocacy group that wanted to cut through the red tape of hospital visitation policy and also accord gay couples equal standing with married people as potential "conservators" of the estates of partners unable to handle their own affairs. Senior citizen cohabitors, upset about being denied hospital visitation privileges, wanted the same rights. The California Commission on Aging, the Congress of California Seniors, and the Older Women's League of California liked the idea of protection for their private relationships, especially for elderly widows who chose not to remarry because they were dependent on their husbands' pensions or on Social Security survivor benefits. In the 1960s, the occasional magazine or newspaper article mentioned unmarried retired couples, and Florida elderly had unsuccessfully backed repeal of the state's criminal law against cohabitation. Cohabitation among the elderly was growing, increasing by a hundred thousand in the decade of the 1990s. What was new in California was that there was a clear coalition of gays and the straight elderly. The chair of the California Commission on Aging characterized domestic partnership as "a sincere and compassionate alternative to matrimony for people who have thoroughly assessed their consciences, and based on cumulative wisdom few people are qualified to challenge have decided that for their purposes, matrimony is impractical."[50]

In 1998, California elected a Democratic governor, and the Democrats controlled both houses of the state legislature. The new governor, Gray Davis, a "media-conscious centrist," had previously represented the gay enclave of West Hollywood in the state assembly. In his gubernatorial campaign, Davis said he favored a domestic partner bill along the lines of one he had voted for as a University of California regent, a benefits policy available only to gays because they were not allowed to marry. Davis did not want to sign a broader bill covering private health care plans as well as those offered by the cities and states. Nor did he want to cover heterosexual as well as homosexual couples. He had been elected with the gay vote and wanted to sign a measure gay activists favored. He worked with Carole Migden, the lesbian and liberal Democratic assemblywoman from San Francisco, in fashioning a compromise. The bill would be the corporate, University of California model (benefits for state and city employees and for gays) to which Migden was able to add elderly straight cohabitors.[51] Subsequently, this definition of domestic partnership became the one used in legislation in New Jersey and Washington state.

Same-Sex Marriage

As domestic partnership was going mainstream, gay legal organizations were debating whether to give much higher priority to arguing for same-sex marriage in state courts. They were flooded with complaints about family issues: child custody and adoption, health benefits coverage, inheritance, and the absence of Social Security survivor benefits coverage.[52] Gay rights litigators, who met twice a year at a legal roundtable, could not agree. In 1989, their behind-the-scenes debate emerged in *Out/Look*, a lesbian and gay journal. Tom Stoddard, a media-friendly fund-raising genius who had built up the Lambda organization and served as its executive director, wrote, "Why Gay People Should Seek the Right to Marry." He argued that legal marriage was cheaper for gay couples than going to a lawyer to fill out a huge number of legal documents protecting their relationship. He further argued that excluding gays from marriage was a symbol of their second-class status. To Stoddard, same-sex marriage was the single most important way to press heterosexuals to grant equality to gays and lesbians because he believed only marriage accorded gay relationships the respect they deserved.

Lesbian activists had always been more critical of marriage than gay men because they saw marriage as a patriarchal institution that underscored the unequal gender roles of men and women.[53] The Lambda legal director, Paula Ettelbrick, countered with her own article, "Since When Is Marriage the Path to Liberation?" She disliked putting before the public the least threatening gay couples, the committed white middle-class homeowners who were raising children and just wanted their rights. She also feared that gay marriage would generate a huge backlash, which would drain resources for other fights. Ettelbrick believed that the highest priority should be given to fighting for universal health care coverage, which would benefit the largest number of people, whatever their sexual orientation. The articles of the two lawyers were often reprinted side by side in anthologies because their opposing arguments seemed to crystallize the two positions in the debate. Both lawyers advocated the right of gays to marry, but they assigned it different priorities.

Evan Wolfson, a Lambda lawyer who coined the term *marriage equality*, had written a paper as a student at Harvard Law School about the arguments on behalf of gay marriage. In 1989, he was still an insider at Lambda who was trying to dampen the bitter internal debates by formulating a compromise between Stoddard and Ettelbrick, which he called "A Family Bill of Rights." In it he espoused the position that, in order to be treated fairly, gays should press for the right to marry *and* the right to have other family forms legally recognized. He favored the domestic partnership benefits employers offered and the local domestic partnership ordinances cities had adopted. He did not think that gay activists should be backed into a corner of favoring either marriage or universal health care, equality or difference, liberation or assimilation. But when it came right down to it, he wrote, "Domestic partnership is indeed second-class. . . . It neither provides the symbolism and substance of marriage, nor resolves the problems of access to needed benefit protections identified by marriage critics."[54]

Still, national gay organizations decided against taking on any gay marriage litigation, because they thought the public was not ready and that such litigation would trigger a national backlash. But they could not stop individual couples who managed to find lawyers and win the first round in court, as a couple did in the Hawaii Supreme Court in 1993. The possibility of same-sex marriage in the Aloha State was frightening enough to trigger a backlash in other states and in Congress. States had always determined their own marriage laws, but with an understanding that they would also recognize marriages contracted under the rules of other states. In this case, however, other states did not want to recognize same-sex marriages contracted in Hawaii, so they passed their own "marriage protection acts." Social conservatives sought a national ban on same-sex marriage. In an election year, Congress passed DOMA (the Defense of Marriage Act) by a whopping margin in anticipation that Hawaii would legalize gay marriage. The purpose of DOMA was to "quarantine" same-sex marriage so that other states would not be forced to recognize same-sex marriage legalized in Hawaii. DOMA further stated that the federal government would not recognize same-sex marriage for any purpose. In 1996, DOMA was passed by both houses of Congress by overwhelming margins, and President Bill Clinton signed the bill into law.

Against the opposition tide, in 2000 Vermont passed a halfway compromise, a civil union registration bill that afforded same-sex couples all the entitlements of legal marriage without attaching the name to it. The first complete victory for same-sex marriage in the United States came in 2003, when the Supreme Court of Massachusetts ruled that gay couples did in fact have the right to marry under the state's constitution. By 2003, the pattern was already clear that a legal victory in the courts for same-sex marriage ignited a backlash—in this case, a deluge of amendments to state constitutions banning same-sex marriage and efforts to ban gay marriage in the federal constitution.

The backlash against gay marriage was the latest wave of the backlash against the sexual revolution. Because state courts could strike down laws banning same-sex marriage, the Christian Right sought stronger protection for traditional marriage at the state as well as national level. State laws banning same-sex marriage seemed an insufficient barrier, which could be overturned by liberal judges. Therefore, opponents of same-sex marriage turned to constitutional amendments, proposed on the ballot for voters in the state to ratify. Except for one temporary victory in Arizona, subsequently reversed, all proposed state amendments banning same-sex marriage passed in the years between 1998 and 2008. The Republican Party used rhetoric about threat to the institution of marriage to encourage ballot measures against same-sex marriage, with the hope of turning out its base of Christian conservatives to vote. In 2004, President George W. Bush endorsed a federal constitutional amendment to outlaw same-sex marriage, and the issue became salient in the presidential campaign. Although both parties had opposed same-sex marriage in the 1990s, it was the Republican Party that sought to use the issue to its advantage. Partisan politics contributed to the high number of ballot measures against same-sex marriage in 2004. Opponents could draw on the rich tradition of opposition to judicial activism dating to Richard Nixon's campaign against the Warren Court and the much longer-standing rhetoric of defending the institution of marriage. In the backlash directed against same-sex marriage, domestic partnership was also targeted for defeat. Beginning in 1997, in response to the passage of the federal DOMA, seven states enacted their own "Super-DOMA statutes" that broadened the prohibition against same-sex marriage and prohibited domestic partnerships as well. Beginning in 2000, seventeen states enacted constitutional amendments prohibiting not only same-sex marriage but also domestic partnership benefits. Although these broader restrictions were passed in more conservative states in the South and Rocky Mountain states, Christian Right advocates also scored important victories for broader restriction in Ohio, largely as a result of mobilization of religious supporters there.

The organizers of these ballot measures built coalitions of Mormons, Catholic bishops, and profamily Christian Right groups. They drew on long-term opponents of gay civil rights, who had made known their opposition to gay civil rights measures even prior to the emergence of the issue of same-sex marriage. By securing signatures from members of church groups, they were able to get these restrictive measures on the ballot. In California, where same-sex couples and the elderly enjoyed many of the same legal rights as married couples because of the domestic partnership laws, activists fighting for legalization of same-sex marriage believed that it was necessary to define domestic partnership as an unpalatable compromise that denied them their full rights as citizens. Matrimony was elevated to the gold standard—the symbolic recognition, the affirmation of lifetime commitment, the natural destination for romantic love, and the source of personal validation same-sex couples were seeking. Nuptials were even claimed to be beneficial because they would increase the revenues for the San Francisco bridal industry. The new legal argument was that denial of same-sex marriage constituted "a dignity harm" by refusing to acknowledge that same-sex couples are entitled to the same dignity and respect as opposite-sex couples. The clear implication of this argument was that there was something undignified about cohabiting. In ruling in favor of same-sex marriage, Judge Vaughn Walker even defended marital privileging as fair, so long as the benefits marriage provided were also extended to same-sex couples. Experts in favor of same-sex marriage testified that domestic partnership, though a well-intentioned legal innovation sponsored by the gay civil rights movement, "marginalizes and stigmatizes gay families."[55]

On the whole, gay activists and legal organizations helped to make cohabitation into an institution possessed of entitlements. They raised questions about the invisibility of relationships other than heterosexual marriage and about what was being done in the name of promoting marriage. In the 1990s, elderly groups emerged as slightly audible voices in a movement dominated by gay rights activists. Although domestic partnership was enormously good for straight cohabitors, it managed to displease both conservatives and gay advocates of same-sex marriage. To conservatives, domestic partnership was one of many threats to the stability of marriage; to advocates of gay marriage, it remained the separate status gays were being offered instead of legal marriage. In fact, public opinion polls showed that the public understood domestic partnership precisely in this manner, as legal recognition for gay couples that provided their relationships with benefits but withheld from them the label *marriage*.[56] As same-sex marriage became a more significant goal within gay political life, domestic partnership proved to be not validating enough. It was created for two contradictory reasons, because gays had nontraditional relationships outside of legal marriage and because gays were not allowed to marry. So long as domestic partnership was associated with the former meaning, it represented coming to grips with the changing reality of the American family. When it was offered as a consolation prize or seen in that light, it was redefined not as a positive reform created by gay union and political leaders, but as the segregated schoolhouse of same-sex marriage, deemed to be separate and inferior.

The fight for same-sex marriage shows that when the battle is truly joined, it is impossible to maintain a nuanced argument that insists on both the right to marriage and the right not to have to marry. Cohabitation throughout American history has existed in the shadow of marriage; it seems altogether fitting that it should now exist in the shadow of same-sex marriage. Virtually every pundit predicts that "someday" (when is left undefined) same-sex marriage will be declared constitutional by the US Supreme Court. But so far as the issue of cohabitation is concerned, the question is whether law and policies for couples who do not marry will receive any interest or attention until that day finally arrives.

ELEVEN

Epilogue

In many west European countries, cohabitation in the 1960s was mainly confined to the student districts, but in the United States, it was part of youth culture, but even more common and rooted in patterns of living among the poor, the less educated, racial minorities, and interracial couples. Cohabitation went mainstream in the 1970s, becoming visible in religious small towns and the suburbs in the 1970s, setting off a number of cultural clashes. Nonetheless, the more couples cohabited, the more favorable attitudes became, especially among young people; the major route to marriage or remarriage lay through cohabiting first; living together became common among the middle aged as well as the young and was even growing among the elderly; it became a family form for bearing and raising children. These developments occurred not because the law was changing, but despite the fact that the law was a roadblock to change. Moreover, for all the publicity and magazine articles that cohabitation generated, it was still the case that as of the mid-1980s, cohabitation was growing despite or because it was concealed, not because landlords, relatives, and employers were explicitly informed about it.

As cohabitation increased in frequency and spread more widely, it was easier to classify into several ideal types: a prelude to marriage, an alternative to marriage, a form of cost-sharing housing, or a serious form of dating. Of these types of cohabitation, living together as an explicit rejection of marriage is actually the least common. The number of couples who are seeking a long-term committed free union because they do not believe in legal marriage remains the smallest group of people living together. To be sure, there has been a substantial number of the population who say that marriage is out-of-date. In 1978, 28 percent of Americans told pollsters that the institution of marriage was obsolete; in 2010, the percentage had risen to 40 percent.[1] But even those who hold to this view are divided between cohabitors defending their way of living and married couples who believe that matrimony is under siege.

A fundamental transformation of sexuality, marriage, and family life transpired in the last three decades of the twentieth century. Cohabitation has introduced more flexibility, churning, complexity, and ambiguity into personal and family life, all the while contributing to changing notions of the institution of marriage. As the result of a series of a linked set of revolutions of the 1960s (sexual, civil rights, youth, feminist, legal, contraceptive), marriage has been redefined as an optional rather than required way of living. Marriage is no longer perceived as necessary for sex, companionship, child-rearing, respect, or moving up the job ladder at work. The origins of these developments lie in the social movements, liberalism, and the counter-culture of the 1960s. Many of the social movements emphasized the importance of the freedom of the individual to make choices and had a critique of the power of institutional authority in regulating the life of the individual. Implicitly what was being contested was the power of established religious authorities to define morality and marriage and of parents, communities, and social institutions to enforce morality through the marriage cure. There is a direct line linking the discussion of personal growth, self-fulfillment to new language about marriage in terms of options, choices, and the still frequently used term, lifestyles. Swept away by such language was the alternative framework of roles, expectations, tradition, and conformity.

Because cohabitation offers some of the same satisfactions once solely confined to marriage and can be seen as an option, choice, or lifestyle, marriage must meet a higher standard. A couple decides to set the date not because family or friends think it is time but because they have paid off their debts, can afford a house, and have reached the level of personal maturity and mutual understanding necessary to make a long-term commitment to each other. The median age at marriage has soared to record highs—there is less of a retreat from a marriage than a delay in postponing the big day.

As cohabitation was diffusing throughout the population, the divorce mania of the 1970s began to slow. Marriage in which both partners had a college degree was accommodating itself to feminist demands for equality within all male/female relationships, including marriage and the emergence of college graduates choosing each other as lifetime partners—they were older than their parent's generation and intent on creating a new form (ours, hers, and his). The divorce rate plateaued in the early 1980s; the rising age of marriage (people who marry later divorce less) was reinforced by the prolongation of education, including the rising level of women's education. Is there such a thing as premarital divorce? Presumably if there was, the actual number of divorces would be considerably higher. More broadly, the relationship of cohabitation to divorce is a complex one; the correlation is weakest for couples who intend to marry when they move in together and strongest for serial cohabitors. Ironically, the link between cohabitation and divorce persisted even as cohabitation became the norm, since those who marry directly without cohabiting are the new countercul-ture, more religious, conservative about gender roles, and committed to lifelong marriage than the much larger group of couples who lived together as prelude to marriage.

Divorce not only left many men and women marriage-shy but made the oft-repeated remark, that if a couple had cohabitated, they would not have gotten a divorce, into a cliché. Cynical guests at a wedding openly specu-lated about whether a marriage would last, and some ministers even raised the prospect as they asked a couple to pledge their faithful love. The specter of divorce seems to act like a yellow blinking caution light on advancing to matrimony. It is seen as worse to marry and get divorced than not to marry at all. The actual trauma of marital disruption added to the attractiveness of cohabitation: the divorced chose to live together before taking the plunge again or opted for cohabitation as an alternative to matrimony. Children who were the products of the world of no-fault divorce, having witnessed parental breakup followed by cohabitation, largely concluded that living together was a very good idea.

Family and relationship styles in postindustrial America reflected the im-press of class and race inequalities as well as the diffusion of living patterns of the poor among the working and lower middle class. As has always been the case, women with higher levels of education are less likely to cohabit than women with less education, creating have and have-not cohabitation. Among the young and well educated, the general pattern is that cohabita-tion is childless and a brief period before marriage, and childbirth takes place only within marriage. Among the young and less well educated, co-habitation often includes childbearing, is also brief, and as often as not does not lead to marriage. Wedding bells are not ringing for those with less edu-cation and income not because they do not value the institution or aspire to its benefits, but because they have a long list of financial and relationship prerequisites before they are willing to say their vows. The weakening of the economic position of young men with limited education, this rising stan-dard for marriage, and the acceptability of single motherhood contributed to the delay in marriage and increases in cohabitation. Despite the impact of feminism on so many aspects of marriage and family life, the belief still holds among both women and men that a man should have a steady job before he can think about pledging his troth. Young men with limited education have had increasing difficulty finding the type of well-paying, secure jobs that enabled their predecessors to fulfill the role of economic provider. A couple no longer marries young and then struggles for success together. They postpone matrimony not just until financial stability appears around the corner but until they can pay for the lavish wedding; meanwhile, the bar for moving in together is far lower.[2]

Rising educational levels for women and greater prospects for them in paid work were inseparable from the availability of a tiny tablet, which weakened the link between marriage and childbearing. The pill diminished a woman's fear that sex outside of marriage would lead to pregnancy. It gave a woman the opportunity to acquire more advanced education by reducing the chance that she would have to drop out of school or abandon her aspirations for a career because of motherhood. Premarital sex came first, living together much later; a college girl usually did not move in with her boyfriend until she had a supply of Enovid. Many doctors in the 1960s did not prescribe the pill for unmarried women; thus, getting a prescription, like cohabitation itself, often involved lying to an adult.

Remarkably the sexual revolution in the United States was characterized by more effective contraception and more unintended pregnancies. Both of these developments, explained more fully in the chapters of this book, were related to the rise of cohabitation, at least indirectly. Not every woman on the pill moved in with her boyfriend, and most single pregnant women were not cohabiting at the time they gave birth. Nonetheless, an increasing number of unwed mothers, often referred to as single mothers, were not single—and were not teenagers either. Cohabiting became a context for childbearing in the 1990s; between 2001 and 2007, 22 percent of American children were born to cohabiting parents, and while this development is fairly uncommon among the college educated, it is spreading upward from the poor to the working class and lower middle class. Many of these pregnancies can be described as accidental rather than planned, although welcome, since children are seen as a positive source of identity for a parent. The cohabiting father's name appears on the child's birth certificate, and he is present at the child's birth. But half of these relationships do not last five years, and the breakup rate among cohabiting parents is much higher than for the legally married. The breakups often appear not directly economic but related to conflict in the relationship, often the man's infidelity. While single motherhood started to become less stigmatized and more common by the 1970s, one factor in the growth of the unwed mother as cohabitor was the increase the Hispanic population of the United States, with cohabiting more common among American-born daughters of Hispanic immigrant parents. Another was the willingness of other relatives to house these couples, most of whom did not live on their own.[3]

Has the stigma against cohabitation disappeared? The evidence in this book has shown that it has lessened considerably but not entirely vanished. Live-in lovers or paramours became POSSLQS, then significant others, and are now being called partners. Had Prince Charles and Diana lived together, as Prince William and Kate Middleton had done before their nuptials, we were told that they might not have gotten divorced. The "elected national leader" measure of stigma toward cohabitation reflects the growth in public acceptance—Governor Andrew Cuomo of New York and Mayor Michael Bloomberg of New York City are residing with their female companions without feeling public pressure to get married, past history of cohabitation is no bar to running for highest office (Hillary and Bill Clinton, with each other and John Kerry who lived with widow Teresa Heinz before they wed). Past behavior is quite different than current living status, and any good campaign manager would tell Andrew Cuomo or Michael Bloomberg that if they choose to run for president, they must get married. Since the French view sexual matters with a wink and nod, it is worth only passing notice that an unwed mother of four in a long-term partnership was a viable candidate for the presidency of that country. But the Australians, who like to refer to the partner of their woman prime minister as the First Bloke, have also decided that their particular twosome is a very modern couple. Because the first family is a symbol of national fidelity to the ideal of marriage and the family, the American electorate is unwilling to accept a presidential cohabitor and seeks reassurance of national ideals in the carefully posed photograph of the happily married candidate and smiling spouse.

Public opinion polls, a more systematic measure of stigma, reveal that the segment of the population who disapprove of cohabitation is most concentrated among older, more religious people living in the most conservative regions of the country. In 2010, a Pew Trust poll asked a representative sample of Americans whether they thought cohabitation was a good thing or a bad thing. Forty-four percent said it was a good thing, 13 percent had no opinion, and 43 percent thought cohabitation was a bad thing. A similar question has been asked going back as early as 1981, with similar results. Those most likely to think cohabitation is a bad thing for society are older, are more frequent churchgoers, tend to be white evangelical Protestants or Mormons, and are political conservatives affiliated with the Republican party. Despite Norman Lear's sitcom suggesting that Republican conservatives were secret cohabitors, they were in fact true to their beliefs and were half as likely to be living together as Democrats. By the 1990s, couples who pledged to love, honor, and obey without having cohabited first reflect the fidelity to the moral values in which they were raised: they come from religious families and have conservative attitudes toward gender roles.[4]

A considerable amount of culture war was conducted over the question of how to define the family. For the stigma of cohabitation to disappear, Americans would have to expect cohabitation not only to be open but also consider such couples a family. Most Americans believe "a family is where the children are." Conversely, the public is not ready to endorse a diversity of living arrangements as a family, especially when there are no children present. Childless cohabitors are regarded as people in a holding pattern, engaged in some temporary arrangement that might evolve into a family. For most of the populace, marriage transforms a childless couple into a family, whereas nonmarriage keeps them outside.[5] A national survey of public attitudes in 2003 confirms these views: the majority of Americans did not define childless cohabitors, straight or gay, as a family, but could be persuaded otherwise by the presence of children; senior citizens, by contrast, told the interviewers that a family consisted of people related by blood, marriage, or adoption.[6] The views of seniors indicate that the same segment of the population that thinks cohabitation is a bad thing has also concluded that it does not meet their definition of a family.

Public attitudes are considerably more negative toward cohabitation among the poor, especially when they are bearing or raising children. The survey in 2003 did not pose the question of what is a family, when the couple had children from several previous relationships, or were living on food stamps or TANF. The social scientists use the term "fragile family" to signal the instability of such a living arrangement, and in public discourse, the question is usually asked, "Why don't they get married?" It remains to be seen if attitudes begin to change as these patterns, once confined to the poor, migrate up the social ladder to the working class and lower middle class. One area of greatest success for the backlash against the sexual revolution was welfare policy, where prejudices about sexuality, marriage, and race were joined with taxpayer desires to cut the welfare rolls. The impetus for changes in welfare had been building since the country turned rightward in the 1970s. Clinton's welfare reform act of 1996 made clear that the basis of a new public policy toward the provision of public assistance was the promotion of marriage. Bush's Healthy Marriage Initiative of 2005 was a continuation of the insistence on marriage promotion under Clinton with the major difference being the amount of federal funding for marriage promotion (including classes in relationship skills) and the growing number of programs for abstinence education as against comprehensive sex education in the schools.

The irony of the backlash against the sexual revolution was that advocates of welfare reform, social conservatism, and gay civil rights ended up being on the side of promoting marriage. The long struggle for same-sex marriage reveals a new constituency that does not believe that marriage is obsolete. In demanding legal marriage gay activists initially attacked and then ended up reinforcing the privileging of citizenship rights through marriage. Vouchsafing the virtues of marriage is favored rhetoric of welfare reform and social conservatives, but for gay rights activists, it is a decided shift in emphasis. When legal marriage was blocked by the courts, gays began to experiment with alternatives such as second-party adoptions. After AIDS and the lesbian baby boom, an institution that offered commitment, stability, a good environment for raising children, and manifold legal benefits acquired new luster; alternatives to marriage seemed to represent acceptance of second-class citizenship. Many gay couples embraced legal marriage not simply as the capstone of the success of a relationship but as an emblem of having achieved full citizenship rights. Gay activists such as Evan Wolfson believed that advocacy of same-sex marriage rights would advance alongside the cause of broader reform in social benefits and family law, that it was possible to fight for the right to marry at the same time as claiming that marriage was only one of several family forms. Wolfson's pluralistic notion of reform in family law was drowned out by demands for same-sex marriage; the former emphasis on marriage as the foundation of society has come at the expense of insistence on family diversity. Indeed, as the fight has continued, same-sex partners have argued for marriage equality on the grounds that their children should not suffer the stigma of "illegitimacy." The successes of same-sex marriage in the courts have come from the plaintiffs stressing their right to the special privileges marriage accords, not from insisting that such benefits are distributed unfairly to the legally married.

So long as the right to marry is denied to same-sex couples, it seems likely that the spotlight will remain on marriage as a social good, and, thus, much of gay discourse will focus on the right to be able to marry rather than on the right not to have to marry. Since the battle over same-sex marriage has attracted most of the attention, there is little interest left over for reforming policies and laws having to do with cohabitation. In theory, at least, cohabitation might find allies in the women's movement, since it insisted on women's equality with men in all relationships. Self-identified feminists have crusaded for student housing rights, palimony, and custody rights for cohabitors on grounds of equality between the sexes, with support from well-known feminists or the National Organization for Women. In paying a personal price for what amounted to a personal or legal attack on the double standard, these women paved the way for other women not to have to suffer as much because of it. But advocating cohabitation was a very minor theme in feminist manifestoes and in pressing for an end to marital status discrimination, they had in mind the plight of single or divorced women. The social movement that has contributed the most to cohabitor's rights has been gay liberation. Gay activists led the fight for domestic partnership, which has brought concrete economic benefits at work to cohabitors, straight or gay. Lacking an identity of their own, cohabitors are attached to the victories won and consolation prizes offered to the gay civil rights movement. There are still some gains being made in terms of domestic partnership registration, but in most other areas of law and policy, cohabitor's rights have not advanced very much. Many areas of law and policy would have to change, but among them are those of the federal government having to do with immigration, inheritance, the military, Social Security, worker's compensation, and health care. Given the political obstacles involved in achieving reform at the state level, only by comparison can it be said that changing federal law is somehow more difficult. Reforming federal law involves Congress voting against a national policy to "put a ring on it"; therefore, the prospect for the passage of a raft of new legislation, especially without a movement pressuring for it, looms far off on the horizon.

Many legal reformers from the American Law Institute to legal scholars such as Cynthia Grant Bowman have advocated some kind of op-out system to impose family obligations on cohabiting couples raising children and allow greater rights as well, even if such couples have not contractually chosen these rights and responsibilities. (The opt-out feature would give long-term cohabiting couples a means of deliberately excluding themselves from having these rights and obligations imposed on them.) An opt-out system is based on the premise that cohabitation, not simply marriage, creates obligations as well as rights. Reforms such as these would bring the United States closer to parity with the family laws for cohabitors already enacted in many of the Commonwealth countries and Western Europe. The historical survey of law and policy in this book has shown that, in the United States, instituting equal rights and benefits for cohabitors would involve far more than a reform of states' family law and changes in benefits. Local and national policies from military stipends reserved for married dependents to welfare reform to sex education in the schools to zoning laws would also have to adapt to reality. Since the 1990s, the United States had experienced a surge in marriage promotion at both the state and federal levels, and it would take a considerable effort to undo what has been done in its name.

Moreover, the problem does not lie simply in family rights or obligations or in reversal of the marriage promotion policies implemented beginning in the 1990s. It also lies in the lack of protection for individual rights. There is no federal civil rights law prohibiting housing discrimination against cohabitors. Civil rights laws that protect singles and the divorced from discrimination on the grounds of marital status do not apply to cohabitation, which is defined as conduct rather than status. Similarly, there is no US Supreme Court ruling on the issue of cohabitors' privacy rights. The shift away from public intervention in intimate relations does not apply to the intimate relations of the poor. Welfare recipients do not have a constitutional right to privacy, but not because they are cohabitating but because they are on welfare. Thus, cohabitors may or may not enjoy a constitutional right to privacy, but only if they are economically privileged. By contrast, the Canadian government took a strong stand in favor of the right of personal privacy in a commission report in 2001, which said, "At its most basic level, privacy requires that the state keep out of the bedrooms of the nation. It also requires that the state avoid, whenever possible the establishment of legal rules that cannot be administered effectively without intrusive examinations into or forced disclosure of, the intimate details of personal adult relationships."[7] That standard is absolutely necessary for fair treatment of cohabitors, because it is the strongest rationale for trumping the state's long-held interest in promoting marriage, forcing it as a cure for cohabitation, and asserting that religious morality must shape public policy toward marriage.

Much of the developed world has proceeded from an understanding that cohabitation is a form of family, and that the question for government is how best to support the kinds of families people actually form. In Sweden and Denmark, where the rates of cohabitation are more than three times higher than in the United States, cohabitors are treated like married couples for purposes of taxation and have the same rights to welfare benefits, inheritance, medical insurance, and child care as married couples. Eligibility for social benefits from the government is not linked to marital status, a reform that would be greatly beneficial to cohabitors and their children in the United States. The French legal system has moved away from the couple to an individual's selection of a designated partner who can be the recipient of benefits and property. The lawyer Nancy Polikoff writes, "All individuals need access to food, housing, and health care. One's attachment to another adult in an intimate, sexual relationship should not be the basis for apportioning these basic necessities."[8] In that respect, the United States lags behind many other developed countries in the legal recognition of and benefits available to cohabitors because it is still committed to bolstering marriage and therefore defines cohabitors as not entitled to fully share in government entitlement programs.[9]

Perhaps it was inevitable that in a nation so committed to freedom of contract, the major legal advance for cohabitation came from a contractual legal framework. *Marvin's* contract approach for cohabiting couples had proved difficult to implement; not many couples spend the time and money to draw up legal contracts, and courts are fairly suspicious of claiming that verbal promises constitute contracts. Eventually, lawyers and judges recognized that such an approach was unworkable and aided a very few. The American Law Institute, the same organization of judges and lawyers that called for decriminalization of the law against cohabitation in 1962, devised what it hoped would become a major new legal approach—a status approach—for cohabiting couples. To be sure, some lawyers argued that the principles did not go far enough. But such principles still went too far for the average state legislator. As of 2011, no state has passed reform of family law incorporating ALI principles. The reason these reforms have failed to pass is the same as the reason so many other laws having to do with cohabitation have been delayed or have not passed; reform on behalf of cohabitors is seen as a threat to the institution of marriage. In addition, it had been argued that many cohabitors do not want quasi-marital obligations imposed on them by the law. As always, changing the law on behalf of cohabitors is not a coherent social movement but, instead, a piecemeal reform of family law led by lawyers and judges. Although the major arguments on behalf of civil rights for cohabitors have been about the right to privacy—being left alone by the state—many of the major difficulties of cohabitation involve the vulnerability of the dependents in such a relationship. In such a situation, the state has a compelling interest in making cohabitation marriage-like, in violating cohabitors' right to privacy by imposing obligations on them that at least some of them hoped to avoid.

In a few areas of law such as removing the disabilities attached to birth outside of wedlock or child custody, the law caught up with and reflected the rapid growth of cohabitation. But on the whole, the major function of law and policy has been to try to strengthen marriage as an institution, propping up what appears to be a shaky foundation. The romance of alternative lifestyles having receded, many social scientists take the same position. A recent report by two major American scholars of the family about cohabitation among the working class calls for, among other policy changes, reintroducing fault grounds in child-custody hearings.[10] Other like-minded social scientists and law professors incorrectly assume that stigma slows the sexual revolution, when in fact, in its early stages the increased frequency of cohabitation was still covert until some tipping point when disclosure, even to relatives, became acceptable. The narrative of family decline, the costs of the sexual revolution, missing all of its benefits, indicates the way that welfare rights and Woodstock continues to shape national debate. We are engaged in a great national experiment to determine whether offering benefits and economic incentives for marriage as well as courses in relationships skills will encourage couples to enter matrimony prior to the moment when they are ready. Fear, compulsion, and long-standing rhetoric about morality and the importance of marriage to the nation have governed public policy toward cohabitation before, during, and since the sexual revolution of the 1960s. It is said that cohabitation leads to divorce, harms children, and contributes to domestic violence. It is claimed that cohabitation lowers the quality of marriages, cheapens women, damages the family, spreads disease, and is even associated with alcoholism. What is remarkable is how little impact these frequently voiced fears have had on attitudes or behavior.

The social issue of cohabitation raises radical questions about the way marriage acts as a gatekeeper to social provision, public and private. Law and policy offer far greater benefits to those who can furnish a wedding certificate. For cohabitation to be something other than second-class citizenship, American laws and social policies would have to terminate the generous and special privileges carved out for the formally married. Many gay activists and feminist law professors have called for an end to these state subsidies for marriage and state regulation of who can marry by replacing our state-regulated system with one of civil unions and benefits and rights bestowed on "dependency relationships" rather than on marriages. The feminist law professor Martha Fineman, for example, favors abolition of marriage as a legal category, taking the state out of the marriage business. She advocates ending all the subsidies that apply to marriage and instead applying them to caretaker relationships such as those between an individual and a sick friend, a sibling, or a roommate. The practical argument against such a view is that it fails to appreciate the depth of the culture war and of the struggle for same-sex marriage, the level of dissatisfaction that would arise among those assigned the legal status of "intimate caregiver" or "committed partner." [11]

In American history, rapid changes in marriage, family, sexuality, and women's roles are perceived as threatening, unwelcome, even frightening and are interpreted as symptoms of national decline. I see no reason to think that most of the country will abandon the belief that the fate of American society rests on the state of marriage. So great is adherence to this notion that the best reformers can hope for is a subtle, less than frontal assault on marital privilege. I like the gentle plea from two demographers who wish for a "more nuanced view of the relative benefits of marriage," which they believe is "essential for the formulation of social policy."[12]

The social policy that represents the most significant change for cohabitors is the availability of domestic partnership benefits, now common at high-tech firms, Fortune 500 companies, and many state and local governments. Before this time, straight cohabitors needed to marry in order to secure health coverage for their partner. Nonetheless, while more employers than ever before offer these important benefits to cohabitors, other firms have been cutting pensions and contributions to health care premiums. Regrettably, much of the equalization of entitlements will come not from greater access for unmarried couples to employer-provided health care but instead from cutting holes in the safety net the married currently enjoy. Although marital privileging is likely to remain, it seems safe to predict there will be fewer privileges for the married and thus, a smaller gap between them and everyone else.

Cohabitors, a large minority group in the American population, even a voting bloc since they are more likely to vote Democratic, have largely achieved change one lawsuit at a time rather than as a social movement. Cohabitors have not been mobilized in other countries either where laws and policies were revised in the direction of equalizing the benefits available to them as against married couples. But such countries do not have as strong and powerful backlash movements as the United States; the United States remains a deeply religious country unusually committed to laws and policies that privilege marriage. The sexual revolution has led to powerful changes in attitudes, behavior, and gender roles as part of a general historical process occurring in many advanced industrial countries in which marriage has become a valued but more optional form. At the same time, law, social policy, and the courts have erected a kind of Maginot Line in the defense of marriage and morality, failing to impede American couples from living together but nonetheless denying them the full benefits of citizenship.

ACKNOWLEDGMENTS

It is lucky that my mother is not alive because she would be embarrassed that her daughter had written a book on this subject. Only about a year into my research did I recall the summer of 1966 when I was sharing a bedroom in a student commune with my boyfriend. I had a separate phone line installed to answer her calls. I found it comforting to learn how common it was to lie to one's mother. A couple of years after that, cohabitation became a part of my family life and not just a distant memory. During the middle of the writing this book, my widowed sister, my nephew, and my postcollege son all became cohabitors; now as I write, all these living relationships have dissolved. Like most people, they think of cohabitation as something one does, not the subject of history, and I think it is both. All of family history is in a sense a personal story writ large, but in this case, my research inspired insight, rather than the other way around.

In writing this book I have received funding for research assistance from the Illinois Research Board and a sabbatical leave from the University of Illinois. Ruth Fairbanks was a superb research assistant who helped me track down leads the first year of research when I began to think it was impossible to learn anything about something so hidden. Katarzyna Balutowski obtained the permissions for some of the photographs reproduced here. Ann Ribstein of the law library at the University of Illinois helped me locate unpublished legal briefs and police reports. I express my thanks to the archivists at Barnard College, the University of Kansas, and the Wisconsin Historical Society. I want to thank the Newberry Gender History Workshop, the Gender History Reading Group of the history department at Illinois, and participants at a session of law and family change at the Social Science History Association in November 2010. Leslie Reagan was an unfailing source of encouragement and an excellent reader. I have benefited from the reading of the manuscript by Alice Echols, Steven Mintz, and Cynthia Grant Bowman. Daniel Rivers shared his research about the history of gay parenting with me. Writing this book taught me that a historian should also be an investigative reporter. I learned that it is impossible to write the history of cohabitation without asking people about their experiences. I want to thank Wayne Homstaad for driving me around Sheboygan's neighborhoods. Unfailingly generous and supportive, Estelle Freedman encouraged me to undertake this study and gave me the benefit of her detailed reading of my chapters. In editing the manuscript, Madeleine Adams caught many an error and taught me the valuable lesson that less is more. Douglas Mitchell at the University of Chicago Press understood the importance of my study, and Mark Reschke did an excellent job of copyediting. My son Dan not only made a stop at the archives for me but also snapped a great photo on his subway ride. My boyfriend became my life partner. I am deeply grateful to Joseph Pleck who accompanied me to Ladue, instructed me about the nature of social science research, and helped me to assemble the photographs for this book.

NOTES

CHAPTER ONE

1. Steven Ruggles estimates the 1960 figure for opposite-sex households as 230,000, using sampling from public use census data. The US Census Bureau puts the figure for 1960 at 439,000. Ruggles believes the higher estimate reflects boarders and domestic servants rather than cohabitors. UC-1, Unmarried Partners of the Opposite Sex/1, by Presence of Children/2: 1960 to the Present, http://www.census/gov/population/socdemo/hh-fam/UC1.xls (accessed September 1, 2011); Daphne Lofquist and Renee Ellis, "Comparison of Estimates of Same-Sex Couple Households," 2011, http://www.census.gov/population/www.socdemo/files/2011Final_PAA_Postu.pdf (accessed September 1, 2011). The thirty-five-fold increase is based on opposite-sex households, since no figures for same-sex couples were available in 1960.

2. For estimates about children, see Larry L. Bumpass and Hsien-Hen Lu, "Trends in Cohabitation and Implications for Children's Family Contexts in the United States," *Population Studies* 54, no. 1 (2000): 29–41; and the follow-up study, Sheela Kennedy and Larry Bumpass, "Cohabitation and Children's Living Arrangements: New Estimates from the United States," *Demographic Research* 19 (2008): 1663–92; CBS News/*New York Times* poll, 1977, http://Webapps.roper.center.uconn.edu/; Connie de Boer, "The Polls: Marriage—a Decaying Institution," *Public Opinion Quarterly* 45, no. 2 (Summer 1981): 265–75; Linda Lyons, "The Future of Marriage: Part II," www.Gallup.com/poll/64Gallup poll, Marriage, 2007 (accessed December 15, 2009); Rose M. Kreeder and Diana B. Elliott, "The Complex Living Arrangements of Children and Their Unmarried Parents," http://www.census.gov/population/www.socdemo/complex-abstract.pdf (accessed July 1, 2010); http://www.gallup.com/poll/117328/Marriage.aspx (accessed May 14, 2010); National Health Marriage Resource Center, "Attitudes toward Cohabitation," 2007, http://www.healthymarriage.info.org (accessed May 15, 2010). The CBS News/*New York Times* poll asked about the "increase in number of couples living together without being married." The question was "do you think this is okay, is it something that's always wrong, or doesn't it matter much to you?" African American public opinion in 1980 was less disapproving, but even so, 61 percent of a nationally representative sample of blacks disapproved of couples living together. Morris Dresner and Tortorello Research Poll: Data Black Study No. 2, March 13–April 9, 1980, http://webapps.ropercenter.uconn.edu (accessed March 14,

2010); Arland Thornton and Linda Young-DeMarco, "Four Decades of Trends in Attitudes toward Family Issues in the United States: The 1960s through the 1990s," *Journal of Marriage and the Family* 63, no. 4 (2001): 1024; Monitoring the Future: A Continuing Study of American Youth (12th-Grade Survey, 1976–2008), "Thirty Years of Change in Marriage and Union Formation Attitudes," 1976–2008," http://ncfmr.bgsu.edu/pdf/family_profiles/files83691-pdf (accessed March 15, 2011). For figures about cohabitation prior to marriage, see Finn Christensen, "The Pill and Partnerships: The Impact of the Birth Control Pill on Cohabitation," Working Papers, Department of Economics, Towson State University, 2010; Larry Bumpass and James A. Sweet, "National Estimates of Cohabitation," *Demography* 26, no. 4 (1989): 615–25.

3. "Bedroom Privacy—Repeal Intrusive States Law Banning Cohabitation," *Detroit Free Press*, December 23, 2005; Rochelle S. Swan, Linda L. Shaw, Sharon Cullity, and Mary Roche, "The Untold Story of Welfare Fraud," *Journal of Sociology and Social Welfare* 35, no. 3 (September 2008): 142; "Documenting Discrimination on the Basis of Sexual Orientation and Gender Identity in State Employment," Williams Institute, UCLA School of Law, 2009, http://www.escholarship.org/uc/ (accessed April 25, 2010); www.foxonline.com/dpp/news/education/local_iuk_appleton_teacher_fired_for_sleeping_over_B200905181714.rev1 (accessed May 19, 2009); "Former Inmate Files Suit, over anti-cohabitation Law," *Charleston West Virginia Record*, October 5, 2006.

4. Susan L. Brown, "Marriage and Child Well-Being: Research and Policy Perspectives," *Journal of Marriage and Family Policy* 72, no. 5 (September 2010): 1072. David T. Evans first used the term "sexual citizenship" in *Sexual Citizenship: The Material Construction of Sexualities* (New York: Routledge, 1993).

5. Larry Bumpass, "What's Happening to the Family: Demography and Institutional Changes," in *Focus on Single-Parent Families*, ed. Annice D. Yarber and Paul M. Sharp (New York: Greenwood Press, 2010), 17.

6. Nancy Cott, *Public Vows: A History of Marriage and the Nation* (Cambridge, MA: Harvard University Press, 2000), 219.

7. Maynard v. Hill, 126 U.S. 190, 211 (1887).

8. The Personal Work and Responsibility Act of 1998, 8 U.S.C. 1612 (1996).

9. Michelle A. Krowl, "'Her Just Dues': Civil War Pensions of African American Women in Virginia," in *Negotiating Boundaries of Southern Womanhood*, ed. Janet L. Coyrell, Thomas H. Appleton, Jr., and Anastasia Sims (Columbia: University of Missouri Press, 2002), 61; Brandi Clay Brimmer, "All Her Rights and Privileges: African-American Women and the Politics of Civil War Widows' Pensions" (PhD diss., University of California at Los Angeles, 2006), 161, 188; Changin Lee, "Beyond Sorrowful Pride: Civil War Pensions and War Widowhood, 1862–1900" (PhD diss., Ohio University, 1997), 100–101. For the higher rejection rate of black applicants for Civil War pensions, see Donald R. Shaffer, "'If I Do Not Suppose That Uncle Sam Looks at the Skin': African Americans and the Civil War Pension System, 1865–1934," *Civil War History* 46, no. 2 (2000): 132–47. African Americans in Mississippi and North Carolina were the targets of increased policing of laws against unlawful cohabitation during Reconstruction. Katherine M. Franke, "Women Imagining Justice," *Yale Journal of Law and Feminism* 14 (2002): 309.

10. Stephen Robertson, "Making Right a Girl's Ruin: Working-Class Legal Cultures and Forced Marriage in New York City, 1890–1950," *Journal of American Studies* 36, no. 2 (2002): 207. On shotgun marriage of cohabitors, see Ellen Messer, *Back Rooms: Voices from the Illegal Abortion Era* (New York: Prometheus Books, 1994), 57. There are some

cases in which government benefits encourage people to divorce. One spouse can become eligible for Medicaid (the government program that pays for medical costs, including nursing home costs) if the other spouse secures a divorce so as to avoid being subjected to the requirement that a couple's assets must be depleted to be eligible for the program.

11. Ariela Dubler coined the term "marriage cure" for what I am calling state-imposed shotgun marriage. Immigration officials often presume that couples marry for fraudulent means, so that, with respect to residence in the United States, government policy does not promote marriage. For her analysis of sham marriages in relation to the marriage cure, see Ariela R. Dubler, "Immoral Purposes: Marriage and the Genus of Illicit Sex," *Yale Law Journal* 115 (2004): 756–812; on the significance of family statutes in criminal law, see Dan Markel, *Privilege or Punish: Criminal Justice and the Challenge of Family Ties* (New York: Oxford University Press, 2009).

12. Cohabitors, same or opposite sex, are two or three times more likely not to have health insurance compared to married couples. In that sense, marital privileging reduces employer's health insurance costs. Michael A. Ash and M. V. Lee Badgett, "Separate and Unequal: The Effect of Unequal Access to Employment Based Health Insurance on Same-Sex and Unmarried Different Sex Couples," *Contemporary Economic Policy* 24, no. 4 (October 2006): 582–99.

13. Mayer N. Zald and Bert Useem, "Movement and Countermovement Interaction: Mobilization, Tactics, and State Involvement," in *Movements in an Organizational Society*, ed. Mayer N. Zald and John McCarthy (New Brunswick, NJ: Transaction, 1987), 249.

14. Jane Mansbridge and Shauna L. Shames, "Toward a Theory of Backlash: Dynamic Resistance and the Central Role of Power," *Politics and Gender* 4 (2008): 625.

15. David Allyn, *Make Love, Not War: The Sexual Revolution; An Unfettered History* (New York: Little Brown, 2000); Beth Bailey, "Sexuality and the Movements for Sexual Liberation," in *The Blackwell Companion to Post-1945 America*, ed. Jean-Christophe Agnew and Roy Rosenzweig (Malden, MA: Blackwell Publishers, 2002), 260–76; John Heidenry, *What Wild Ecstasy: The Rise and Fall of the Sexual Revolution* (New York: Simon and Schuster, 1970); Beth Bailey, *Sex in the Heartland* (Cambridge, MA: Harvard University Press, 2002); Joanna L. Grossman and Lawrence M. Friedman, *Inside the Castle: Law and Family in 20th Century America* (Princeton, NJ: Princeton University Press, 2011), 109–120; Alan Petigny, "Illegitimacy, Postwar Psychology, and the Reperiodization of the Sexual Revolution," *Journal of Social History* 38, no. 1 (2004): 63–79; and Petigny, *The Permissive Society: America, 1941–1965* (New York: Cambridge University Press, 2009).

16. Claudia Goldin and Lawrence Katz, "The Power of the Pill: Oral Contraceptives and Women's Career and Marriage Decisions," *Journal of Political Economy* 110, no. 4 (2002): 730–70; R. Kelley Raley, "Recent Trends in Marriage and Cohabitation: The United States," in *Ties That Bind: Perspectives on Marriage and Cohabitation*, ed. Linda Waite, Christine Bachrach, Michelle Hindin, Elizabeth Thomson, and Arland Thornton (Hawthorne, NY: Aldine de Gruyter, 2000), 19–39.

17. For higher rates of cohabitation among lesbians than gay men, see Christopher Carpenter and Gary J. Gates, "Gay and Lesbian Partnership: Evidence from California," *Demography* 45 (2008): 573–90.

18. Although this broader movement is now called LGBT (lesbian, gay, bisexual, and transgender), the issues of gender identity and bisexuality rarely emerged in relation to cohabitor's rights.

19. Erving Goffman, *Stigma: Notes on the Management of Spoiled Identity* (Englewood Cliffs, NJ: Prentice-Hall, 1963), 15.

20. For the view that marriage is inherently stigmatizing to those who do not enter it, see Michael Warner, *The Trouble with Normal: Sex, Politics, and the Ethics of Queer Life* (New York: Free Press, 2000). For a similar critique, see Judith Butler, "Is Kinship Always Already Heterosexual," *differences: A Journal of Feminist Cultural Studies* 13, no. 1 (2002): 14–44.

21. Anna Clark prefers the term "Twilight moments" as a general classification for secret sexual practices occurring prior to the twentieth century that did not lead to a distinct sexual identity and could not be publicly acknowledged because of social stigma. Anna Clark, "Twilight Moments," *Journal of the History of Sexuality* 14, nos. 1–2 (January– April 2005): 139–61. On disinheritance and cutting off allowances, see Paul Green, *Peter Duel* (Jefferson, NC: McFarland, 2007), 123; Perri Klass, *A Not Entirely Benign Procedure: Four Years as a Medical Student* (New York: Plume, 1994), 33; Paul Hightower, "Senior Forum," *Lewiston (ME) Sun Journal*, July 23, 1971; "Dear Abby," *Bend (OR) Bulletin*, January 29, 1979; Ione Quinby Griggs, "Should Daughter's Live-In Boyfriend Be Invited Home for Holiday Dinner," *Milwaukee Journal*, November 28, 1980; Alison E. Hatch, "Saying 'I Don't' to Matrimony: An Investigation of Heterosexual Couples Who Resist Marriage" (PhD diss., University of Colorado, 2009), 116.

22. State of New Jersey v. Charles Saunders, 130 N.J. 234, 326 A.2d 84 (1974).

23. Betsy L. Fife and Eric R. Wright, "The Dimensionality of Stigma: A Comparison of Its Impact on the Self of Persons with HIV/AIDS and Cancer," *Journal of Health and Social Behavior* 41, no. 1 (March 2000): 50–67.

24. For the most comprehensive history of common-law marriage, see Goran Lind, *Common Law Marriage: A Legal Institution for Cohabitation* (New York: Oxford University Press, 2008).

25. Ibid., 5–6. The common-law tradition in French colonial law included acknowledgment of the legitimacy of the child of the relationship. Thomas Jay Vaughan, "The Tendency of Affections: Natural Families in Nineteenth-Century Louisiana" (PhD diss., Northern Illinois University, 2008).

26. Rebecca Probert, *Marriage Law and Practice in the Long Eighteenth Century* (Cambridge: Cambridge University Press, 2009); William G. Burgin, "Concubinage: Revolutionary Response or Last Resort? The Attitudes of Town Authorities and of Couples Rejected in Their Marriage Suits in Nineteenth Century Germany," *Consortium on Revolutionary Europe, 1750–1860: Proceedings* (Tallahassee, FL: Institute on Napoleon and the French Revolution, 1983), 271–87; Lynn Abrams, "Concubinage, Cohabitation and the Law: Class and Gender Relations in Nineteenth Century Germany," *Gender and History* 5 (Spring 1993): 81–100; Jeffrey Kaplow, "Concubinage and the Working Class in Early Nineteenth Century Paris," in *Vom Ancien Regime Zur Franzosichen Revolution*, ed. Ernst Hinrichs, Eberhard Schmitt, and Rudolf Vierhaus (Gottingen, West Germany: Vandenhoeck and Ruprecht, 1978), 366–67; Lenard R. Berlandstein, "Illegitimacy, Concubinage, and Proletaranization in a French Town, 1760–1914," *Journal of Family History* 5 (Winter 1980): 369–73; John R. Gillis, *For Better, For Worse: British Marriages, 1600 to the Present* (New York: Oxford University Press, 1985), 190–228; Anne Skevik, "A Gilded Cage? Help and Control in Early Norwegian Social Policy," *Journal of Family History* 29 (2004): 211–24; Barrie M. Ratcliffe, "Popular Classes and Cohabitation in Mid-Nineteenth Century Paris," *Journal of Family History* 21 (1996): 316–50; Ginger S. Frost, *Living in Sin: Cohabiting as Husband and Wife in Nineteenth-Century England* (Manchester: Manchester University Press, 2009).

27. Michael Grossberg, *Governing the Hearth: Law and the Family in Nineteenth-Century America* (Chapel Hill: University of North Carolina Press, 1988), 86–90, 95–99.

28. Clare Lyons, *Sex among the Rabble: An Intimate History of Gender and Power in the Age of Revolution* (Philadelphia: University of Pennsylvania Press, 2006), 275; Kristin A. Collins, "Administering Marriage: Marriage-Based Entitlements, Bureaucracy, and the Legal Construction of the Family," *Vanderbilt Law Review* 62, no. 4 (May 2009): 1085–1167.

29. Abigail Van Buren, "Living Together Is a Must," *San Francisco Chronicle*, February 21, 1993.

30. The percentage of nonmarital births occurring to cohabiting couples increased from 29 percent in the early 1980s to 39 percent a decade later. Bumpass and Lu, "Trends in Cohabitation and Implications for Children's Family Contexts in the United States."

31. Diane N. Lye and Ingrid Waldron, "Attitudes toward Cohabitation, Family, and Gender Roles: Relationships to Values and Political Ideology," *Social Perspectives* 40, no. 2 (1997): 199–225.

CHAPTER TWO

1. "Supreme Court on the Spot," *Pittsburgh Courier*, October 31, 1964.

2. Michelle Brittain, "Miscegenation and Competing Definitions of Race in Twentieth-Century Louisiana," *Journal of Social History* 71, no. 3 (August 2005): 19–20.

3. She claimed not to have legally married Gonzalez because she was not divorced, suggesting that she might have been legally married prior to the relationship with Gonzalez. Testimony of Dorothy Kaabe, In the Criminal Court Record in and for Dade County, Florida, No. 62-1385, June 28, 1962, 83–84.

4. When he was arrested, he first told the police he was married, then single, then separated. Identification and Records Division, Miami Beach Police Department, Arrests of Dewey McLaughlin and Connie Hoffman, Docket No. 110953, No. 110954, No. 110955. By December of 1964, Dora Goodnick and her husband informed a *Jet* reporter that they liked Dewey McLaughlin, but the police forced them to demand the couple's arrest. Larry Still, "'What Is a Negro' Court Case," *Jet*, December 17, 1964.

5. Testimony of Dora Goodnick, In the Criminal Court Record in and for Dade County, Florida, No. 62-1385, June 28, 1962, 23.

6. Ibid., 24.

7. Mary Douglas, *Purity and Danger: An Analysis of Concepts of Pollution and Taboo* (New York: Praeger, 1996).

8. Elizabeth Fee, "Venereal Disease: The Wages of Sin?," in *Passion and Power: Sexuality in History*, ed. Kathy Peiss and Christina Simmons (Philadelphia: Temple University Press, 1989), 180.

9. Testimony of Dora Goodnick, 24.

10. Testimony of Nicholas Valeriani, In the Criminal Court of Record in and for Dade County, Florida, No. 62-1385, June 28, 1962, 36.

11. Marvin Dunn, *Black Miami in the Twentieth Century* (Gainesville: University Press of Florida, 1997), 171.

12. Testimony of Nicholas Valeriani, 44.

13. Testimony of Detective Stanley Marcus in the Criminal Court of Record in and for Dade County, Florida, No. 62-1385, June 28, 1962, 521.

14. Ibid., 48.

15. Identification and Records Division, Miami Beach Police Department, Arrest Report, Dewey McLaughlin and Connie Hoffman, February 23, 1962; Complaint 12443, February 28, 1962.

16. Deborah Dash Moore, *To the Golden Cities: Pursuing the American Jewish Dream in Miami and L.A.* (New York: Free Press, 1994), 155.

17. I. B. Singer, *My Love Affair with Miami Beach* (New York: Simon and Schuster, 1991), vii; Joann Biondi, *Miami Beach Memories: A Nostalgic Chronicle of Days Gone By* (Guilford, CT: Globe Pequot Press, 2007), 29.

18. Raymond A. Mohl, "'South of the South': Jews, Blacks, and the Civil Rights Movement in Miami, 1945–1960," *Journal of American Ethnic History* 18, no. 2 (Winter 1999): 21.

19. Moore, *To the Golden*, 64–66; Robert Sherrill, "Miami Beach, the All-Too-American City," *New York Times*, August 4, 1968, 8, 9, 34; Abby Goodnough, "For Shtetl by the Sea, Only a Few Fading Signs Remain," *New York Times*, April 3, 2007. Television footage in the mid-1950s showed African Methodist Episcopal conventioneers eating at Miami Beach kosher restaurants. Afterward, many Jewish patrons of these restaurants refused to eat there because blacks had used the utensils in the establishment. Moore, *To the Golden*, 170.

20. Interview with Mark Naison, November 17, 2004; "Social Security Effect: Elderly Unwed Couples," *New York Times*, January 12, 1965; Sanford Schneir, "I Think We'll Get Married Now," *Miami News*, August 6, 1965.

21. Moore, *To the Golden*, 78.

22. Ibid., 32.

23. Ibid.; Biondi, *Miami Beach*, 17.

24. Biondi, *Miami Beach*, 17.

25. For an overview of this case, see Ariela Dubler, "From *McLaughlin v. Florida* to *Lawrence v. Texas*: Sexual Freedom and the Road to Marriage," *Columbia Law Review* 106 (2006): 1165–87; Phyl Newbeck, *Virginia Hasn't Always Been for Lovers: Interracial Marriage Bans and the Case of Richard and Mildred Loving* (Carbondale: Southern Illinois University, 2005), 117–31; Peggy Pascoe, *What Comes Naturally: Miscegenation Law and the Making of Race in America* (New York: Oxford University Press, 2009), 246–83.

26. Mississippi passed a new law against interracial cohabitation in 1960 after the state's supreme court struck down a previous law because of a technicality. The law was enforced in the state—in one case, to punish interracial adultery. *Greenville (MS) Delta Democrat-Times*, February 3, 1960; *Greenville (MS) Delta Democrat-Times*, June 24, 1960.

27. Charles Frank Robinson II, *Dangerous Liaisons: Sex and Love in the Segregated South* (Little Rock: University of Arkansas Press, 2003), 103.

28. Law professor Andrew Koppelman argues that *McLaughlin v. Florida* offers precedent for overturning sodomy statutes on the grounds of sex discrimination. The argument is that sodomy laws make certain offenses crimes based on the sex of those who commit the act. The Supreme Court struck down interracial cohabitation statutes because cohabitation was a special offense based on the race of those who committed the act. The Court overruled the "equal protection claim" in *McLaughlin v. Florida* in holding that special offenses based on the "invidious distinction of race" specified in the nature of the crime violated the equal protection clause of the Fourteenth Amendment. In *Lawrence v. Texas* (2003), the Court found such laws unconstitutional on the grounds that they violated the due process clause of the Fourteenth Amendment.

But one could extend the argument that equal protection had been violated on the grounds of sex rather than on the grounds of race. Lawrence and Garner v. Texas, 539 U.S. 558 (2003). Andrew Koppelman, "Defending the Sex Discrimination Argument for Lesbian and Gay Rights: A Reply to Edward Stein," *ULCA Review* 49 (December 2001): 519–38.

29. Carter G. Woodson, "The Beginnings of the Miscegenation of the Whites and Blacks," *Journal of Negro History* 3, no. 4 (October 1918): 341.

30. 1832 Fla. Laws 4, 5. The law of 1832 was clearly designed to curb concubinage of slave owners. It applied only to black women and white men; the black woman partner in an interracial couple was not punished while her white lover was fined and barred from public office. The assumption was that a white man had disgraced himself in the eyes of his community and rendered himself unfit for public service.

31. There was no crime if a person older than fifteen was present. *The Acts and Resolutions Adopted by the Legislature of Florida at Its Eleventh Session* (Tallahassee, FL: Charles Dyke, 1907), 83.

32. Robinson, *Dangerous Liaisons*.

33. "Mississippi High Court Throws Out Laws against Mixed Cohabitation," *Jet*, January 1, 1959, 6–7; "Mississippi White Woman Admits 'Loving' Handy Man," *Jet*, March 6, 1958, 20–23.

34. "Cohabitation Case Hearing Is Delayed," *Palm Beach (FL) Post*, July 17, 1961.

35. Chang Moon Sohn, "Principle and Expediency in Judicial Review: Miscegenation Cases in the Supreme Court" (PhD diss., Columbia University, 1970), 96.

36. State *ex rel.* Hawkins v. Board of Control, 93 So. 2d 354, 359 (Fla. 1957).

37. At the criminal court trial, he had not objected to the judge's instructions to the jury when the judge argued that the couple could not claim a common-law marriage. According to Florida law, he was supposed to register an objection then in order to have a valid basis for an appeal regarding common-law marriage.

38. 172 So. 2d, 460 (Fla. 1965). For more on the Florida Supreme Court, see Walter W. Manley II and Canter Brown, Jr., eds., *The Supreme Court of Florida, 1917–1977* (Gainesville: University Press of Florida, 2006).

39. "Marriage by Choice," *Time*, May 9, 1964.

40. Pascoe, *What Comes Naturally*, 263.

41. Sohn, "Principle," 84; Alex Lubin, *Romance and Rights: The Politics of Interracial Intimacy, 1945–1954* (Jackson: University Press of Mississippi, 2005), 40–41. For the increasing homophobia within black communities as part of the claim to respectable citizenship, see Thaddeus Russell, "The Color Discipline: Civil Rights and Black Sexuality," *American Quarterly* 90, no. 1 (March 2008): 101–28.

42. McLaughlin v. Florida, 31906, Appeal from the Criminal Court of Record in and for Dade County, Florida, Brief of Appellee, 1963.

43. Scott v. Georgia, 39 Ga. 321, 323 (1869).

44. *United States Law Week* 53, no. 12 (October 20, 1964): 3437–38.

45. Del Dickson, ed., *The Supreme Court in Conference (1940–1985)* (New York: Oxford University Press, 2001), 694.

46. Reva B. Siegel, "Equality Talk, Equality Talk: Antisubordination and Anticlassification Values in Constitutional Struggles over *Brown*," *Harvard Law Review* 117 (2004): 1483, 1504.

47. Still, "What Is a Negro?," 18; "Marriage by Choice," *Time*, May 8, 1964.

48. Jacquin Sanders, "Trying to Make the System Work," *St. Petersburg (FL) Times*, January 30, 1990; E-mail from Askia Muhamma Aquil, May 30, 2010.

49. Favors v. City of Tampa, 246 So. 2d 172 (Fla. Dist. Ct. App. 1971); Patti Bridges, "Unmarried Couple May Face Charges," *St. Petersburg (FL) Evening Independent,* February 15, 1980; Jeff Cull, "Illegal?," *Florida Weekly,* fortmyers.floridaweekly.com/news/2007-05-03/top-news/001>html (accessed January 2, 2010).

50. Siegel, "Equality Talk," 1503–4.

51. Tinsley E. Yarborough, *John Marshall Harlan: The Great Dissenter of the Warren Court* (New York: Oxford University Press, 1992), 269.

52. "The Supreme Court," *New York Times,* March 27, 2003.

53. Kathleen Haughney, "Unmarried? Living Together? You're Breaking the Law in Florida," *Ft. Lauderdale Sun Sentinel,* August 31, 2011.

54. George Meyer, "Code and Policemen Run into Conflicts," *St. Petersburg (FL) Times,* August 12, 1974; "Policeman to Fight Penalty on Girl Friend Curb," *New York Times,* July 16, 1974; George Bayliss, "For This Man, It's Married or Go to jail," *Gainesville (FL) Sun,* November 6, 1983; "Indiscretion in Clearwater," *St. Petersburg (FL) Evening Independent,* June 6, 1974; Chevon Thompson, "Fired Police Couples Meets with City Manager," *Lakeland (FL) Ledger,* August 16, 1977; Neil Skene, "Living Together Gains Acceptance, but It's Still against the Law," *St. Petersburg (FL) Times,* January 8, 1978; Cheryl Harrison, "Clearwater Overruled on Discrimination Complaint," *Evening Independent,* August 25, 1981; *Ledger,* November 7, 1983; Tim Johnson, "Couple Calls Refusal to Rent to Them Discrimination," *St. Petersburg (FL) Times,* August 31, 1983; *St. Petersburg (FL) Times,* July 2, 1984; *Gainesville (FL) Sun,* November 18, 1986; J. Sanders, "Trying to Make the System Work," *St. Petersburg (FL) Times,* January 30, 1990; State of Florida v. Tiffany Cara Coyle and Cherry Che Flatley, Case No. 96-04073, 718 So.2d 218 (Fla. Dist. Ct. App. 1998); Eric Ernst, "Activism of Charlotte's Interim Sheriff Upholds a local Tradition," *Sarasota (FL) Herald Tribune,* February 22, 2004; "Condominium Board Defends Exclusion of Unmarried Couple, Cites Obscure Law," *Miami Herald,* May 2, 1990; "Cohabiting Law Officers Find No-Sweetheart Deal," *Tampa Tribune,* October 26, 1994; "Cohabitation Policy Voided," *Palm Beach (FL) Post,* September 25, 1981; "School Board Sanctions against Cohabitation," *St. Petersburg (FL) Times,* October 6, 1973; "Two Accused of Hacking into Teamsters Database," *St. Petersburg (FL) Times,* November 16, 2000.

55. Jamie Thompson, "She's the Other Woman in Michael Schiavo's Heart," http://www.sptimes.com/2005/03/26/new-pd (accessed July 31, 2008); "Mike Schiavo Sets Up PAC," August 16, 2006, http://blastfurnacecanada.spaces.live .comblogcmsDB745086233C67DA1302.entry (accessed May 15, 2010); In the Circuit Court for Pinellas County, Florida, Probate Division, File No. 90-29086D-003, *In re* The Guardianship of Theresa Marie Schiavo, 2002.

56. "Living Together," *Miami News,* November 16, 1977.

57. Tina Fetner, *How the Religious Right Shaped Lesbian and Gay Activism* (Minneapolis: University of Minnesota Press, 2008), xv; Tina Fetner, "Why Anita Bryant: The Impact of Christian Anti-Gay Activism on the Lesbian and Gay Movement Claims," *Social Problems* 48, no. 3 (2001): 411–28.

58. "Court Tests Lie Ahead for Privacy Amendment," *Palm Beach (FL) Post,* November 16, 1980. An HUD bureaucrat, almost on her own, ruled in 1977 that public housing could not discriminate against gays and unmarried couples. The House and Senate tried to strike back by prohibiting funding for any enforcement of these provisions. Two Democrats, Senator Lawton Chiles of Florida, a supporter of Bryant's, and William Proxmire of Wisconsin, favored the provision, but were outvoted by Democrats and Republicans alike who did not believe that Congress should explicitly endorse

discrimination in federal legislation. The whole episode indicates that the spillover from Bryant's campaign led to efforts to deny rights to gays and straight cohabitors. "No Gay-Rights Debate," *Chicago Tribune,* June 25, 1977.

59. "Outdated Laws Need Quiet Reform," *St. Petersburg (FL) Times,* August 14, 1972; "Marriage and Family Task Force," *Palm Beach (FL) Post,* December 4, 1975; "Dade County's Policewoman Ousted for Living with a Deputy," *St. Petersburg (FL) Times,* November 12, 1975; "Panel on Family Discusses Laws on Cohabitation," *Palm Beach (FL) Post,* December 4, 1975.

60. Haughney, "Unmarried?"

61. Campbell v. State, 331 So. 2d 389 (Fla. 1976); "Former State Employee Protests 1–4-Year Law," *Fort Walton (FL) Playground Daily News,* August 4, 1972; "Police Chief Backs Code," *Naples (FL) Daily News,* August 12, 1974; Craig Allsopp, "Silver Haired Legislature Begins Work on Proposals Concerning Aged," *St. Petersburg (FL) Times,* July 17, 1979; Pat Fenner, "Independent Action," *St. Petersburg (FL) Independent,* August 21, 1981; "Parolee Lives with Lover, May Face Jail," *Miami Herald,* November 7, 1983; "Retirees Test 1886 Law That Bars Live-In Couples," *Orlando Sentinel,* April 7, 1990; "Old Law Is Key in Eviction Case at Trailer Park," *Miami Herald,* April 7, 1990; Robert L. Steinback, "State Shouldn't Get Involved in Consensual Sex," *Miami Herald,* March 21, 1977; "Judge Throws Out Challenge to State's Sex Laws," *Vero Beach (FL) Press Journal,* June 25, 1999; Karen Testa, "Challenge to Sex Laws Tossed: Lawyers Miss Procedural Deadline," *Ft. Lauderdale (FL) Sun Sentinel,* June 24, 1998; *Fort Walton (FL) Playground Daily News,* December 7, 1975; Fla. Stat. §31.43 (2009), http://www.leg.state.fl.us (accessed January 10, 2010).

CHAPTER THREE

1. Johnnie Tillmon, as quoted in Premilla Nadasen, "'We Do Whatever Becomes Necessary': Johnnie Tillmon, Welfare Rights, and Black Power," in *Want to Start a Revolution? Radical Women in the Black Freedom Struggle,* ed. Jeanne Theoharis, Komozi Woodward, and Dayo Gore (New York: New York University Press, 2009), 321.

2. "New York Welfare Search and Interrogation Challenged," *Welfare Law Bulletin,* no. 10 (October 1967): 8–9.

3. Dorothy Gilliam, "Fear of the Helping Hand Haunts Our Poor," *Washington Post,* May 23, 1965.

4. Martha L. Fineman, "Law and Changing Patterns of Behavior: Sanctions on Non-Marital Cohabitation," *Wisconsin Law Review* 1981 (1981): 291.

5. The states were Alabama, Arkansas, Arizona, Connecticut, Indiana, Louisiana, Maine, Michigan, Mississippi, Missouri, New Hampshire, New Mexico, North Carolina, South Carolina, Oklahoma, Tennessee, Texas, Vermont, Virginia, and the District of Columbia.

6. Fineman, "Law," 297. City attorneys also investigated fraud at Philadelphia municipal hospitals: mothers giving birth who were allegedly involved in "common-law marriages" had been charged a lower fee because they claimed to be single mothers. Lisa Levenstein, *A Movement without Marches: African American Women and the Politics of Poverty in Postwar Philadelphia* (Chapel Hill: University of North Carolina Press, 2009), 178.

7. Ronald J. Chilton, "Social Control through Welfare Legislation: The Impact of a State 'Suitable Home Law,'" *Law and Society Review* 5, no. 2 (November 1960): 220; Tanya Lindhorst and Leslie Leighninger, "'Ending Welfare as We Know It' in 1960: Louisiana's Suitable Home Law," *Social Science Review* 71, no. 4 (December 2003): 571.

8. Scott Briar, "Welfare from Below: Recipients' Views of the Public Welfare System," *California Law Review* 54 (1966): 370; Karen Seccombe, *"So You Think I Drive a Cadillac": Welfare Recipient's Perspectives on the System and Reform* (Boston: Allyn and Bacon, 1999), 129–30.

9. Lisa Marie Levenstein, "The Gendered Roots of Modern Urban Poverty: Poor Women and Public Institutions in Post–World War II Philadelphia" (PhD diss., University of Wisconsin, 2002), 84, 85.

10. Briar, "Welfare from Below," 370; Cynthia Edmonds-Cady, "Mobilizing Motherhood: Race, Class, and the Uses of Maternalism in the Welfare Rights Movement," *WSQ: Women's Studies Quarterly* 37, nos. 3–4 (Fall/Winter 2009): 206–22. In addition to searching the home, investigators also interviewed friends, neighbors, relatives, and ministers, and searched bank accounts and records of insurance companies.

11. William Stringfellow, *My People Is the Enemy: An Autobiographical Polemic* (New York: Holt, Rinehart and Winston, 1964), 75; Dorothy Gilliam and Willard Clopton, "3500 Here Given Help by Antipoverty Legal Service," *Washington Post*, February 21, 1966, B1.

12. Frances Fox Piven and Richard A. Cloward, *Regulating the Poor: The Functions of Public Welfare* (New York: Pantheon Books, 1971), 106.

13. Martin Garbus, *Ready for the Defense* (New York: Farrar, Straus and Giroux, 1971), 182; Dorothy Gilliam, "Fear of the Helping Hand Haunts Our Poor," *Washington Post*, May 23, 1965. The actual extent of the policing of cohabitation among welfare mothers in the 1960s is not known, but information from one state, New Jersey, suggests it was extensive. In the late 1950s and early 1960s, New Jersey welfare rolls were rising much more rapidly than those of neighboring states. The state established a commission that compiled elaborate statistics about the extent of welfare fraud. It was acceptable for a woman to have a live-in partner so long as she reported his income. In 1962, the commission determined that there were 3,261 incidents of illegal cohabitation with intent to deceive or defraud—presumably this involved 3,261 separate visits to the homes of welfare mothers.

14. Martin Smith, "Investigators Hold Down Cost of Aid to Needy Children Program," *Modesto (CA) Bee*, December 30, 1960; Julius Paul, "The Return of Punitive Sterilization Proposals: Current Attacks on Illegitimacy and the AFDC Program," *Law and Society Review* 3, no. 1 (August 1968): 77–106; Rickie Solinger, *Beggars and Choosers: How the Politics of Choice Shapes Adoption, Abortion, and Welfare in the United States* (New York: Hill and Wang, 2001), 139–82.

15. "Special Squad 'Stamps' Pair," *Philadelphia Sunday Herald*, March 12, 1961; "Mother of Five Probed," *Sunday Herald*, November 6, 1960; "Welfare Raiders Find Unlisted Males in Bed," *Times-News*, January 1, 1962; "11 Women Arrested in Welfare Fraud Cases," *Los Angeles Times*, May 13, 1962; Howard Kennedy, "'Raids' to End on Recipients on Welfare," *Los Angeles Times*, January 25, 1963; Levenstein, *A Movement*, 110.

16. Use of the form was discontinued in 1965. Applicant's Statement, Form 3-44, Alameda County Welfare Department, Edward V. Sparer, *Materials on Public Assistance Law* (Philadelphia: University of Pennsylvania Law School, 1969), 2:8–111; *Oakland (CA) Tribune*, January 16, 1963.

17. Phyllis Osborn, "Aid to Dependent Children: Realities and Possibilities," *Social Service Review* 28, no. 2 (1954): 153–72.

18. Parrish v. Civil Service Commission of County of Alameda, 57 Cal. Rptr. 623 (1967); "Five Take Aim at Supervisor Brink," *Modesto (CA) Bee*, May 26, 1970.

19. Parrish v. Civil Service Commission.

20. Richard A. Chikota, "Pre-Dawn Welfare Inspections and the Right of Privacy," *Journal of Urban Law* 44 (1966–67): 119–35.

21. The California decision only applied to welfare searches in that state. Other states were still able to conduct such searches. A Supreme Court decision the same year, having to do with warrantless searches to prosecute violations of San Francisco's housing code, seemed to rule that warrantless administrative searches were unconstitutional. Camara v. Municipal Court, 397 U.S. 523 (1967). In the liberal college town of Madison, caseworkers called before visiting a recipient's home; in Milwaukee, they did not. Although mothers in welfare rights organizations were militantly opposed to invasions of their privacy, most recipients did not object to such searches. Joel F. Handler and Ellen Jane Hollingsworth, "Stigma, Privacy and Other Attitudes of Welfare Recipients," *Stanford Law Review* 22 (1969–70): 10, 12; Albert M. Jennings, "Welfare Fraud Costly Problem for Oregon," *Eugene (OR) Register-Guard*, July 17, 1967.

22. Kyle Farmbry, *Administration and the Other* (Lanham, MD: Lexington Books, 2009), 131.

23. Fulton Lewis, Jr., "Washington Report," *Reading (PA) Eagle*, June 20, 1968.

24. Jonathan Spivak, "Welfare Contract," *Wall Street Journal*, April 9, 1963.

25. Garbus, *Ready*, 151; Winifred Bell, "The Rights of the Poor: Welfare Witchhunts in the District of Columbia," *Social Work* 13 (January 1968): 60–67; Anne M. Valk, *Radical Sisters: Second-Wave Feminism and Black Liberation in Washington, D.C.* (Urbana: University of Illinois Press, 2008); "Welfare Suit Demands Snoopers Get Warrant," *Washington Post*, June 4, 1966.

26. Kris Shepard, *Rationing Justice: Poverty Lawyers and Poor People in the Deep South* (Baton Rouge: Louisiana University Press, 2006), 38. For a general survey of surveillance of contemporary welfare mothers, see John Gilliom, *Overseers of the Poor: Surveillance, Resistance, and the Limits of Privacy* (Chicago: University of Chicago Press, 2001).

27. Testimony of Sylvester Smith, In the Supreme Court of the United States October Term, 1967, No. 949, Ruben K. King, et al. v. Mrs. Sylvester Smith et al.

28. Garbus, *Ready*, 164.

29. Martha F. Davis, *Brutal Need: Lawyers and the Welfare Rights Movement, 1960–1973* (New Haven, CT: Yale University Press, 1993), 64; Walter Goodman, "The Case of Mrs. Sylvester Smith: A Victory for 400,000 Children," *New York Times Magazine*, August 25, 1968, 62.

30. Shepard, *Rationing Justice*, 39; Lee Albert, "Choosing the Test Case in Welfare Litigation: A Plea for Planning," *Clearinghouse Review* 2 (November 1968): 4–6, 28.

31. Smith v. Board of Commissioners, 259 F. Supp. 423, 424 (D.C. 1966). Irene Robinson was the mother of six who had a continuing relationship with the father of two of her children. The man was observed entering her home and leaving early in the morning. Robinson and the man both denied that he lived with her. Carola Honsa, "Suit Challenges Regulation on 'Man in the House,'" *Washington Post*, December 19, 1966, B1.

32. King v. Smith, Brief for Appellants, 392 U.S. 309 (1968), 5.

33. King v. Smith, Records and Briefs, 392 U.S. 309 (1968), 77, 103–4.

34. For a general narrative of the case and the impact of poverty lawyers on the development of welfare rights litigation, see Davis, *Brutal Need*, and Felicia Kornbluh, *The Battle over Welfare Rights* (Philadelphia: University of Pennsylvania Press, 2007). For an analysis of the case in relationship to a broader definition of reproductive rights, see Rickie Solinger, "The First Welfare Case: Sex, Marriage, and White Supremacy

in Selma, 1966; A Reproductive Justice Analysis," *Journal of Women's History* 22, no. 3 (Fall 2010): 13–38. Additional reviews of this case can be found in Anna Marie Smith, *Welfare Reform and Sexual Regulation* (Cambridge: Cambridge University Press, 2007), and Alison Lefkovitz, "Men in the House: Race, Welfare, and the Regulation of Men's Sexuality in the United States, 1961–1972," *Journal of the History of Sexuality* 20, no. 4 (September 2011), forthcoming. A general history of the civil rights movement in Selma is found in Richie Jean Sherod Jackson, *The House by the Side of the Road: The Selma Civil Rights Movement* (Tuscaloosa: University of Alabama Press, 2011). For other histories of rights and the courts, see Susan E. Lawrence, *The Poor in Court: The Legal Services Program and Supreme Court Decision Making* (Princeton, NJ: Princeton University Press, 1990); Elizabeth Bussiere, *(Dis)entitling the Poor: The Warren Court, Welfare Rights, and the American Political Tradition* (University Park: Pennsylvania State University Press, 1997). For the development of the OEO (Office of Economic Opportunity) in the Alabama Black Belt in the aftermath of the civil rights movement, see Susan Youngblood Ashmore, *Carry It On: The War on Poverty and the Civil Rights Movement in Alabama, 1964–1972* (Athens: University of Georgia Press, 2008).

35. William Chapman, "Court Bars Bias in All Housing," *Washington Post*, June 18, 1968, A1–A2.

36. Alan W. Houseman, "Symposium: The Legacy of *Goldberg v. Kelly*; A Twenty Year Perspective; The Vitality of *Goldberg v. Kelly* to Welfare Advocacy in the 1990s," *Brooklyn Law Review* 56 (Summer 1990): 831–58.

37. Shirley Mesher, Oral History, Ralph J. Bunche Oral History Collection, Civil Rights Documentation Project, Stanley Smith, Interviewer, File 388, Moorland-Spingarn Research Library, Howard University, Washington, DC.

38. Fineman, "Law," 290; Goodman, "The Case of Mrs. Sylvester Smith," 68. In the late sixties, Los Angeles investigators were making home visits as late as 10 p.m. and as early as 6:30 a.m. in order to be able to locate a male cohabitor who could be forced to contribute to a woman's support. States also found other ways to make the cohabiting man pay for support—but within the new administrative rules laid down by the Supreme Court.

39. Jerry L. Marshaw, "Welfare Reform and Local Administration of Aid to Families with Dependent Children in Virginia," *Virginia Law Review* 57 (1971): 828–30; Jacobus tenBroek, "California's Dual System of Family Law," Part I, *Stanford Law Review* 16, no. 2 (1964): 619; Paul Wellstone, *How the Rural Poor Got Power: Narrative of a Grass-Roots Organizer* (Minneapolis: University of Minnesota Press, 2003), 186; Jack Jones, "Poverty War Lawyers Try Reshaping Welfare," *Los Angeles Times*, October 19, 1968, B1; "Eligibility Determinations in Public Assistance: Selected Problems and Proposals for Reform in Pennsylvania," *University of Pennsylvania Law Review* 115 (1967): 1327. Nine states, mainly in the North and West, had such rules.

40. Martin Smith, "Investigators Help Hold Down Cost of Aid to Needy Children Program," *Modesto (CA) Bee*, December 30, 1960.

41. The states in 1970 were Arizona, California, New Hampshire, New Jersey, New York, Oklahoma, South Dakota, Tennessee, and Washington. "Comment: Man-in-the-House Rules after King v. Smith: New HEW Regulations," *Welfare Law Bulletin*, no. 4 (September 1968): 19–23; In the Supreme Court of the United States, October Term, 1969, No. 829, Genever Lewis et al. v. John Montgomery, Amicus Curiae Brief, Center on Social Welfare Policy and Law, the Roger Baldwin Foundation of the American Civil Liberties Union, National Welfare Rights Organization, and the State Office of Legal Services.

42. David Rosen, "Enforcement of California's Man Assuming the Role of Spouse Statute: Empirical Findings," May 1969, in *Materials on Public Assistance*, Edward V. Sparer (Philadelphia, University of Pennsylvania Press, 1969), 1:5-132-5-141.

43. Circulate Letter No. 1570, California Department of Social Welfare, California: Man in the House Ruling, 1965, Elizabeth Wickenden Papers, Box 7, Folder 4, Wisconsin State Historical Society, Madison, WI. For an unsuccessful challenge, see People v. Gilbert, 1 Cal. 3d 475, 464 P.2d 580, 82 Cal. Rptr. 724 (1969).

44. New York had a similar but more novel view of the cohabitor. He was redefined as a "lodger" who should contribute something to the family's housing expenses. In *Van Lare v. Hurley*, the Supreme Court ruled that the welfare department could not automatically assume that a cohabitor had to contribute to a family's housing. Van Lare v. Hurley, 421 U.S. 338 (1975).

45. Robert A. Moffitt, Robert T. Reville, and Anne E. Winkler, "State AFDC Rules Regarding the Treatment of Cohabitors: 1993," *Social Security Bulletin* 57, no. 4 (October 1994): 6–33.

46. Robert A. Moffitt, Robert T. Reville, and Anne E. Winkler, "Beyond Single Mothers: Cohabitation and Marriage in the AFDC Program," *Demography* 35, no. 3 (August 1998): 266.

47. Marjorie Hunter, "Welfare Reform in Capitol Sought," *New York Times*, May 31, 1965, 4.

48. New Jersey Welfare Rights Organization et al. v. Cahill, Governor of New Jersey, 411 U.S. 619 (1972); Robert E. Riggs and Thomas D. Proffitt, "The Judicial Philosophy of Justice Rehnquist," *Akron Law Review* 16 (Spring 1983): 555–605.

49. Bussiere, *(Dis)entitling*; Solinger, *Beggars and Choosers*, 145–52; Kaaryn Gustafson, "The Criminalization of Poverty," *Journal of Criminal Law and Criminology* 99 (2009): 1653; Michael W. Flamm, *Law and Order: Street Crime, Civil Unrest, and the Crisis of Liberalism* (New York: Columbia University Press, 2005).

50. Erik G. Luna, "Welfare Fraud and the Fourth Amendment," *Pepperdine Law Review* 24 (1996): 1260; Fineman, "Law," 275–332; Reyes v. Edmunds, 472 F. Supp. 1218 (Minn. 1979); Tannette Johnson-Elie, "Suit Alleges 'Warrantless Home' 'Searches,'" *Milwaukee Sentinel*, June 4, 1991; S. L. v. Whitburn, 67 F.3d 1299, 1301–3 (7th Cir. 1995); "Court Restricts Welfare Searches," *Spokane (WA) Spokesman Review*, October 19, 1990. In Dayton, Ohio, between 1980 and 2000, the district attorney who headed a special welfare fraud unit prosecuted about 110 men a year for living with their partner but not reporting their income. *Prosecutor*, April 2005.

51. Espinosa Solis, "Vallejo Housing Project Raided," *San Francisco Chronicle*, March 14, 1997.

52. Amy Mulzer, "The Doorkeeper and the Grand Inquisitor: The Central Role of Verification Procedures in Means-Tested Welfare Programs," *Columbia Human Rights Law Review* 36 (Summer 2005): 663–711.

53. Richelle S. Swan, Linda L. Shaw, Sharon Cullity, and Mary Roche, "The Untold Story of Welfare Fraud," *Journal of Sociology and Social Welfare* 25, no. 3 (September 2008): 133–51.

54. Preston L. Morgan, "Public Assistance for the Price of Privacy: Leaving the Door Open on Welfare Home Searches," *McGeorge Law Review* 40 (2009): 227–60.

55. "Tactics of State Welfare Study Assailed," *San Francisco Chronicle*, August 21, 1995, C12; Lisa Richardson, "O.C. Welfare Recipients Subject of Random Fraud Investigations Assistance," *Los Angeles Times*, August 20, 1995, 1; Gustafson, "The Criminalization of Poverty," 1–64.

56. Melanie Heath, "State of Our Unions: Marriage Promotion and the Contested Power of Heterosexuality," *Gender and Society* 23, no. 1 (February 2009): 27–48; Katherine Boo, "The New Marriage Cure: Is Wedlock Really a Way Out of Poverty?," *New Yorker*, August 18, 2003, 105–21.

57. Laura Duberstein, John S. Lindberg, and Susheela Singh Santelli, "Changes in Formal Sex Education: 1995–2002," *Perspectives on Sexual and Reproductive Health* 38, no. 4 (2006): 182–89; Choosing the Best, http://www.choosingthebest.org/curricula/index.html (accessed July 1, 2010).

58. There is more evidence that welfare reform actually increased cohabitation, since the rate of cohabitation among welfare mothers was about 6 percent in 1987, 7 percent in 1992, and doubled within the space of seven years. The primary explanation is that as a result of welfare reform, women were more eager to find a man to help pay the rent and the utilities and provide some child care when they went to work—the man was not necessarily the father of the woman's children. However, these relationships tended to break up rather quickly and lead to another cohabitation. T. Gave, "Demographic Trends Affecting AFDC Caseload: CRS Report to Congress" (Washington, DC: Congressional Research Service, 1992); Sheila R. Zedlewski and Donald W. Alderson, "Before and After Reform: How Have Families on Welfare Changed?" (Washington, DC: Urban Institute, April 2001), http://www.urban.org/uploadedPDF/ant-b32.pdf; David J. Fein, Nancy R. Burstein, Oreta G. Fein, and Laura D. Lindberg, "The Determinants of Marriage and Cohabitation among Disadvantaged Americans: Marriages and Family Formation, Data Analysis Project," http://www.acf.hhs.gov/programs/opie/strengthen/marr_family/reports/determinants_findings/datafindings_title.html (accessed December 1, 2007).

59. Three sociologists concluded that marriage was good for the mental health of single mothers only if they managed to stay married. They found that it was worse for a woman's mental health to get married and divorced than to stay unmarried. Kristi Williams, Sharon Sassler, and Lisa M. Nicholson, "For Better or For Worse? The Consequences of Marriage and Cohabitation for Single Mothers," *Social Forces* 86, no. 4 (June 2008): 1481–1511.

60. Gustafson, "The Criminalization of Poverty," 708.

61. Smith, *Welfare and Sexual Regulation*, 172.

CHAPTER FOUR

1. Judy Klemesrud, "An Arrangement: Living Together for Convenience, Security, Sex," *New York Times*, March 4, 1968, 40.

2. For the view that LeClair was "boastful," see David Allyn, *Make Love, Not War: The Sexual Revolution; An Unfettered History* (New York: Routledge, 2001), 96. Allyn devotes several pages in his chapter on *in loco parentis* to LeClair. Beth Bailey, in both *Sex in the Heartland* (Cambridge, MA: Harvard University Press, 1999), and "Sexual Revolution(s)," in *The Sixties: From Memory to History*, ed. David Farber (Chapel Hill: University of North Carolina Press, 1994), 235–62, emphasizes the feminism in LeClair's protest against Barnard's rules. Rosalind Rosenberg is the most sympathetic to Barnard deans, administrators, and President Peterson in Rosalind Rosenberg, *Changing the Subject: How the Women of Columbia Shaped the Way We Think about Sex and Politics* (New York: Columbia University Press, 2004), 231–36. Her discussion is marred by a number of errors, including the statement that LeClair had not told her parents she was living with Behr until the story appeared in the *New York Times* and the assumption, unwarranted from the evidence, that LeClair dropped out of

college because she had had an abortion. Sara Evans does not mention LeClair but examines the relationship of the "generation of 1968" to the sexual revolution and the emergence of women's liberation. Sara M. Evans, "Sons, Daughters, and Patriarchy: Gender and the 1968 Generation," *American Historical Review* 114, no. 3 (April 2009): 331–47.

3. Annie Gottlieb, *Do You Believe in Magic* (New York: Times Book, 1987), 341.

4. "Students: Linda the Light Housekeeper," *Time*, April 26, 1968, 51.

5. "Cornell Ponders Rules of Conduct: University Code Reviewed after Student Is Ousted," *New York Times*, October 4, 1962.

6. Susan E. Tifft and Alex S. Jones, *The Trust: The Private and Powerful Family behind the New York Times* (Boston: Little, Brown and Company, 1999), 438.

7. Gay Talese, *The Kingdom and the Power* (New York: World Publishing Company, 1969), 54.

8. Tifft and Jones, *The Trust*, 56, 438.

9. Stanley Cohen, *Folk Devils and Moral Panics: The Creation of the Mods and Rockers* (London: MacCobb and Kee, 1972), 6.

10. "Unstructured Relations," *Newsweek*, July 4, 1966, 78–79; Kenneth R. Clark, "Housing Shortage Governs Morals at Pan Am," *Brownsville (TX) Herald*, May 26, 1968.

11. Robert R. Bell and Kathleen Coughey, "Premarital Sexual Experience among College Females, 1958, 1968, and 1978," *Family Relations* 29, no. 3 (July 1980): 353–57; Kenneth L. Cannon and Richard Long, "Premarital Sexual Behavior in the Sixties," *Journal of Marriage and the Family* 33, no. 1 (February 1971): 36–49; Robert R. Bell and Jay B. Chaskes, "Premarital Sexual Experience among Coeds, 1958 and 1968," *Journal of Marriage and the Family* 32, no. 1 (February 1970): 81–96; Tom W. Smith, "A Report: The Sexual Revolution," *Public Opinion Quarterly* 54, no. 3 (Autumn 1990): 415–35.

12. Elaine Tyler May, *America and the Pill: A History of Promise, Peril, and Liberation* (New York: Basic Books, 2010), 88.

13. Finn Christensen examined the relationship between legal access to the pill and increased likelihood of cohabitation. He pointed out that the use of the pill was greater among young women in states with more liberal rules about access to contraception for unmarried women. Finn Christensen, "The Pill and Partnerships: The Impact of the Birth Control Bill on Cohabitation," January 2010, http://pages.towson.edu/FChriste/PillPart072809.pdf (accessed May 1, 2011); May, *America and the Pill*, 88; "Revolution in Morals: The Barnard Response," *Barnard Bulletin*, April 8, 1964; *Barnard Bulletin*, March 8, 1967.

14. Interview with Peter Behr, October 27, 2004; *Nashua (NH) Telegraph*, March 3, 1960; "Hudson Choir in Easter Service," *Nashua (NH) Telegraph*, April 6, 1960; *Nashua (NH) Telegraph*, December 12, 1961; *Nashua (NH) Telegraph*, January 25, 1963; *Nashua (NH) Telegraph*, November 30, 1967.

15. "Hudson PTA to Discuss Budget," *Nashua (NH) Telegraph*, February 10, 1960; *Nashua (NH) Telegraph*, February 17, 1965.

16. Deirdre Carmody, "Head of Barnard Asks Parents of Defiant Girl for Their Views," *New York Times*, April 19, 1968, 1; Grace (Linda) LeClair, "Feminist Legacies of 1968," "Columbia 1968," http://www.columbia1968.com/conference/ (accessed December 5, 2009).

17. Rose Weitz, *Rapunzel's Daughters: What Women's Hair Tells Us about Women's Lives* (New York: Farrar, Straus, and Giroux, 2004), 114.

18. William A. McWhirter, "'The Arrangement' at College," *Life* 64 (May 31, 1968): 56–62.

19. Laura Kavesh, "An Unmarried Couple's Memories of a Scandal," *Chicago Tribune*, July 3, 1984, 4.

20. Kenneth Kenniston, *Young Radicals: Notes on Committed Youth* (New York: Harcourt, Brace and World, 1968).

21. Mary Breasted, "Dr. Peterson Retires as Barnard President," *New York Times*, January 25, 1975, 49.

22. Martha Elizabeth Peterson, "An Evaluation of Relationships between Test Data and Success as a Residence Hall Counselor" (PhD diss., University of Kansas, 1959).

23. Interview with Estelle Freedman, June 12, 2003. For her recollections of Barnard at this time, including memories of acquaintance rape, see "Reckonings: Coming of Age at Barnard, 1968," *The Sixties: A Journal of History, Politics and Culture* 1, no. 2 (December 2008): 209–21; Dennis Hevesi, "Martha Peterson, 90, Barnard President in Vietnam War Era," *New York Times*, July 20, 2006.

24. Rosenberg, *Changing*, 226; LeClair, "Feminist Legacies."

25. But Barnard's housemothers were not all kindly widows from genteel New England backgrounds. Miss Lutton from Jamaica also made bail for Barnard students after they were arrested at protests at Columbia. Interview with Kathy Seal, November 16, 2004.

26. Rosenberg, *Changing*, 236–237.

27. Deirdre Carmody, "Barnard Eases Its Rules for Off-Campus Housing," *New York Times*, August 23, 1968, 41. A Radcliffe a senior, who had been denied permission to live off campus, figured out that she could succeed if she claimed to be married. She advertised in the *Crimson*, seeking a one-year marriage partner. Unlike at Barnard, however, no administrator ever sought her out. "Girl Student Uses Ad for Marriage Bid," *Reading (PA) Eagle*, April 20, 1966.

28. Interview with Kathy Seal, November 16, 2004.

29. Ti-Grace Atkinson, *Amazon Odyssey: The First Collection of Writings by the Political Pioneer of the Women's Movement* (New York: Links Books, 1974), 32; E-mail from Helen Longino, November 23, 2004; Karla Jay, *Tales of the Lavender Menace: A Memoir of Liberation* (New York: Basic Books, 1999), 6; "Love Chronicles: Groovy Kind of Love," A&E Television Network, 2000; "Linda vs. Locksmiths at Barnard," *New York Post*, March 15, 1968, 6.

30. Interview with Peter Behr, October 27, 2004.

31. "Illegal Abortions," *Washington Post*, April 13, 1964, B5; Jay, *Tales*, 8–9; Lawrence Lader, *Abortion* (Boston: Beacon Press, 1966), 6.

32. Interview with Nancy Biberman, November 18, 2004.

33. McWhirter, "'The Arrangement,'" 60.

34. Deirdre Carmody, "Co-Ed Disciplined by College Becomes a Dropout at Barnard," *New York Times*, September 4, 1968, 51.

35. Michael S. Foley, *Confronting the War Machine: Draft Resistance during the Vietnam War* (Chapel Hill: University of North Carolina Press, 2003), 8–9.

36. E-mail from Marty Jezer, November 21, 2004. There is no examination of draft resistance in New York City; for a study of the draft resistance movement in Boston, see Foley, *Confronting the War Machine.*

37. Gretchen Lemke-Santangelo, *Daughters of Aquarius: Women of the Sixties Counterculture* (Lawrence: University of Kansas, 2009), 136.

38. Interview with Peter Behr, October 27, 2004.

39. Todd Gitlin, *The Sixties: Years of Hope, Days of Rage* (New York: Bantam, 1969), 222.

40. Charles Perry, *The Haight-Ashbury: A History* (New York: Random House, 1984); Joel Selvin, *Summer of Love: The Inside Story of LSD, Rock and Roll, Free Love, and High*

Times in the Wild West (New York: Dutton, 1994). For the Diggers and masculinity, see Timothy Hodgdon, *Manhood in the Age of Aquarius* (New York: Columbia University Press, 2008).

41. Interview with Peter Behr, October 27, 2004.

42. Donald Boch, MD, with Sam Blum, "Unwed Couples: Do They live Happily Ever After," *Redbook*, April 1969, 140.

43. Klemesrud, "An Arrangement."

44. Unpublished article, July 1968, in the possession of Peter Behr.

45. Anne Hoffman, "Columbia Student Refuses Induction," *Barnard Bulletin* 82, no. 28 (March 13, 1968): 1.

46. Interview with Nancy Biberman, November 18, 2004.

47. E-mail from Peter Behr, January 16, 2005.

48. Steven Marx, www.columbia1968.com/stevenmarx/ (accessed July 1, 2009).

49. Interview with Linda Kerber, April 16, 2005; Renne N. Lansley, "College Women or College Girls: Gender, Sexuality, and In Loco Parentis on Campus" (PhD diss., Ohio State University, 2004).

50. "At Barnard, Sin Is Now Sensible," *Benton Harbor (MI) News-Palladium*, April 18, 1968, 1.

51. Deirdre Carmody, "Barnard Unit against Expelling Girl Who Lives with Boyfriend," *New York Times*, April 18, 1968, 1; "60 More Barnard Girls Insist They've Been Naughty, Too," *New York Post*, April 12, 1968, Linda LeClair clipping files, Barnard College Archives.

52. Maggie Astor, "In Another Era, a Barnard Student Makes National Headlines after Moving in with Boyfriend," *Columbia Spectator*, April 27, 2008.

53. "Student Objects to Rules," *Washington Post*, April 15, 1968; Frank Mazza, "Minister, Rabbi Rally to Linda in Love Trial," *New York Daily News*, April 17, 1968.

54. Jerry L. Avrorn, *University in Revolt: A History of the Columbia Crisis* (London: Macdonald, 1968), 186; A. Wu, "The Secularization of the Chaplaincy: A Brief History of the Columbia University Chaplaincy, 1908–1969," in *History of Universities*, ed. Mordechai Feingold (New York: Oxford University Press, 2009), 9:23; LeClair, "Feminist Legacies."

55. Deirdre Carmody, "Barnard Considering Decision on Student Living With Man," *New York Times*, April 17, 1968, 51; Michael E. Staub, *Torn at the Roots* (New York: Columbia University Press, 2002), 2.

56. Deirdre Carmody, "Barnard Protest Follows 'Affair,'" *New York Times*, March 15, 1968, 42.

57. "Testimony Given by Linda LeClair at Judicial Council Hearing," April 16, 1968, Linda LeClair Collection, Barnard College Archives.

58. Jean Crafton, "Barnard's Live-In Girl Tells Story in Tears," *New York Post*, April 16, 1968, 2.

59. McWhirter, "The Arrangement," 56.

60. "Girl Living with Boy Friend Says It's Not College's Affair," *Milwaukee Journal*, April 17, 1968, 1, 3; Lindsay Van Gelder, "Coed Facing Ouster for Unwedded Bliss," *Long Beach (CA) Press Telegram*, April 17, 1968; "Coed Facing Expulsion for Living with Boyfriend," *El Paso (TX) Herald Post*, April 17, 1968, 1; "Coed Defends Right to Share Room with Beau," *Boise Idaho State Journal*, January 17, 1968, 1; "Coed Wins Fight to Live with her Boyfriend," *Bryan (OH) Times*, April 19, 1968, 1.

61. Letter from Mrs. C. Petrus, April 16, 1968, Linda LeClair Collection, Barnard Archives.

62. Letter in the personal collection of Peter Behr, n.d.

63. Letters, Mrs. Harriette B. Wagner, *Time*, May 10, 1968; Dorothy Denburg, *Record*, April 20, 1968.

64. Unsigned letter in the personal collection of Peter Behr, n.d.

65. Letter from Mrs. Eleanor Christiansen, Freeport, NY, April 17, 1968, Linda LeClair Collection, Barnard Archives.

66. *America*, a liberal Catholic magazine, believed that a student living off campus should not be punished by a college. "Barnard College Affair and Campus Regulations," *America* 118 (May 4, 1968): 592.

67. William F. Buckley, Jr., "The Linda LeClair Case: Is The Moral Code Dead?" *Los Angeles Times*, April 29, 1968, 11A.

68. Harriet Van Horne, "The Case against Linda," *New York Post*, April 19, 1968, 46; Max Lerner, "The Value Rebels," *New York Post*, April 19, 1968, 46.

69. Roy Wilkins, "Non-Thinkers Just Turned on Patter Learned by Rote," *Bend (OR) Bulletin*, April 26, 1968.

70. "Barnard Girl Claims Victory," *Bridgeport (CT) Post*, April 18, 1968.

71. *Lowell (MA) Sunday Sun*, April 21, 1968; Frank Mazza, "Dad Cuts Off Linda's Allowance," *New York Daily News*, April 20, 1968.

72. Jean Crampton, "Banker Dad Punishes Linda Fiscally," *New York Post*, April 19, 1968, 3. The headline of the *Portsmouth Herald* was "Dad Wants Coed Home, Doesn't Approve," *Portsmouth (NH) Herald*, April 20, 1968; John F. Fenton, "Father Despairs of Barnard Daughter," *New York Times*, April 20, 1968, 27.

73. Atkinson, *Amazon Odyssey*, 32; Mark Rudd, *Underground: My Life with SDS and the Weathermen* (New York: William Morrow, 2009), 50; Bread and Roses, Manifesto, Declaration of Women's Independence (1970), in *The New Left: Declaration of Women's Independence*, ed. Rosalyn Baxandall and Linda Gordon (New York: Basic Books, 2000), 45.

74. Martha Weinman Lear, "The Second Feminist Wave," *New York Times*, March 10, 1968, 24–25, 50–56; LeClair, "Feminist Legacies."

75. Roger Kahn, *The Battle for Morningside Heights: Why Students Rebel* (New York: William Morrow, 1968), 214; Robert D. McFadden, "Remembering Columbia," *New York Times*, April 25, 2008; George Keller, "Six Weeks: That School Morningside," *Columbia College Today*, Spring 1968, 22.

76. "Barnard President Reverses Decision on Linda LeClair," *Washington Post*, May 18, 1968, C2; *Bridgeport (CT) Telegram*, April 19, 1968, 9; "Barnard President Reverses Decision on Linda LeClair," *Washington Post*, May 18, 1968, C2.

77. LeClair, "Feminist Legacies."

78. Interview with Peter Behr, October 27, 2004.

79. E-mail from Peter Behr, January 16, 2005.

80. Gail Collins, *When Everything Changed: The Amazing Journey of American Women from 1960 to the Present* (New York: Little, Brown, and Company, 2009), 399.

81. Gottlieb, *Do You*, 341–42.

82. LeClair, "Feminist Legacies."

83. Kavesh, "An Unmarried Couple's Memories."

CHAPTER FIVE

1. Tracey Shatek, "Cohabitation Pits Morality vs. Legality," *Grand Forks (ND) Herald*, January 26, 1991; *Clovis (NM) News-Journal*, September 6, 1976; Doe and Doe v. Duling, 782 F.2d 1202 Fourth Circuit, U.S. Appeals 1986.

2. "Cohabitation Legal in Culver," *Bend (OR) Bulletin,* May 15, 1979; Marjorie Fine Knowles, "Legal Status of Women in Alabama: A Crazy Quilt," *Alabama Law Review* 29 (1977–78): 504; Mary C. Schwartz and Laura Zeisel, "Unmarried Cohabitation: A National Study of a Parole Policy," *Crime and Delinquency* 22, no. 2 (April 1976): 139. Schwartz and Zeisel incorrectly included Massachusetts as a state that prohibited cohabitation by a parolee, thus bringing their count of the number of states to twenty-one.

3. "Note, Constitutional Barriers to Civil and Criminal Restrictions on Pre and Extramarital Sex," *Harvard Law Review* 104, no. 7 (May 1991): 1662.

4. Many laws against cohabitation were passed or reintroduced in the last 1940s as an attempt to clamp down on the sexual revolution during World War II. Thus, in 1947 Alabama passed a law making it unlawful for an unmarried couple to check into a tourist camp or motel. Alinder v. City of Homewood, 254 Ala. 525, 49 So. 2d 108 (1950).

5. Elizabeth Lutes Hillman, *Defending America: Military Culture and the Cold War Court-Martial* (Princeton, NJ: Princeton University Press, 1995), 196–97. For a navy court-martial in 1985, see Steve Rubenstein, "An Affair Could Cost Navy Man 17 Years," *San Francisco Chronicle,* April 30, 1985. The other military benefits only for the married were legal counseling, access to base commissaries, and subsidized life and health insurance. In 1979, the Spokane tribe, a tribe of Christian Indians, enacted an ordinance making cohabitation illegal and imposing a jail term of thirty days against it because it violated their Christian beliefs. *Akwesasne Notes* 2, no. 4 (Autumn 1974): 20.

6. Ill. Ann. Stat., 38.11 (1961), Committee Comments at 290.

7. Warner v. State, 202 Ind. 479, 175 N.E. 661 (1931). For an earlier attempt to define cohabitation, see State v. Chandler, 96 Ind. 591 (1884).

8. Gerhard Mueller, *Legal Regulation of Sexual Conduct* (New York: Oceana Publications, 1961), 46–47.

9. "Unwed Teachers Fired," *Kennewick (WA) Tri-City Herald,* February 11, 1971; "People in the News," *Pittsburgh Press,* January 25, 1975; "Worker Seeks $60,000 in Cohabitation Case," *Toledo (OH) Blade,* July 22, 1976; Thompson v. Southwest School District, No. 79-5112-CV-SW, 483 F. Supp. 1170 (1980); Bill McAllister, "Dispute Flares in Tazewell," *Washington Post,* April 3, 1977; "Ruling Due on Firing Teacher for Cohabitation," January 8, 1980, http://lexis.nexus (accessed July 1, 2009); "Reinstated Teacher May Get $81,814," *Orlando (FL) Sentinel,* April 12, 1985; "Victorious Professor Says She Is No Feminist," *Fredericksburg (VA) Free Lance-Star,* March 27, 1980; "East Hartford Police Chief Pulls Back on Guidelines," *Hartford (CT) Courant,* March 29, 1979. In Montana, an all-Hutterite school board fired teachers for cohabiting. The teachers fought back and won in the courts. In response, the state legislature tried but failed in passing a law to fire cohabiting teachers or prohibit school boards from hiring them. "Montana Teachers Battle Right to 'Live in Sin,'" *Spokane (WA) Spokesman Review,* March 20, 1979; "Vote Is Set Back for 'Cohabit' Bill," *Spokane (WA) Spokesman Review,* March 21, 1979; "Sheriff Targets Unwed Couples Living Together," *Spokane (WA) Spokesman Review,* April 1, 1987. Despite the failure of the law to pass, school boards in small Montana towns did fire teachers for cohabiting. For more examples, see Michael Martizen, "Arlington Police Deny Race Discrimination Charges," *Washington Post,* August 14, 1983; *Anchorage (AK) Daily News,* August 7, 1978. For probation officers in Orange County, California, denied promotion, see "Lived Together Prior to Their Marriage," *Los Angeles Times,* April 29, 1975. For the firing and reinstatement of a single New York City policeman for cohabiting with his

girlfriend, see Anthony V. Bouza, "The Policeman's Character Investigation: Lowered Standards of Changing Times," *Journal of Criminal Law, Criminology, and Police Science* 60, no. 1 (1972): 121. For the dismissal of a policeman in Peotone, Illinois, in 1985 for living together with a dispatcher, whom he subsequently married, see Kukla v. Village of Antioch, F. 647 Supp. 799 (1986).

10. Frank R. Kent, "Sex Offenses Weighed for New Moral Code," *Washington Post*, May 20, 1955, 44; Anthony Lewis, "Model Penal Code Is Approved by the American Law Institute," *New York Times*, May 25, 1962, 1; Frank P. Grad, "The A.L.I. Model Penal Code," *Crime and Delinquency* 4 (1958): 127–38.

11. Wallace Turner, "Hawaii Expected to Ease Sex Laws," *New York Times*, August 4, 1971; John Darnton, "Hartford Supports Homosexuality Bill," *New York Times*, June 3, 1969.

12. Stanford N. Sesser, "Some Officials Invoke Ancient Sex Statutes—Selectively, Critics Say," *Wall Street Journal*, July 5, 1968, 1.

13. Ibid.

14. Ibid.

15. "'Most Arrests Made' for Sex Law Offenses in Smaller Cities," *Sheboygan Press*, July 5, 1968, 15.

16. Richard Rhodes, "Sex and Sin in Sheboygan," *Playboy*, August 1972, 186.

17. Martha Fineman, "Law and Changing Patterns of Behavior: Sanctions on Non-Marital Cohabitation," *Wisconsin Law Review* 275 (1981): 282; Clarke Morrison, "Adoption Denied to Unmarried Couple," *Asheville (NC) Citizen-Times*, September 17, 2006; Joanna L. Grossman and Lawrence M. Friedman, *Inside the Castle: Law and the Family in 20th Century America* (Princeton, NJ: Princeton University Press, 2011), 123; Interview with Linda R. Brumken, August 23, 2011.

18. Ann Marie Lipinski, "Trouble for Birds and Bees in the Land of Curds and Whey," *Chicago Tribune*, May 2, 1982; "Two Cops Fired for Living Together Are Reinstated," *Chicago Tribune*, October 14, 1978; "2 Engaged Officers Spied Upon, Fired," *Milwaukee Journal*, September 13, 1978.

19. Gerald A. Layton, "La Crosse, Wisconsin, 1862–1882: Crime, the Police Court, the Newspapers" (master's thesis, University of Wisconsin–La Crosse, 1971); Parker McCobb Reed, *The Bend and the Bar of Wisconsin* (Green Bay, WI: P. M. Reed, 1882), 9.

20. "B-Day Pros, Cons Debated," *Sheboygan Press*, February 15, 1966.

21. *Sheboygan Press*, September 27, 1968. For more on the alternative press, see John McMillian, *Smoking Typewriters: The Sixties Underground Press and the Rise of Alternative Media* (New York: Oxford University Press, 2011).

22. Birth Record of Julia Decko, August 12, 1965, Register of Deeds Office, Filed August 25, 1965, Wisconsin State Board of Health, Original Certificate of Live Birth, Sheboygan County Register of Deeds.

23. Interview with Peter Bjork, March 9, 2005; "Tennis," *Sheboygan Press*, July 19, 1969, 14; "Decko Named Recreation Supervisor," *Sheboygan Press*, July 17, 1964, 3; "LWV Officers Re-Elected," *Sheboygan Press*, April 6, 1967, 11; "Wonderful Wisconsin Week Plans Set," *Sheboygan Press*, September 12, 1968, 5.

24. "James Decko to Head Recreation Department," *Sheboygan Press*, March 11, 1967.

25. *Sheboygan Press*, September 21, 1966, 12.

26. "Ted Hook to Direct Follies,'" *Sheboygan Press*, September 4, 1968.

27. Interview with Wayne Homstaad, May 19, 2005.

28. Ibid.; *Olwein (IA) Daily Register*, May 12, 1963; *Olwein (IA) Daily Register*, June 12, 1969; *Fayette County (IA) Leader*, February 24, 1966.

29. Rhodes, "Sex," 130.
30. "Former Police Chief Frank Dies," *Sheboygan Press*, October 12, 1992.
31. "'Rec' Director, Decko Resigns," *Sheboygan Press*, September 5, 1970.
32. Ibid.
33. "Jones Takes Office as D.A.," *Sheboygan Press*, May 1, 1969.
34. Rhodes, "Sex," 186.
35. Interview with Richard Rhodes, May 2, 2005.
36. Ibid.
37. "The Decko Resignation," *Sheboygan Press*, September 11, 1970.
38. Editor's Mail Box, *Sheboygan Press*, September 15, 1970.
39. Interview with Peter Bjork, March 8, 2005.
40. Rhodes, "Sex," 186.
41. Peter Bjork, letter, *Playboy*, April 1972, 72, 189.
42. Interview with Peter Bjork, March 8, 2005.
43. Rhodes, "Sex," 190; "Death in Park Ruled Suicide," *Carroll County (IL) Mirror Democrat*, December 2, 1971; Rhodes, "Sex," 90.
44. Peter Bjork, letter, *Playboy*, April 1972, 72, 189.
45. Ibid.
46. Notes, Richard Rhodes Collection, University of Kansas, Lawrence.
47. Rhodes, "Sex," 190.
48. Ibid.; "D.A. Raps Playboy Article," *Sheboygan Press*, August 10, 1972.
49. Griswold v. Connecticut, 381 U.S. 479 (1965), Goldberg concurring.
50. Marc Stein, *Sexual Injustice: Supreme Court Decisions from Griswold to Roe* (Chapel Hill: University of North Carolina Press, 2010), 102–4, 120–21.
51. Shwago v. Spradlin, 701 F.2d 470 (5th Cir. 1983); Hollenbaugh v. Carnegie Library et al., No. 78-5519 (U.S. December 11, 1978); City of North Muskegon v. Briggs, No. 84-1230 (U.S. July 1, 1985).
52. Jason C. Long, "Housing Discrimination and the Status of Unmarried Cohabitants: Living with *McCready v. Hoffus*," *University of Detroit Mercy Law Review* 76 (1999–2000): 99–126; Leonard J. Eichbauer v. Commissioner of Internal Revenue, Docket No. 6987-70SC (T.C., 1971); Nevitt F. Ensmeyer v. Commissioner of Internal Revenue, Docket No. 77-2302, Docket No. 77-2302 (T.C. 1979); "Revised Code Won't Intrude on Private Life," *Eugene (OR) Register-Guard*, February 5, 1971; *Bend (OR) Bulletin*, May 15, 1979; "House Repeals Sex Laws," *Anchorage (AK) Daily News*, March 14, 1975; "WCTU Lobbyist Speaks Out," *Modesto (CA) Bee*, February 21, 1973; Jerry Gillan, "Dymally Breaks Tie, Senate Ok's Sex Measure," *Los Angeles Times*, May 2, 1975.
53. For the 1996 information, see Richard A. Posner and Katherine B. Silbaugh, *A Guide to America's Sex Laws* (Chicago: University of Chicago Press, 1996), 98–102. The five states that criminalized cohabitation as of 2011 were Florida, Michigan, Mississippi, South Carolina, and Virginia.
54. "Criminologist Urges Repeal of Morality, Conduct Laws," *Sheboygan Press*, November 17, 1971, 11; Interview with David Clarenbach, July 20, 2010.
55. "Legalize Pot, Abolish Some Sex Crimes," *Wisconsin Rapids Daily Tribune*, November 13, 1972, 1; "Judicial Recommendations Given to Lucey by Panel," *Sheboygan Press*, February 23, 1972, 1.
56. "Legalize Pot," 1.
57. William B. Turner, "The Gay Rights State: Wisconsin's Pioneering Legislation to Prohibit Discrimination Based on Sexual Orientation," *Wisconsin Women's Law Journal*, 22 (2007): 28–55; Interview with David Clarenbach, July 20, 2010.

58. Fineman, "Law," 282, 299; "Revisions in Sex Laws Supported," *Milwaukee Journal*, February 28, 1980; Interview with David Clarenbach, July 20, 2010.

59. Interview with David Clarenbach, July 20, 2010; *Milwaukee Sentinel*, April 20, 1983; "Legislature Should Note Iowa Cohabitation Ruling," *Milwaukee Sentinel*, April 21, 1983; "Fear of Cohabitation Law," *Milwaukee Sentinel*, January 1, 2009; *Bryan (OH) Times*, June 13, 1983.

60. "Legislature Spent Time Patching Old Laws," *Prescott (AZ) Courier*, June 13, 1975; "Legislature Considers Removal of Sex Laws," *Casa Grande (AZ) Dispatch*, February 8, 2000; Paul Davenport, "House Votes to Repeal Sex Laws," *Casa Grande (AZ) Dispatch*, March 15, 2001; "Legislature at a Glance," *Casa Grande (AZ) Dispatch*, March 21, 2001; Thomas F. Coleman, *The Domino Effect* (Glendale, CA: Spectrum Institute, 2009), 188; "Fundamentalist Preachers Scorn Sex-Act Bill," *Milwaukee Journal*, March 27, 1981.

61. http://www.sodomylaws.org/usa/arizona/aznewszo.htm (accessed June 25, 2005). The one additional element in the liberal repeal coalition in Utah was polygamists. "ACLU Is Helping Pro-Polygamy Group," *Salt Lake City (UT) Deseret News*, July 16, 1999.

62. "Cohabitation Repeal Squeaks By," *Grand Forks (ND) Herald*, March 2, 2007; Janell Cole, "Panel Changes, OKs Cohabitation Bill," *Grand Forks (ND) Herald*, February 8, 2007; Tom Dennis, "Living Together in Harmony," *Grand Forks (ND) Herald*, February 9, 2007.

63. Cece Von Kolnitz, "Denied Compensation for Injury, Death," *Wilmington (NC) Star-News*, April 25, 1999; "Task Force to Study Effects of Domestic Upsets," *Lundington (NC) Daily News*, March 31, 1979; "Legislators Meet Opposition to Change in N.C. Sex Statutes," *Wilmington (NC) Star News*, October 4, 1984; *Mountain Torch*, Fall 2006, 3–6.

CHAPTER SIX

1. "Leftists and War Foes Set Up Center in Capital," *New York Times*, February 16, 1968; Sam Brinkley, *Getting Loose: Lifestyle Consumption in the 1970s* (Durham, NC: Duke University, 2007).

2. Eleanor Dorsey Macklin, "Evaluation of a Program Designed to Affect the Language Development of Young Disadvantaged Children" (PhD diss., Cornell University, 1973); Eleanor D. Macklin, John Harding, and Eugene Michael Fodor, *Cornell Story Book Reading* (Ithaca, NY: Cornell Research Program in Early Childhood Education, 1968).

3. "Michael Douglas and Brenda Vaccaro: Is Out of Wedlock No Longer In?," *People*, September 2, 1974; Anthony Summers and Robbyn Swan, *Sinatra: The Life* (New York: Vintage, 2005), 152.

4. "Off Campus Morals Stir Cornell Storm," *Tuscaloosa (AL) News*, November 13, 1962; "Cornell Drops 4 after New Riots," *New York Times*, May 25, 1958; Michael Lerner, "Cornell Rejects Plea from Student Council for Social Freedom," *Harvard Crimson*, December 19, 1962.

5. Shulamith Firestone, *The Dialectic of Sex: The Case for Feminist Revolution* (New York: William Morrow, 1970), 258–59; Anonymous, "Barbarous Rituals: 84 Ways to Feminize Humans," Pittsburgh Know, Inc., n.d., Documents from the Women's Liberation Movement, an On-Line Archival Collection, Special Collections Library, Duke University, http://scriptorium.lib.duke.edu/wlm/barbar (accessed February 2, 2011).

6. Betty Fang, "Swinging: In Retrospect," *Journal of Sex Research* 12 (1976): 220–37.

7. Eleanor D. Macklin, "Going Very Steady," *Psychology Today* 8 (November 1974), 53–59.

8. Unsigned letter to Eleanor Macklin, November 14, 1974, Personal Files of Eleanor Macklin.

9. Unsigned letter to Eleanor Macklin, October 21, 1971, Personal Files of Eleanor Macklin.

10. *Cohabitation Research Newsletter*, no. 4, June 1974, 26.

11. Letter from John Chappell, Jr., to Eleanor Macklin, November 10, 1974, Personal Files of Eleanor Macklin.

12. Letter to Eleanor Macklin, January 21, 1974, Personal Files of Eleanor Macklin.

13. John D'Emilio and Estelle B. Freedman, *Intimate Matters: A History of Sexuality in America*, 2nd ed. (Chicago: University of Chicago Press, 1997), 241.

14. Eleanor D. Macklin, "Heterosexual Cohabitation among Unmarried College Students," *Family Coordinator* 21, no. 4 (October 1972): 470.

15. Eleanor D. Macklin, "Nontraditional Family Forms: A Decade of Research," *Journal of Marriage and the Family* 42, no. 4 (November 1980): 905–22.

16. Eleanor Macklin, "Nonmarital Heterosexual Cohabitation," *Marriage and Family Review* 1 (1978): 3–12.

17. *Binghamton (NY) Evening Press*, October 20, 1971, n.p.

18. Eleanor Dorsey Macklin, "Unmarried Heterosexual Cohabitation on the University Campus," in *The Social Psychology of Sex*, ed. J. P. Wiseman (New York: Harper and Row, 1976), 119.

19. *Trenton (NJ) Evening News*, July 26, 1982.

20. Eleanor Macklin to Mrs. Haskin, February 17, 1974, Personal Files of Eleanor Macklin.

21. *Binghamton (NY) Evening Press*, October 20, 1971, n.p.

22. Interview with Eleanor Macklin, July 22–23, 2003.

23. Letter of Pat to her parents, August 1, 1972, in *Women's Letters: America from the Revolutionary War to the Present* (New York: Dial Press, 2005), 660.

24. *Love American Style* (1969; Los Angeles, CA: CBS Studios, 2007), DVD. *God Bless Mr. Ferguson* (1971) was a spin-off of *Love American Style*. It involved a minister and his wife who try to persuade a young couple not to live together.

25. Ione Quinby Griggs, "Lifestyle of Grown Son Accepted by His Mother," *Milwaukee Journal*, December 19, 1978, 4.

26. "Unstructured Relations," *Newsweek*, July 4, 1966, 78; Jonathan Randall, "Relaxed Campus Rules Reflect Liberalized Attitudes on Sex," *New York Times*, April 25, 1966.

27. Macklin, "Unmarried Heterosexual Cohabitation on the University Campus," 138.

28. Ibid., 118–19.

29. Letter to Eleanor Macklin from Robert E. Gardner, Director, Advising and Counseling, College of Engineers, October 25, 1974, Personal Files of Eleanor Macklin.

30. Jo Tucker to Eleanor Macklin, February 21, 1975, Personal Files of Eleanor Macklin.

31. Unsigned letter to Eleanor Macklin, March 7, 1975, Personal Files of Eleanor Macklin.

32. John Doris, "Letter to the Editor," *Cornell Daily Sun*, March 17, 1975, 4.

33. Unpublished paper of Tom Rhodes, HDFS, 1975, Personal Files of Eleanor Macklin.

34. Donna Zahorik, Judith Long Laws, Antonia Glasse, and Charlotte Farris v. Cornell University, 729 F.2d 85 (2nd Cir. 1984).

35. Interview with Eleanor Macklin, July 22–23, 2003.

36. Jim Nyers, "Popular Controversial Teacher Loses Job," *Ithaca (NY) Journal*, March 4, 1975, Personal Files of Eleanor Macklin.

37. Urie Bronfenbrenner, curriculum vita, http://www.peopleell.edu/pages.ubii/ (accessed July 1, 2008).

38. E-mail from Eleanor Macklin, January 15, 2003.

39. Interview with Eleanor Macklin, July 22–23, 2003.

40. Tony Schwartz, Mary Lord, Dewey Gram, Pamela Ellis Simons, and Lisa Whitman, "Living Together," *Newsweek*, August 1, 1977, 46–50; Urie Bronfenbrenner, "The Calamitous Decline of the American Family," *Washington Post*, January 2, 1977.

41. "Comments on Macklin, Prof. Henry N. Ricciuti," *Cornell Daily Sun*, March 12, 1975, 4.

42. E-mail from Eleanor Macklin, January 15, 2003.

43. *Cornell Daily Sun*, March 13, 1975, 5.

44. Interview with Eleanor Macklin, July 22–23, 2003.

45. Macklin, "Nontraditional Family Forms."

46. Ibid.

47. Macklin, "Nonmarital Heterosexual Cohabitation: An Overview," 70.

48. Paul C. Glick and Arthur J. Norton, "Marrying, Divorcing and Living Together in the U.S. Today," *Population Bulletin* 32, no. 1 (1977): 4–34.

49. Interview with Arthur Norton, August 25, 2005.

50. Ibid.; "Study Downs Unwed 'Live-Ins,'" *Hartford (CT) Courant*, November 21, 1976.

51. Nancy Moore Clatworthy, "Living Together," in *Old Family/New Family*, ed. Nona Glazer-Malbin (New York: Devan Nostrand, 1975), 88. The defining element of moral panic, fear of venereal disease, combined with the oft-repeated hope that cohabitation was a fad that would disappear. The more conservative the commentator, the more likely the prediction of the demise of cohabitation. Nancy Moore Clatworthy, "The Nontraditional Family and the Child," *Capital University Law Review* 12 (1983): 345–54.

52. Charles and Bonnie Remsberg, "The Case against Living Together," *Seventeen* 36 (November 1977): 132–33, 162–63.

53. Ibid., 133.

54. Rebecca Stafford, Elaine Backman, and Pamela Dibona, "The Division of Labor among Cohabiting and Married Couples," *Journal of Marriage and the Family* 39, no. 1 (February 1977): 43–57.

55. Richard R. Clayton and Harwin L. Ross, "Shacking Up: Cohabitation in the 1970s," *Journal of Marriage and the Family* 39, no. 2 (May 1977): 273–83.

56. Kazuo Yamaguchi and Denise Kandel, "Dynamic Relationships between Premarital Cohabitation and Illicit Drug Use: An Event-History Analysis of Role Selection and Role Socialization," *American Sociological Review* 50 (August 1985): 544.

57. Jan E. Stets and Murray A. Straus, "The Marriage License as a Hitting License: A Comparison of Assaults in Dating, Cohabiting, and Married Couples," in *Physical Violence in American Families: Risk Factors and Adaptations to Violence in Families*, ed. Murray A. Straus and Richard J. Gelles (Lanham, MD: Transaction Books, 1989), 33–52.

58. Catherine J. Kenney and Sara S. McLanahan argue that cohabitors during the first year of living together are no more violent than recently wed couples, but long-term cohabitors have more violent relationships than married couples. Catherine J. Kenney and Sara S. McLanahan, "Are Cohabiting Relationships More Violent Than Marriage?," Center for Research on Child Wellbeing, Working Paper 01-22, January 8, 2002.

59. Kersti Yllo and Murray A. Straus, "Interpersonal Violence among Married and Co-habiting Couples," *Family Relations* 30, no. 3 (July 1981): 345; Catherine Kenney and Sara McLanahan, "Why Are Cohabiting Relationships More Violent Than Marriage?," *Demography* 43, no. 1 (2006): 127–40.

60. Kenney and McLanahan, "Why Are Cohabiting Relationships More Violent Than Marriage?"

61. Ben B. Lindsey, *The Companionate Marriage* (Garden City, NY: Garden City Publishers, 1927); Ben B. Lindsey, "The Companionate Marriage," *Redbook*, October 1926; Ben B. Lindsey, "The Companionate Marriage," *Redbook*, March 1927.

62. Margaret Mead, "Marriage in Two Steps," *Redbook*, July 1966, 48.

63. Alfred DeMaris, "A Comparison of Remarriages with First Marriages on Satisfaction in Marriage and Its Relationship to Prior Cohabitation," *Family Relations* 33, no. 3 (July 1984): 443–49.

64. Ibid., 448.

65. Alan Booth and David Johnson, "Premarital Cohabitation and Marital Success," *Journal of Family Issues* 9, no. 2 (June 1988): 255–72.

66. Andrew Cherlin, *Marriage, Divorce, Remarriage* (Cambridge, MA: Harvard University Press, 1981), 15–16.

67. Philip Blumstein and Pepper Schwartz, *American Couples: Money, Work, Sex* (New York: William Morrow and Company, 1983), 321.

68. Julia A. Ericksen, with Sally A. Steffen, *Kiss and Tell: Surveying Sex in the Twentieth Century* (Cambridge, MA: Harvard University Press, 1999), 228.

69. Charles Mohr, "Carter, in New Hampshire, Promises to Seek to Restore Respect for Family," *New York Times*, August 4, 1976; "The American Family: Bent but Not Broken," *U.S. News and World Report*, June 16, 1986, 50. For an analysis of the significance of Carter's contribution to the debate about family values, see J. Brooks Flippen, *Jimmy Carter, the Politics of the Family, and the Rise of the Religious Right* (Athens: University of Georgia Press, 2011).

70. Natasha Zaretsky, *No Direction Home: The American Family and the Fear of National Decline, 1968–1980* (Chapel Hill: University of North Carolina Press, 2007).

71. Col. Stephen Bauer, *At Ease in the White House: Social Life as Seen by a Presidential Military Aide* (Lanham, MD: Rowman and Littlefield, 2004), 225.

72. Eleanor Clift, "Setting the Style," *Newsweek*, February 21, 1977; Thomas M. DeFrank, "The Really New Faces," *Newsweek*, March 14, 1977; "Just Call Him Mister," *Time*, February 21, 1977.

73. *Public Papers of the Presidents of the United States, Jimmy Carter* (Washington, DC: US Government Printing Office, 1977), 138.

74. "Pr. George's 'Living in Sin' Bill Debated," *Washington Post*, May 9, 1977.

75. "Hearings Gather Views on Family Life in Oregon," *Portland Sun Oregonian*, December 9, 1979.

76. Nadine Brozan, "Conference on Family Turns into a Feud," *Chicago Tribune*, June 15, 1980; "What Makes a Family Stirs Debate," *Boston Globe*, February 20, 1980; Sandy Banisky, "Right, Left Gird for Battle over Families Conference," *Baltimore (MD) Sun*, June 1, 1980.

77. What's a Family? N.H. Squabbles over Definition," *Nashua (NH) Telegraph*, February 11, 1990; Weyrich, as quoted in Rebecca E. Klatch, *Women of the New Right* (Philadelphia: Temple University, 1987), 125. For general discussion of the conference, see Leo Ribuffo, "Family Past as Prologue: Jimmy Carter, the White House Conference on Families, and the Mobilization of the New Christian Right," *Review of Policy Research*,

23, no. 2 (April 2006): 311–38, and William Martin, *With God on Our Side: The Rise of the Religious Right in America* (New York: Broadway, 2005), 168–91. Laura Kalman provides an overview of the Ford and Carter administrations in *Right Star Rising: A New Politics, 1974–1980* (New York: W. W. Norton, 2010). For an assessment of the significance of backlash and mass mobilization of the New Right's interest in family values, see Matthew D. Lassiter, "Inventing Family Values," in *Rightward Bound: Making America Conservative in the 1970s,* ed. Bruce Schulman and Julian Zelizer (Cambridge, MA: Harvard University Press, 2007), 13–29. For other general surveys about the rise of the Right, see Clyde Wilcox, *God's Warriors: The Christian Right in Twentieth-Century America* (Baltimore: Johns Hopkins University Press, 1992); Kenneth J. Heineman, *God Is a Conservative: Religion, Politics, and Morality in a Christian America* (New York: New York University Press, 1998); Ruth Murray Brown, *For a "Christian America": A History of the Religious Right* (New York: Prometheus Books, 2002).

78. James Davison, *Culture Wars: The Struggle to Define America* (New York: Basic Books, 1992), 179; *Daily News,* June 17, 1977.

79. Zaretsky, *No Direction Home,* 232; Letter from W. Kennard Lacy, Letters, *Milwaukee Journal,* June 17, 1980; "What Makes Up a family?," *Fredericksburg (VA) Free Lance-Star,* November 28, 1979.

CHAPTER SEVEN

1. Her story was that she was stopped by the police for speeding when the couple were in Oregon. The police asked her why her driver's license listed her as Michelle Triola when she was known in town as Mrs. Marvin. She hired Mitchelson, who put through the legal papers to change her name. Nonetheless, it is also the case that legal papers were procured one week prior to her breakup with Marvin. Roger Ebert, *Awake in the Dark: The Best of Roger Ebert* (Chicago: University of Chicago Press, 2006), 29.

2. He claimed that he stopped payments because she told a gossip columnist that his second marriage was failing. She claimed he stopped payments because his second wife wanted him to reduce his outlays to her and his first wife.

3. "'Divorce without Marriage' Suits Today's Life-Style, Argues Attorney Marvin Mitchelson," *People,* August 24, 1978, 67. See also John A. Jenkins, *Ladies' Man: The Life and Trials of Marvin Mitchelson* (New York: St. Martin's, 1972).

4. Amy Dockser and Gay Jervey, "Mitchelson," *American Lawyer,* September 1988, 125.

5. *Chicago Sun-Times,* October 9, 1979.

6. The courts also held that Lee Marvin could not make a promise of financial support to Michelle Marvin in 1964 because at the time he was still married to Betty Marvin. Mitchelson then changed his argument to claim that Lee Marvin renewed his promise for support in 1967 after he was divorced.

7. Marvin v. Marvin, 18 Cal. 3d 600 (1976).

8. Ibid.

9. Ariela Dubler, "Wifely Behavior: A Legal History of Acting Married," *Columbia Law Review* 100, no. 4 (2000): 957–1021.

10. Walter O. Weyrauch, "Informal Marriage and Common Law Marriage," *Sexual Behavior and the Law,* ed. Ralph Slovenko (Springfield, IL: Charles C. Thomas, 1965), 297–340; Charlotte K. Goldberg, "The Schemes of Adventuresses: The Abolition and

Revival of Common-Law Marriage," *William and Mary Journal of Women and Law* 13 (2006–7): 483–538.

11. Anders Walker, *The Ghost of Jim Crow: How Southern Moderates Used* Brown v. Board of Education *to Stall Civil Rights* (New York: Oxford University Press, 2009), 41–42.

12. Marriage of Cary, 109 Cal. Rptr. 862 (Ct. App. 1973).

13. Grace Ganz Blumberg, "The Regularization of Nonmarital Cohabitation: Rights and Responsibilities in the American Welfare State," *Notre Dame Law Review* 76 (2000–2001): 1303.

14. Joanna Lublin, "Trailblazing Bench," *Wall Street Journal,* July 20, 1972.

15. Marvin v. Marvin, 18 Cal. 3d 600 (1976).

16. "Mathew Tobriner: Justice for 18 Years on Coast High Court," *New York Times,* April 9, 1982, 86; Michael A. Willemsen, "Justice Tobriner and the Tolerance of Evolving Lifestyles: Adapting the Law to Social Change," *Hastings Law Journal* 29 (1977): 73–99. Tobriner was consistent in his views, as in his concurring opinion supporting overnight visitation of prisoners by girlfriends, not just by wives. In re Cummings, 30 Cal. 3d 870 (1982).

17. Senate Committee on Judiciary, *Marvin v. Marvin and the Rights of Unmarried Parties* (Los Angeles: n.p., 1977), 110.

18. Herma Hill Kay and Carol Amyx, "*Marvin v. Marvin*: Preserving the Options," *University of California Law Review* 65 (1977): 945.

19. Michael Grossberg, *Governing the Hearth: Law and Family in Nineteenth-Century America* (Chapel Hill: University of North Carolina Press, 1985), 86–102.

20. William Knoedelseder, Jr., and Ellen Farley, "Marvin's 'Idle Male Promises,'" *Washington Post,* January 27, 1979.

21. Marvin Mitchelson, *Living Together* (New York: Simon and Schuster, 1980), 50.

22. Claudia Luther, "Gene Kelly Denies Offering Musical Role to Ms. Marvin," *Los Angeles Times,* February 16, 1979.

23. Jenkins, *Ladies' Man,* 142.

24. Claudia Luther, "Testimony on Lee Marvin Sex Life Barred by Judge," *Los Angeles Times,* March 15, 1975.

25. "The Marvins at Home," *San Francisco Chronicle,* January 17, 1979.

26. Jenkins, *Ladies' Man,* 139; Eileen Keerdoja, "The Trials of the Unmarried," *Newsweek,* October 8, 1979.

27. "Reaction to Marvin Decision," *Los Angeles Times,* April 19, 1979, IV-12.

28. Luther, "Testimony," 1–20.

29. Nora Ephron, "The Gold-Digger Standard," *Washington Post,* April 20, 1979.

30. Pamela Marvin, *Lee* (London: Faber and Faber, 1997), 266.

31. "A Free Ride," Letters to the Editor, *San Francisco Chronicle,* January 17, 1979.

32. *Saturday Night Live,* March 16, 1979.

33. "The Marvin Case," *Pittsburgh Press,* April 20, 1979; *Nevada (MO) Daily Mail,* April 20, 1979; *Los Angeles Times,* April 19, 1979; "The Real Winners," *Garden City (KA) Telegram,* April 19, 1979.

34. *Atlanta Daily World,* June 11, 1982.

35. "They Deserved Each Other," *San Francisco Chronicle,* April 19, 1979, 44.

36. Jenkins, *Ladies' Man,* 140.

37. The decision was two to one, with the female judge dissenting from the majority opinion. "Newsmakers," *Newsweek,* August 21, 1981, 41.

38. Bob Baker and Patti Morrison, "Lee Marvin, Menacing Gunman of Films, Dies," *Los Angeles Times,* August 30, 1987.

39. William K. Knoedelseder, Jr., and Ellen Farley, "*Marvin v. Marvin*: The Price of Living Together," *Washington Post*, January 10, 1979; Whorton v. Dillingham, 248 Cal. Rptr. 405 (Ct. App. 1998).

40. LaBarbara Bowman, "From Altar to Palimony," *Washington Post*, July 3, 1979; Bob Greene, "Divorce Suits Very Ladylike," *Pittsburgh Press*, July 6, 1978. For the opposite point of view, see Sharmila Roy Grossman, "Illusory Rights of *Marvin v. Marvin* for the Same-Sex Couple versus the Preferable Canadian Alternative," *California Western Law Review* 38 (2001–2): 548–68.

41. Myrna Oliver, "Marvin Cases Hard to Win," *Los Angeles Times*, January 30, 1986, 1; Ann Laquer Estin, "Unmarried Partners and the Legacy of *Marvin v. Marvin*: Ordinary Cohabitation," *Notre Dame Law Review* 76 (2001): 1383.

42. Oliver, "Marvin Cases Hard to Win," 1.

43. Cynthia Grant Bowman, "Legal Treatment of Cohabitation in the United States," *Law and Policy* 26, no. 1 (January 2004): 127.

44. Oliver, "Marvin Cases Hard to Win," 1.

45. Ira Mark Ellman, Paul M. Kurtz, and Elizabeth S. Scott, *Family Law: Cases, Text, Problems* (Charlottesville, VA: Lexis Law Publishing, 1998), 966–67; Katherine C. Gordon, "Note: The Necessity and Enforcement of Cohabitation Agreements; When Strings Will Attach and How to Prevent Them; A State Survey," *Brandeis Law Journal* 37 (Winter 1998): 259–72.

46. Lee Strobel, "'Palimony' Case: 'Live In' at Own Risk," *Chicago Tribune*, September 23, 1979.

47. Daniel Egler and Mark Polzin, "Bill Requires Pacts for Unwed Couples," *Chicago Tribune*, May 2, 1979; Charles Mount, "Domiciled but Unwed Women Win Court Case," *Chicago Tribune*, July 14, 1978. For more about the history of no-fault divorce legislation in Illinois, see Alison Lekfovitz, "The Problem of Marriage in the Era of Women's Liberation" (PhD diss., University of Chicago, 2010), chap. 3.

48. He claimed that he presented himself as her husband to be respectable and to make the children legitimate. He argued that he did not intend marriage when they were students at Grinnell because he was unable to undertake the financial responsibility for a wife and child. Robert Mapplethorpe, the live-in lover of singer Patti Smith, asked a friend visiting Aruba to mail a letter to his Catholic parents, postmarked Aruba, telling them that he had eloped. Patti Smith, *Just Kids* (New York: Harper/Collins, 2010), 73.

49. *Champaign-Urbana, Illinois City Directory* (Champaign, IL: Johnson Publishing Co., 1975), n.p.

50. Judith Michaelson, "Marvin Rule: Revolution in Getting 'Split,'" *Los Angeles Times*, May 17, 1979.

51. Carol Kleiman, "Playing House: The Stakes Are Rising," *Chicago Tribune*, October 11, 1978.

52. *Urbana-Champaign, Illinois City Directory* (Champaign, IL: Johnson Publishing Co., 1981), 459; Kleiman, "Playing House," D1; E-mail from Cynthia Bowman, May 14, 2009.

53. The order was 15 percent of gross income; in Illinois, the standard guideline amount is 20 percent of net for two children, which turns out to be roughly similar. E-mail from Cynthia Bowman, May 13, 2009.

54. Hewitt v. Hewitt, 20 Ill. Dec. 476, 380 N.E.2d 454 (1978).

55. Hewitt v. Hewitt, 77 Ill. 2d 49, 394 N.E.2d 1204, 31 Ill. Dec. 827 (1979).

56. "Down with Hopkinsville Divorcing Dad," *Hopkinsville Kentucky New Era*, September 21, 1979; *Mt. Prospect (IL) Daily Herald*, September 21, 1979.

57. Cynthia Grant Bowman, *Unmarried Couples, Law, and Public Policy* (New York: Oxford University Press, 2010); Richard A. Wilson, "State of the Law of Protecting and Securing the Rights of Same-Sex Partners in Illinois without Benefit of Statutory Rights Accorded Heterosexual Couples," *Loyola University Chicago Law Journal* 38 (2006–7): 323–49.

58. Cynthia Gorney, "Loved and Left: The Palimony Question," *Washington Post*, January 30, 1989.

59. Blumberg, "Regularization," 1302; Barbara Hunt Lazeron, "Marvinizing Can Lead to Palimony," *American Speech* 63, no. 2 (Summer 1988): 188–92.

60. Ira Mark Ellman, "Contract Thinking Was Marvin's Fatal Flaw: Unmarried Partners and the Legacy of *Marvin v. Marvin*," *Notre Dame Law Review* 76 (2001): 1368.

61. Martha Fineman, *The Autonomy Myth* (New York: New Press, 2005); Lois Harder, "Rights of Love: The State and Intimate Relationships in Canada and the United States," *Social Politics* 14, no. 2 (Summer 2007): 144–81.

62. Lawrence Van Gelder, "Lawyers Troubled by Rehabilitation Concept in Marvin Decision," *New York Times*, April 20, 1979.

63. Estin, "Unmarried Partners," 383.

64. Goran Lind, *Common Law Marriage* (New York: Oxford University Press, 2009), 824.

65. William Knoedelseder and Ellen Parley, "The Split Decision," *Washington Post*, April 19, 1979, B1.

66. "Michelle Marvin Pleads Innocent to Shoplifting," *Los Angeles Times*, September 30, 1980; "Court Reverses $104,000 Award for Ex-Companion of Lee Marvin," *New York Times*, August 13, 1980, 12; Jenkins, *Ladies' Man*, 146.

CHAPTER EIGHT

1. Transcript, *60 Minutes*, vol. 12, no. 28, as broadcast over the CBS Television Network, March 23, 1980.

2. Both of the parents deliberately kept their daughters out of the interview. Thus, the *60 Minutes* program consisted of adult commentary on the question of a mother's cohabitation.

3. Monroe Anderson, "Mom Who Lost Kids: I'd Change," *Chicago Tribune*, October 22, 1980; "Parents in Court," *Palm Beach (FL) Post*, October 14, 1980; "Excerpts from Platform to Be Submitted to Republican Delegates," *New York Times*, July 13, 1980.

4. For a historical overview about changing attitudes toward child custody, see Mary Ann Mason, *From Father's Property to Children's Rights: The History of Child Custody in the United States* (New York: Columbia University Press, 1994), 121–60.

5. On alimony, see Jim Young, "Alimony Cutoff Upheld by the Court," *Daily Oklahoman*, January 22, 1983; "Alimony Modification: Cohabitation of Ex-Wife with Another Man," *Hofstra Law Review* 7 (1978–79): 471–98; Wendy Ricketts, "The Relevance of Premarital and Postmarital Cohabitation in Awarding Spousal Support," *Divorce Litigation* 7 (July 1996): 150; J. Thomas Oldham, "The Effect of Unmarried Cohabitation by a Former Spouse upon His or Her Right to Continue to Receive Alimony," *Journal of Family Law* 17, no. 2 (1978–79): 249–73; Note, "The Effect of Third Party Cohabitation on Alimony Payments," *Tulsa Law Journal* 5 (1980); and J. Thomas Oldham, "Cohabitation by an Alimony Recipient Revisited," *Journal of Family Law* 20 (1982): 615; Newton M. Galloway, "An Analysis of the Georgia

'Live-In Lover' Law," *Mercer Law Review* 32, no. 1 (Fall 1980): 375–92; "Court Rules for Ex-Wife," *Ironwood (MI) Daily Globe*, January 6, 1983; "Ruling in Live-In Lover Case May Hearten Gays," *Atlanta Constitution*, February 11, 1993; "The Divorced Man Gets Help from New Laws?," *Norwalk (CT) Hour*, February 3, 1979. What was remarkable about the denial of alimony to Patricia Craissati in 2008 was that a Florida Appellate Court judge ruled in her ex-husband's favor, claiming that living with a cellmate in a Florida jail because of her drunk driving conviction constituted cohabitation. "Ex-Wife's Alimony Cut Off Because She Has Cellmate," *Palm Beach (FL) Post*, December 11, 2000. Robert McAnerney, a savvy lawyer from Darien, Connecticut, pioneered the idea that was called the McAnerney clause in divorce agreements. He had lost in his effort to stop paying alimony to his ex-wife, who had been living with her boyfriend for three years. A state court in Connecticut held that cohabitation was not the same as remarriage, and McAnerney still had to make his payments. As a result, divorce lawyers in Connecticut began inserting clauses into divorce settlements specifying that a wife would forfeit alimony if she cohabited for a specific length of time.

6. Ketron v. Ketron, 15 Ark. App. 325, 692 S.W.2d 261 (1985).

7. In his survey of eighty-one attorneys in thirty-six states and the District of Columbia, Donald H. Stone put the figure at 30 percent. Donald H. Stone, "Just Molly and Me and Baby Makes Three—or Does It? Child Custody and the Live-In Lover: An Empirical Study," *Pace Law Review* 11, no. 1 (Fall 1980): 4; Larry Bumpass and H. Lu, "Trends in Cohabitation and Implications for Children's Family Contexts in the United States," *Population Studies* 54 (2000): 29–41.

8. Jessica Pearson, Paul Munson, and Nancy Thoennes, "Legal Change and Child Custody Awards," *Journal of Family Issues* 3, no. 1 (March 1982): 8. Lenore J. Weitzman put the figure at one in ten in *The Divorce Revolution: The Unexpected Social and Economic Consequences for Women and Children in America* (New York: Free Press, 1985); Larry L. Bumpass and James A. Sweet, "National Estimates of Cohabitation," *Demography* 26, no. 3 (November 1989): 615–25.

9. Although these cases dealt with two parents who were divorcing, children's protective services also sent caseworkers to insure that a mother did not engage in "child neglect" by having a live-in boyfriend in the home. The case was *In re* Burrell, 58 Ohio St. 2d 37, 358 N.E.2d 738 (1979). For discussion of this case, see "The Effect of Custodial Parents' Sexual Conduct in Dependency Determinations: *In re Burrell*," *Ohio State Law Journal* 40 (1979): 1017–23.

10. Jeff Atkinson, "Criteria for Deciding Child Custody in the Trial and Appellate Courts," *Family Law Quarterly* 18 (1984–85): 8; Julie E. Artis, "Judging the Best Interests of the Child: Judges' Accounts of the Tender Years Doctrine," *Law and Society Review* 38, no. 4 (2004): 798.

11. Rippon v. Rippon, 64 Ill. App. 3d 465, 381 N.E.2d 70 (1970).

12. Jarrett v. Jarrett, 64 Ill. App. 3d 932, 382 N.E.2d 12 (1978); Bagents v. Bagents, 419 So. 2d 460, 1092 (La. 1982).

13. Holman v. Wellman, 104 Cal. App. 3d 992, 164 Cal. Rptr. 148 (1980); Jill Lindeman Sanford, "Contested Custody and the Judicial Decision-Making Process" (PhD diss., Florida State University, 1977), 145.

14. Cheryl Crane, with Cliff Jahn, *Detour: A Hollywood Story* (New York: Avon, 1988).

15. Sue Miller, *The Good Mother* (New York: Harper and Row, 1986).

16. Reply Brief of Defendant—Appellant, Jarrett v. Jarrett, September 1979.

17. Susan Axelrod, "'60 Minutes' of Anguish," *Washington Post*, March 25, 1980.

18. Judy Foreman, "In *Jarrett v. Jarrett*: New Battle Lines Drawn," *Boston Globe*, October 21, 1980.

19. Defendant-Appellant, Testimony, Jarrett v. Jarrett, July 1976.

20. Jarrett v. Jarrett, 78 Ill. 2d 447, 400 N.E.2d 421 (1979); 40 Ill. Comp. Stats., 610 (b) (1977).

21. "Archive," *People*, February 18, 1980; "Children Up for Grabs," *Washington Post*, November 7, 1980; Joyce Brown, "Women Facing 'Backlash" in Divorce Courts," *Chicago Tribune*, May 17, 1981; *Mt. Prospect (IL) Sunday Herald*, November 2, 1980.

22. "Child Custody Ruling Unrealistic," *Kokomo (IN) Tribune*, October 31, 1980.

23. "Moral Standards Upheld," *Chicago Tribune*, November 23, 1979,; "Child Custody, Morals . . . ," *Chicago Tribune*, October 22, 1980.

24. Lee Strobel, "Judicial Rivals Clash on Child Custody Case," *Chicago Tribune*, October 12, 1980.

25. Lee Strobel, "Council of Lawyers Says Sklodowski Is Unqualified," *Chicago Tribune*, October 16, 1980.

26. Lee Strobel, "Supreme Court Foes Come Off Bench Swinging," *Chicago Tribune*, October 18, 1980; Lee Strobel, "High Court Race Is Called Embarrassing," *Chicago Tribune*, November 2, 1980; Lee Strobel, "Simon Links Supreme Court Win to Foe's 'Ugly' Tactics," *Chicago Tribune*, November 6, 1980.

27. *In re* Marriage of Thompson and Thompson, 96 Ill. 2d 67, 449 N.E.2d 88, 93 (1983). For additional questioning of the decision of Jarrett, see Brandt v. Brandt, 99 Ill. App. 3d 1089, 425 N.E.2d 1252 (1981).

28. *Mt. Prospect (IL) Daily Herald*, September 24, 1979; *Mt. Prospect (IL) Sunday Herald*, April 17, 1983.

29. Joseph R. Tybor, "Custody Decision Overturns History," *Chicago Tribune*, April 17, 1983.

30. Other appellate court cases in Illinois made the same point. An appellate court overruled a decision that had restricted a father's visitation to the daytime hours so long as he had a live-in lover. Another appellate court removed the restriction that had prohibited overnight visitation in the father's home if he had a woman living with him. *In re* Marriage of Lawler, 82 Ill. App. 198, 402 N.E.2d 430 (1980); *In re* Marriage of Hanson, 111 Ill. App. 3d 544, 445 N.E.2d 912 (1983).

31. Hackley v. Hackley, 380 So. 2d 446 (Fla. Dist. Ct. Appl. 1979). Other appellate court judges in Illinois also decided in favor of cohabiting fathers in several rulings about visitation. A trial court judge had limited a father's visits with his son to two daytime visits per month, with meetings prohibited at the girlfriend's house where father was living. An Illinois Appellate Court ruled that such a decision was too harsh. The courts made these rulings not because visitation was different than cohabitation but because they did not want to punish fathers as harshly as mothers. A father who had moved from Illinois to San Francisco could retain custody despite having a girlfriend, a divorcée with children, who stayed over at his apartment two nights a month while his five-year-old son was living with him. The court approved of the good relationship between the boy and the woman's children. Moreover, like Jackie Jarrett, the father had told his son that sometimes Dad had woman friends who did on occasion sleep in his bed. The father was not asked if he was planning to marry nor told that he must stop seeing the woman. In re Custody of Blonsky, 84 Ill. App. 3d 810, 405 N.E.2d 1112 (1980).

32. Jessica Pearson and Maria A. Luchesi Ring, "Judicial Decision-Making in Contested Custody Cases," *Journal of Family Law* 21 (1982–83): 720; Mary Ann Mason and Ann

Quirk, "Are Mothers Losing Custody—Read My Lips: Trends in Judicial Decision-Making in Custody disputes—1920, 1960, 1990, and 1995," *Family Law Quarterly* 3 (1997–98): 215–17; "Cohabiting, Custody," *Boston Globe*, September 12, 1981.

33. Mason and Quirk, "Are Mothers Losing Custody," 215–17.

34. Brown v. Brown, 218 Va. 196, 237 S.E.2d 89 (1977); Rhonda R. Rivera, "Our Straight-Laced Judges: Twenty Years Later," *Hastings Law Journal* 50, no. 4 (April 1999): 1196.

35. Johnson v. Johnson, 422 So. 2d 1013 (Fla. Dist. Ct. Appl. 1982); Gayet v. Gayet, 92 N.J. 149, 456 A.2d 102 (1983).

36. Shioji v. Shioji, 712 P.2d 197 (Utah 1985). On surprisingly conservative attitudes of superior court judges in California in the 1980s, see Thomas J. Reidy, Richard M. Silver, and Alan Carlson, "Child Custody Decision: A Survey of Judges," *Family Law Quarterly* 23 (1989–90): 75–88.

37. Stone, "Just Molly."

38. Roe v. Roe, 228 Va. 772, 324 S.E.2d 691 (1985); Robert L. Gottsfield, "Child Custody and Sexual Lifestyle," *Conciliation Courts Review* 23, no. 1 (June 1985): 43.

39. Kimberly D. Richman, *Courting Change: Queer Parents, Judges, and the Transformation of American Family Law* (New York: New York University Press, 2010); Daniel Rivers, "'In the Best Interests of the Child': Lesbian and Gay Parenting Custody Cases, 1967–1985," *Journal of Social History* 43, no. 4 (Summer 2010): 917–45.

40. Reidy, Silver, and Carlson, "Child Custody Decisions," 85; Marc J. Ackerman and Linda J. Steffen, "Child Custody Evaluation Practices: A Survey of Family Law Judges," *American Journal of Family Law* 15 (2001): 12–23.

41. Kathryn Katz, "Majoritarian Morality and Parental Rights," *Albany Law Review* 62 (1987–88): 405.

42. Beck v. Beck, 341 So. 2d 580 (La. Ct. App. 1977).

43. Shirley A. Settle and Carol R. Lowery, "Child Custody Decisions: Content Analysis of a Judicial Survey," *Therapists, Lawyers, and Divorcing Spouses*, ed. Esther Oshiver Fisher and Mitchell Salem Fisher (New York: Haworth Press, 1982), 132.

44. McRae v. McRae, 381 So. 2d 1052 (Miss. 1980).

45. Gibson v. Pierce, 176 Ga. App. 287, 335 S.E.2d 658 (Ga. Ct. App. 1985).

46. Bagents v. Bagents, 419 So. 2d 460 (La. 1982).

47. Robinson v. Robinson, 5 Va. App. 22, 361 S.E.2d 356 (Va. Ct. App. 1987).

48. Appellate court decisions regarding cohabiting parents were based on cases identified by Julie E. Artis and June Carbone and Naomi Cahn. June Carbone and Naomi Cahn, "Judging Families," *University of Missouri Kansas City Law Review* 77 (Winter 2008): 267–305; Julie E. Artis, "What Makes a Good Parent? An Examination of Child Custody Statutes: Case Law and Judges" (PhD diss., Indiana University, 1999).

49. http://www.divorcesource.com/ubbthreads0show (accessed March 1, 2010). On Utah, see Tucker v. Tucker, 910 P.2d 1209, (Utah 1996). For barring a mother from having overnight guests while her child was present, see Carrico v. Blevins, 12 Va. App. 47, 402 S.E.2d 235(Va. 1991); Parker v. Parker, 986 S.W. 2d 557 (Tenn. App. 1999). See also Campbell v. Campbell, 63 Ark. App. 136, 975 S.W.2d 869 (Ark. Ct. App. 1998). For Arizona, see Higgins v. Higgins, 194 Ariz. 266, 981 P.2d 134 (Ariz. Ct. App. 1999). For a review of recent appellate court decisions related to child custody involving heterosexual or gay cohabitors, see Naomi Cahn and June Carbone, *Red Families v. Blue Families: Legal Polarization and the Creation of Culture* (New York: Oxford, 2010), 139–54.

50. Alphin v. Alphin, 19 S.W.3d 160 (Ark. 2005); Carbone and Cahn, "Judging Families," 268–305.

51. Tybor, "Custody Decision"; "Damaged Healed in Custody Dispute," *Seattle Times*, April 17, 1983.

CHAPTER NINE

1. Carl Danzinger, *Unmarried Heterosexual Cohabitation* (San Francisco: R and E Associates, 1978), 73.

2. Don Mitchell, *Cultural Geography: A Critical Introduction* (Oxford: Blackwell, 2000), 289. On stereotypes of cohabitors as less stable tenants, see Bella DePaulo, *Singled Out: How Singles Are Stereotyped, Stigmatized, and Ignored, and Still Live Happily Ever After* (New York: St. Martin's Press, 2006), 213–14; Beverly Solochek, "Unmarried Couples Look for Equity in Co-ops," *New York Times*, September 4, 1977; "Council Hedges on Explosive Human Relations Bill," *University Park (PA) Daily Collegian*, May 31, 1975.

3. Barbara Riker, "Unwed Sharing a Home: It Works for Some," *Los Angeles Times*, April 13, 1975; Thomas F. Coleman, "Single-Minded Change Agent," *Psychology Today*, August 27, 2009, http://psychologytoday.com/blog/living-single/200908; "Young Unwed Couples Enjoy the Benefits of Marriage but Fear Its Pitfalls," *Bend (OR) Bulletin*, June 16, 1974.

4. "House Upholds Barring Unmarried Couples," *Hartford (CT) Courant*, March 3, 1977; Leslie Gourse, "Now, When Unmarried Register, Hotels Just Turn the Other Way," *Chicago Tribune*, August 17, 1980; "Apartments in Orlando Rented to Unmarrieds," *Fort Walton Beach (FL) Playground Daily News*, January 9, 1977; Fahizah Alim, "Anti-Gay Practices Renter Study Reports Sex Bias," *Sacramento (CA) Bee*, April 10, 1984. There is much more study of the extent of discrimination against same-sex couples, but the comparison group is not usually distinguished by marital status. Despite higher levels of discrimination, same-sex couples are more likely to own homes than straight cohabitors because they have higher levels of incomes and are older. Karen Leppel, "Home-Ownership among Opposite- and Same-Sex Couples in the U.S." *Feminist Economics* 13, no. 1 (January 2007): 1–30.

5. "Cohabiting Couples Keep Arrangements Concealed," *Lawton (OK) Constitution*, November 22, 1972; *Los Angeles Times*, March 25, 1968.

6. "Bill Could Limit Housing to Married Couples," *Washington Post*, February 3, 1977; "Rights Ordinance Draws Criticism," *University Park (PA) Daily Collegian*, April 18, 1975; Rose Mary Lentz, "Cohabiting Couples Keep Arrangements Concealed," *Lawton (OK) Constitution*, November 22, 1972; Henry Allen, "Freaks in the Suburbs: Seeking Middle Class Amenities," *Washington Post*, January 21, 1971; Jane Doe, "I Wish They'd Do Right," *New York Times*, September 23, 1977; *Charlottesville (VA) Cavalier Daily*, September 14, 1976; Loretta Tofani, "Complaints Test Rent Law Barring Unmarried Pairs," *Washington Post*, July 24, 1980; Sunny Schubert, "Unmarried Couples Find No Hassle," *Wisconsin State Journal*, July 29, 1979; David J. Grzesek, *Financial Independence: Through Buying and Investing in Single Family Homes* (Gretna, LA: Pelican Publishing, 1985), 233.

7. *Spokane (WA) Spokesman Review*, August 12, 1974; Wendy Schuman, "Singles Becoming More Stable Tenants," *New York Times*, July 14, 1974; Bernard C. Meltzer, "Dialogue on Real Estate Topics," *Washington Post*, March 6, 1971; "Proposal Would Ban Rentals to Unwed," *Hartford (CT) Courant*, October 7, 1981; "Just Living

Together," *Eugene (OR) Register-Guard*, February 14, 1976; "U.S. Questions Legality of Virginia Loan Policy," *Washington Post*, February 20, 1996.

8. Doe, "I Wish They'd Do Right."

9. "Rental Barrier Removed," *Milwaukee Journal*, March 17, 1977.

10. Daniel Curry, "State High Court Refuses to Hear Cohabit Case," *Mt. Prospect (IL) Daily Herald*, October 4, 1990.

11. Kenneth D. Wald, James W. Button, Barbara A. Rienzo, "The Politics of Gay Rights in American Communities: Explaining AntiDiscrimination Ordinances and Policies," *American Journal of Political Science* 4, no. 4 (November 1996): 1152–78; Simon Hall, "The American Gay Rights Movement and Patriotic Protest," *Journal of the History of Sexuality* 19, no. 3 (September 2010): 550.

12. Ted Gregory, "'Live-Ins' Sue to Get Apartment," *Mt. Prospect (IL) Daily Herald*, August 12, 1989.

13. The trial court had found the ordinance constitutional, but an appeals court disagreed.

14. Marsha Ritzdorf, "Sex, Lies, and Urban Life: How Municipal Planning Marginalizes African American Women and Their Families," in *Gender and the City* (New York: Rowman and Littlefield, 2009), 176; Village of Belle Terre v. Boraas, 416 U.S. 1 (1974).

15. Gerald Fairs, "Commune Living Restriction Law to be Readied," *Los Angeles Times*, November 16, 1975.

16. Moore v. City of East Cleveland, 431 U.S. 494 (1977); Philip Hager, "Woman Fights to Keep Family," *Los Angeles Times*, October 31, 1976.

17. Frank S. Alexander, "The Housing of America's Families: Control, Exclusion, and Privilege," *Emory Law Journal* 54 (2005): 1231–70; Shawn G. Kennedy, "Family Zoning Ruling Challenged," *New York Times*, July 20, 1980.

18. "Shore Towns Reluctant to Ban 'Group Rentals,'" *New York Times*, January 23, 1971.

19. Marsha Brown Ritzdorf-Brozovsky, "The Impact of Family Definitions in American Municipal Zoning Ordinances" (PhD diss., University of Washington, 1983), 107, 207, 225.

20. Ritzdorf, "Sex, Lies."

21. *Fredericksburg (VA) Free-Lance Star*, March 17, 1989; Larson v. The Mayor and Council of the Borough of Spring Lake Heights, New Jersey, 99 N.J. Super. 365, 240 A.2d 31 (N.J. 1968).

22. Thomas Maier, *The Masters of Sex: The Life and Times of William Masters and Virginia Johnson, the Couple Who Taught America How to Love* (New York: Basic Books, 2010), 270–80.

23. Interview with E. Terrence Jones, July 25, 2009.

24. "Town Takes Brave Stand against Sin," *Mother Jones Magazine* 2 (February–March, 1987), 18.

25. Interview with Joan Kelly Horn, July 24, 2009; Mark Schlenkman, "Woman behind the Upset: Horn Is Called Calm, Focused," *St. Louis Post Dispatch*, November 11, 1990.

26. *Boston Globe*, January 12, 1980.

27. *St. Louis Post Dispatch*, November 2, 1985.

28. Michael Tachett, "An Imperfect Family Circle Squares Off with Zoning Law," *Chicago Tribune*, November 9, 1986.

29. Robbi Courtaway, "Ladue 'Cohabitation' OK with Some Residents," *Clayton (MD) Citizen-Journal*, November 12, 1986.

30. Interview with E. Terrence Jones, July 25, 2009; *Clayton (MD) Citizen Journal*, November 12, 1986.

31. Editorial, "Shame," *St. Louis Post-Dispatch*, March 8, 1986.

32. "La-De-Dah in La-De-Due," *St. Louis Dispatch*, October 25, 1985.

33. Interview with Joan Kelly Horn, July 24, 2009; *St. Louis Globe-Democrat*, February 8, 1986.

34. City of Ladue v. Horn, 720 S.W. 2d 745 (1986).

35. Ruling, Missouri Court of Appeals, Eastern District, No. 51415, Opinion, William H. Crandall, Jr., n.d.; J. B. Cullingworth *The Political Culture of Planning: American Land Use Planning in Comparative Perspective* (New York: Routledge, 1983), 5.

36. "2 Bills Affecting Large Houses, Concept of 'Family' Gain Council's Approval," *St. Louis Post-Dispatch*, September 21, 1958.

37. Nancy Larson, "Gay Families, Keep Out," *Advocate*, July 18, 2006; "Co-Habitating Couple Unwelcome as Tenants," *Washington-Times*, August 11, 1998.

38. Dinan et al. v. Board of Zoning Appeals of the Town of Stratford, No. 142088, 220 Conn. 61, 595 A.2d 864 (1991); Douglas Root, "Move Over, Mom and Pop: New Families Are Here," *Pittsburgh-Post Gazette*, January 19, 1992; McMinn v. Town of Oyster Bay et al., 66 N.Y.2d 544, 488 N.E.2d 120, 498 N.Y.S. 128 (1985); *Gazette*, September 1, 1990.

39. Zavala and Dotson v. City and County of Denver, Case No. 855A300, 759 P.2d 664, 1988 Colo. 113 (1988).

40. "Denver 'Living in Sin' Law Repealed," *Washington Post*, May 2, 1989; "Denver Fight Turns on Defining a Family," *New York Times*, May 26, 1989; Dorothy Nelkin, David P. Willis, and Scott V. Parris, eds., *A Disease of Society: Cultural and Institutional Responses to AIDS* (Cambridge: Cambridge University Press, 1991), 60; "Denver Ends Ban on Unrelated People Sharing Home," *San Francisco Chronicle*, May 3, 1989.

41. "Victory for Family Diversity in Black Jack, Missouri," http://www.unmarried.org/black-jack-missouri.html (accessed March 19, 2011); Introductory Provisions and Definition, Winnetka, Illinois, Village Code, Chap. 17,04, http://wwww.amlegal.com/next/gateway/dll (accessed August 3, 2009); Title IV, Land Use, Huntleigh, Missouri, http://www.huntleigh.org; "Local Occupancy Codes in Northeast Ohio," Housing Research and Advocacy Center, 2010, http://www.thehousingcenter.org (accessed August 5, 2011).

42. For a gay man successfully winning a housing discrimination fight, charging marital status discrimination, see Loveland v. Leslie, 21 Wash. App. 74 (1978).

43. "Rights Ordinance Draws Criticism," *University Park (PA) Daily Collegian*, July 10, 1974. The first college town to explicitly prohibit discrimination against cohabitors was Madison in 1988, but the law was struck down by the state supreme court six years later. Rita M. Neuman, "Note: Closing the Door on Cohabitants under Wisconsin's Open Housing Law," *Wisconsin Law Review* 1995, no. 4 (1995): 965–1002.

44. Beverly Solochek, "Unmarried Couples Look," *New York Times*, September 4, 1977. Interview with Arthur Emil, September 1, 2009; Emil v. Dewey, 66 A.D.2d 758, 411 N.Y.S.2d 865 (N.Y. App. Div. 1978); Emil v. Dewey, 49 N.Y.2d 968, 406 N.E.2d 744, 428 N.Y.S.2d 887 (1980).

45. Richard Levine, "Living Together Is Suddenly Risky," *New York Times*, May 15, 1983; Daniel A. Lee, "Owners Consider Appeal of Ruling on Cohabitation," *New York Times*, August 2, 1980; Susan Chira, "Unrelated Apartment Sharers May Be Evicted," *New York Times*, May 11, 1983; "Unwed Couple Wins Stay from Eviction in Appellate Ruling," *New York Times*, February 12, 1982. While cohabitation does not constitute

marital status discrimination in New York, it does in California, Massachusetts, Michigan, Alaska, and New Jersey.

46. Andrew Brooks, "Talking Roommates: No Mass Evictions Foreseen," *New York Times*, May 25, 1983; Shawn G. Kennedy, "Leaders in Albany Agree on Measure to Shield Tenants," *New York Times*, June 18, 1983; Georgia Dullea, "Apartment Sharer's Fret over Lease Ruling," *New York Times*, May 16, 1983; Arthur S. Leonard, "Lesbian and Gay Families and the Law: A Progress Report," *Fordham Urban Law Journal* 21 (1993): 927–72. However, in response to the AIDS crisis, a New York state supreme court in 1983 held that a gay couple who considered themselves married were "a family" and therefore the surviving partner was entitled to inherit survivors' rights to remain in a rent-controlled apartment. Braschi v. Stahl Associates, 543 N.E.2d (1989).

47. Bob Nelson, "Court Ruling Bans Eviction of Gay Couples," *Gay Community News*, August 28, 1982.

48. Neil H. Mehler, "Landlord to Fight Court Order on Religious Grounds," *Chicago Tribune*, January 13, 1989.

49. For this history, with a defense of religious landlords, see David E. Bernstein, *You Can't Say That: The Growing Threat to Civil Liberties from Antidiscrimination Laws* (Washington, DC: Cato Institute, 2003), 121–30; Thomas F. Coleman, *The Domino Effect* (Glendale, CA: Spectrum Institute, 2009), 140–51; Jerry DeMuth, "No Children, No Pets, No Sinners," *Advocate*, April 18, 1995, 34.

50. Art Barnum, "Rental Ban on Unmarried OK," *Chicago Tribune*, April 27, 1990.

CHAPTER TEN

1. "Unmarried Union," *New Orleans Times Picayune*, March 21, 1975.

2. Ariela R. Dubler, "Sexing Skinner: History and the Politics of the Right to Marry," *Columbia Law Review* 110, no. 5 (June 2010): 1376.

3. Rory McVeigh and Maria-Elena D. Diaz, "Voting to Ban Same-Sex Marriage: Interests, Values and Communities," *American Sociological Review* 74, no. 4 (2009): 891–915.

4. "More Employers Providing Domestic Partner Benefits," *Journal of Employee Assistance*, 35, no. 3 (July 2005); Walecia Konrad, "For Gay Couples, Obstacles to Health Insurance," *New York Times*, May 9, 2009.

5. The other benefits were relocation assistance, family medical leave, employee discounts, adoption assistance, dental and vision insurance, disability and retirement benefits, and sickness, bereavement, and parenting leave.

6. Valerie Richardson, "Domestic Partners Don Gay Apparel," *Washington Times*, February 15, 1991.

7. Roman Catholic archbishops were the major opponents of domestic partnership law in Boston, New York, and the District of Columbia and also major opponents of gay rights bills in several cities. On Roman Catholic opposition to domestic partnership in Boston in 1991, see Kenneth L. Karst, *Law's Promise, Law's Expression: Visions of Power in the Politics of Race, Gender, and Religion* (New York: Yale University Press, 1993), 69–70.

8. By the end of the 1980s, gay and lesbian plaintiffs in those regions were also enjoying the greatest success in winning child custody and visitation rights and rights to adoption of children. Daniel R. Pinello, *Gay Rights and the American Law* (Cambridge: Cambridge University Press, 2003), 26.

9. However, the major growth in domestic partnership coverage at Fortune 500 companies occurred since 2000.

10. One social survey of cohabitating straight couples who registered with a city determined that their major motivation was economic—they wanted health insurance, state residency status for college tuition, residence in university-owned family housing, a family discount on football tickets, or the family rate at the local health club. Marion Willetts also found that most heterosexual couples obtain domestic partnership certificates as a step toward marriage. One cohabiting engineer in Huntington Beach, California, explained, "But we're young and don't feel the need to get married yet. It was a great way for us to have the same doctor, the same dentist, and it worked out financially." Marion C. Willetts, "An Exploratory Investigation of Heterosexual Licensed Domestic Partners," *Journal of Marriage and the Family* 65, no. 4 (November 2003): 939–52; Martin Wisckol, "Finding Benefits in Partnership," *Orange (CA) City Register*, May 2, 1999.

11. Domestic partnership benefits were considered taxable to the employed partner and therefore less valuable than the untaxed benefit married couples enjoyed. Heterosexuals and homosexuals who were not legally married faced adverse taxation. Therefore, the taxation of benefits could not have been a reason why gays were less likely to utilize domestic partner benefits than straights.

12. Marion Christine Willetts, "Innovative Dyadic Relationships: A Quantitative and Qualitative Analysis" (PhD diss., University of Florida, 1997), 63.

13. David L. Chambers, "Couples: Marriage, Civil Union, and Domestic Partnership," *Creating Change: Sexuality, Public Policy, and Civil Rights*, ed. John D'Emilio, William B. Turner, and Urvashi Vaid (New York: St. Martin's Press, 2000), 281–304.

14. George Chauncey, *Why Marriage: The History Shaping Today's Debate over Gay Equality* (New York: Basic Books, 2004), 91.

15. Carl Wittman, "A Gay Manifesto," in *Out of the Closets: Voices of Gay Liberation*, ed. Karla Jay and Allen Young (New York: New York University Press, 1997), 330. *A Different Story* (1978) was a film about a lesbian and a gay man who cohabited as friends and had sex. After the woman got pregnant, the couple got married, and moved to the suburbs. Ruthe Stein, "When Gays Are Just Roommates," *San Francisco Chronicle*, June 22, 1978.

16. The 1972 Gay Rights Platform, http://www.reslevinson.com/gaylesissues/features/collective/onetime/bl_platform1972.htm (accessed January 11, 2008).

17. Chambers, "Couples," 281–304; Lynn Sweet, "Prison Can't Crush Lesbians' Marriage Crusade," *Chicago Sun-Times*, February 10, 1977.

18. A gay man was rejected when he applied to the AAA for associate family membership. "AAA Denies Gay Spouse Coverage," *Advocate*, August 28, 1974. Social Security pensions, railroad retirement pensions, and veterans' compensation programs provided benefits for a spouse, but not for a cohabiting parent. Marjorie Dick Rombauer, "Marital Status and Eligibility for Federal Statutory Income Benefits: A Historical Survey," *Washington Law Review* 52, no. 2 (April 1977): 227–88.

19. William J. Waitrowski, "Family-Related Benefits in the Workplace," *Monthly Labor Review* 113, no. 3 (March 1990): 28–34; Ed Mickens, *The 100 Best Companies for Gay Men and Lesbians* (New York: Pocket Books, 1994). The more often quoted figure of 40 percent included all forms of benefits, including contributions to retirement.

20. Doug Ireland, "Remembering Herbert Marcuse," July 20, 2005, http://2mag.org/content/showarticle.cfm?ItemID=8336 (accessed February 1, 2008); Jeff Weinstein's Cultural Mixology, http:///www.artsjournal.com/outhere/2007/08/jeff_weinstein.html (accessed July 5, 2009).

21. Jeff Weinstein, "Uneasy Days on Old Cape Cod," *Body Politic* 55 (August 1979): 23–26.

22. Jeff Weinstein, "Political Activism and Personal Pleasure," http://www.artistswith aids.org/artery/centerpieces/centerpieces_weinstein.html (accessed February 1, 2008).

23. "Voice Contract Includes Pro-Gay Provisions," *New York Native*, July 19, 1982; "Gay Spouses Covered in New 'Voice' Pact," *Advocate*, September 16, 1982; Miriam Frank, "Lesbian and Gay Caucuses in the U.S. Labor Movement," *Laboring for Rights: Unions and Sexual Diversity across Nations*, ed. Gerald Hunt (Philadelphia: Temple University Press, 1999); Kitty Krupat, "Out of Labor's Dark Age: Sexual Politics Comes to the Workplace," *Out at Work: Building a Gay-Labor Alliance*, ed. Kitty Krupat and Patrick McCreery (Minneapolis: University of Minnesota Press, 2001), 11; Miriam Frank and Desma Holcomb, *Pride at Work: Organizing for Lesbian and Gay Rights in Unions* (New York: Lesbian and Gay Labor Network, 1990), 3.

24. Interview with Jeff Weinstein, October 3, 2003; Claudia H. Deutsch, "Managing Insurance for Domestic Partners," *New York Times*, July 28, 1991. The contract provided immediate coverage for current union members but required a one-year waiting period for new hires. Employees were required to file a notarized affidavit. Martha McDonald, "Domestic Partner Benefits Changes—Insurance Policy on Significant Others," *Business and Health*, October 1990.

25. Donald P. Haider-Markel, Mark R. Joslyn, and Chad J. Kniss, "Minority Group Interest and Political Representation: Gay Elected Officials in the Policy Process," *Journal of Politics* 62, no. 2 (2000): 568–77; Lewis Becker, "Recognition of Domestic Partnerships by Governmental Entities and Private Employers," *National Journal of Sexual Orientation Law* 1, no. 1 (1995), http://www.biblioorg/gaylaw/index.html (accessed February 22, 2008).

26. Charles Burress, "Berkeley's Leftist Council Gets Off to a Splashy Start," *San Francisco Chronicle*, December 15, 1984.

27. Susan Goldfarb, "Church Pleased with Mayor's Veto," *United Press International*, December 10, 1982; "Benefits for Live-In Lovers, Gay and Otherwise Studied," *Miami Herald*, November 12, 1982; Dawn Garcia, "A Reluctant Politician Will Lead S.F. Supervisors," *San Francisco Chronicle*, December 28, 1998; Leland Traiman, "A Brief History of Domestic Partnerships," *Gay and Lesbian Review*, July–August 2003, http://w.equalitywithoutmarriage.org (accessed September 3, 2010).

28. Susan Goldfarb, "Gays Rally to Protest Health-Benefits Veto," *Syracuse Herald*, December 10, 1982; Philip Hager, "Benefits May Go to Gay Survivors," *Los Angeles Times*, November 11, 1982.

29. *Casa Grande (AZ) Dispatch*, April 26, 1989.

30. "Board in San Francisco Backs Couples' Benefits," *New York Times*, November 30, 1982. Two members of the board of supervisors did want coverage for other relationships "such as business partners, fathers and sons, and other kin relationships." "S.F. Supervisors Nod Measure for Unwed Couples," *Los Angeles Daily Journal*, November 24, 1982; Philip Hager, "S.F. OKs Ordinance to Bestow Recognition on Gay Couples," *Los Angeles Times*, November 25, 1982.

31. Cynthia Gorney, "Making It Official: The Law and Live-Ins," *Washington Post*, July 5, 1989; Philip Hager, "S.F. Mayor Vetoes 'Live-In Lovers' Law," *Los Angeles Times*, December 10, 1982.

32. Lisa Levitt, "Domestic News," *Associated Press*, December 9, 1982; Goldfarb, "Church Pleased with Mayor's Veto."

33. "Gay, Straight Partners Get Full Job Benefits," *San Francisco Chronicle*, August 2, 1984; Will Evans, "Organization Honors Trailblazer," *Berkeley Daily Californian*, February 1, 2008.

34. One of the fourteen who testified also made the point that straight cohabitors often lied and said they were married in order to receive benefits reserved for married couples. Hearings before the Human Relations Welfare Committee, City of Berkeley, October 1983, Box 86, Folder 13, 1983–93, Reel 13, Gay and Lesbian Task Force Records, 1973 to 2000 from the Holdings of the Human Sexuality Collection, Division of Rare and Manuscript Collections, Cornell University.

35. Barbara J. Cox, "The Little Project: From Alternative Families to Domestic Partnerships to Same-Sex Marriage," *Wisconsin Women's Law Journal* 15, no. 77 (2000): 77–92; Barbara J. Cox, "Alternative Families: Obtaining Traditional Family Benefits through Litigation, Legislation and Collective Bargaining," *Wisconsin Women's Law Journal* 2 (1986): 1–51; Jessica Gwynn, "Benefits in Partnership," *Contra Costa (CA) Times*, September 12, 1999.

36. Robert W. Bailey, *Gay Politics, Identity and Economics in the Urban Setting* (New York: Columbia University Press, 1999), 313.

37. Jonathan Mandell, "Those 'Married Folks Who Aren't Married,'" *Newsday*, October 9, 1987; Heather Murray, *Not in This Family: Gays and the Meaning of Kinship in Postwar North America* (Philadelphia: University of Pennsylvania Press, 2010), 136–78; Peter Nardi, "AIDS and Obituaries: The Perception of Stigma in the Press," in *When AIDS Began: San Francisco and the Making of an Epidemic*, ed. Michelle Cochran (New York: Routledge, 2004), 159–68.

38. Casey Charles, *The Sharon Kowalski Case: Lesbian and Gay Rights on Trial* (Lawrence: University Press of Kansas, 2003); Karen Thompson and Julie Andrzejew, *Why Can't Sharon Kowalski Come Home* (San Francisco: Spinsters/Aunt Lute, 1998).

39. Linda Wheeler, "2,000 Gay Couples Exchange Vows in Ceremony of Rights," *Washington Post*, October 11, 1987.

40. Evelyn Gilbert, "Major N.Y. Hospital Offers Domestic Partner Benefits," *National Underwriter Property and Casualty—Risk and Benefits Management*, no. 12 (April 8, 1991): 2–3; James Barron, "Bronx Hospital Gives Gay Couples Spouse Benefits," *New York Times*, March 27, 1991; K. A. O'Hanlan, "Domestic Partnership Benefits at Medical Universities," *Journal of the American Medical Association* 282, no. 13 (October 6, 1999): 1289–92.

41. In 1989, Ben and Jerry's Homemade Ice Cream, a progressive company in liberal Vermont, offered health insurance coverage to same- and opposite-sex partners, but they charged straight cohabitors more for their share of the coverage. Jay Mathews, "Gay Partners Gain Benefits; Big Firms Quietly Agree to Pay Medical Bills," *Washington Post*, October 2, 1993; Jennifer J. Laabs, "Unmarried . . . with Benefits," *Personnel Journal* (December 1991), 64. For the general distinction between the corporate model of domestic partnership benefits and the union model, see Desma Holcomb, "Domestic Partner Health Benefits: The Corporate Model vs. the Union Model," in *Laboring for Rights*, 103–21.

42. "Corporations Snubbing Unwed Couples," *San Francisco Chronicle*, July 27, 1977.

43. Barbara Presley Noble, "At Work: Benefits for Domestic Partners," *New York Times*, June 21, 2008.

44. Davis Stripp, "Lotus Extends Company Benefits to Cover Domestic Partners of Homosexual Staff," *Wall Street Journal*, September 9, 1991; Laabs, "Unmarried . . . with Benefits."

45. Bruce D. Butterfield, "Gay Couples Get Benefits at Lotus," *Boston Globe* (September 6, 1991). For opposition to Apple's domestic partnership benefits in Williamson County, Texas, in 1993, see John Gallagher and Chris Bull, *Perfect Enemies: The Battle between the Religious Right and the Gay Movement* (Lanham, MD: Madison Books, 1996), 191–95.

46. When Oracle instituted domestic partner benefits, it required employees to sign an affidavit stating that "we should legally marry each other if we could, and we intend to do so if marriage becomes available to us in our state of residence." Nancy Polikoff, *Beyond (Straight and Gay) Marriage: Valuing All the Families under the* Law (Boston: Beacon Press, 2008), 81.

47. David J. Jefferson, "Family Matters: Gay Employees Win Benefits for Partners at More Corporations—Cost Is Less Than Expected, but Customer Reaction Worries Some Executives—It's a Validation of Sorts," *Wall Street Journal*, March 18, 1994.

48. William M. Bulkeley, "Lotus Flap Over Extending Benefits to Partners of Gay Employees," *Wall Street Journal*, October 25, 1991. Lotus said that 80 percent of the three hundred letters they received were positive, and some people even promised to buy more from them because of their action. Kenneth H. Hammonds, "Lotus Opens a Door for Business Partners," *Business Week*, November 4, 1991; "Benefits Parity for Gays," *Newsday*, September 7, 1991; Catherine Iannunzzo and Alexandra Pinck, "Benefits for the Domestic Partners of Gay and Lesbian Employees at Lotus Development Corporation," November 1991, http://www.qrd.org/qrd/dp/bus/1991/Lotus-11.91 (November 5, 2007).

49. Cindy Richards, "Mass. Firm Offers Benefits for 'Spousal Equivalents,'" *Chicago Sun-Times*, September 7, 1991.

50. "Public Forum-Domestic Partnerships," *Daily News of LA*, June 11, 1994; Thomas F. Coleman, *The Domino Effect* (Glendale, CA: Spectrum Institute, 2009), 64; Susan L. Brown, Jennifer Roebuck Bulanda, and Gary R. Lee, "The Significance of Nonmarital Cohabitation: Marital Status and Mental Health Benefits among Middle-Aged and Older Adults," *Journal of Gerontology: Social Sciencies* 60B (2005): 521–29.

51. Grace Ganz Blumberg, "Legal Recognition of Same-Sex Conjugal Relationships: The 2003 California Domestic Partner Rights and Responsibilities Act in Comparative Civil Rights and Family Law Perspective," *UCLA Law Review* 51 (2004): 1555–1617. See also Megan E. Callan, "The More, the Not Marry-Er: In Search of a Policy behind Eligibility for California Domestic Partnerships," *San Diego Law Review* 40 (2003): 427–54; Marion C. Willetts, "Registered Domestic Partnerships, Same-Sex Marriage, and the Pursuit of Equality in California," *Family Relations* 60, no. 2 (April 2011): 135–49.

52. *In Renshaw v. Heckler*, a US Court of Appeals decided that a "long term cohabitor" was entitled to Social Security survivors' benefits because they considered her a common-law wife, according to the law of Pennsylvania. Renshaw v. Heckler, 787 F.2d 50 (2nd Cir. 1986). A government commission was unable to succeed in passing the modest reform of restoring a widow's Social Security benefits if she divorced within a year of remarrying. Alice Kessler-Harris, *In Pursuit of Equity: Women, Men, and the Quest for Economic Citizenship in 20th-Century America* (New York: Oxford University Press, 2001), 164.

53. Paula Ettelbrick, "Since When Is Marriage a Path to Liberation?," *Lesbians, Gay Men, and the Law*, ed. William B. Rubenstein (New York: New Press, 1993), 401–6; Nancy D. Polikoff, "We Will Get What We Ask For: Why Legalizing Gay and Lesbian Marriage Will Not 'Dismantle the Legal Structure,'" *Virginia Law Review* 79, no. 7 (Octo-

ber 1993): 1553–50. After the 2004 election and the passage of so many antimarriage bans, an influential group of gay intellectuals wrote a statement opposing the movement's emphasis on "marriage equality." Beyond Marriage, "Beyond Same-Sex Marriage: A New Strategic Vision for All Our Families and Relationships," http://www.beyondmarriage.org/full_statement.html (accessed February 1, 2008). For an analysis of both sides of the argument, see Gust A. Yep, Karen E. Lovaas, and John P. Elia, "A Critical Appraisal of Assimilationist and Radical Ideologies Underlying Same-Sex Marriage in LGBT Communities in the United States," *Journal of Homosexuality* 45, no. 2 (2003): 45–65.

54. Evan Wolfson, "Crossing the Threshold: Equal Marriage Rights for Lesbians and Gay Men and the Inter-Community Critique," *New York University Review of Law and Social Change* 21 (1993–95): 567–615.

55. Perry et al. v. Schwarzenegger et al., 2010 U.S. District Lexis 78817, Case No. C 09-2292 VRW.

56. Daniel R. Pinello, *America's Struggle for Same-Sex Marriage* (Cambridge: Cambridge University Press, 2006).

CHAPTER ELEVEN

1. Brenda Luscombe, "Marriage: What's It Good For," *Time*, November 29, 2010, 51.

2. Ibid.

3. Sheela Kennedy and Larry Bumpass, "Cohabitation and Trends in the Structure and Stability of Children's Family Lives," unpublished paper, 2010, http://paa2011.princeton.edu/download.aspx?submissionid=111757 (accessed September 1, 2011). For lower figures, see Fertility of American Women: 2008, P20-563, http://www.census-gov/prod/2010pubs/p2-563.pdf (accessed September 1, 2011); Pamela J. Smock and Fiona Rose Greenland, "Diversity in Pathways to Parenthood: Patterns, Implications, and Emerging Research Directions," *Journal of Marriage and Family* 72 (June 2010): 576–93.

4. Paul Taylor, Cary Funk, and April Clark, *As Marriage and Parenthood Drift Apart, Public Is Concerned about Social Impact* (Washington, DC: Pew Research Center, 2007), 40; Arland Thornton and Linda Young-DeMarco, "Four Decades of Trends in Attitudes toward Family Issues in the United States: The 1960s through the 1990s," *Journal of Marriage and Family* 63 (November 2002): 1–23; Jeni Loftus, "America's Liberalization in Attitudes toward Homosexuality, 1973 to 1998," *American Sociological Review* 66, no. 5 (October 2001): 764. The attitudes of high school students were from the Detroit area study of white youths, beginning with those born in 1961.

5. Brian Powell, Catherine Bolzendahl, Claudia Gesit, and Lala Carr Steelman, *Counted Out: Same-Sex Relations and Americans—Definitions of Family* (New York: Russell Sage, 2010), 75; Pew Research Center, *The Decline of Marriage and the Rise of New Families* (Washington, DC: Pew Research Center, 2010), 14, 66.

6. Powell et al., *Counted Out*, 37–70.

7. Goran Lind, *Common Law Marriage: A Legal Institution for Cohabitation* (New York: Oxford University Press, 2009), 1047.

8. Nancy D. Polikoff, "Why Lesbians and Gay Men Should Read Martha Fineman," *American Journal of Gender, Social Policy and the Law* 8, no. 1 (2000), 176. Even so, the EU still promotes marriage in some social policies, such as free courses for the legal wives of farmers.

9. Lynne Prince Cooke and Janeen Baxter, "Families," in "International Context: Comparing Institutional Effects across Western Societies," *Journal of Marriage and the Family* 72 (June 2010): 521.

10. W. Bradford Wilcox and Andrew J. Cherlin, *The Marginalization of Marriage in Middle America* (Washington, DC: Brookings Institution, 2011), 6.

11. Martha Albertson Fineman, *The Neutered Mother, The Sexual Family and Other Twentieth Century Tragedies* (New York: Routledge, 1995). See also Tamara Metz, *Untying The Knot: Marriage, the State, and the Case for Their Divorce* (Princeton, NJ: Princeton University Press, 2010).

12. Kelly Musick and Larry Bumpass, "Re-Examining the Case for Marriage: Variation and Change in Well-Being and Relationships," CCPR Working Paper No. 2006-003, UCLA, http://papers.ccpr.ucla.edu/papers/PWP-CCPR-2006-003/PWP-CCPR-2006-003.pd (accessed March 15, 2011).